Hello, Amélie here.
Sunlight feels great, doesn't it? I
store up my energy by sleeping a
lot, eating breakfast, going back
to sleep for a bit and sunbathing.
All so I can get the old guy, who's
sleeping comfortably over there, to
go outside and watch how fast I
can run around. Heh heh heh...

—*Yūki Tabata's dog, 2019*

YŪKI TABATA

was born in Fukuoka Prefecture
and got his big break in the 2011
Shonen Jump Golden Future Cup
with his winning entry, *Hungry
Joker*. He started the magical fantasy
series *Black Clover* in 2015.

BLACK CLOVER
VOLUME 20
SHONEN JUMP Manga Edition

Story and Art by YŪKI TABATA

Translation ✱ TAYLOR ENGEL, HC LANGUAGE SOLUTIONS, INC.

Touch-Up Art & Lettering ✱ ANNALIESE CHRISTMAN

Design ✱ KAM LI

Editor ✱ ALEXIS KIRSCH

First published in Japan in 2015 by SHUEISHA Inc., Tokyo.
English translation rights arranged by SHUEISHA Inc.

Printed in the U.S.A.

Published by VIZ Media, LLC
P.O. Box 77010
San Francisco, CA 94107

10 9 8 7 6 5 4 3 2 1
First printing, March 2020

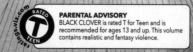

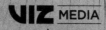

Gauche Dorothy

Charmy

Gordon

Asta

Fana

Henry

Marie

Grey

Vetto

Black ✣ Clover

YŪKI TABATA **20** WHY I LIVED SO LONG

Yuno

| Member of:
The Golden Dawn | | Magic: Wind |

Asta's best friend, and a good rival who's also been working to become the Wizard King. He controls Sylph, the spirit of wind.

Asta

 Member of: The Black Bulls
Magic: None (Anti-Magic)

He has no magic, but he's working to become the Wizard King through sheer guts and his well-trained body. He fights with anti-magic swords.

Magna Swing

 Member of:
The Black Bulls
Magic: Flame

He has the temperament of a delinquent, but he's quite manly and logical, and good at taking care of others.

Vanessa Enoteca

 Member of:
The Black Bulls
Magic: Thread

She has an unparalleled love of liquor. During battle, she uses her magic to manipulate fate, changing the future.

Luck Voltia

 Member of:
The Black Bulls
Magic: Lightning

A battle maniac. Once he starts fighting, he gets totally absorbed in it. Smiles constantly.

Charmy Pappitson

 Member of:
The Black Bulls
Magic: Cotton

She eats like a maniac, and when food is involved, she uses absolutely insane magic. She has a big crush on Yuno.

Grey

Member of:
The Black Bulls
Magic: Transformation

She has a shy personality, and always acts timid. She can transform to look like whoever she's with.

Gordon Agrippa

Member of:
The Black Bulls
Magic: Poison

He looks scary, but he's actually just incredibly bad at communicating. He wants to get closer to everybody else.

Gauche Adlai

Member of:
The Black Bulls
Magic: Mirror

A former convict with a blind, pathological love for his little sister. Both he and his sister have had their bodies taken over by elves.

Henry Legolant

Member of:
The Black Bulls
Magic: Recombination

His strange constitution absorbs magic from the people around him. He uses the vast amount of accumulated magic to pilot the hideout.

Rill Boismortier

Member of:
The Aqua Deer
Magic: Picture

A young captain with outstanding talent. His body has been taken over by an elf named Lira.

Dorothy Unsworth

Member of:
The Coral Peacocks
Magic: Dream

A brigade captain. She's usually fast asleep. She's able to use Dream Magic to make a world that's exactly how she wants it to be.

✿ ✿ ✿

STORY

In a world where magic is everything, Asta and Yuno are both found abandoned on the same day at a church in the remote village of Hage. Both dream of becoming the Wizard King, the highest of all mages, and they spend their days working toward that dream.

The year they turn 15, both receive grimoires, magic books that amplify their bearer's magic. They take the entrance exam for the Magic Knights, nine groups of mages under the direct control of the Wizard King. Yuno, whose magic is strong, joins the Golden Dawn, an elite group, while Asta, who has no magic at all, joins the Black Bulls, a group of misfits. With this, the two finally take their first step toward becoming the Wizard King...

In the tower floating above the royal castle, the elves conduct the ritual to open the Shadow Palace in order to make their reincarnation complete. The Black Bulls charge in as it was happening, but their group is split up by Dorothy, whose body has been taken over by an elf. Vanessa and the others summoned into Dorothy's dream world now try their best to escape. Meanwhile, what's happening to Asta and the members who've been left behind at the castle?!

BLACK ✿ CLOVER

CONTENTS

BLACK ✣ CLOVER

20

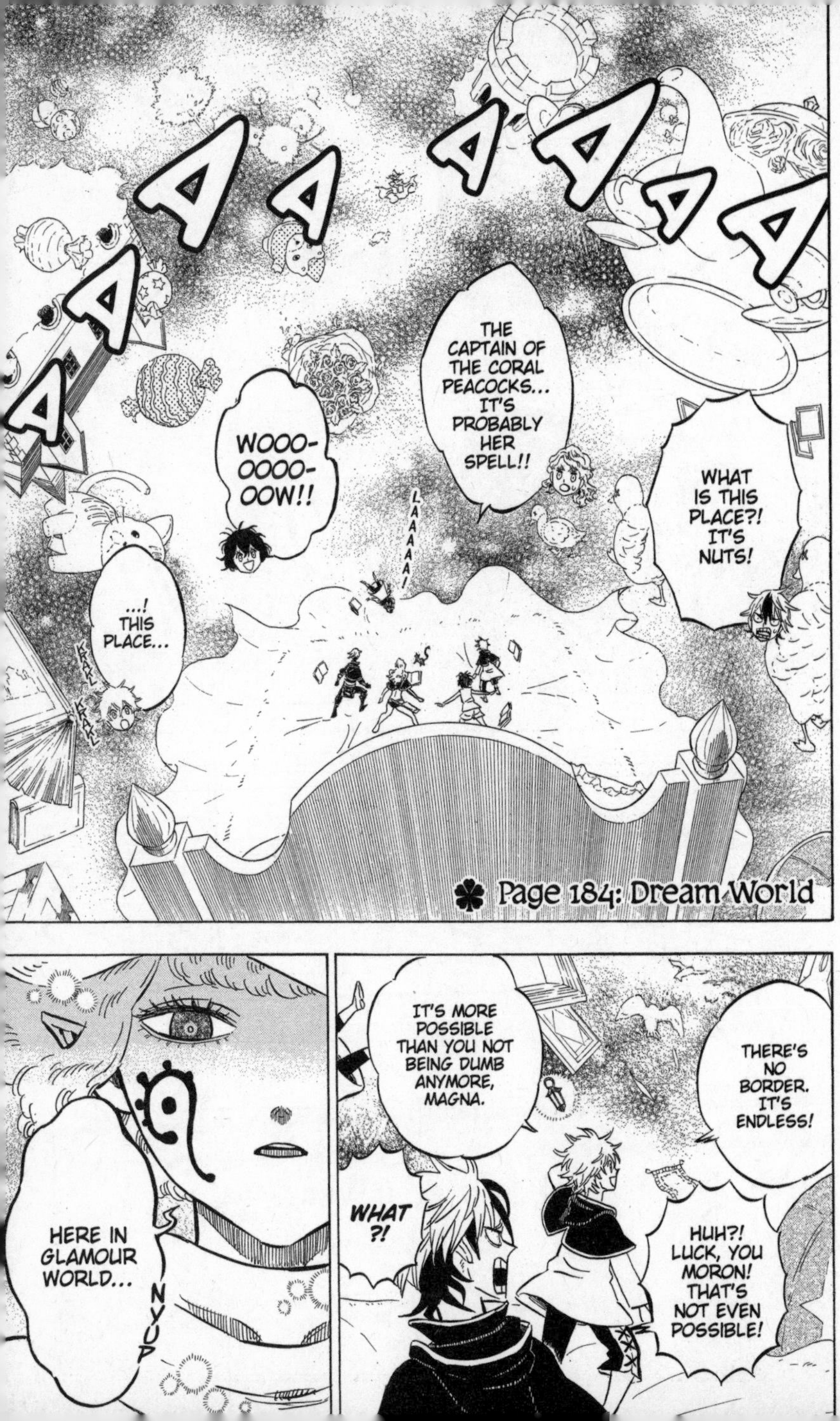
AAAAAAAAAA
WHAT IS THIS PLACE?! IT'S NUTS!
THE CAPTAIN OF THE CORAL PEACOCKS... IT'S PROBABLY HER SPELL!!
WOOO-OOOO-OOW!!
LAAAAAA!
...! THIS PLACE...
KRAKL KRAKL
Page 184: Dream World
THERE'S NO BORDER. IT'S ENDLESS!
HUH?! LUCK, YOU MORON! THAT'S NOT EVEN POSSIBLE!
IT'S MORE POSSIBLE THAN YOU NOT BEING DUMB ANYMORE, MAGNA.
WHAT?!
HERE IN GLAMOUR WORLD...
NYUP

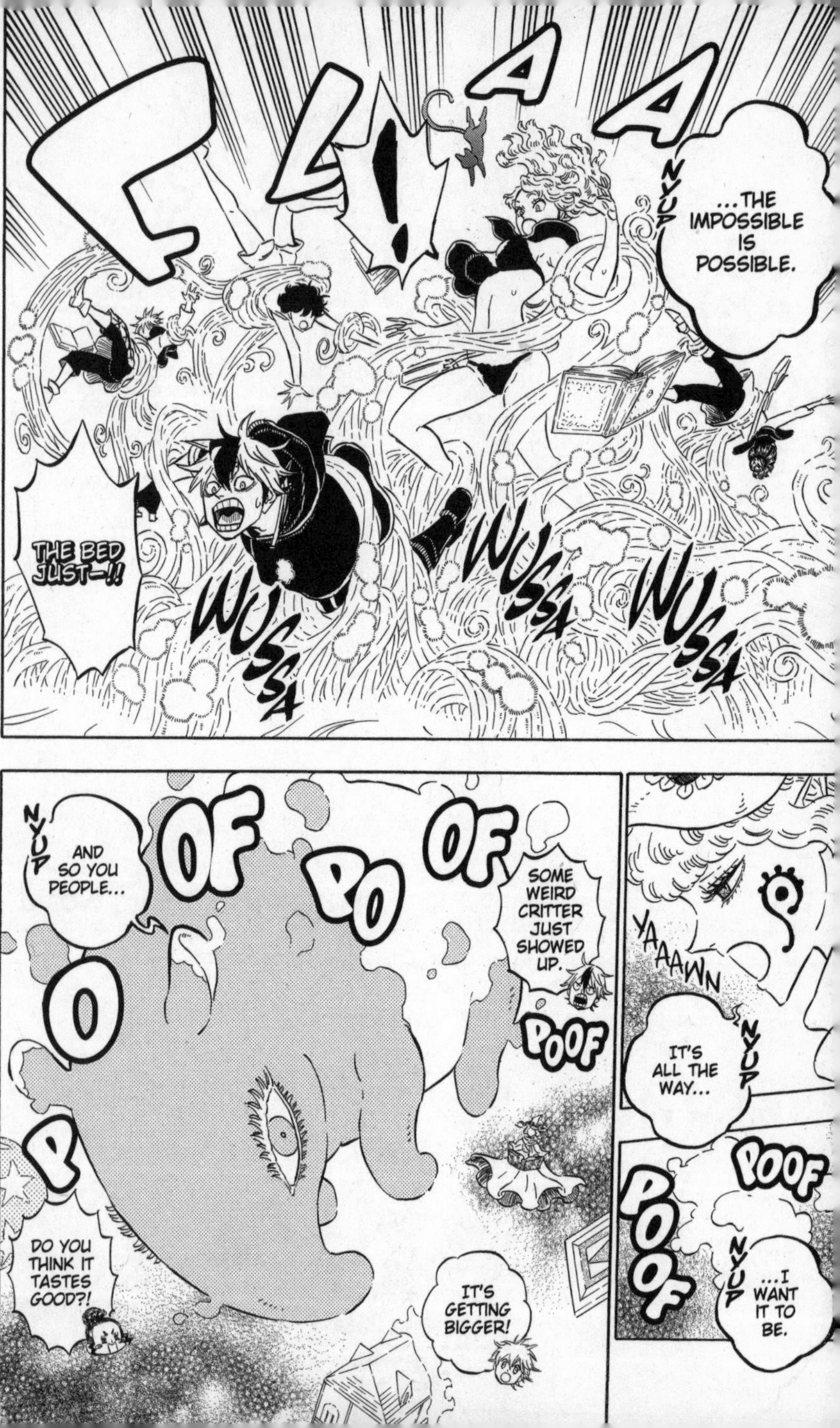
NYUP
...THE IMPOSSIBLE IS POSSIBLE.
THE BED JUST—!!
WUSSA
WUSSA
WUSSA
YAAAWN
NYUP
IT'S ALL THE WAY...
POOF
POOF
NYUP
...I WANT IT TO BE.
SOME WEIRD CRITTER JUST SHOWED UP.
POOF
NYUP
AND SO YOU PEOPLE...
IT'S GETTING BIGGER!
DO YOU THINK IT TASTES GOOD?!

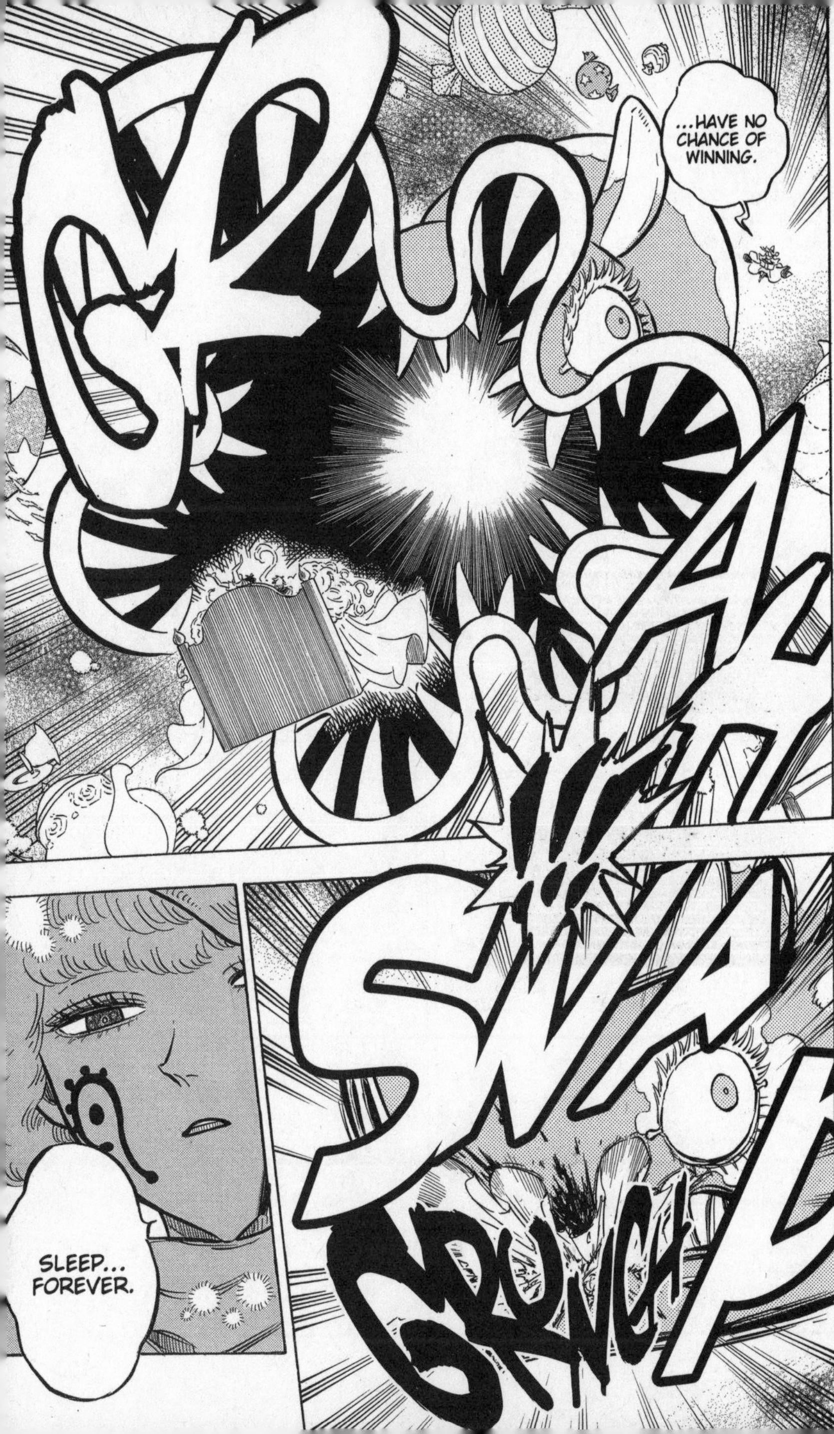
...HAVE NO CHANCE OF WINNING.
SLEEP... FOREVER.

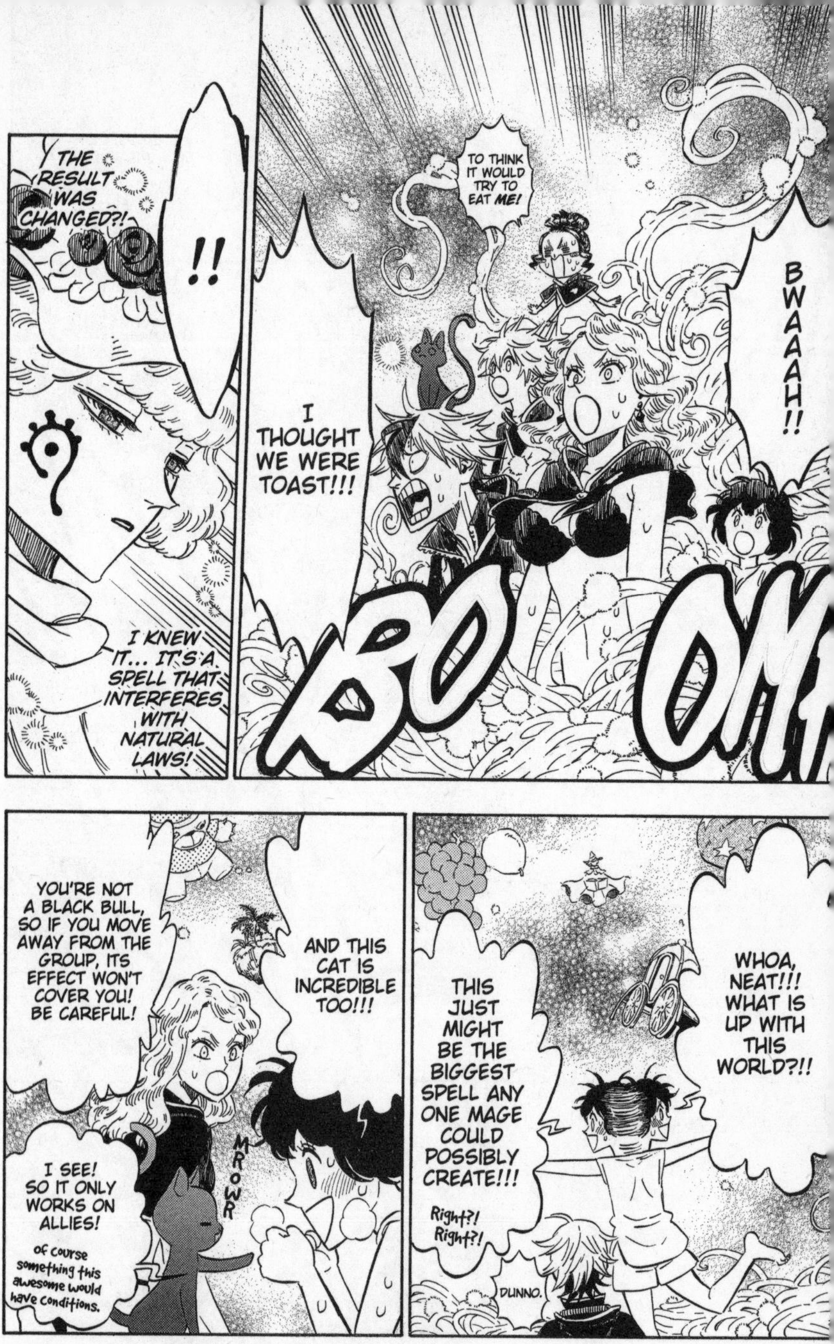
BWAAAAH!!
TO THINK IT WOULD TRY TO EAT ME!
I THOUGHT WE WERE TOAST!!!
BO OM
!!
THE RESULT WAS CHANGED?!
I KNEW IT... IT'S A SPELL THAT INTERFERES WITH NATURAL LAWS!
WHOA, NEAT!!! WHAT IS UP WITH THIS WORLD?!!
THIS JUST MIGHT BE THE BIGGEST SPELL ANY ONE MAGE COULD POSSIBLY CREATE!!!
Right?! Right?!
DUNNO.
AND THIS CAT IS INCREDIBLE TOO!!!
YOU'RE NOT A BLACK BULL, SO IF YOU MOVE AWAY FROM THE GROUP, ITS EFFECT WON'T COVER YOU! BE CAREFUL!
MROWR
I SEE! SO IT ONLY WORKS ON ALLIES!
of course something this awesome would have conditions.

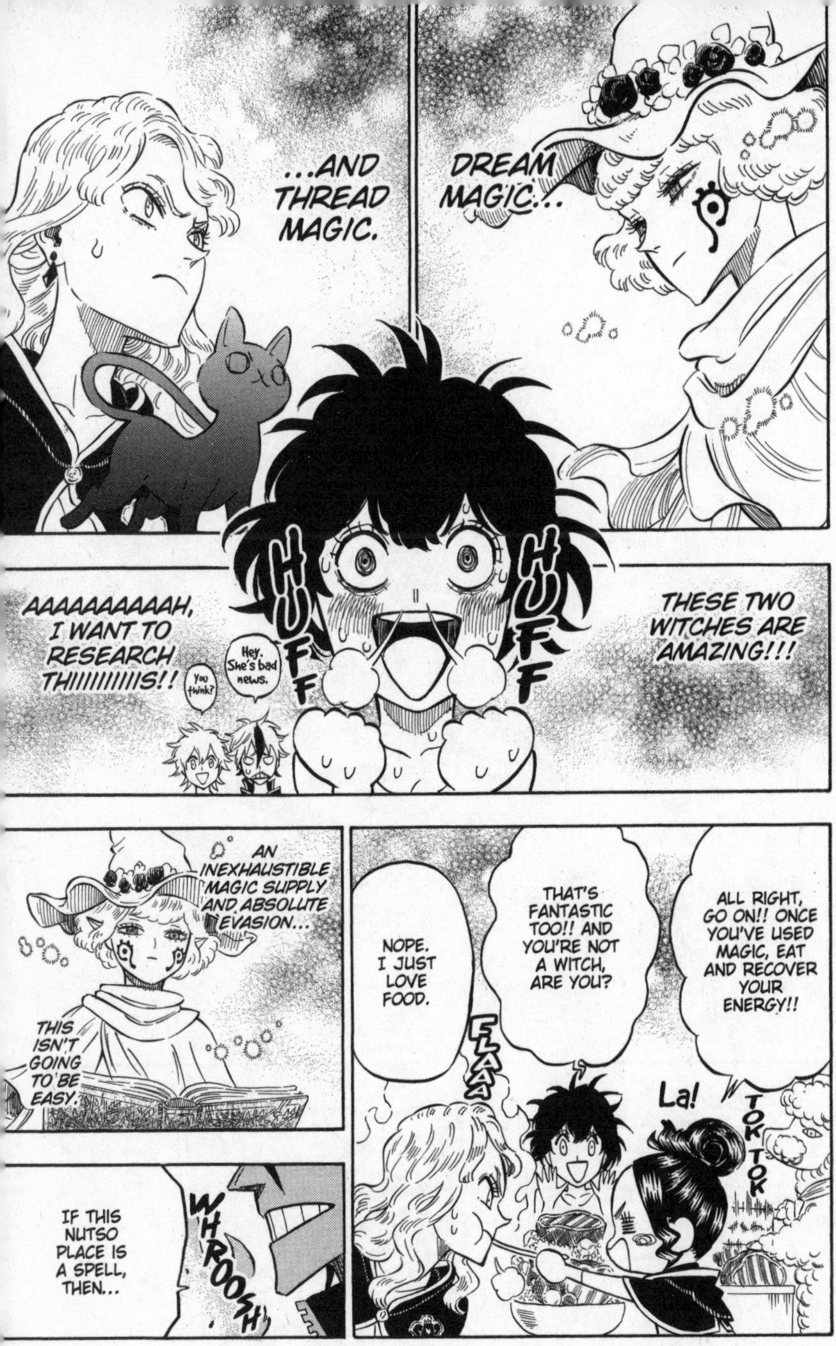
DREAM MAGIC...
...AND THREAD MAGIC.
THESE TWO WITCHES ARE AMAZING!!!
HUFF
HUFF
AAAAAAAAAAH, I WANT TO RESEARCH THIIIIIIIIIS!!
Hey. She's bad news.
You think?
ALL RIGHT, GO ON!! ONCE YOU'VE USED MAGIC, EAT AND RECOVER YOUR ENERGY!!
THAT'S FANTASTIC TOO!! AND YOU'RE NOT A WITCH, ARE YOU?
NOPE. I JUST LOVE FOOD.
La!
TOK TOK
FLAAA
AN INEXHAUSTIBLE MAGIC SUPPLY AND ABSOLUTE EVASION...
THIS ISN'T GOING TO BE EASY.
IF THIS NUTSO PLACE IS A SPELL, THEN...
WHROOSH

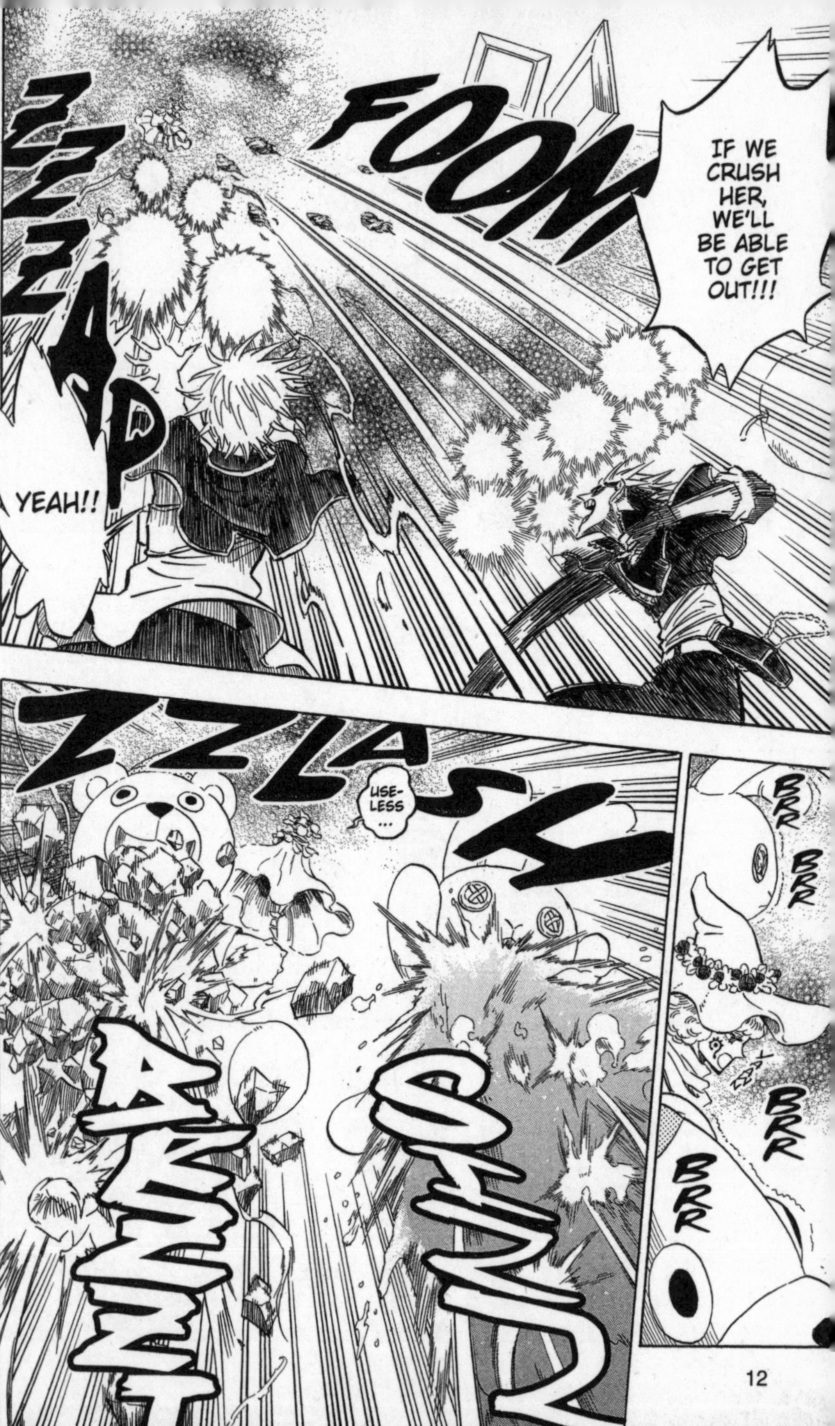
IF WE CRUSH HER, WE'LL BE ABLE TO GET OUT!!!
FOOM
ZZZZAP
YEAH!!
BRR BRR
BRR
BRR
ZZLASH
USE-LESS ...

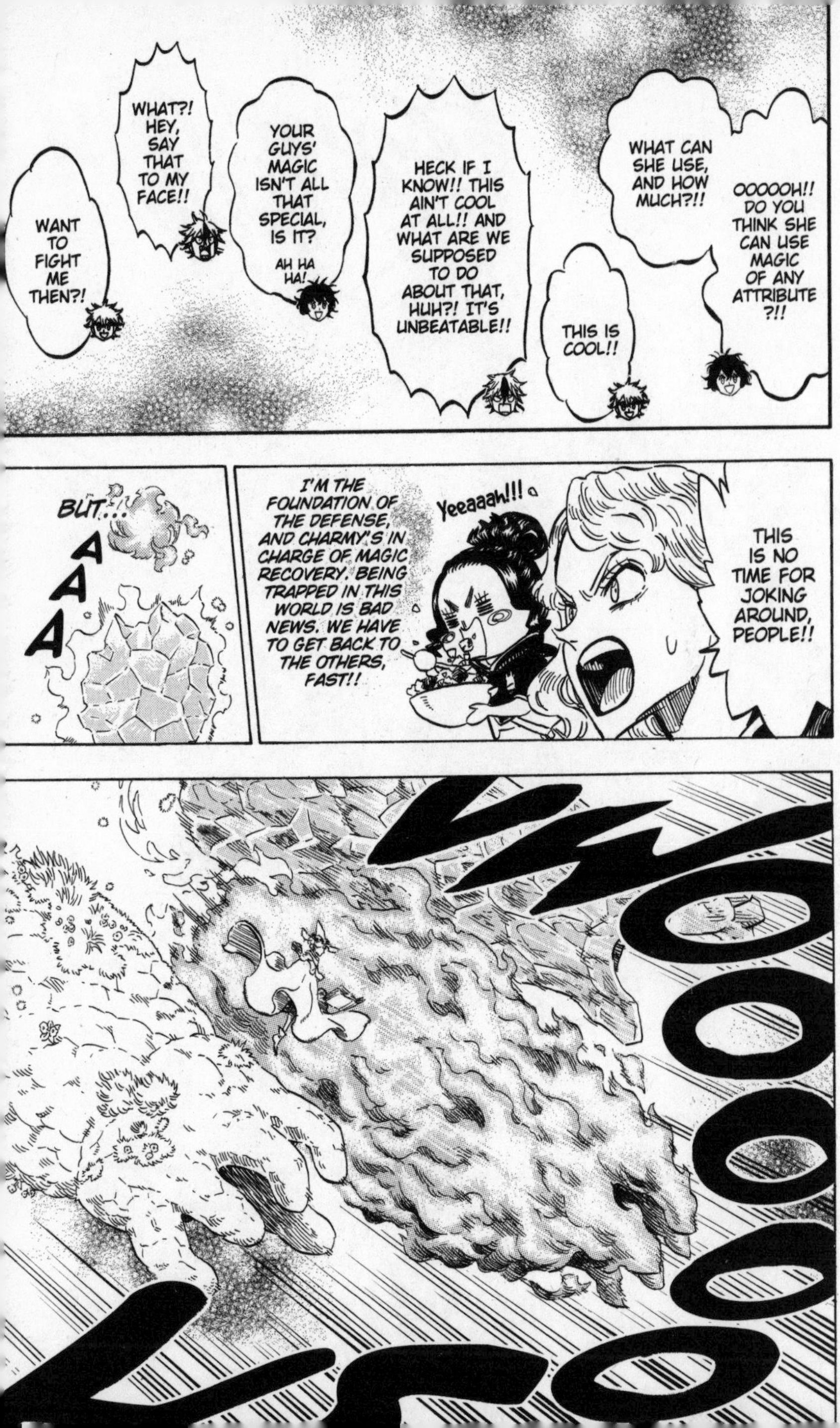
OOOOOH!! DO YOU THINK SHE CAN USE MAGIC OF ANY ATTRIBUTE ?!!
WHAT CAN SHE USE, AND HOW MUCH?!!
THIS IS COOL!!
HECK IF I KNOW!! THIS AIN'T COOL AT ALL!! AND WHAT ARE WE SUPPOSED TO DO ABOUT THAT, HUH?! IT'S UNBEATABLE!!
YOUR GUYS' MAGIC ISN'T ALL THAT SPECIAL, IS IT?
AH HA HA!
WHAT?! HEY, SAY THAT TO MY FACE!!
WANT TO FIGHT ME THEN?!
THIS IS NO TIME FOR JOKING AROUND, PEOPLE!!
Yeeaaah!!!
I'M THE FOUNDATION OF THE DEFENSE, AND CHARMY'S IN CHARGE OF MAGIC RECOVERY. BEING TRAPPED IN THIS WORLD IS BAD NEWS. WE HAVE TO GET BACK TO THE OTHERS, FAST!!
BUT...!!
AAA

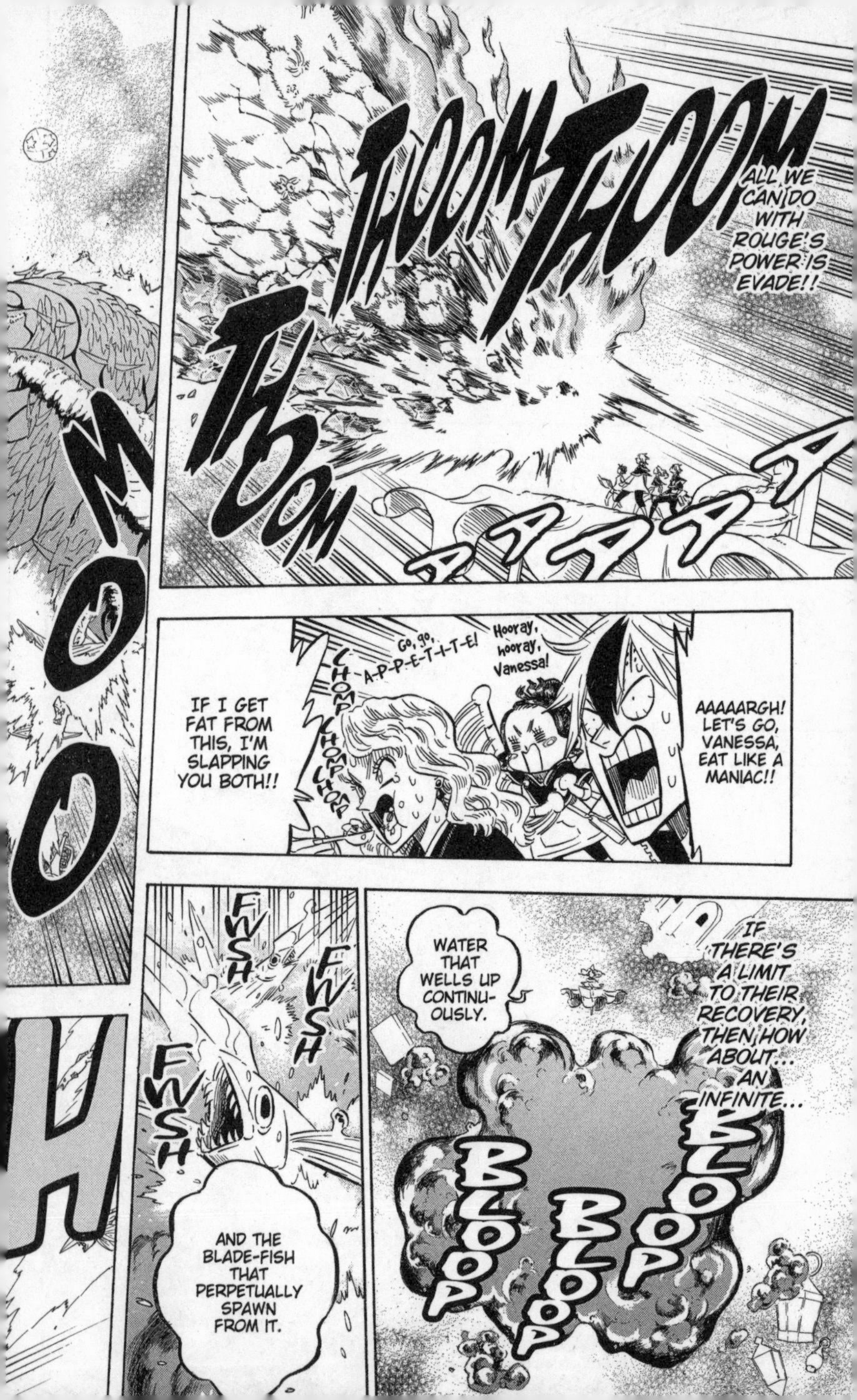
ALL WE CAN DO WITH ROUGE'S POWER IS EVADE!!
THOOM THOOM
THOOM
AAAAAA
AAAAARGH! LET'S GO, VANESSA, EAT LIKE A MANIAC!!
Hooray, hooray, Vanessa!
Go, go, A-P-P-E-T-I-T-E!
CHOMP CHOMP CHOMP
IF I GET FAT FROM THIS, I'M SLAPPING YOU BOTH!!
IF THERE'S A LIMIT TO THEIR RECOVERY, THEN HOW ABOUT... AN INFINITE...
BLOOP BLOOP BLOOP
WATER THAT WELLS UP CONTINU-OUSLY.
FWSH FWSH
FWSH
AND THE BLADE-FISH THAT PERPETUALLY SPAWN FROM IT.

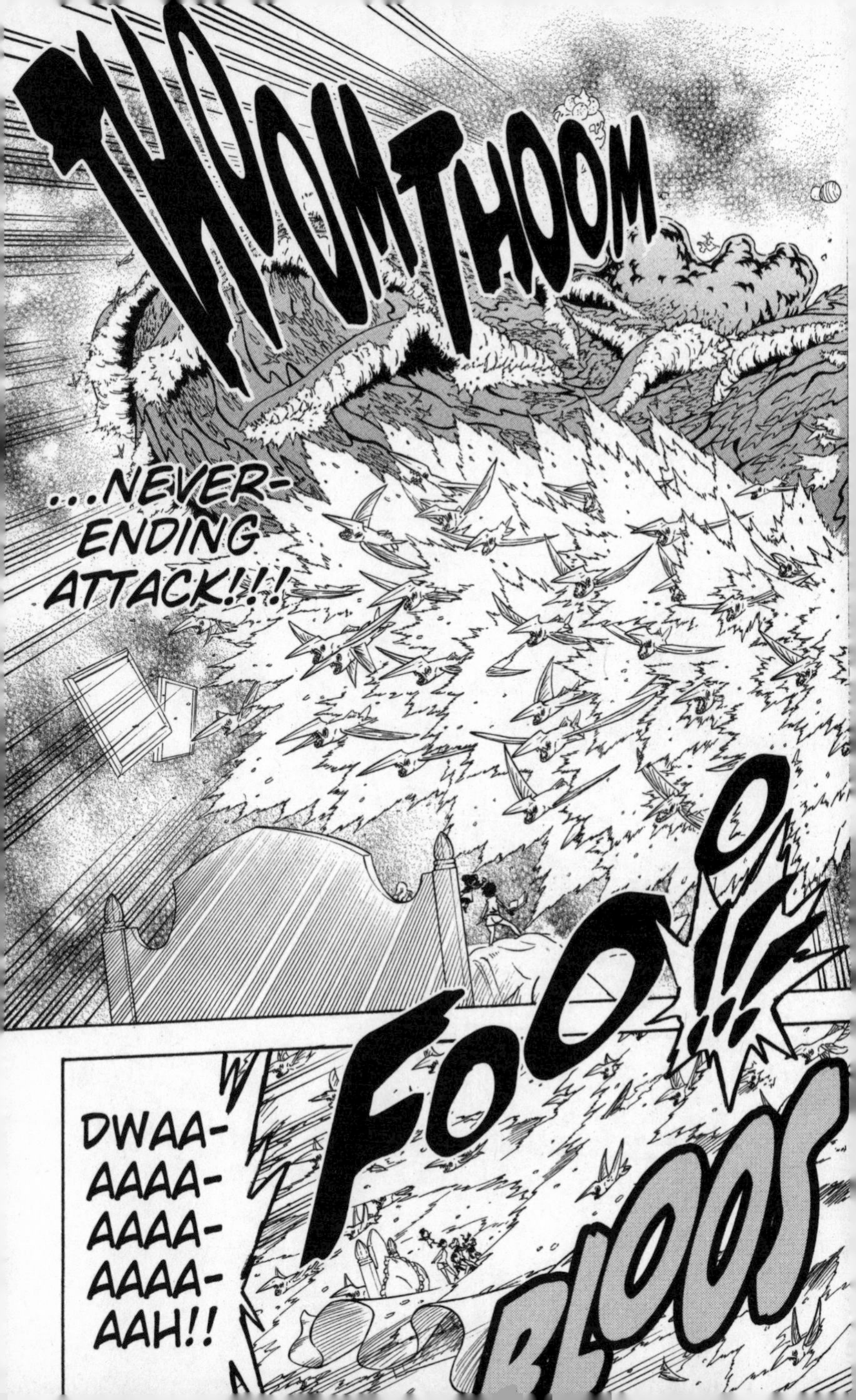
THOOM THOOM
...NEVER-ENDING ATTACK!!!
FOOO!!
BLOOOS
DWAA-AAAA-AAAA-AAAA-AAH!!

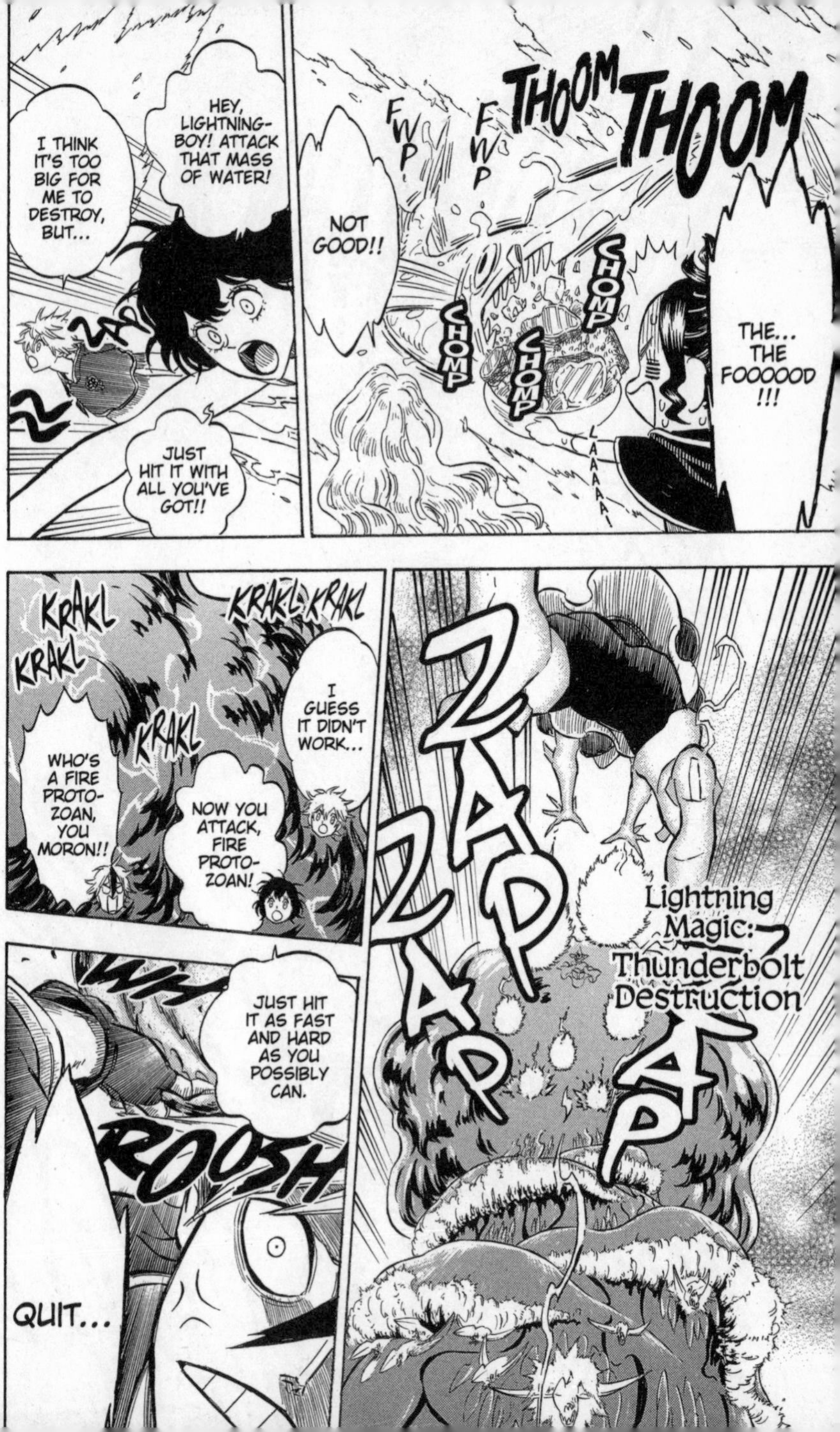
THOOM THOOM
FWP
FWP
THE... THE FOOOOOD!!!
CHOMP
NOT GOOD!!
CHOMP
CHOMP
LAAAAA!
HEY, LIGHTNING-BOY! ATTACK THAT MASS OF WATER!
I THINK IT'S TOO BIG FOR ME TO DESTROY, BUT...
JUST HIT IT WITH ALL YOU'VE GOT!!
ZAP
ZAP
Lightning Magic: Thunderbolt Destruction
ZAP
KRAKL KRAKL
I GUESS IT DIDN'T WORK...
KRAKL
KRAKL
KRAKL
NOW YOU ATTACK, FIRE PROTOZOAN!
WHO'S A FIRE PROTOZOAN, YOU MORON!!
JUST HIT IT AS FAST AND HARD AS YOU POSSIBLY CAN.
ROOSH
QUIT...

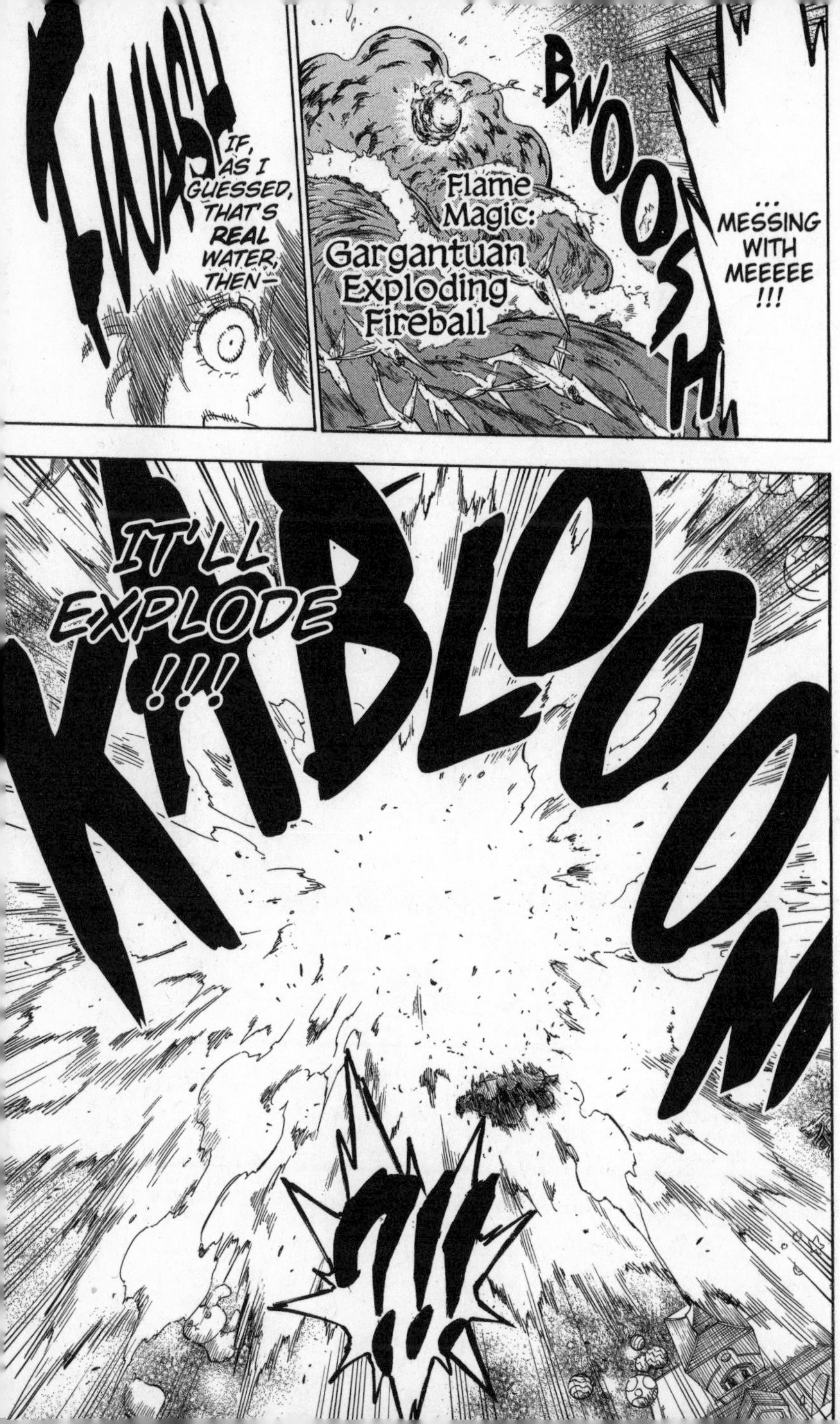
...MESSING WITH MEEEEE!!!
BWOOOSH
Flame Magic: Gargantuan Exploding Fireball
IF, AS I GUESSED, THAT'S REAL WATER, THEN—
KABLOOOM
IT'LL EXPLODE!!!
!!!

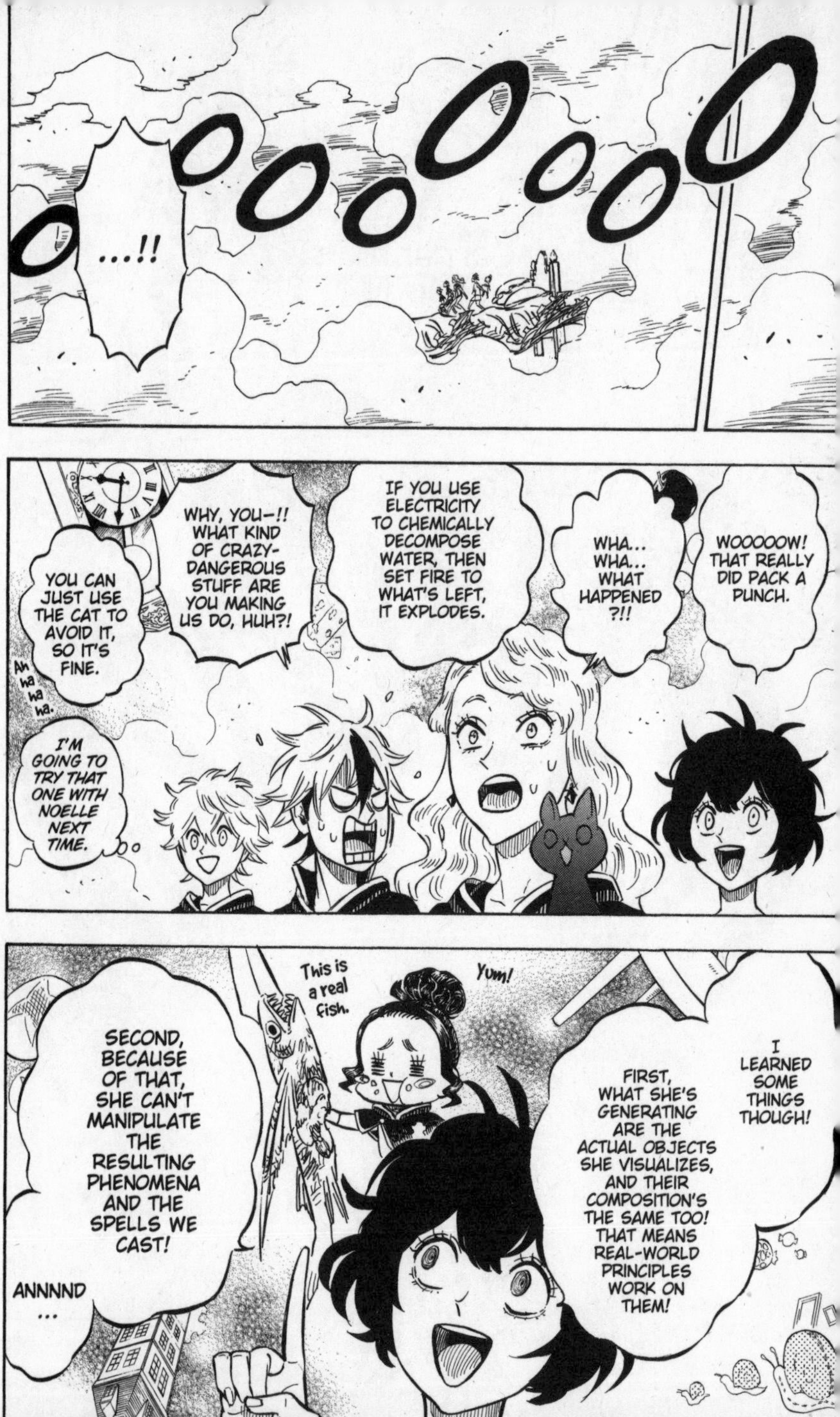
OOOOOOOO
...!!
WOOOOOW! THAT REALLY DID PACK A PUNCH.
WHA... WHA... WHAT HAPPENED?!!
IF YOU USE ELECTRICITY TO CHEMICALLY DECOMPOSE WATER, THEN SET FIRE TO WHAT'S LEFT, IT EXPLODES.
WHY, YOU—!! WHAT KIND OF CRAZY-DANGEROUS STUFF ARE YOU MAKING US DO, HUH?!
YOU CAN JUST USE THE CAT TO AVOID IT, SO IT'S FINE.
Ah ha ha ha.
I'M GOING TO TRY THAT ONE WITH NOELLE NEXT TIME.
I LEARNED SOME THINGS THOUGH!
FIRST, WHAT SHE'S GENERATING ARE THE ACTUAL OBJECTS SHE VISUALIZES, AND THEIR COMPOSITION'S THE SAME TOO! THAT MEANS REAL-WORLD PRINCIPLES WORK ON THEM!
Yum!
This is a real fish.
SECOND, BECAUSE OF THAT, SHE CAN'T MANIPULATE THE RESULTING PHENOMENA AND THE SPELLS WE CAST!
ANNNND ...

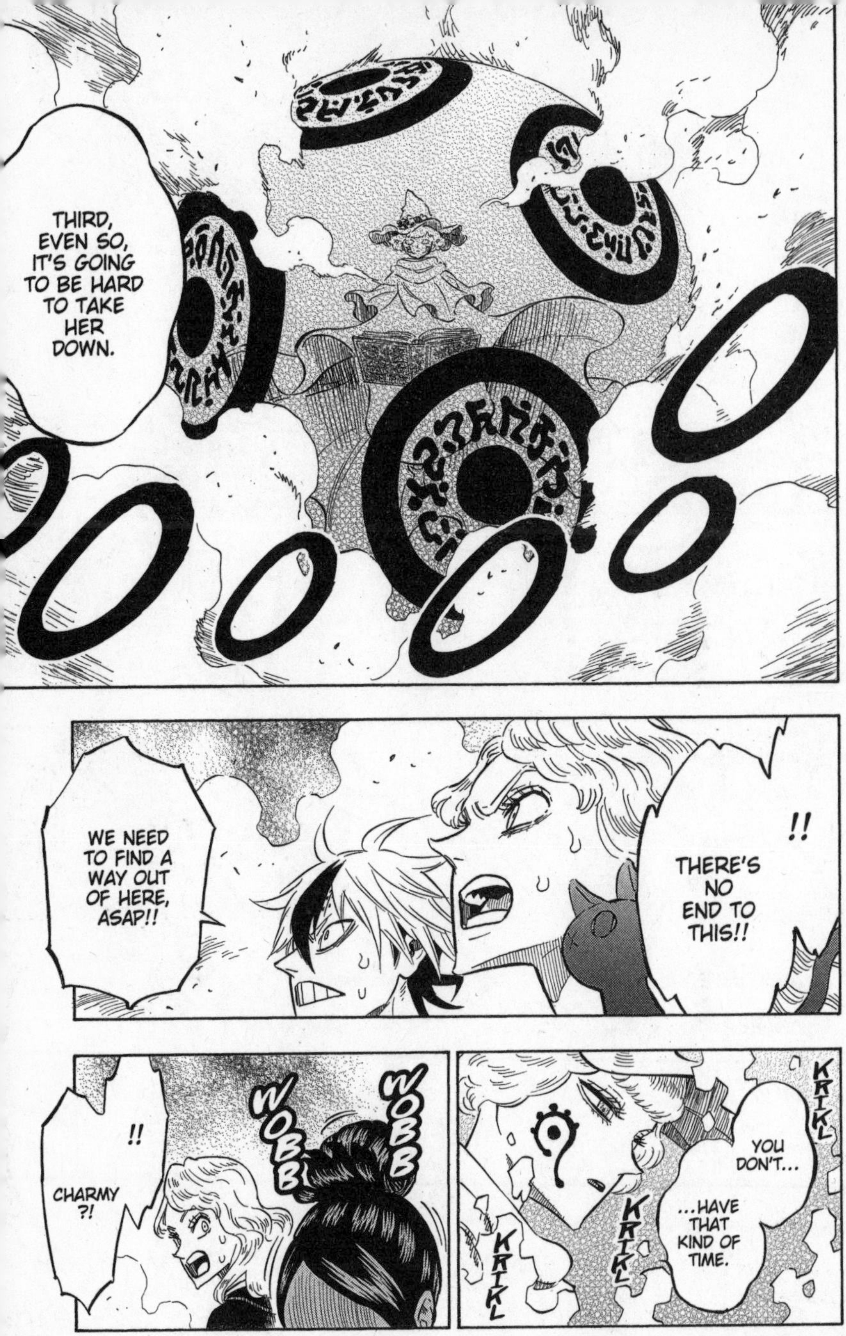
THIRD, EVEN SO, IT'S GOING TO BE HARD TO TAKE HER DOWN.
!!
THERE'S NO END TO THIS!!
WE NEED TO FIND A WAY OUT OF HERE, ASAP!!
KRIKL
YOU DON'T...
...HAVE THAT KIND OF TIME.
KRIKL
KRIKL
WOBB
WOBB
!!
CHARMY ?!

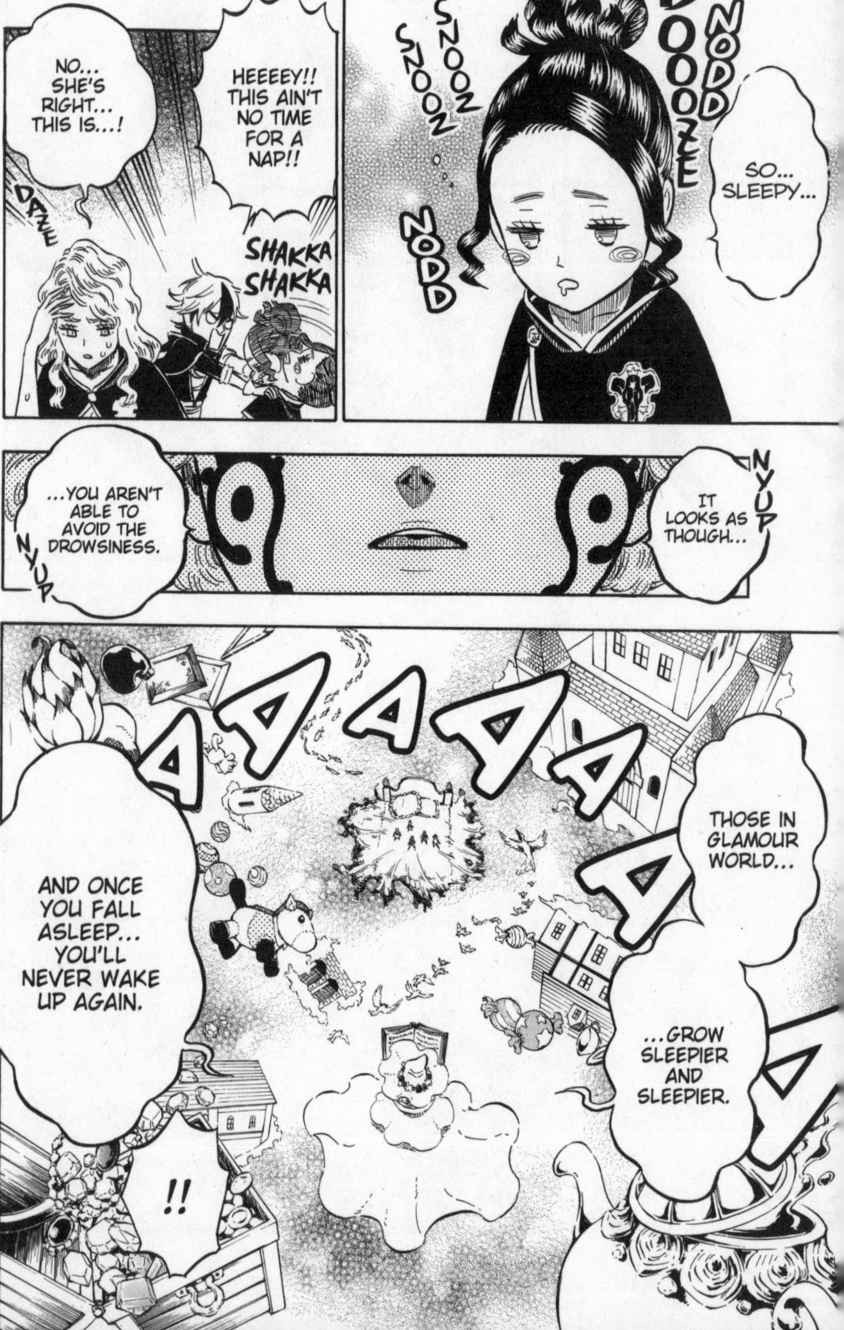
NODD
DOOOOZE
SO... SLEEPY...
SNOOZE
SNOOZE
NODD
HEEEEY!! THIS AIN'T NO TIME FOR A NAP!!
SHAKKA SHAKKA
NO... SHE'S RIGHT... THIS IS...!
DAZE
IT LOOKS AS THOUGH...
NYUP
...YOU AREN'T ABLE TO AVOID THE DROWSINESS.
NYUP
AAAAAAAA
THOSE IN GLAMOUR WORLD...
...GROW SLEEPIER AND SLEEPIER.
AND ONCE YOU FALL ASLEEP... YOU'LL NEVER WAKE UP AGAIN.
!!

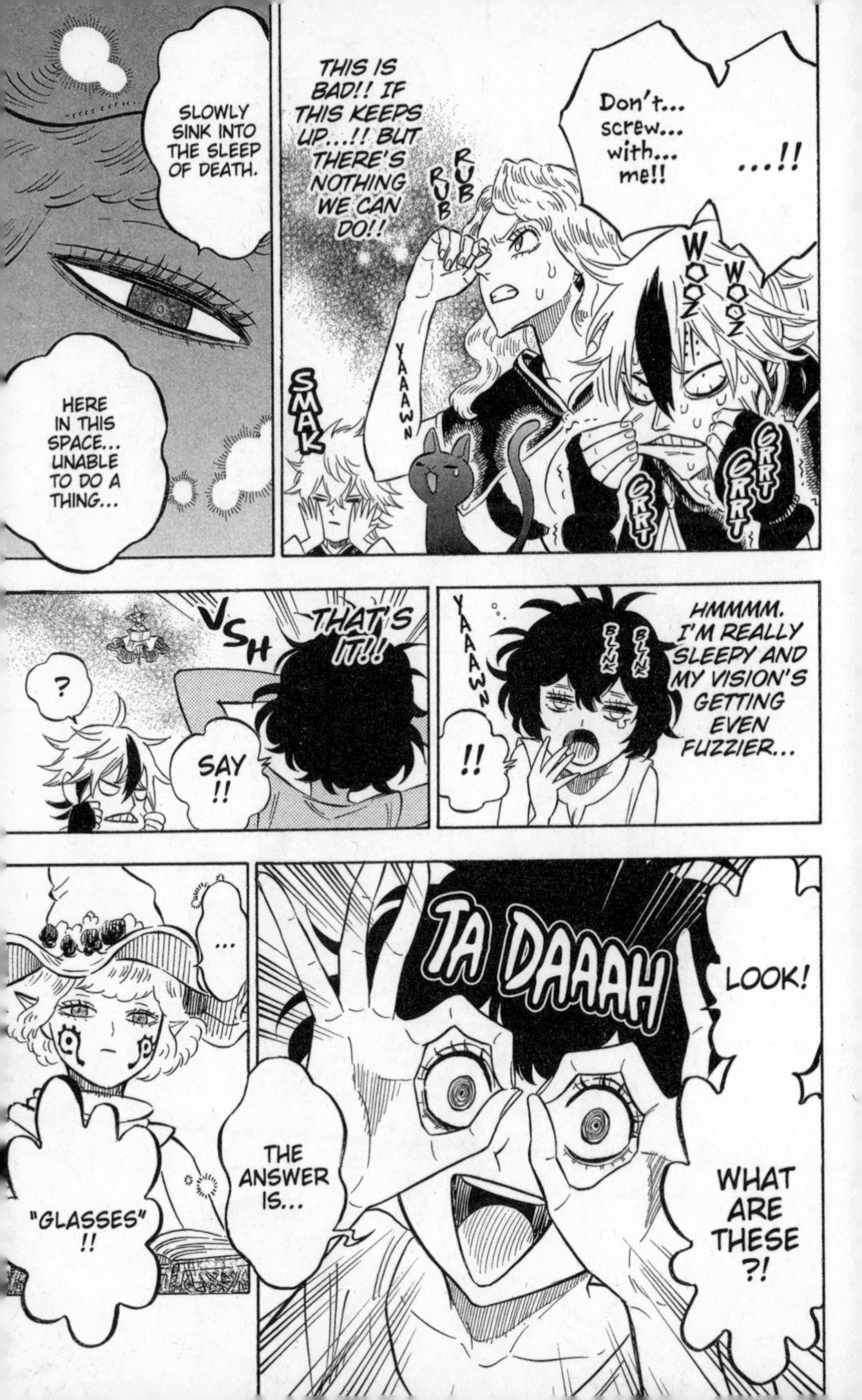
Don't... screw... with... me!!
...!!
WOOZ WOOZ
GRRT GRRT GRRT
THIS IS BAD!! IF THIS KEEPS UP...!! BUT THERE'S NOTHING WE CAN DO!!
RUB RUB
YAAAAWN
SMAK
SLOWLY SINK INTO THE SLEEP OF DEATH.
HERE IN THIS SPACE... UNABLE TO DO A THING...
HMMMM. I'M REALLY SLEEPY AND MY VISION'S GETTING EVEN FUZZIER...
BLINK BLINK
YAAAAWN
!!
THAT'S IT!!
VSH
SAY !!
?
LOOK!
TA DAAAH
WHAT ARE THESE ?!
THE ANSWER IS...
...
"GLASSES" !!

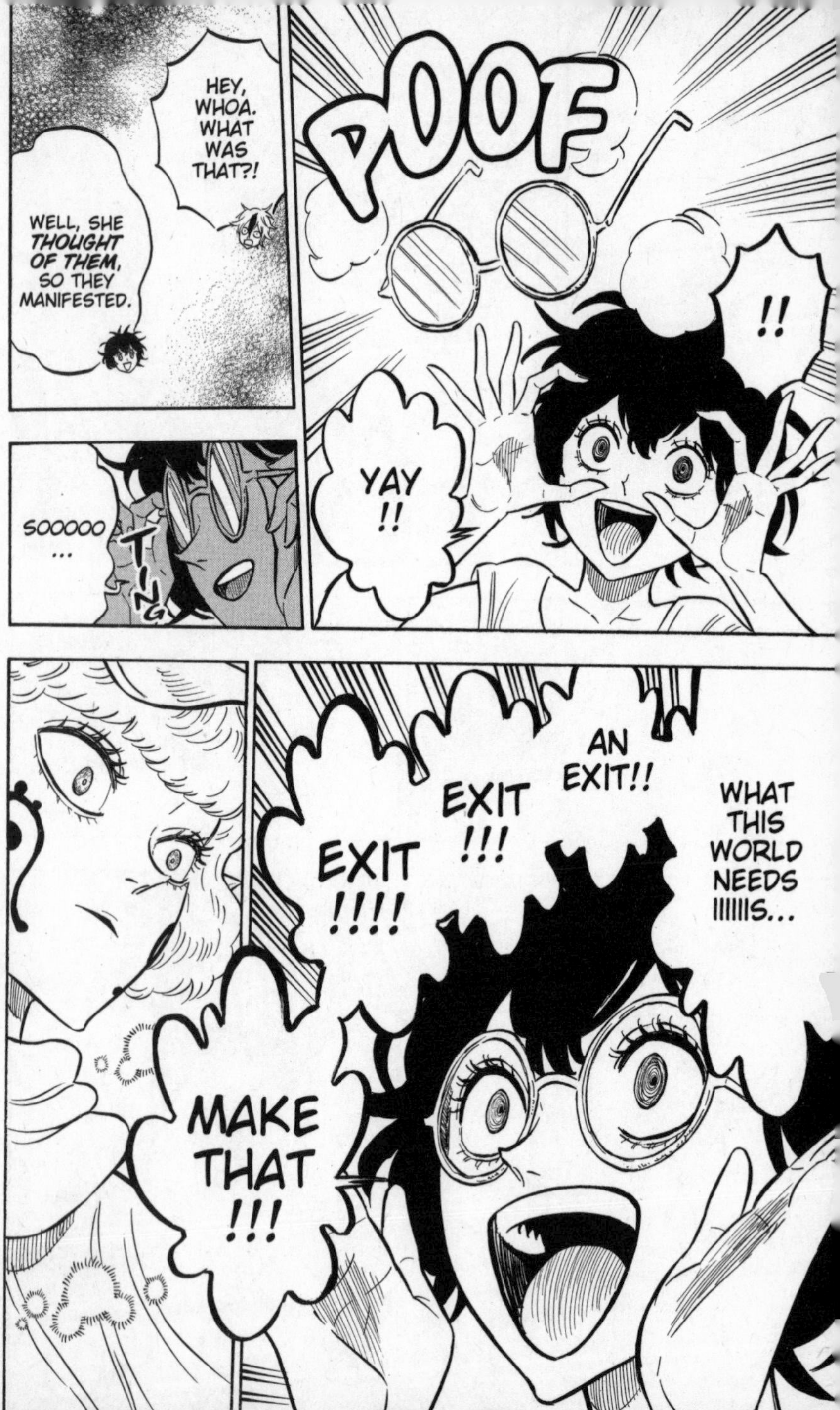
POOF
!!
YAY !!
HEY, WHOA. WHAT WAS THAT?!
WELL, SHE *THOUGHT OF THEM*, SO THEY MANIFESTED.
SOOOOO ...
TING
WHAT THIS WORLD NEEDS IIIIIIS...
AN EXIT!!
EXIT !!!
EXIT !!!!
MAKE THAT !!!

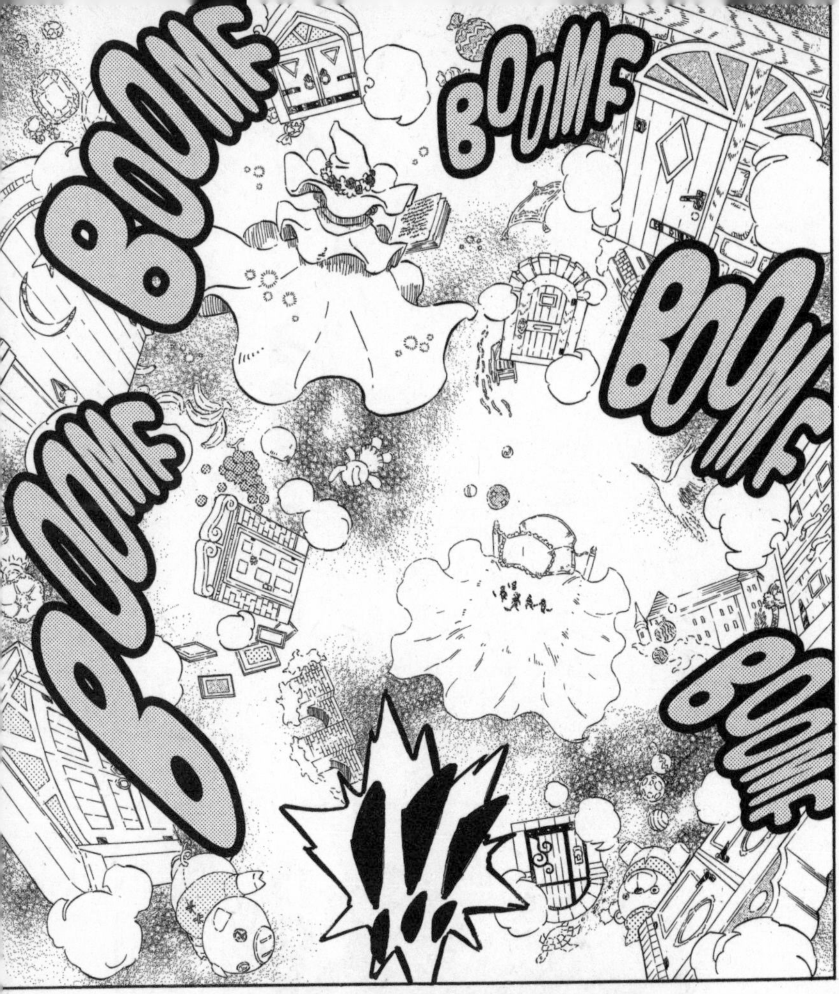
BOOMF
BOOMF
BOOMF
BOOMF
BOOMF
!!

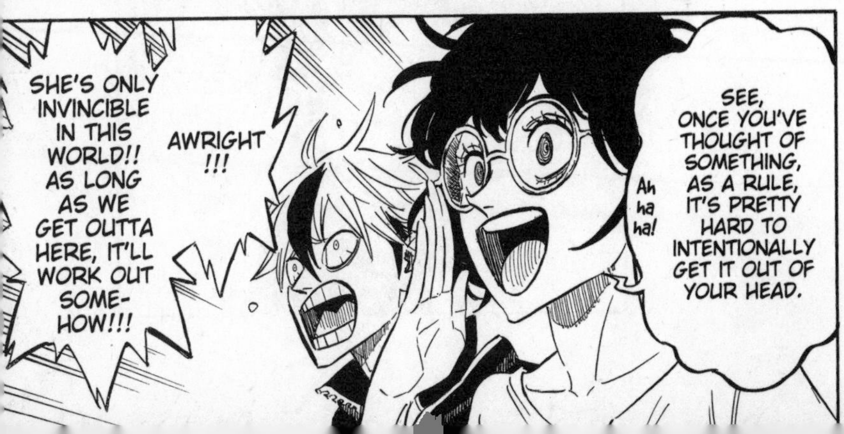
SEE, ONCE YOU'VE THOUGHT OF SOMETHING, AS A RULE, IT'S PRETTY HARD TO INTENTIONALLY GET IT OUT OF YOUR HEAD.
Ah ha ha!
AWRIGHT!!!
SHE'S ONLY INVINCIBLE IN THIS WORLD!! AS LONG AS WE GET OUTTA HERE, IT'LL WORK OUT SOME-HOW!!!

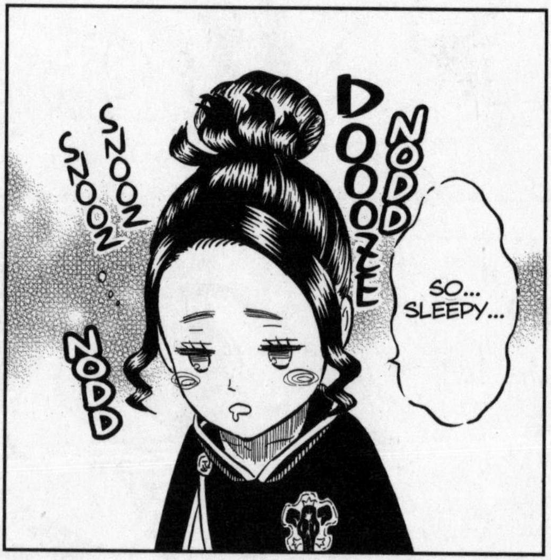
SO... SLEEPY...
NODD
DOOOOZE
SNOOZ
SNOOZ
NODD

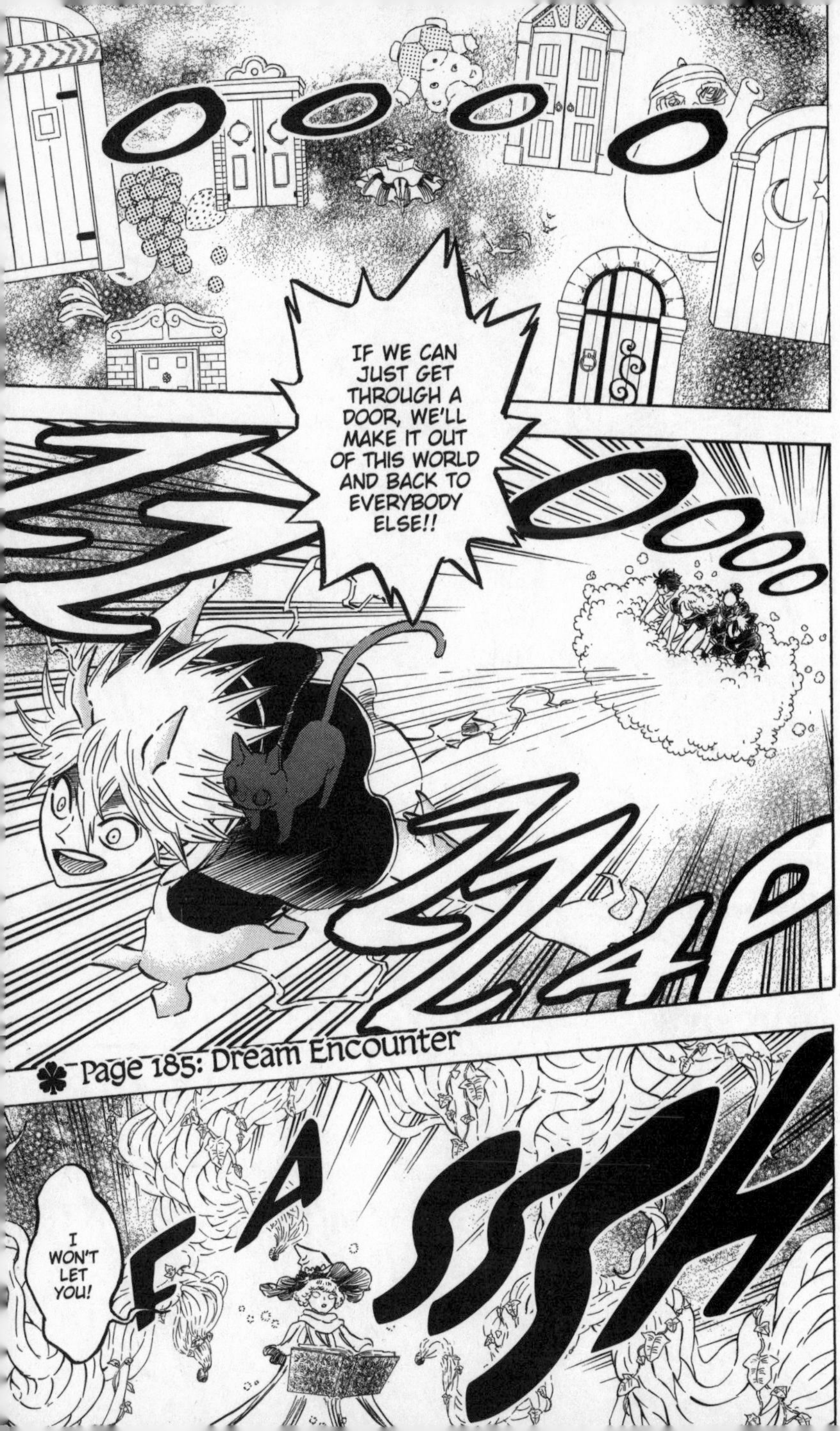
IF WE CAN JUST GET THROUGH A DOOR, WE'LL MAKE IT OUT OF THIS WORLD AND BACK TO EVERYBODY ELSE!!
Page 185: Dream Encounter
I WON'T LET YOU!

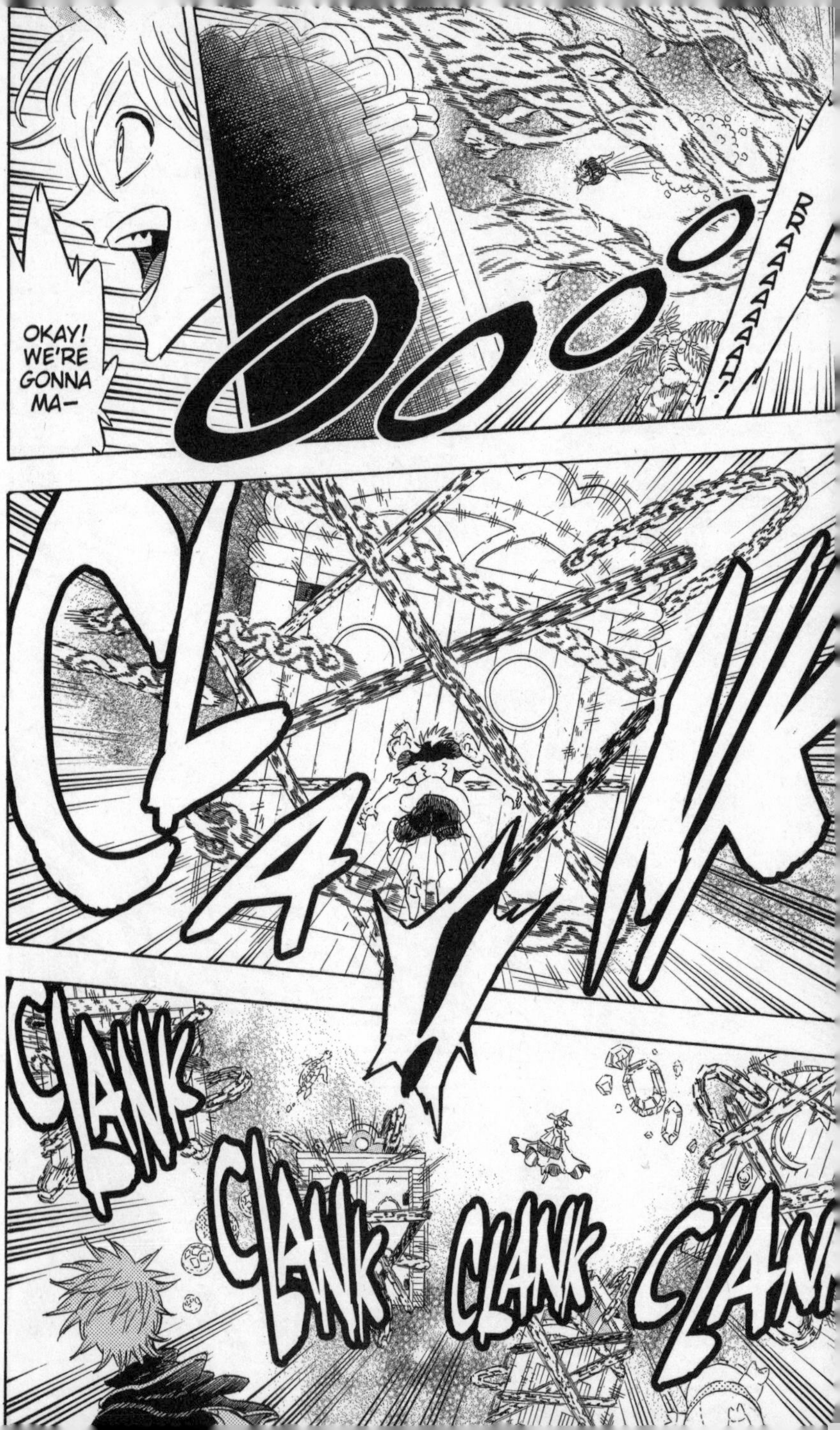
RRAAAAAAAH!
OOOO
OKAY! WE'RE GONNA MA—
CLANK
CLANK
CLANK
CLANK
CLAN...

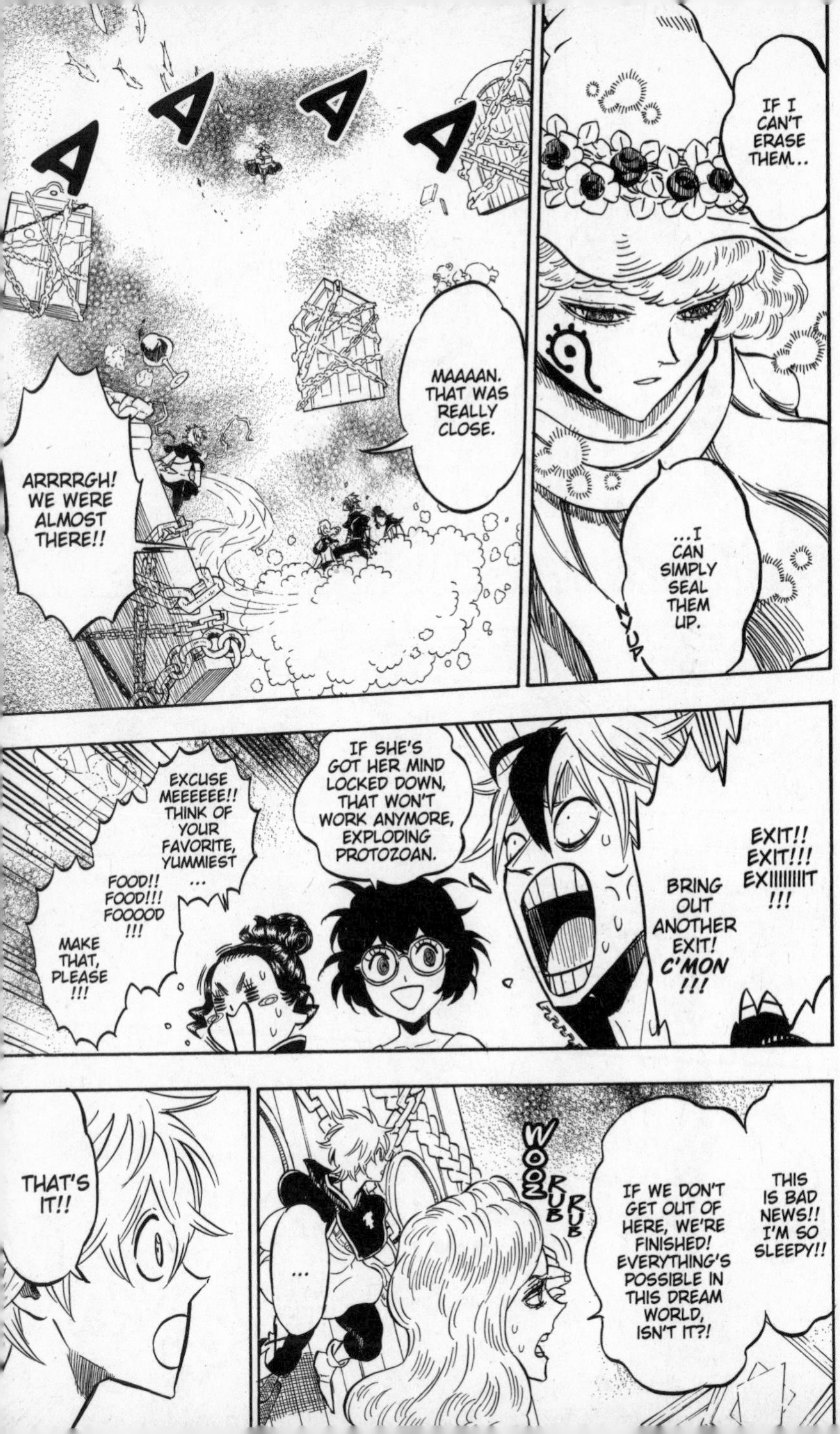
IF I CAN'T ERASE THEM...
...I CAN SIMPLY SEAL THEM UP.
NYUP
A A A A
MAAAAN. THAT WAS REALLY CLOSE.
ARRRRGH! WE WERE ALMOST THERE!!
EXIT!! EXIT!!! EXIIIIIIIIT!!!
BRING OUT ANOTHER EXIT! C'MON!!!
IF SHE'S GOT HER MIND LOCKED DOWN, THAT WON'T WORK ANYMORE, EXPLODING PROTOZOAN.
EXCUSE MEEEEEE!! THINK OF YOUR FAVORITE, YUMMIEST...
FOOD!! FOOD!!! FOOOOD!!!
MAKE THAT, PLEASE!!!
THIS IS BAD NEWS!! I'M SO SLEEPY!!
IF WE DON'T GET OUT OF HERE, WE'RE FINISHED! EVERYTHING'S POSSIBLE IN THIS DREAM WORLD, ISN'T IT?!
WOOZ
RUB RUB
...
THAT'S IT!!

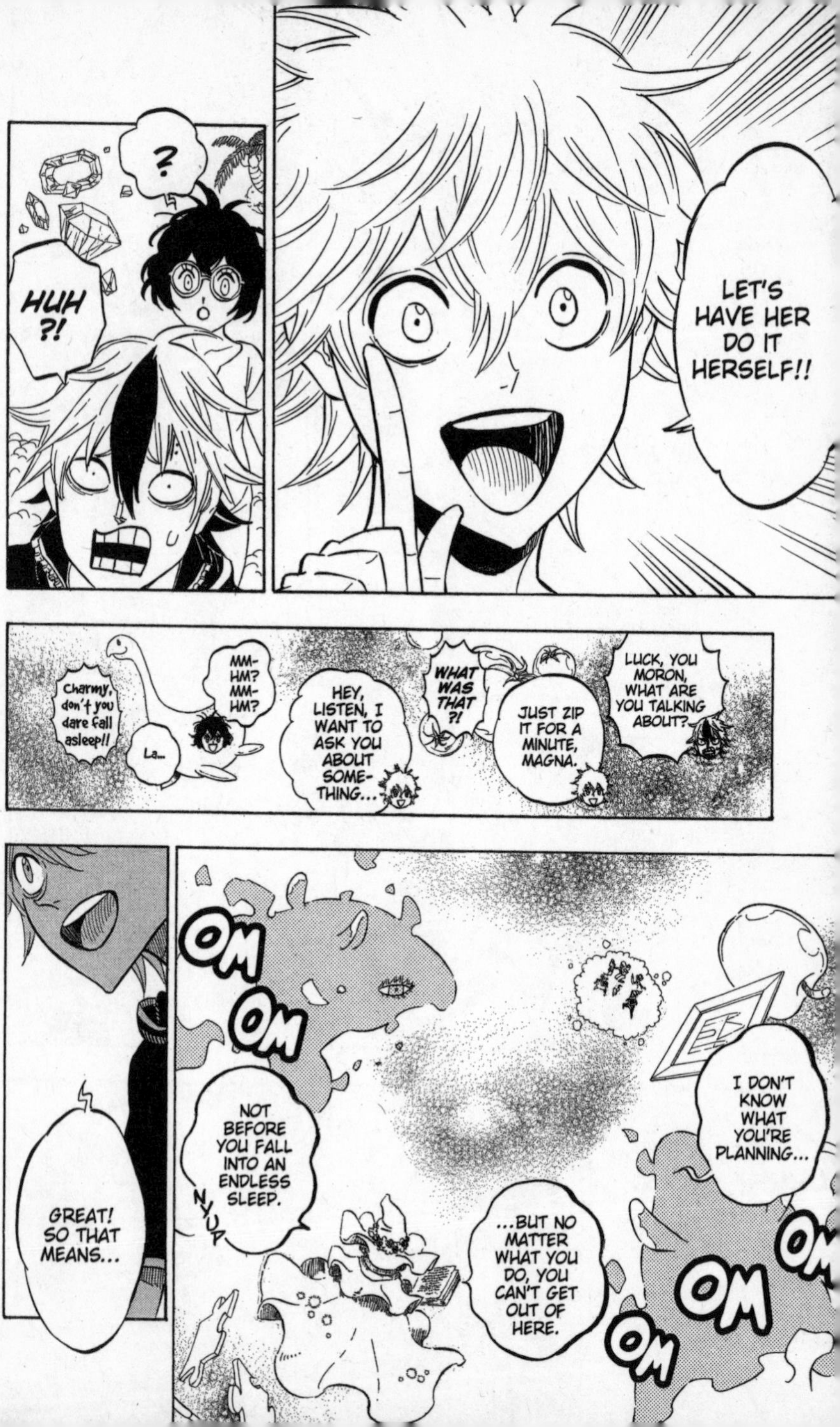
LET'S HAVE HER DO IT HERSELF!!
?
HUH ?!
LUCK, YOU MORON, WHAT ARE YOU TALKING ABOUT?
JUST ZIP IT FOR A MINUTE, MAGNA.
WHAT WAS THAT ?!
HEY, LISTEN, I WANT TO ASK YOU ABOUT SOME-THING...
MM-HM? MM-HM?
La...
Charmy, don't you dare fall asleep!!
OM OM OM
I DON'T KNOW WHAT YOU'RE PLANNING...
...BUT NO MATTER WHAT YOU DO, YOU CAN'T GET OUT OF HERE.
NOT BEFORE YOU FALL INTO AN ENDLESS SLEEP.
NYUP
OM OM
GREAT! SO THAT MEANS...

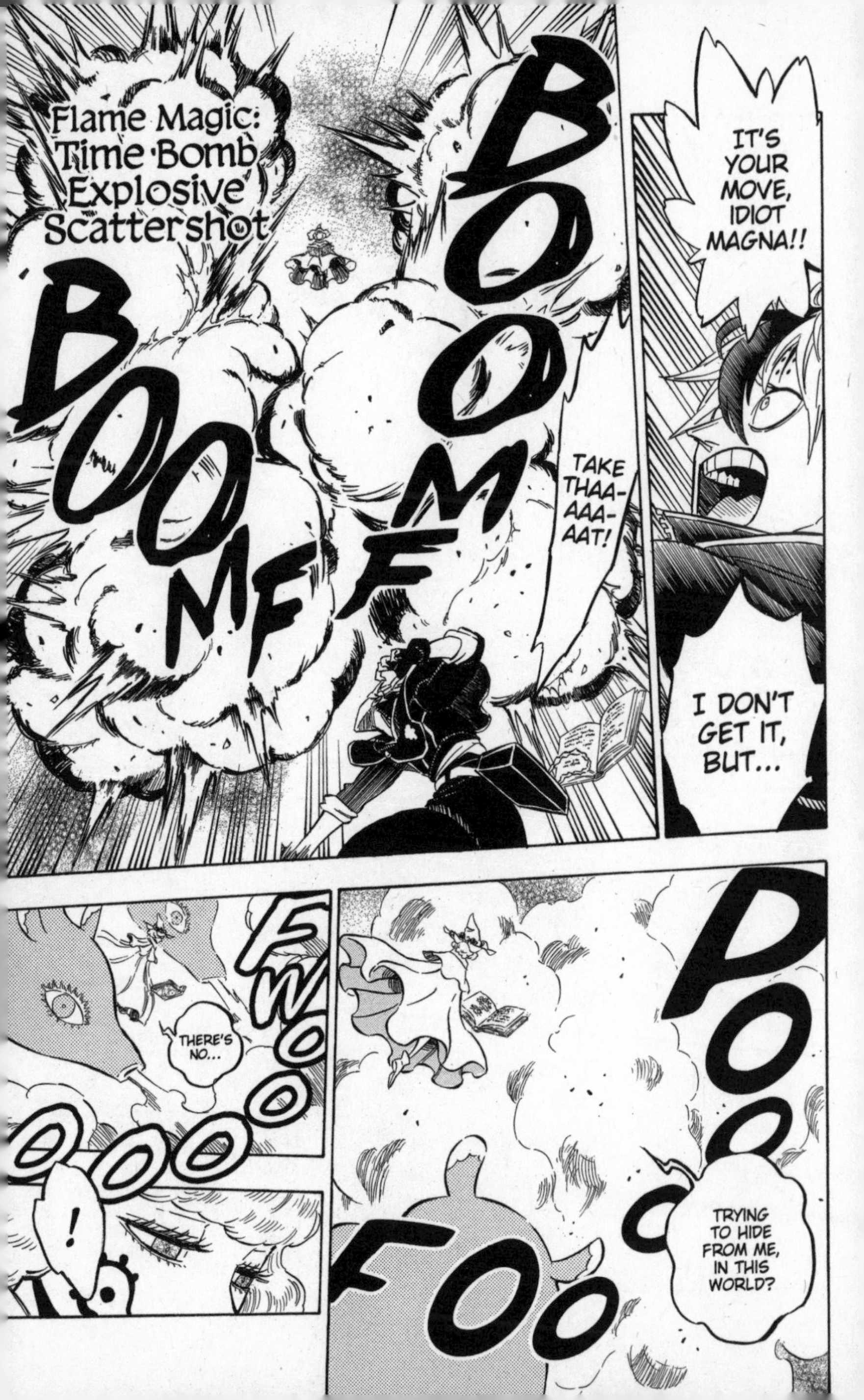
IT'S YOUR MOVE, IDIOT MAGNA!!
I DON'T GET IT, BUT...
Flame Magic: Time Bomb Explosive Scattershot
BOOOMF
BOOOMF
TAKE THAA-AAA-AAT!
POOO
TRYING TO HIDE FROM ME, IN THIS WORLD?
FOO
FWOOOOOOO
THERE'S NO...
!

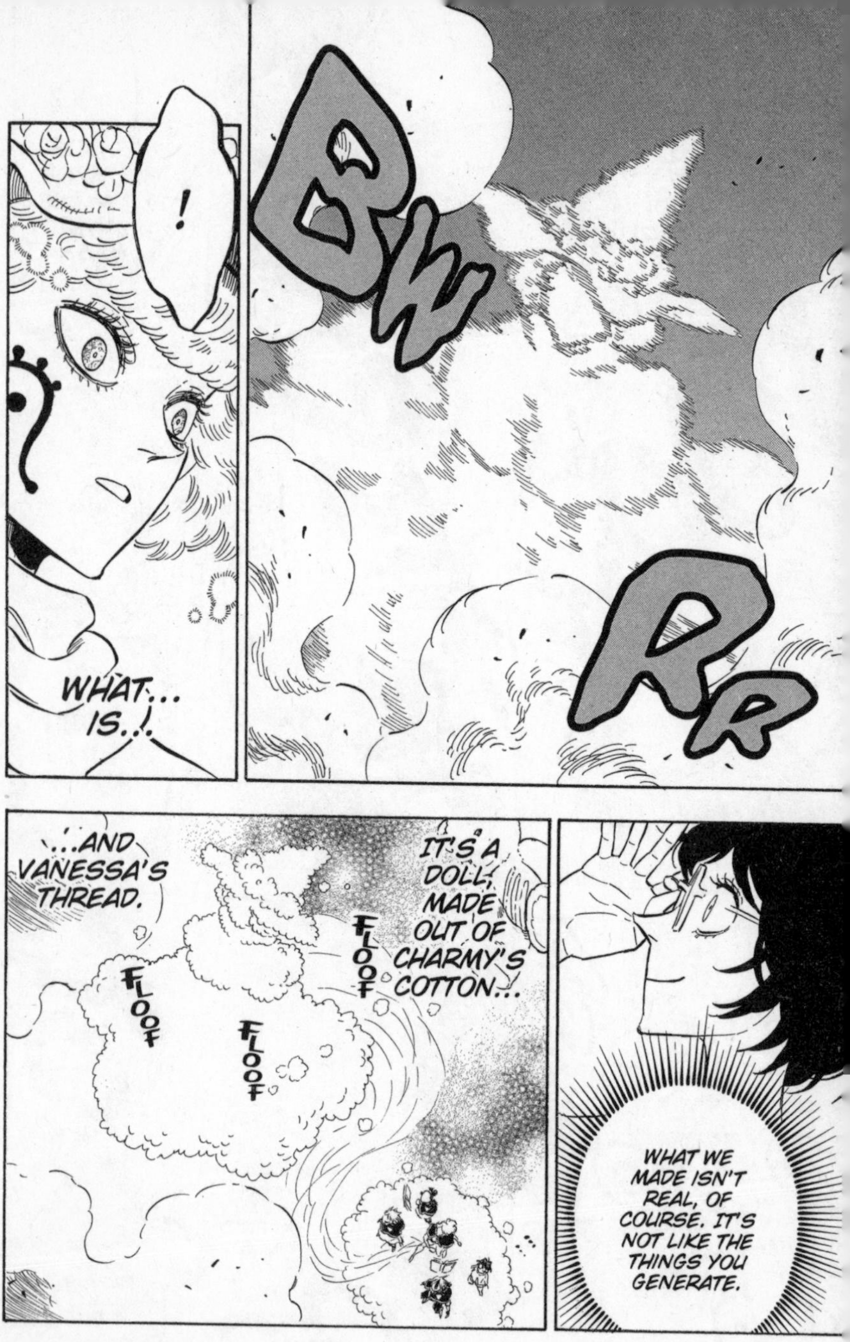
BWRR
!
WHAT... IS...
WHAT WE MADE ISN'T REAL, OF COURSE. IT'S NOT LIKE THE THINGS YOU GENERATE.
IT'S A DOLL, MADE OUT OF CHARMY'S COTTON...
...AND VANESSA'S THREAD.
FLOOF
FLOOF
FLOOF

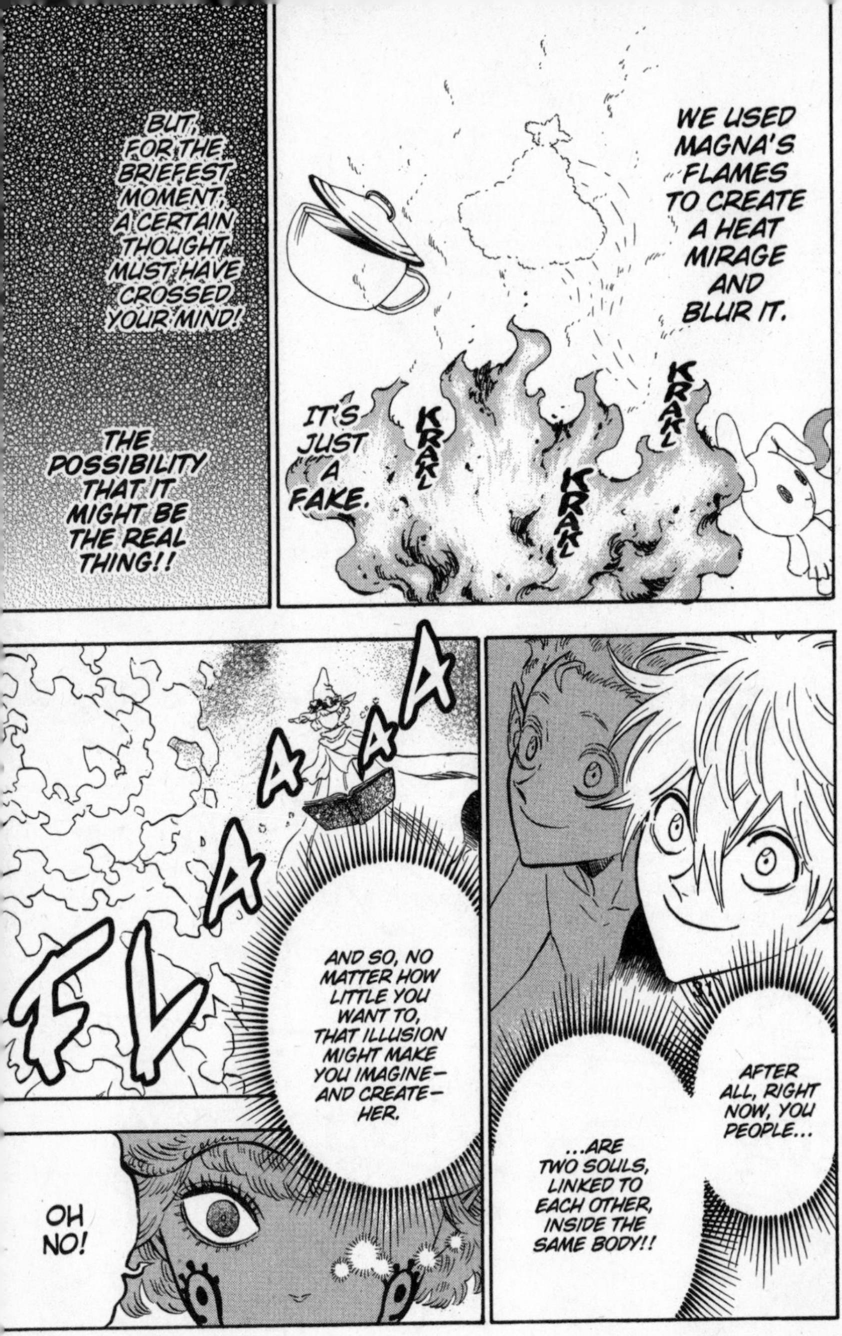
WE USED MAGNA'S FLAMES TO CREATE A HEAT MIRAGE AND BLUR IT.
KRAK
KRAK
KRAK
IT'S JUST A FAKE.
BUT, FOR THE BRIEFEST MOMENT, A CERTAIN THOUGHT MUST HAVE CROSSED YOUR MIND!
THE POSSIBILITY THAT IT MIGHT BE THE REAL THING!!
AFTER ALL, RIGHT NOW, YOU PEOPLE...
...ARE TWO SOULS, LINKED TO EACH OTHER, INSIDE THE SAME BODY!!
FLAAAAA
AND SO, NO MATTER HOW LITTLE YOU WANT TO, THAT ILLUSION MIGHT MAKE YOU IMAGINE—AND CREATE—HER.
OH NO!

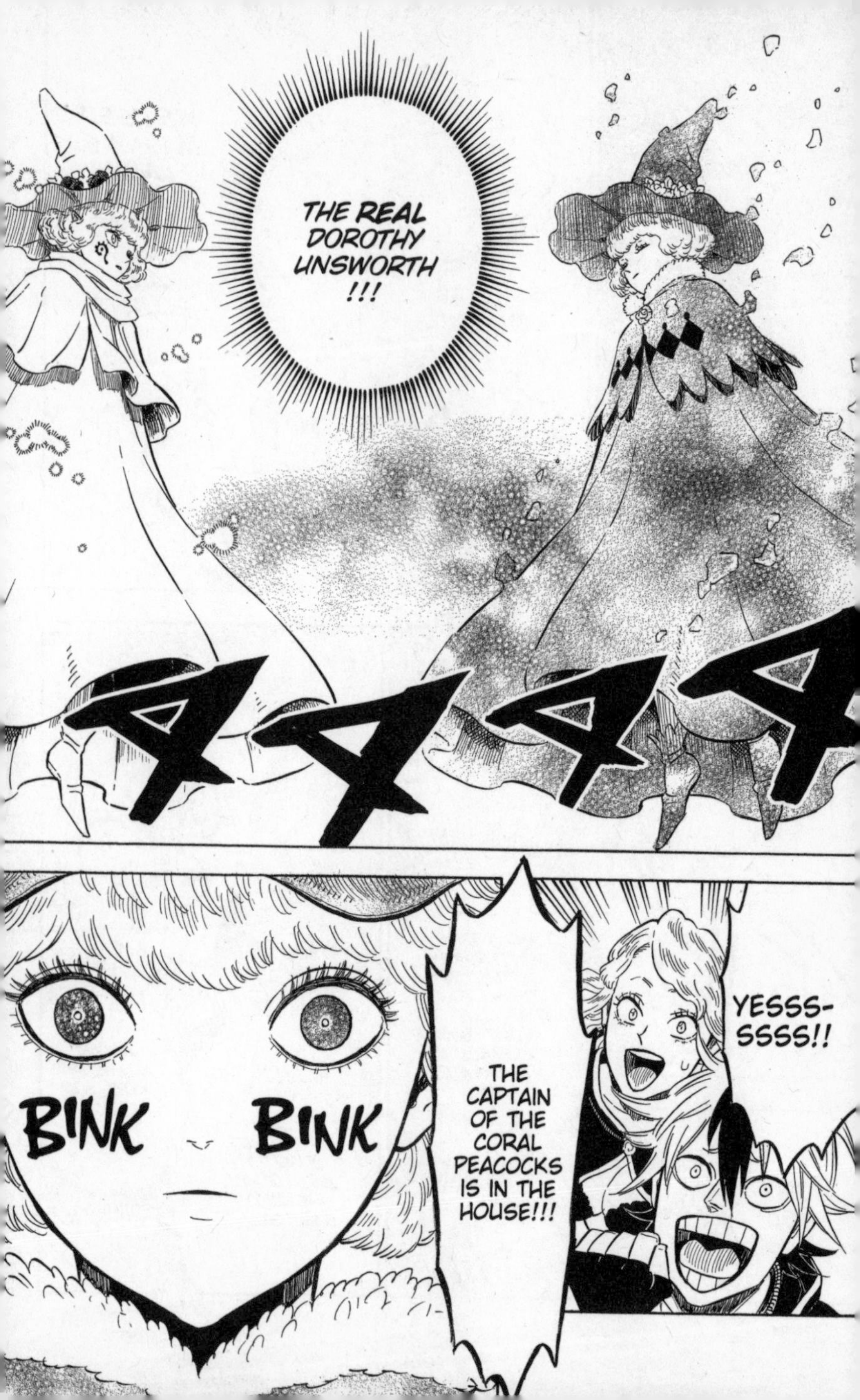
THE REAL DOROTHY UNSWORTH!!!
YESSS-SSSS!!
THE CAPTAIN OF THE CORAL PEACOCKS IS IN THE HOUSE!!!
BINK
BINK

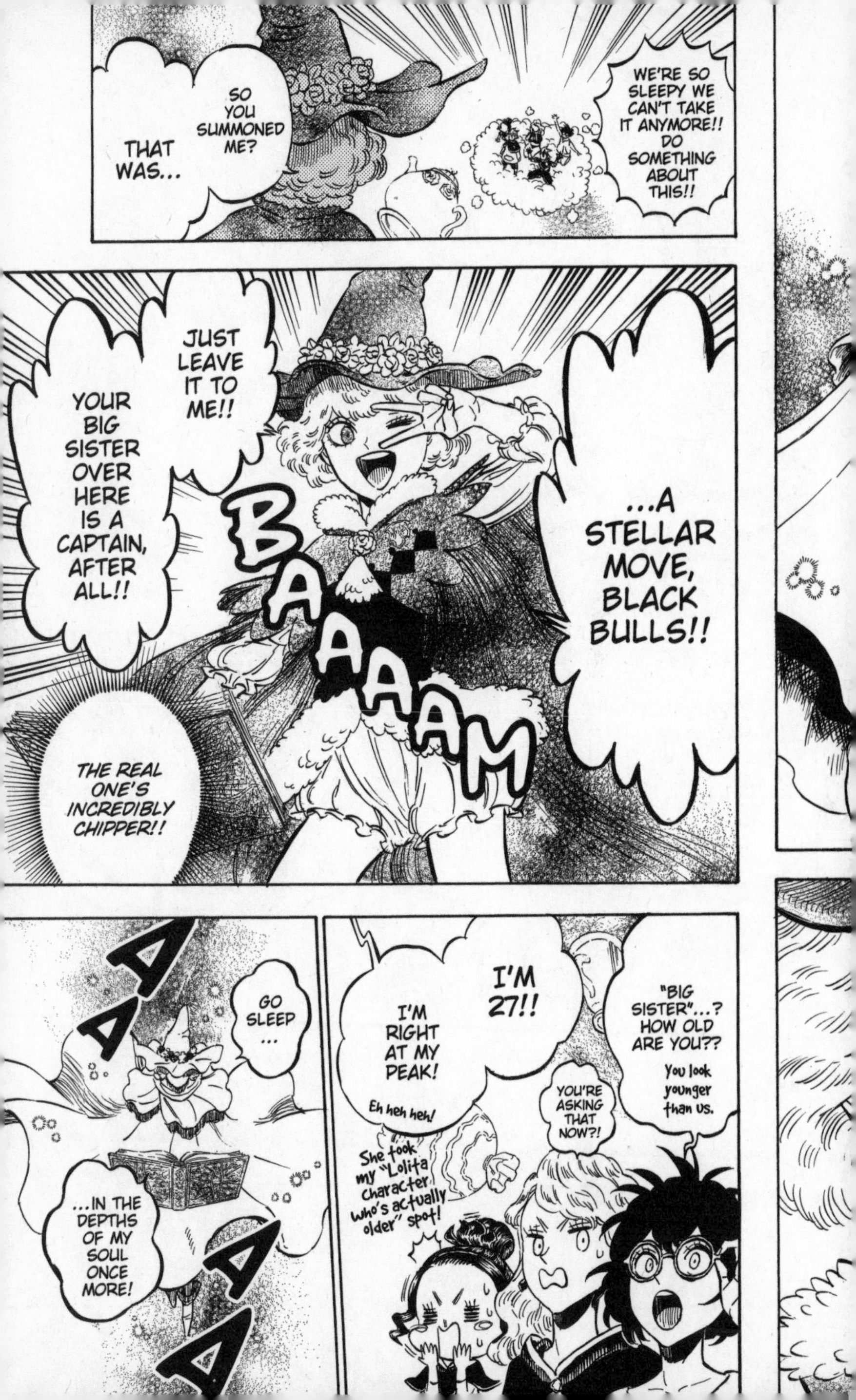
WE'RE SO SLEEPY WE CAN'T TAKE IT ANYMORE!! DO SOMETHING ABOUT THIS!!
SO YOU SUMMONED ME?
THAT WAS...
...A STELLAR MOVE, BLACK BULLS!!
JUST LEAVE IT TO ME!!
YOUR BIG SISTER OVER HERE IS A CAPTAIN, AFTER ALL!!
BAAAAAM
THE REAL ONE'S INCREDIBLY CHIPPER!!
"BIG SISTER"...? HOW OLD ARE YOU??
You look younger than us.
I'M 27!!
I'M RIGHT AT MY PEAK!
Eh heh heh!
YOU'RE ASKING THAT NOW?!
She took my "Lolita character who's actually older" spot!
AA
GO SLEEP...
...IN THE DEPTHS OF MY SOUL ONCE MORE!
AAA

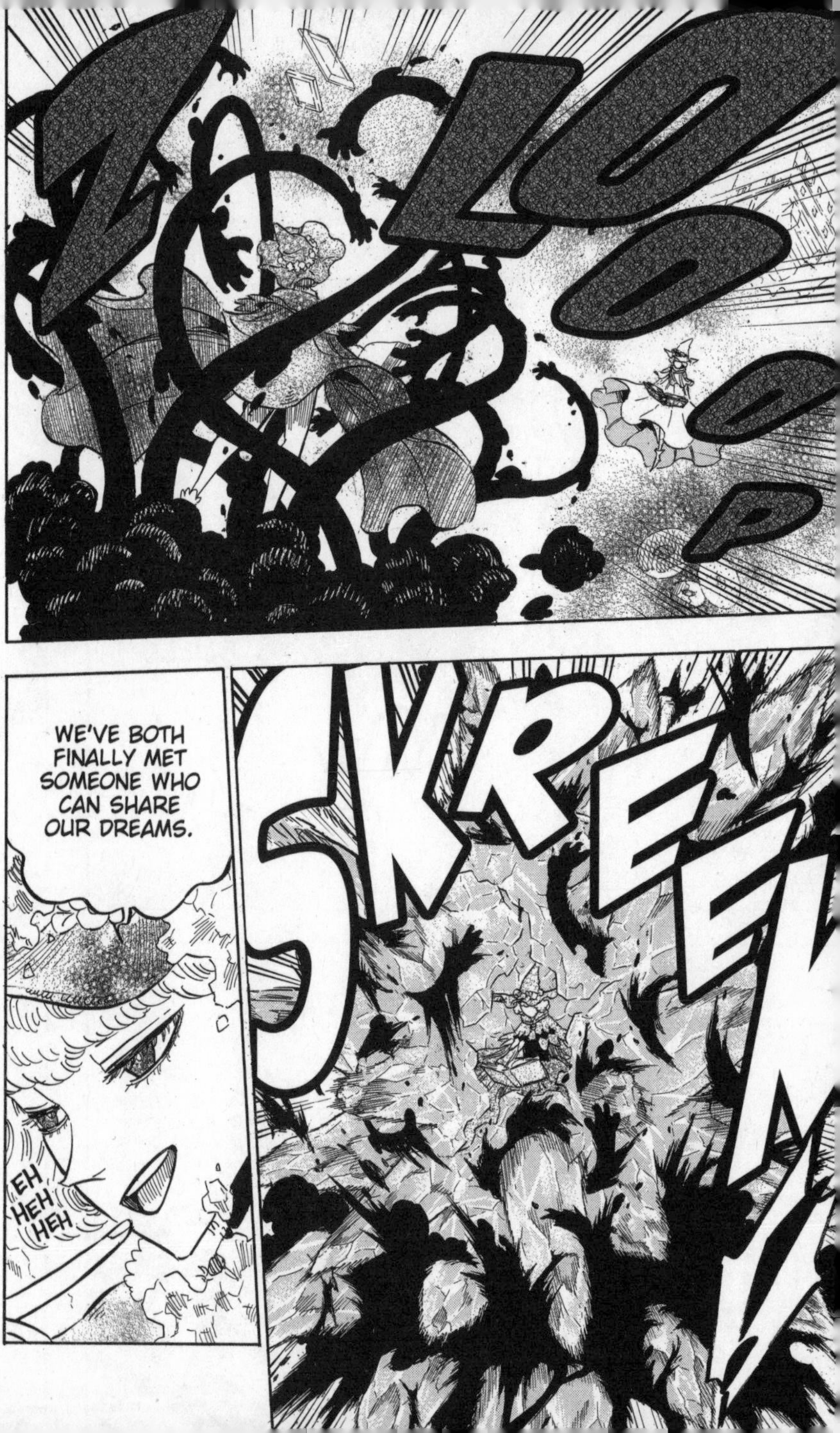
WE'VE BOTH FINALLY MET SOMEONE WHO CAN SHARE OUR DREAMS.
EH HEH HEH

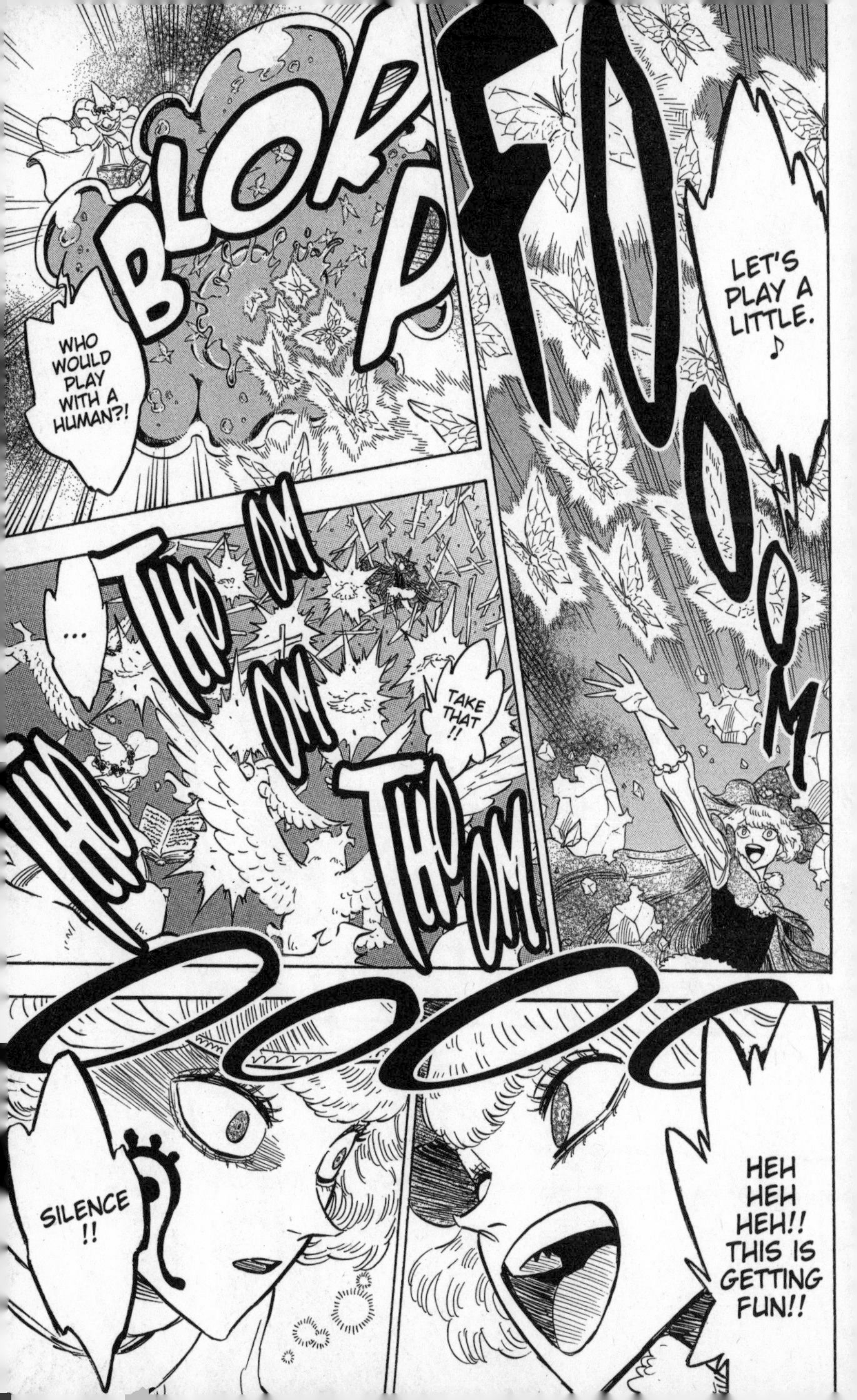
LET'S PLAY A LITTLE. ♪
FOOOOM
BLOP
WHO WOULD PLAY WITH A HUMAN?!
TAKE THAT!!
THOOM
THOOM
THOOM
...
HEH HEH HEH!! THIS IS GETTING FUN!!
SILENCE!!

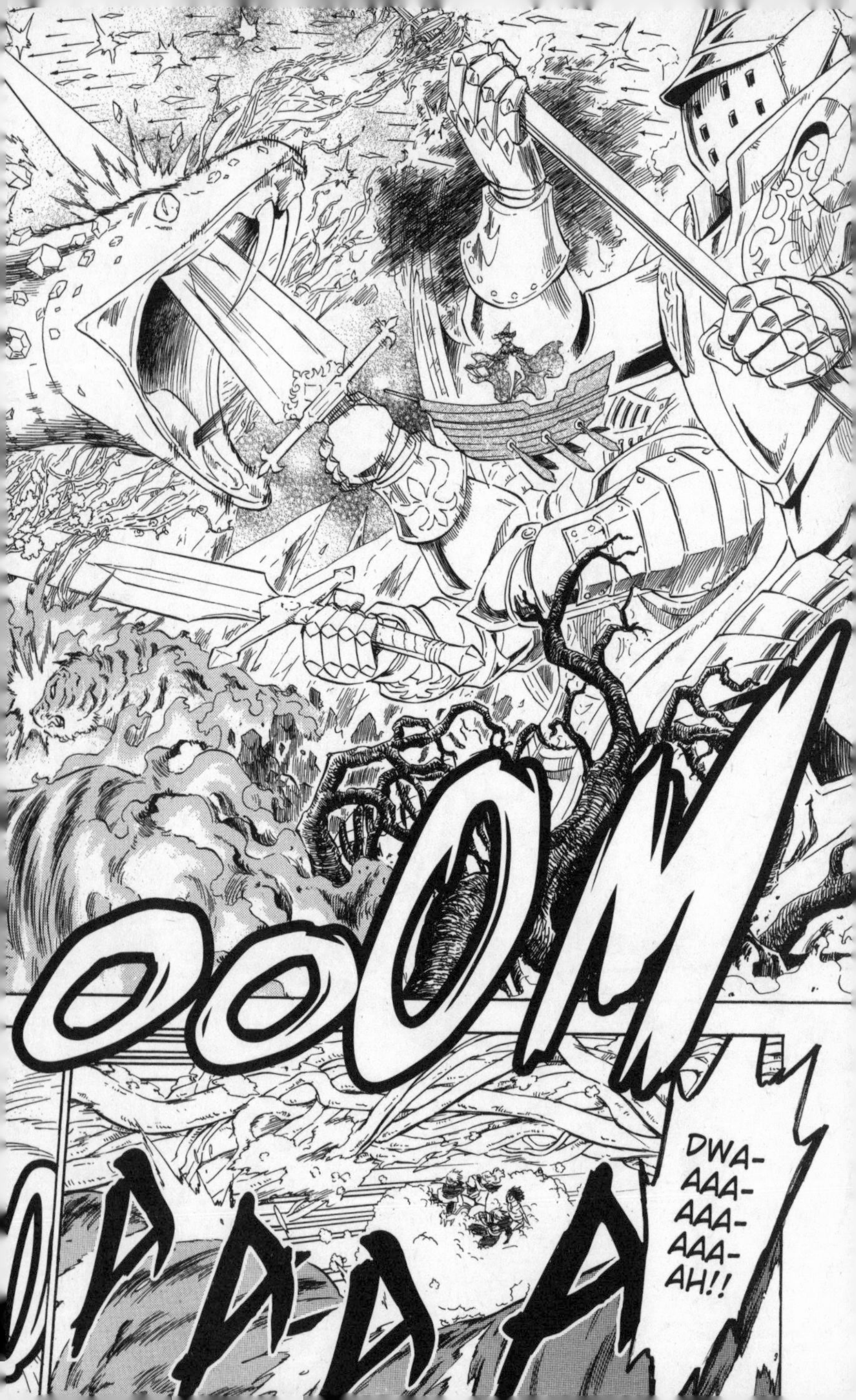

BOOOM
DWA-AAA-AAA-AAA-AH!!

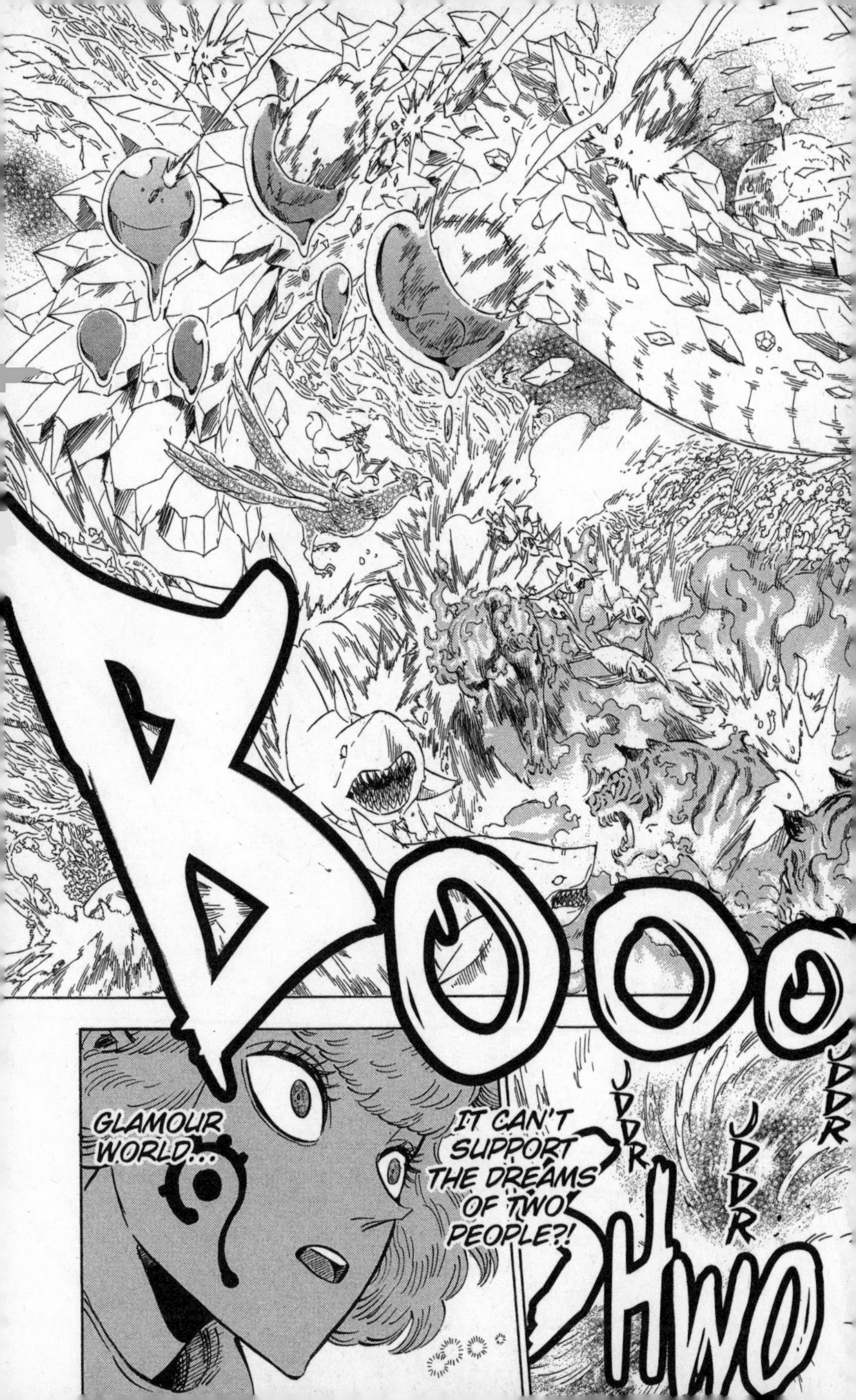
BOOOO
JDDR
JDDR
JDDR
IT CAN'T SUPPORT THE DREAMS OF TWO PEOPLE?!
GLAMOUR WORLD...
SHWO

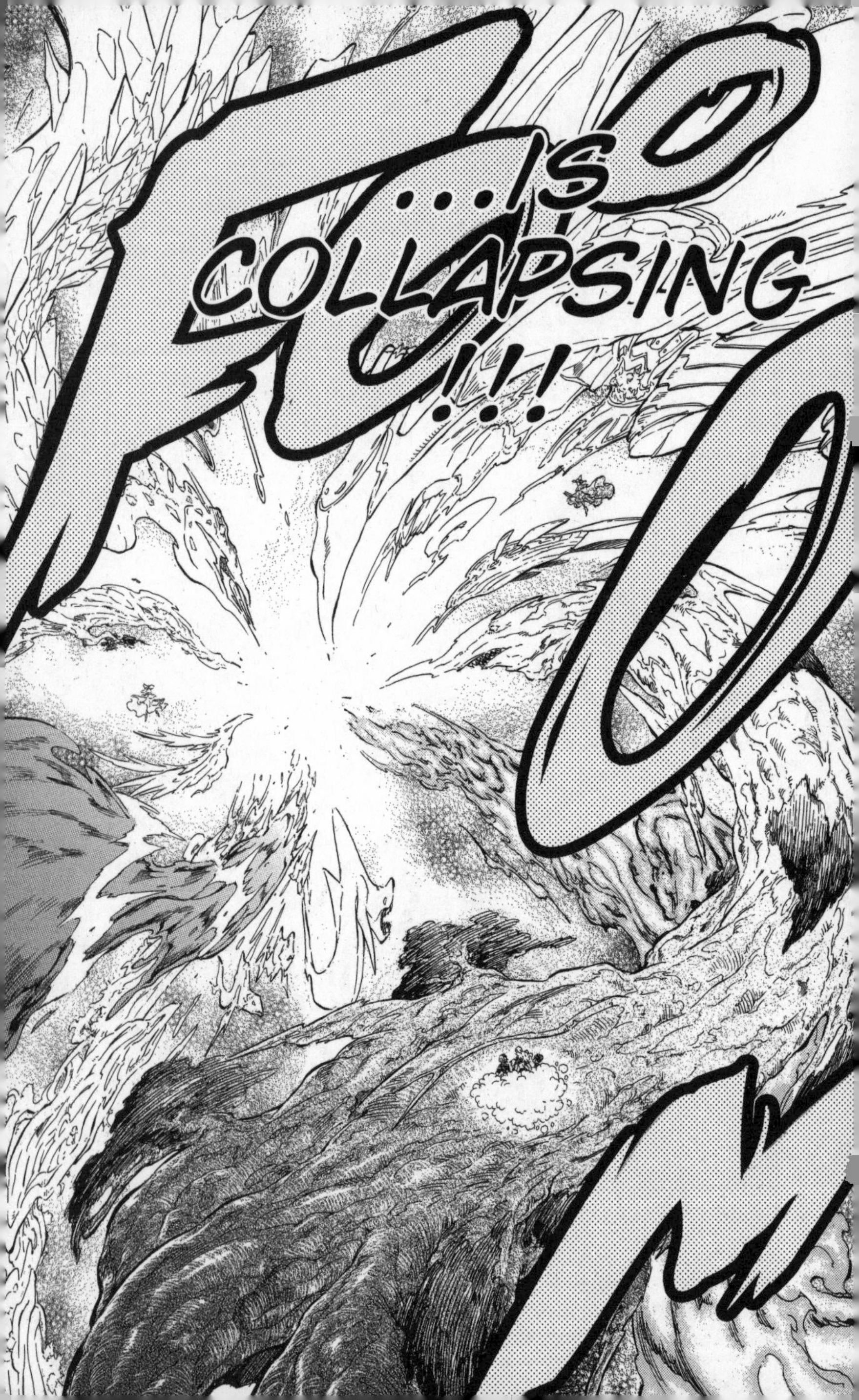
...IS COLLAPSING...!!!

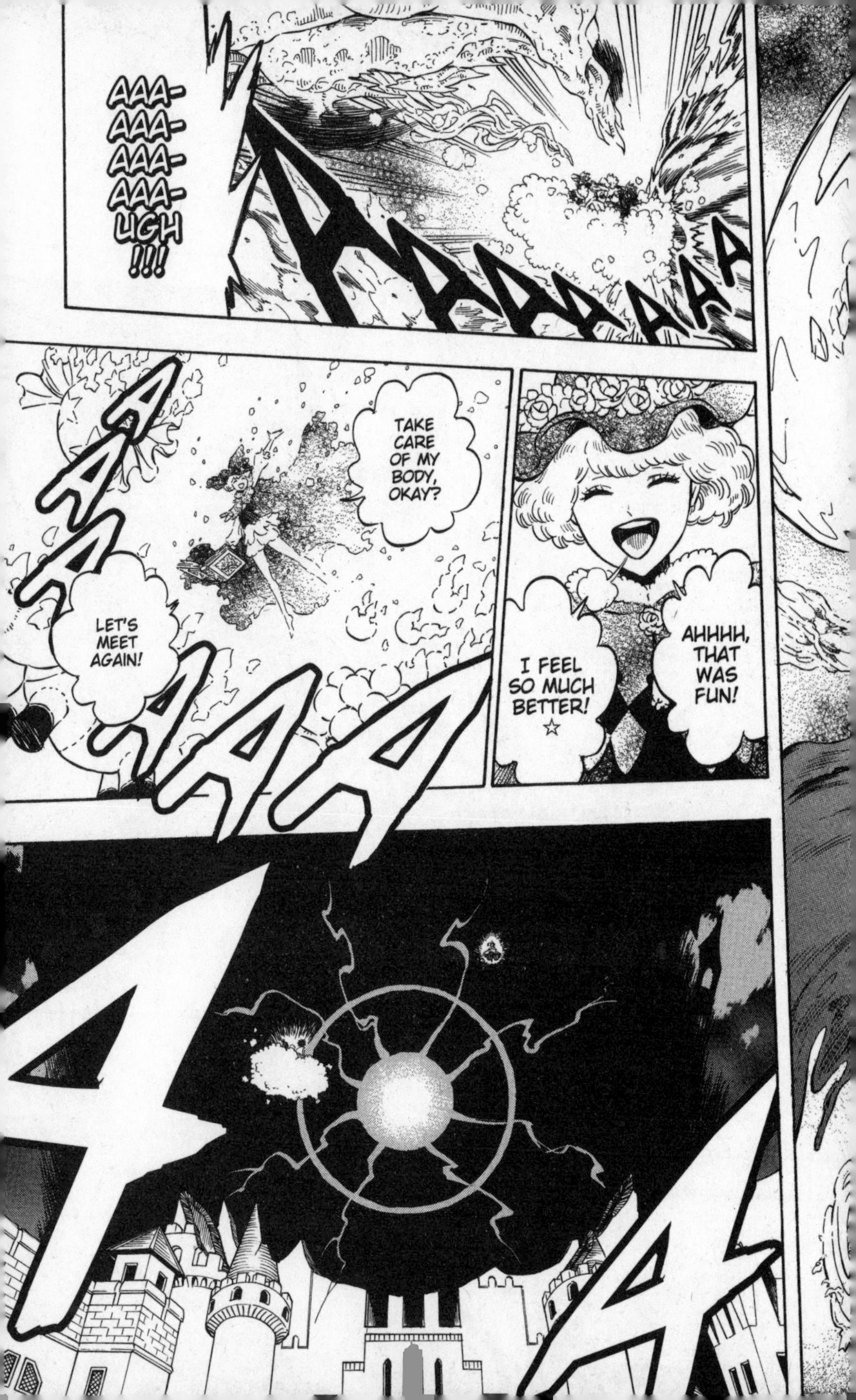
AAA-AAA-AAA-AAA-UGH!!!
AHHHH, THAT WAS FUN!
I FEEL SO MUCH BETTER! ☆
TAKE CARE OF MY BODY, OKAY?
LET'S MEET AGAIN!

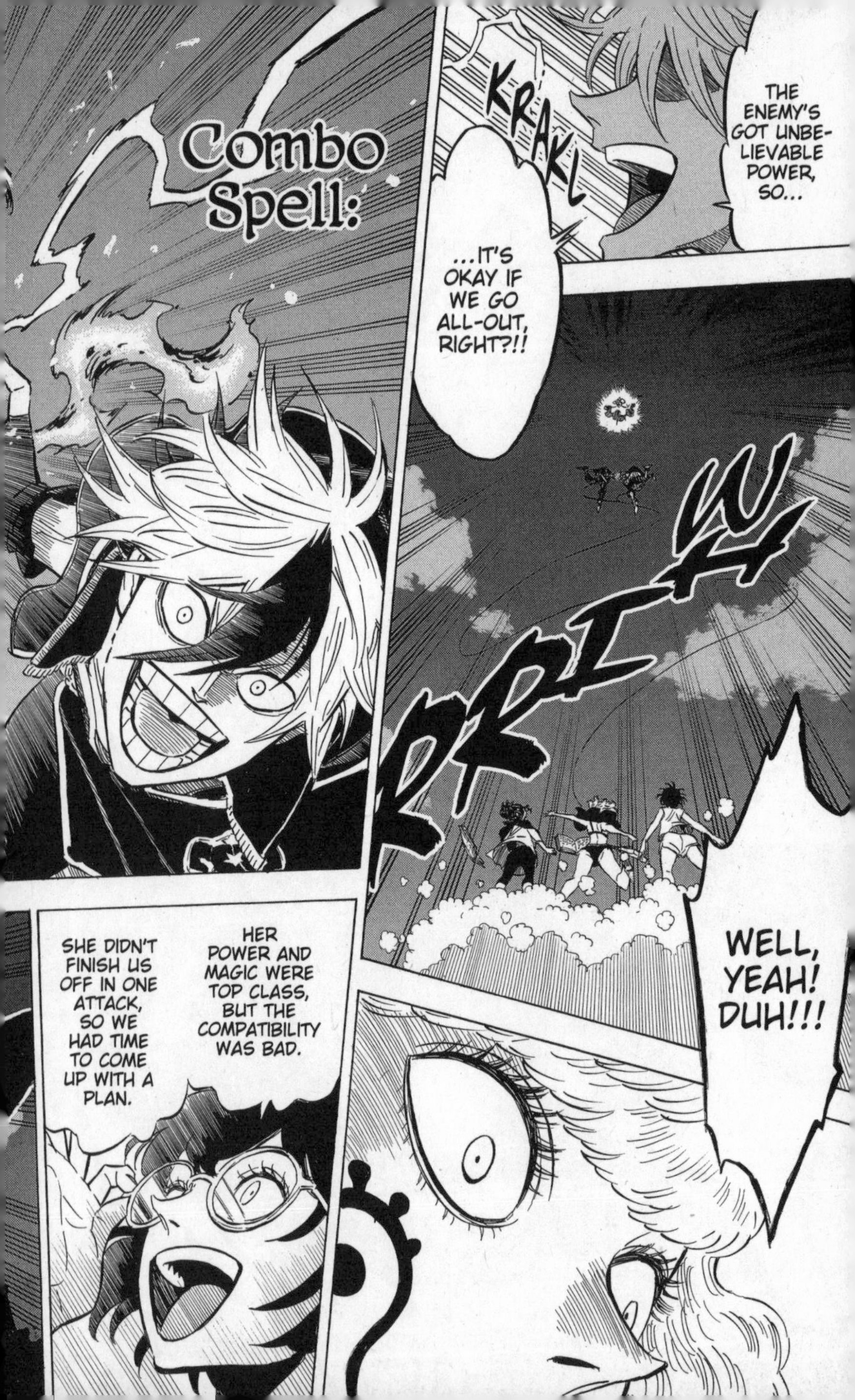
THE ENEMY'S GOT UNBE-LIEVABLE POWER, SO...
KRAKL
...IT'S OKAY IF WE GO ALL-OUT, RIGHT?!!
WELL, YEAH! DUH!!!
Combo Spell:
HER POWER AND MAGIC WERE TOP CLASS, BUT THE COMPATIBILITY WAS BAD.
SHE DIDN'T FINISH US OFF IN ONE ATTACK, SO WE HAD TIME TO COME UP WITH A PLAN.

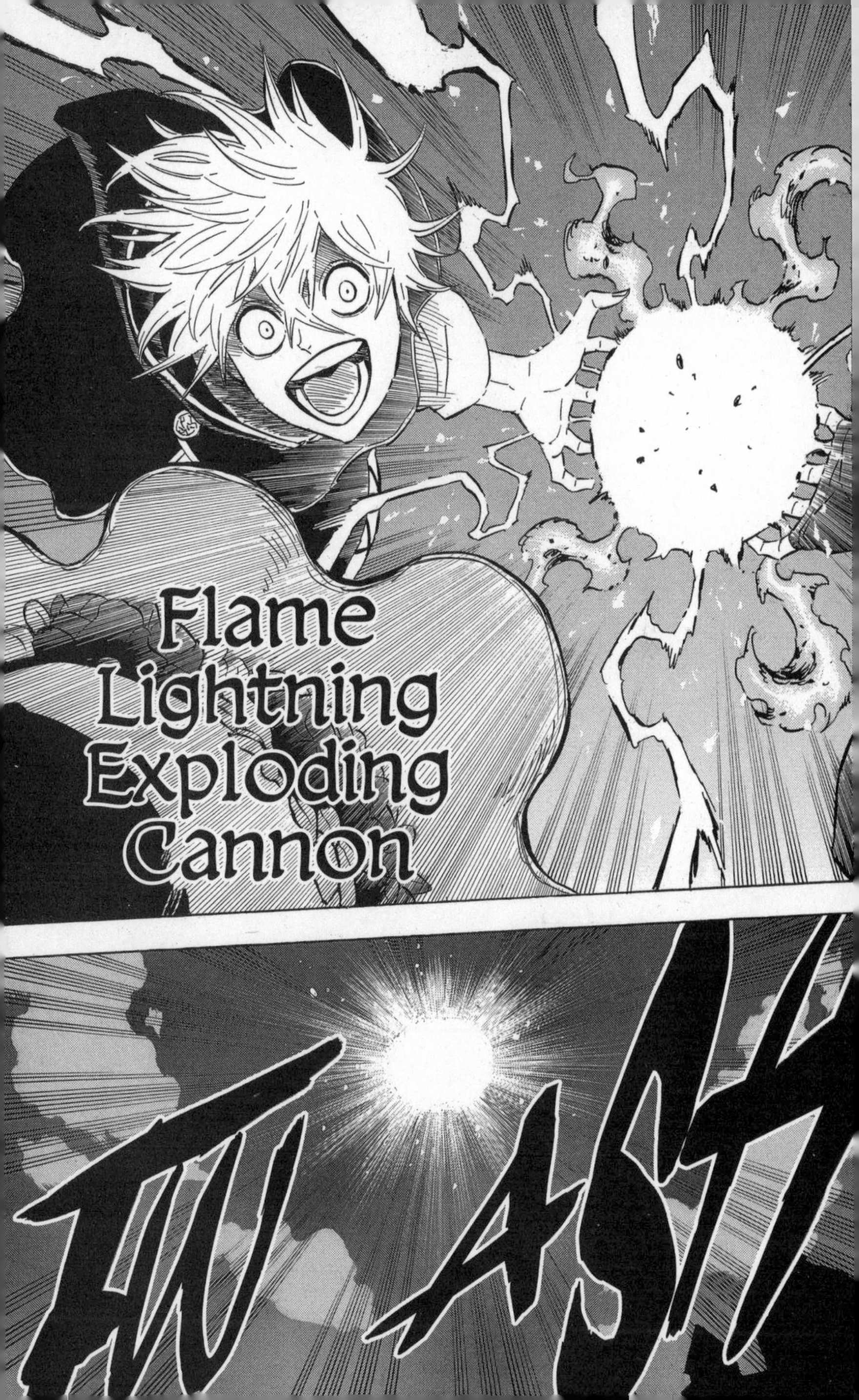
Flame Lightning Exploding Cannon
FWOOSH

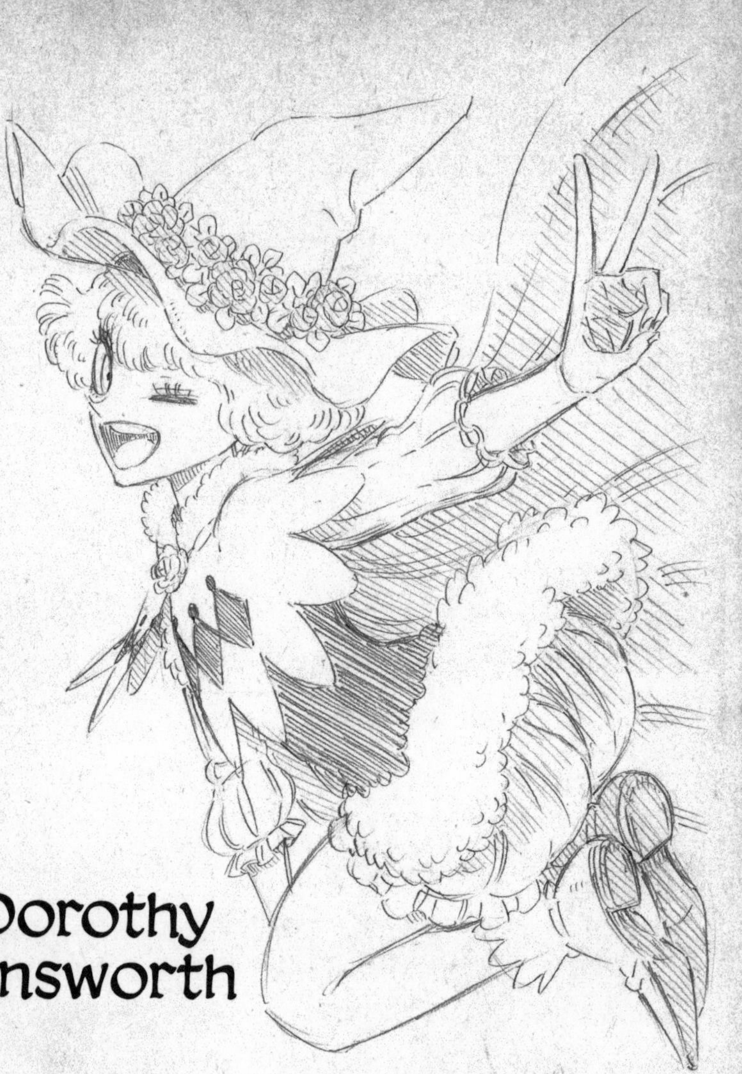

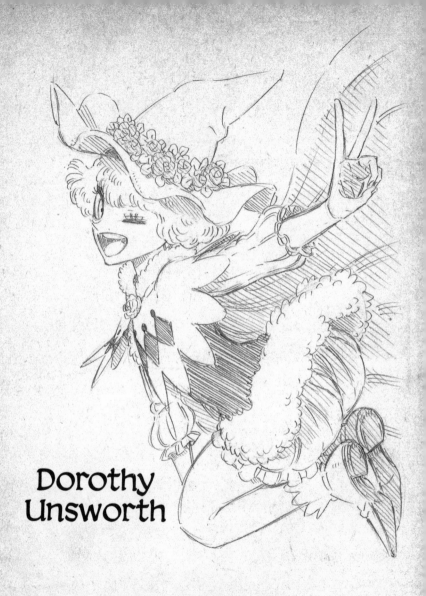

Dorothy Unsworth

Age: 27 Height: 145 cm
Birthday: March 21 Sign: Aries Blood Type: O
Likes: Colorful things, macarons

Character Profile

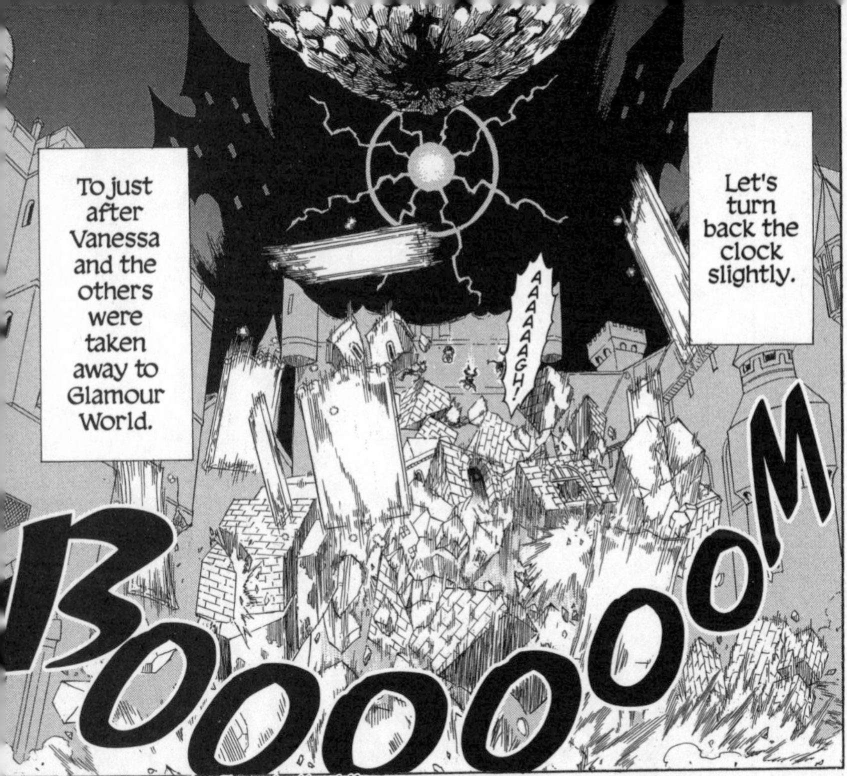
Let's turn back the clock slightly.
To just after Vanessa and the others were taken away to Glamour World.
AAAAAAAAGH!
BOOOOOOOOM

Page 186: The Eyes in the Mirror

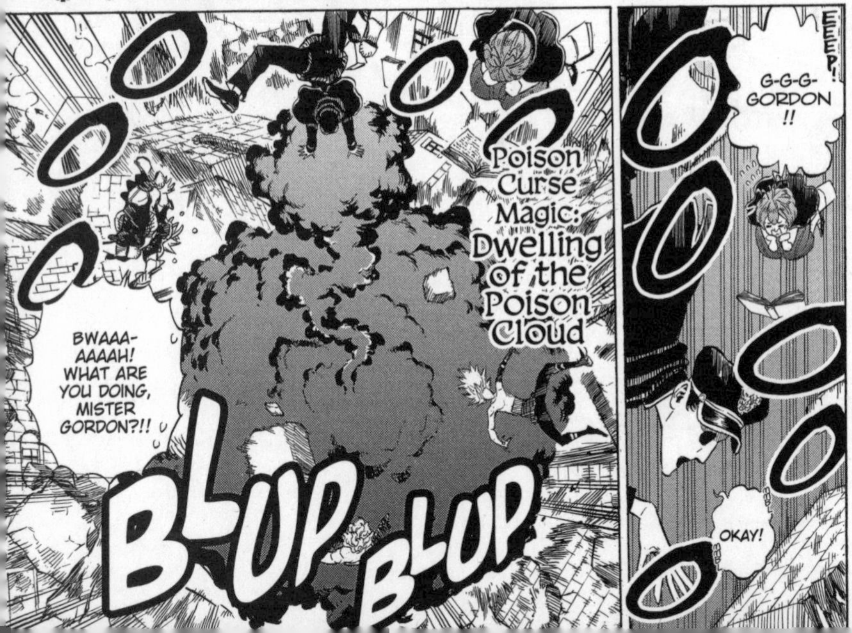
EEEP!
G-G-G-GORDON!!
OKAY!
Poison Curse Magic: Dwelling of the Poison Cloud
BWAAA-AAAAH! WHAT ARE YOU DOING, MISTER GORDON?!!
BLUP BLUP

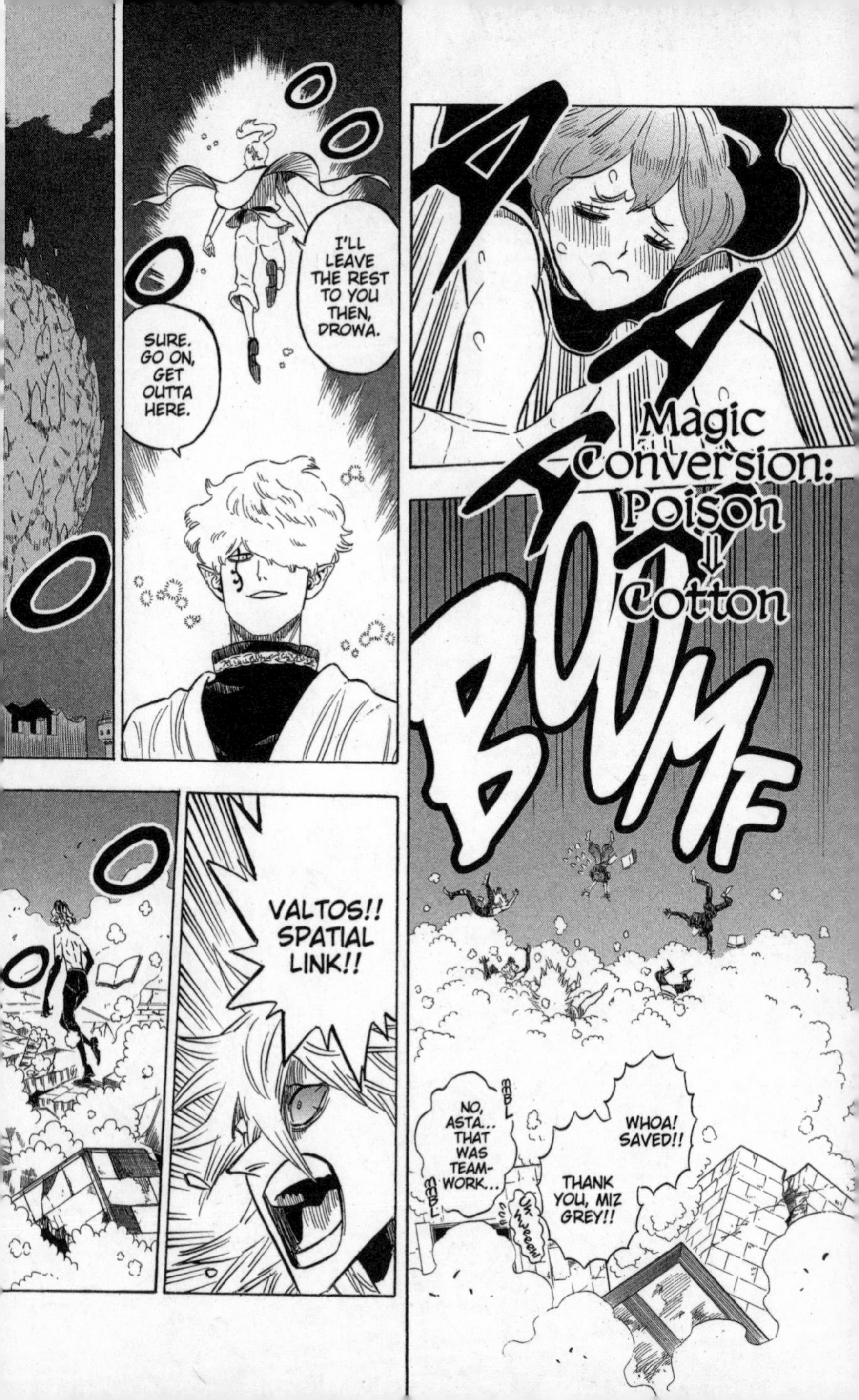
Magic Conversion: Poison ⇓ Cotton
BOOMF
WHOA! SAVED!!
THANK YOU, MIZ GREY!!
NO, ASTA... THAT WAS TEAMWORK...
MMBL
MMBL
Uh wheeee!
I'LL LEAVE THE REST TO YOU THEN, DROWA.
SURE. GO ON, GET OUTTA HERE.
VALTOS!! SPATIAL LINK!!

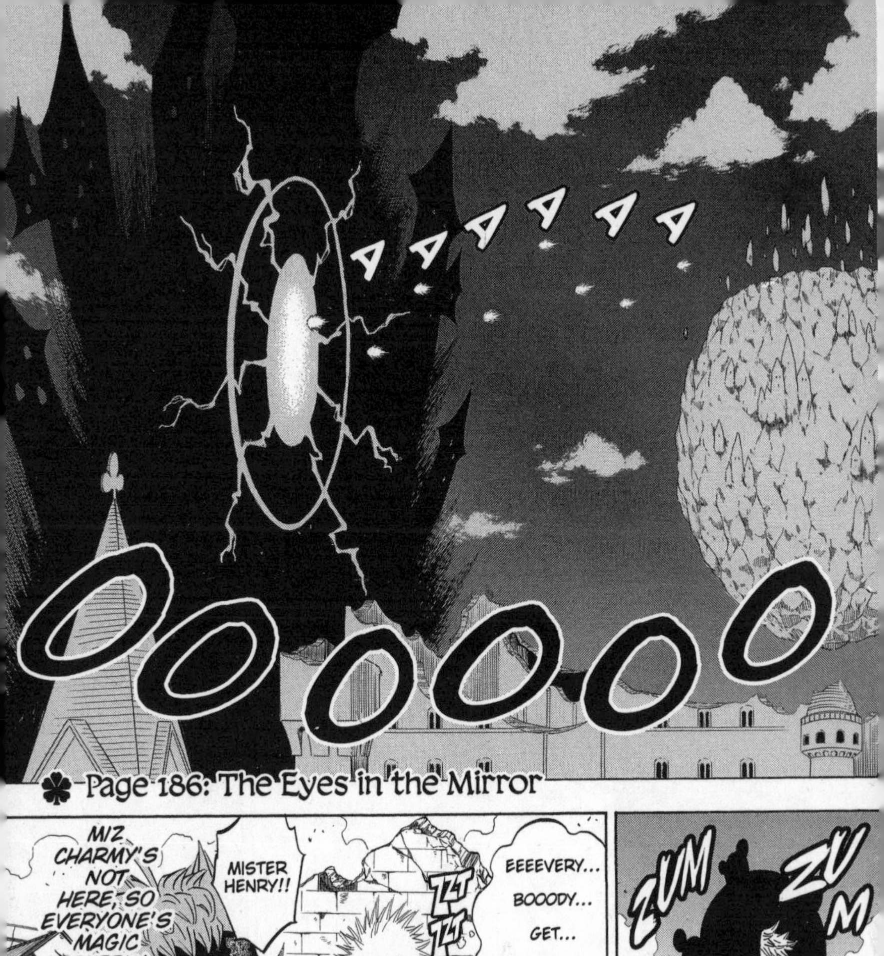
AAAAAA
OOOOOO

Page 186: The Eyes in the Mirror

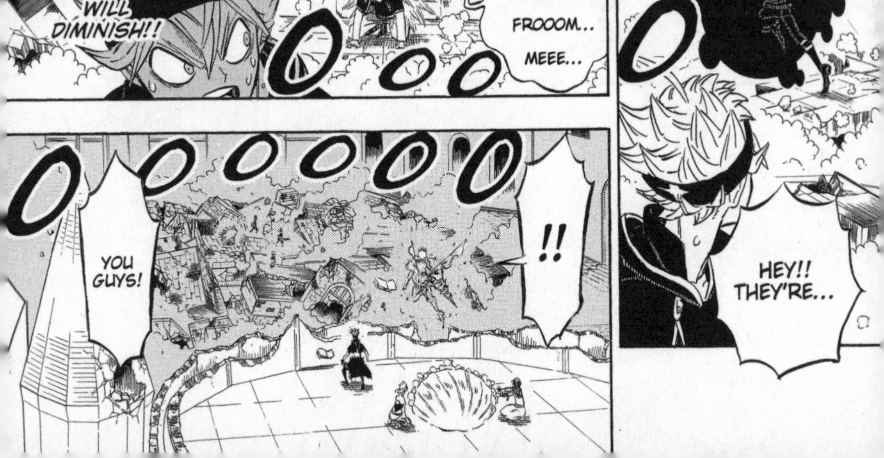
ZUM ZUM
O
HEY!! THEY'RE...
EEEEVERY... BOOODY... GET... AWAAAAY... FROOOM... MEEE...
ZZT ZZT
OOOO
MISTER HENRY!!
MIZ CHARMY'S NOT HERE, SO EVERYONE'S MAGIC SUPPLY WILL DIMINISH!!
!!
OOOOOO
YOU GUYS!

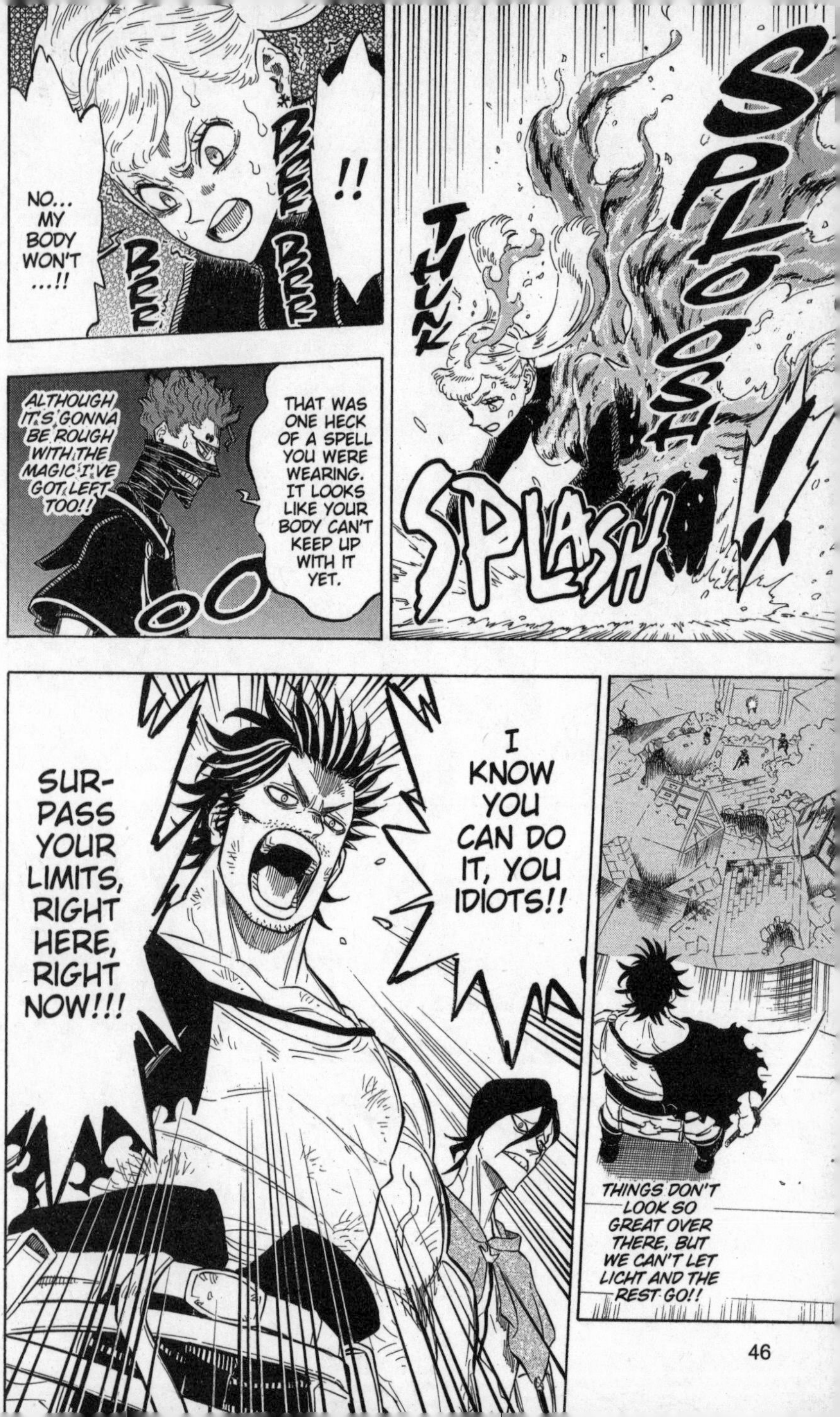
SPLOOSH
THUNK
SPLASH!!
NO... MY BODY WON'T ...!!
!!
THAT WAS ONE HECK OF A SPELL YOU WERE WEARING. IT LOOKS LIKE YOUR BODY CAN'T KEEP UP WITH IT YET.
ALTHOUGH IT'S GONNA BE ROUGH WITH THE MAGIC I'VE GOT LEFT TOO!!
THINGS DON'T LOOK SO GREAT OVER THERE, BUT WE CAN'T LET LIGHT AND THE REST GO!!
I KNOW YOU CAN DO IT, YOU IDIOTS!!
SUR-PASS YOUR LIMITS, RIGHT HERE, RIGHT NOW!!!

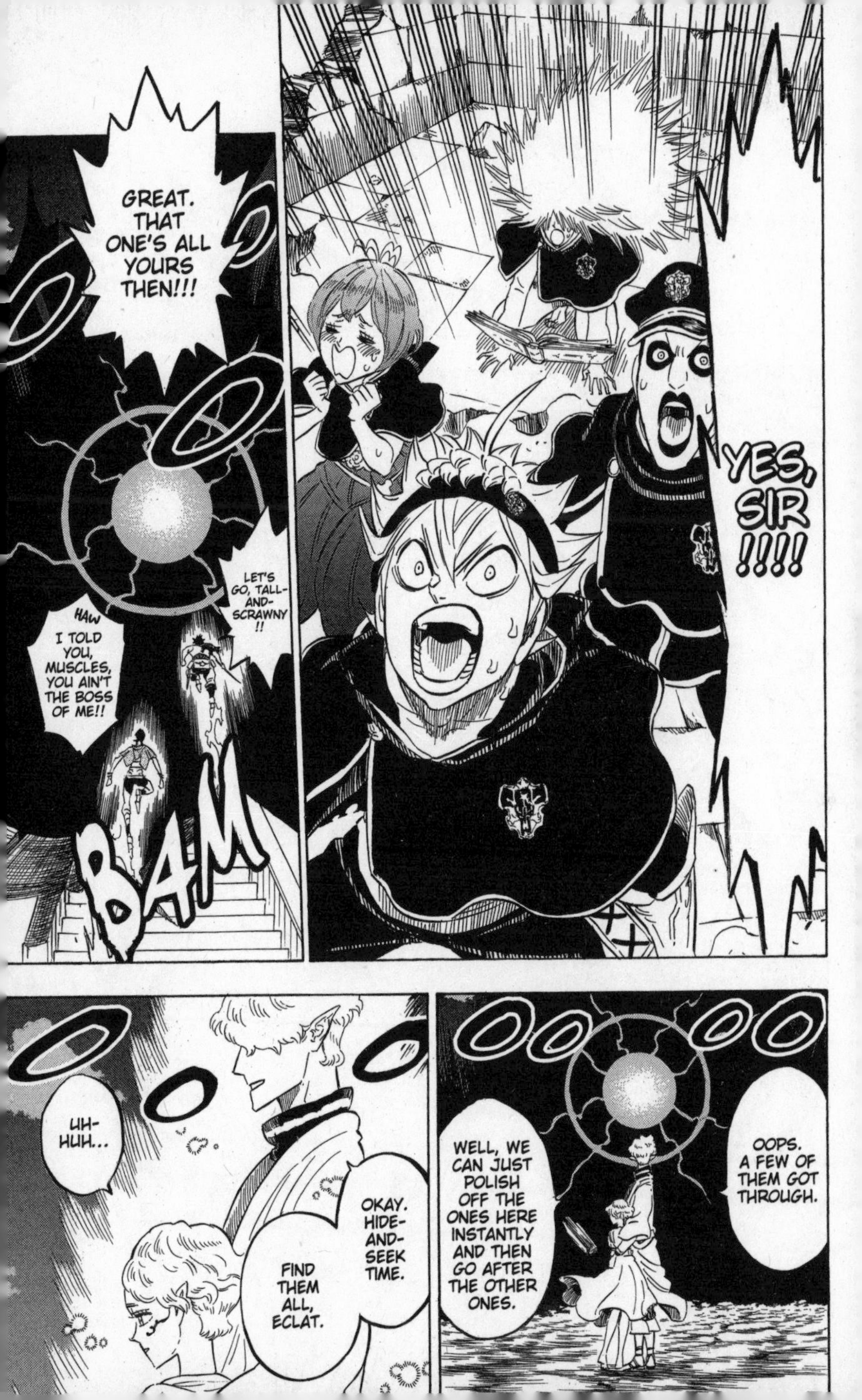
YES, SIR!!!!
GREAT. THAT ONE'S ALL YOURS THEN!!!
LET'S GO, TALL-AND-SCRAWNY!!
HAW
I TOLD YOU, MUSCLES, YOU AIN'T THE BOSS OF ME!!
BAM
OOPS. A FEW OF THEM GOT THROUGH.
WELL, WE CAN JUST POLISH OFF THE ONES HERE INSTANTLY AND THEN GO AFTER THE OTHER ONES.
OKAY. HIDE-AND-SEEK TIME.
FIND THEM ALL, ECLAT.
UH-HUH...

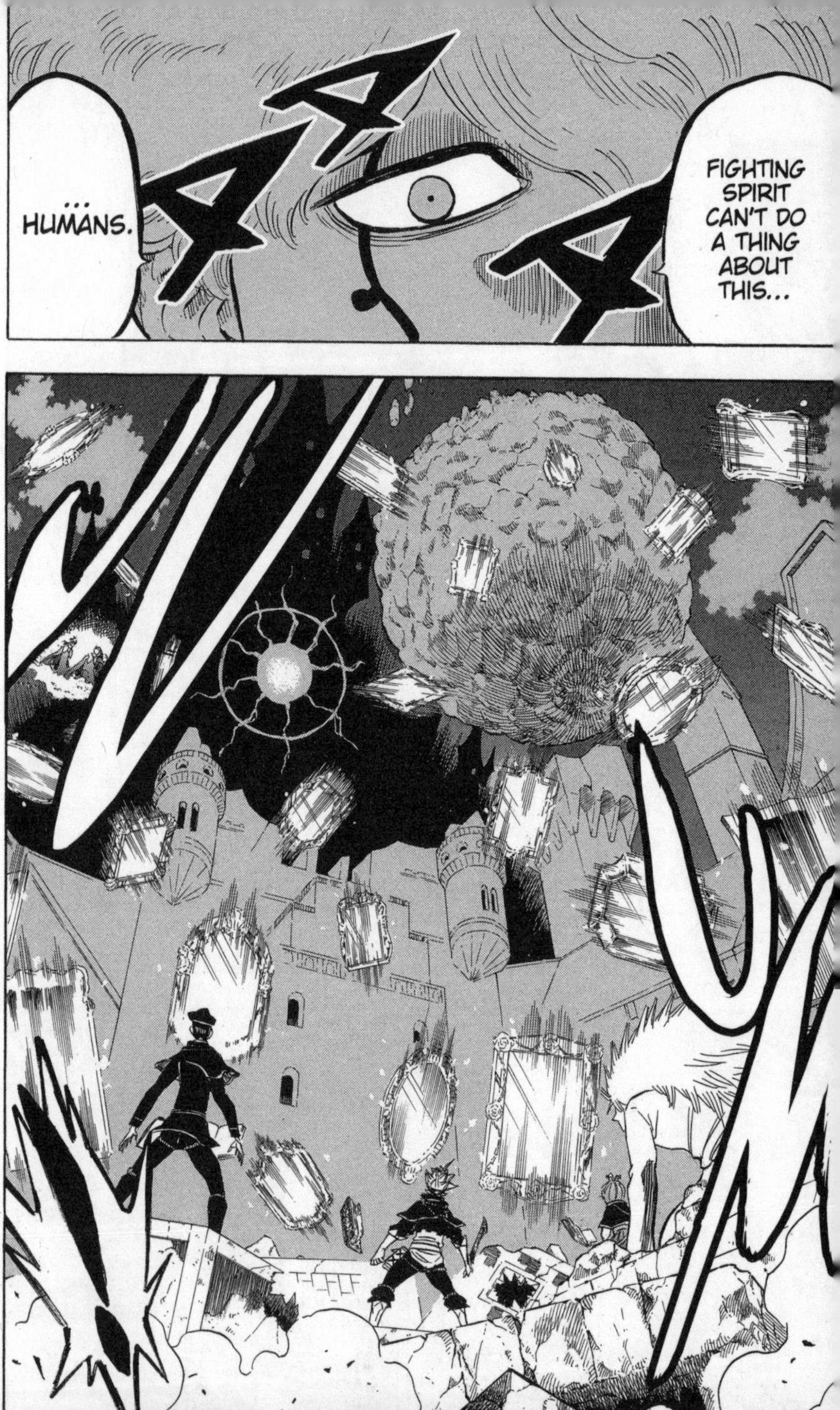
FIGHTING SPIRIT CAN'T DO A THING ABOUT THIS...
...HUMANS.

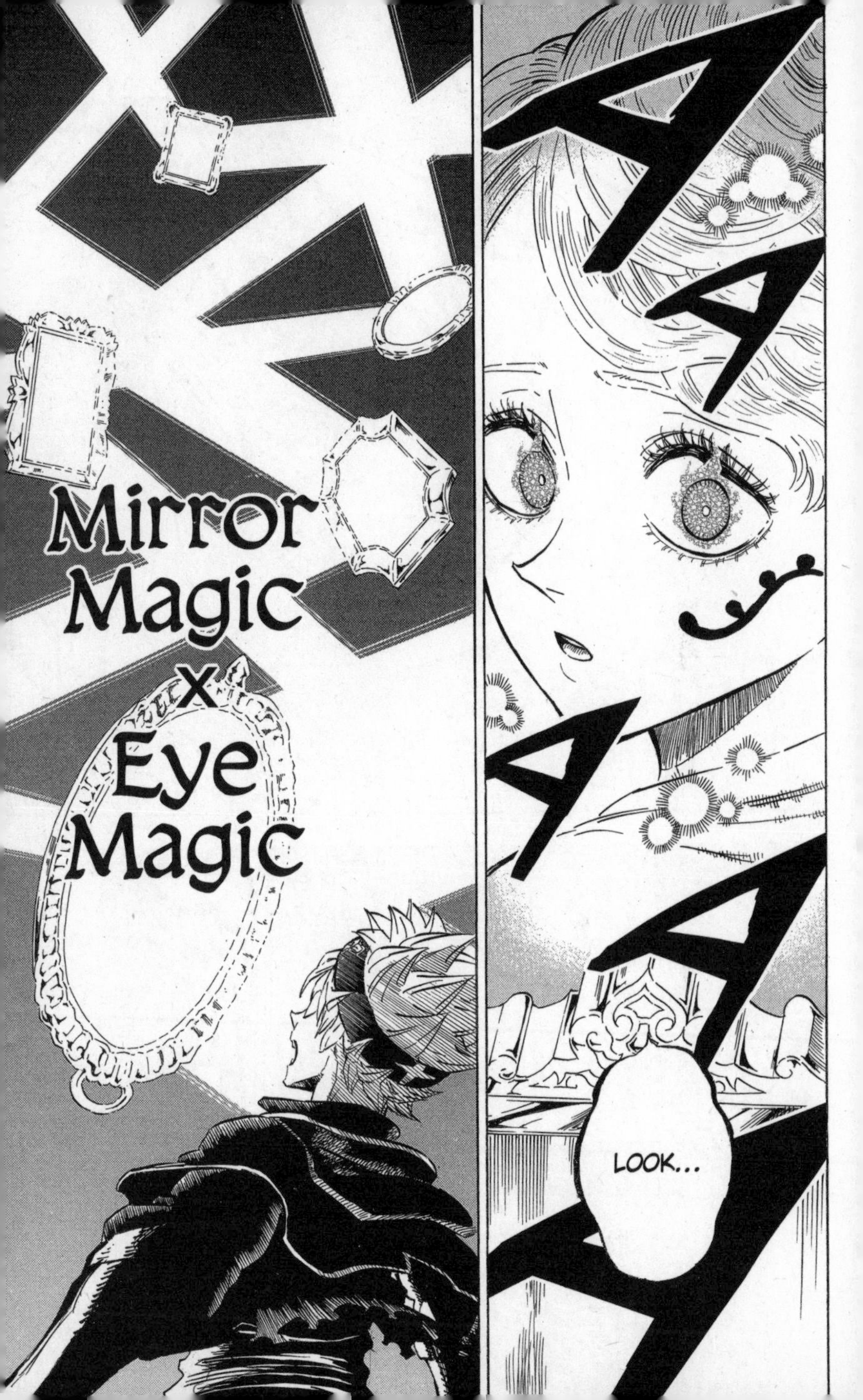
LOOK...
Mirror Magic x Eye Magic

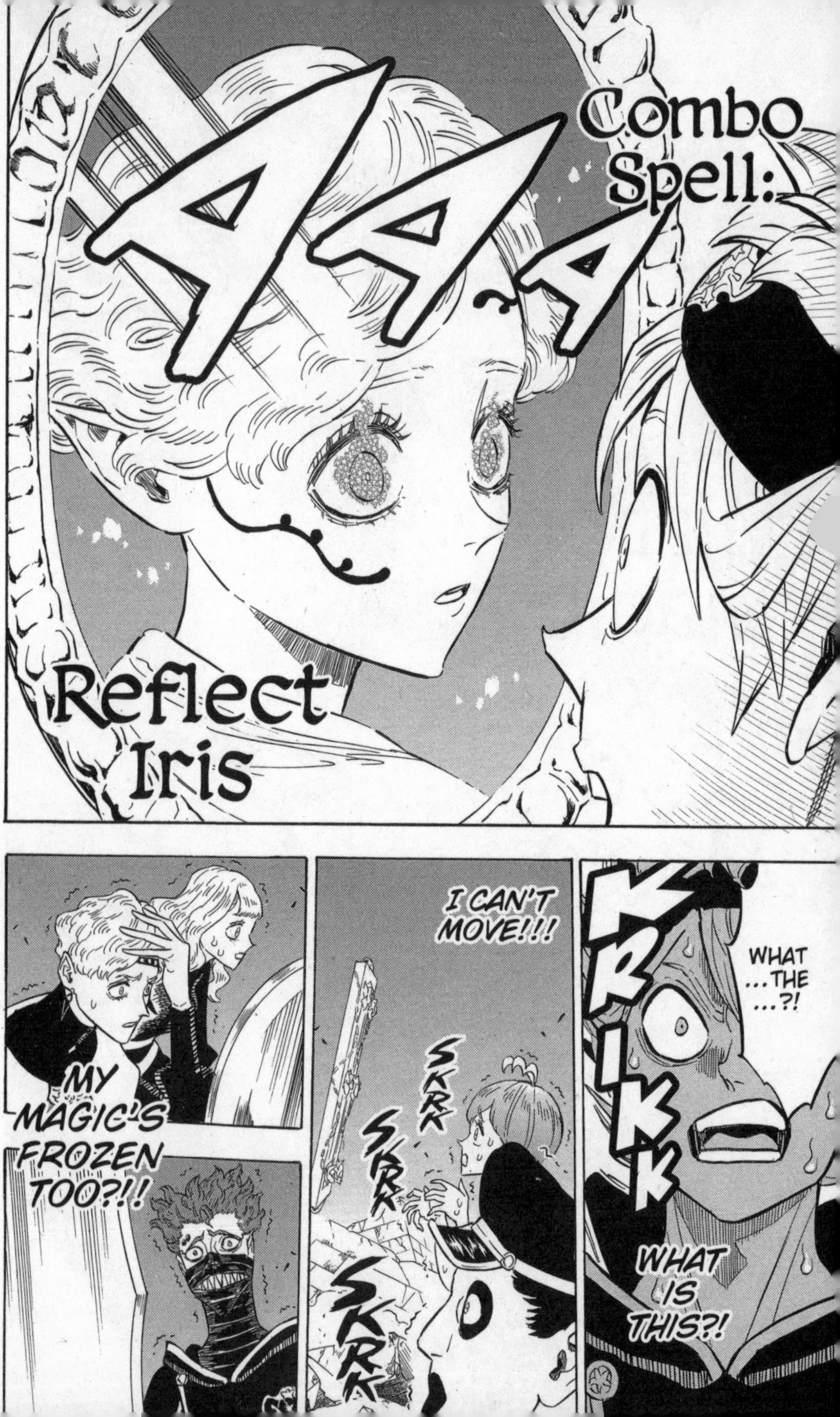
Combo Spell:
AAA
Reflect Iris
KRIKK
WHAT ...THE ...?!
WHAT IS THIS?!
I CAN'T MOVE!!!
SKRK
SKRK
SKRK
MY MAGIC'S FROZEN TOO?!!

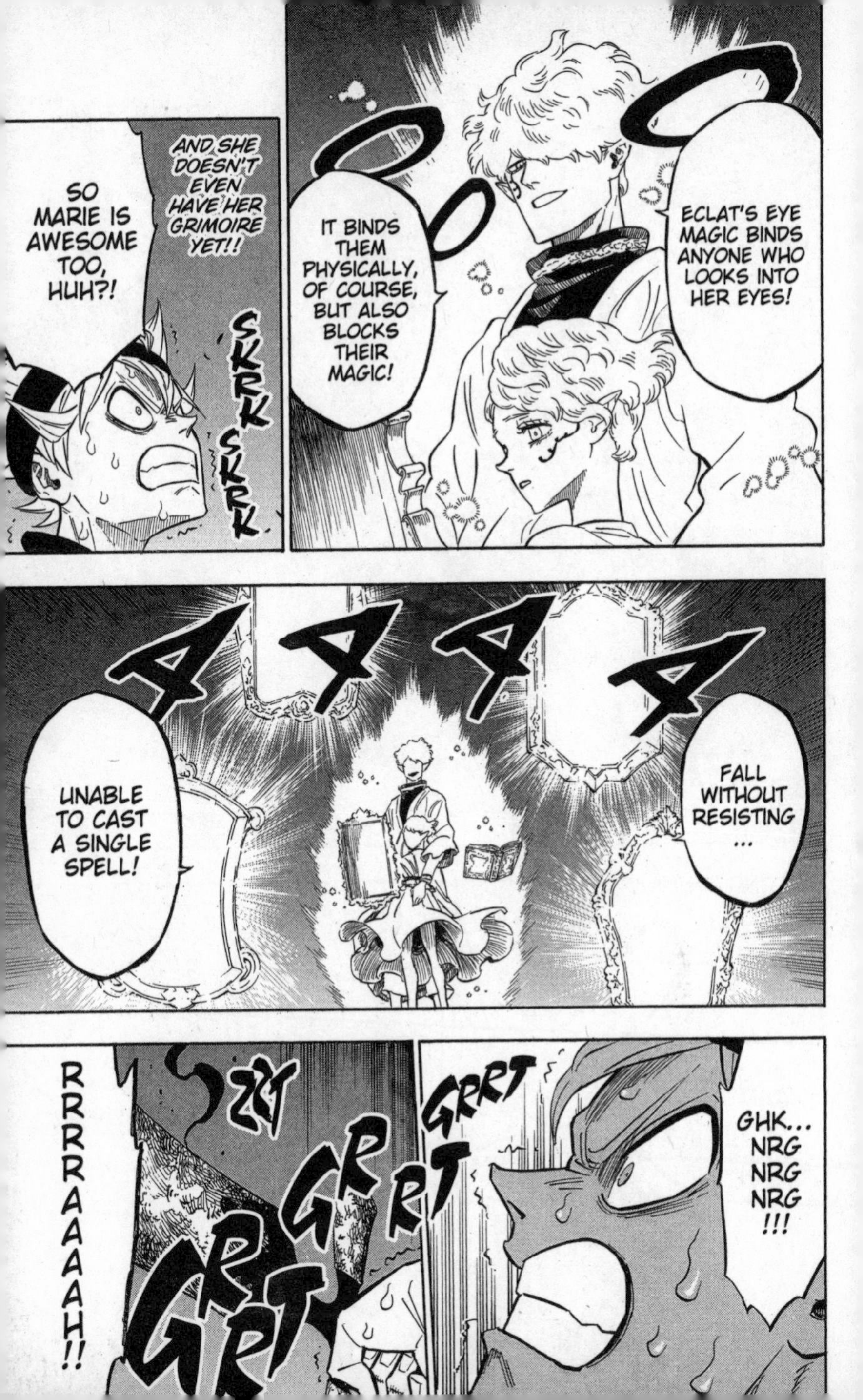
ECLAT'S EYE MAGIC BINDS ANYONE WHO LOOKS INTO HER EYES!
IT BINDS THEM PHYSICALLY, OF COURSE, BUT ALSO BLOCKS THEIR MAGIC!
AND SHE DOESN'T EVEN HAVE HER GRIMOIRE YET!!
SO MARIE IS AWESOME TOO, HUH?!
SKRK SKRK
FALL WITHOUT RESISTING ...
UNABLE TO CAST A SINGLE SPELL!
GHK... NRG NRG NRG !!!
GRRT
GR RT
GRRT
RRRRAAAAH!!

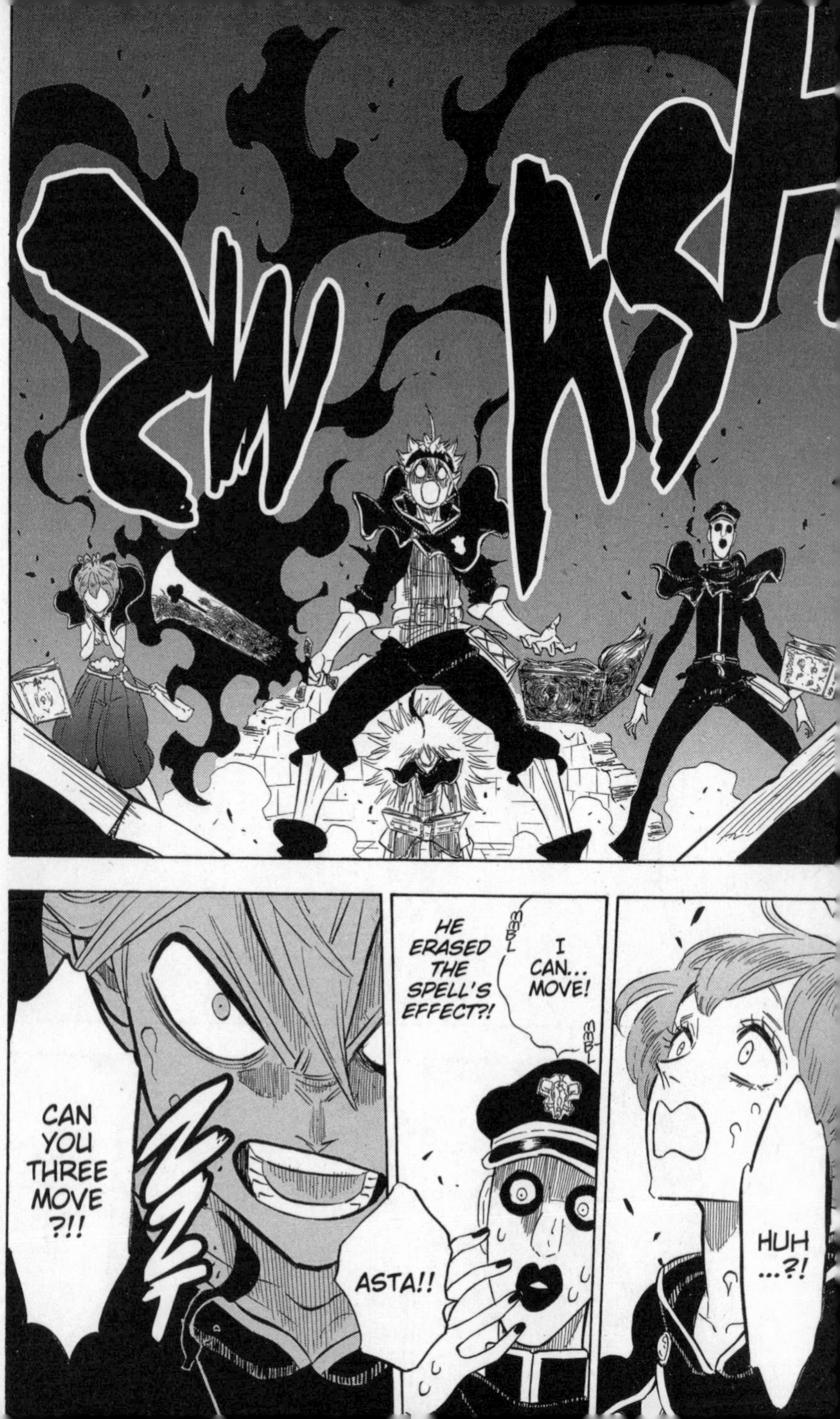
SWASH
HUH ...?!
MMBL
I CAN... MOVE!
MMBL
HE ERASED THE SPELL'S EFFECT?!
ASTA!!
CAN YOU THREE MOVE ?!!

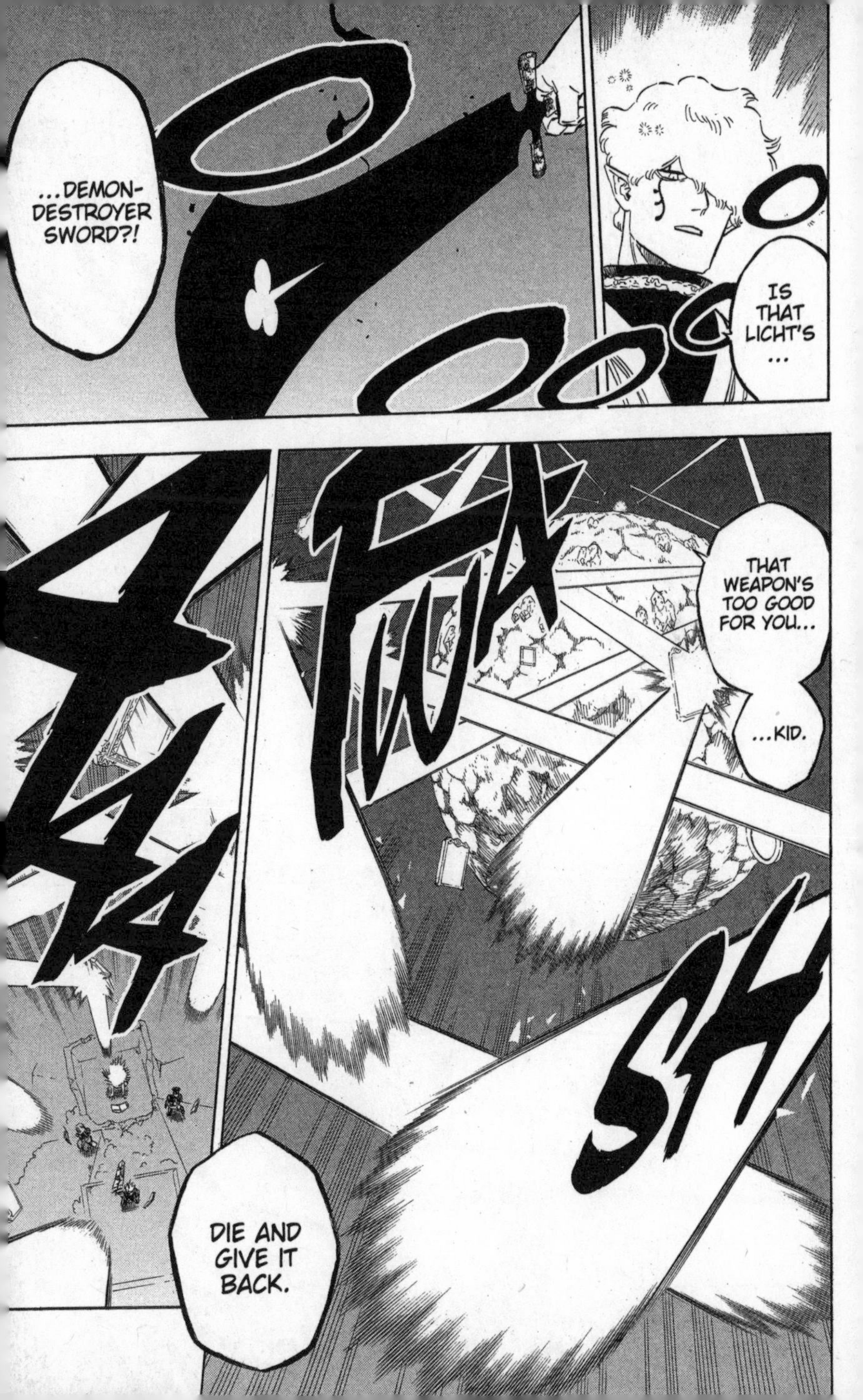
IS THAT LICHT'S ...
...DEMON-DESTROYER SWORD?!
THAT WEAPON'S TOO GOOD FOR YOU...
...KID.
DIE AND GIVE IT BACK.

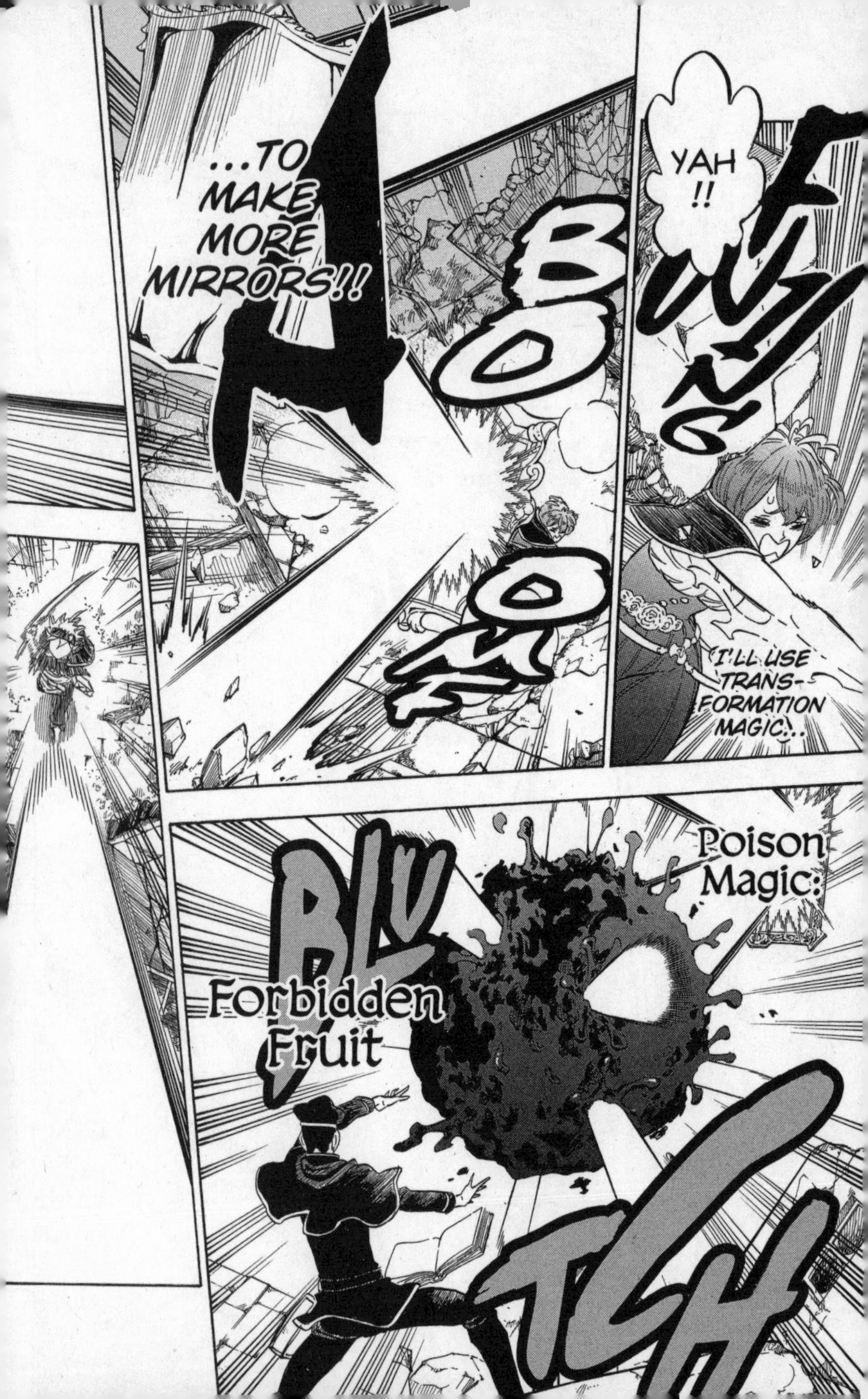
YAH!!
I'LL USE TRANSFORMATION MAGIC...
BOOM
...TO MAKE MORE MIRRORS!!
Poison Magic:
Forbidden Fruit
BLU
TCH

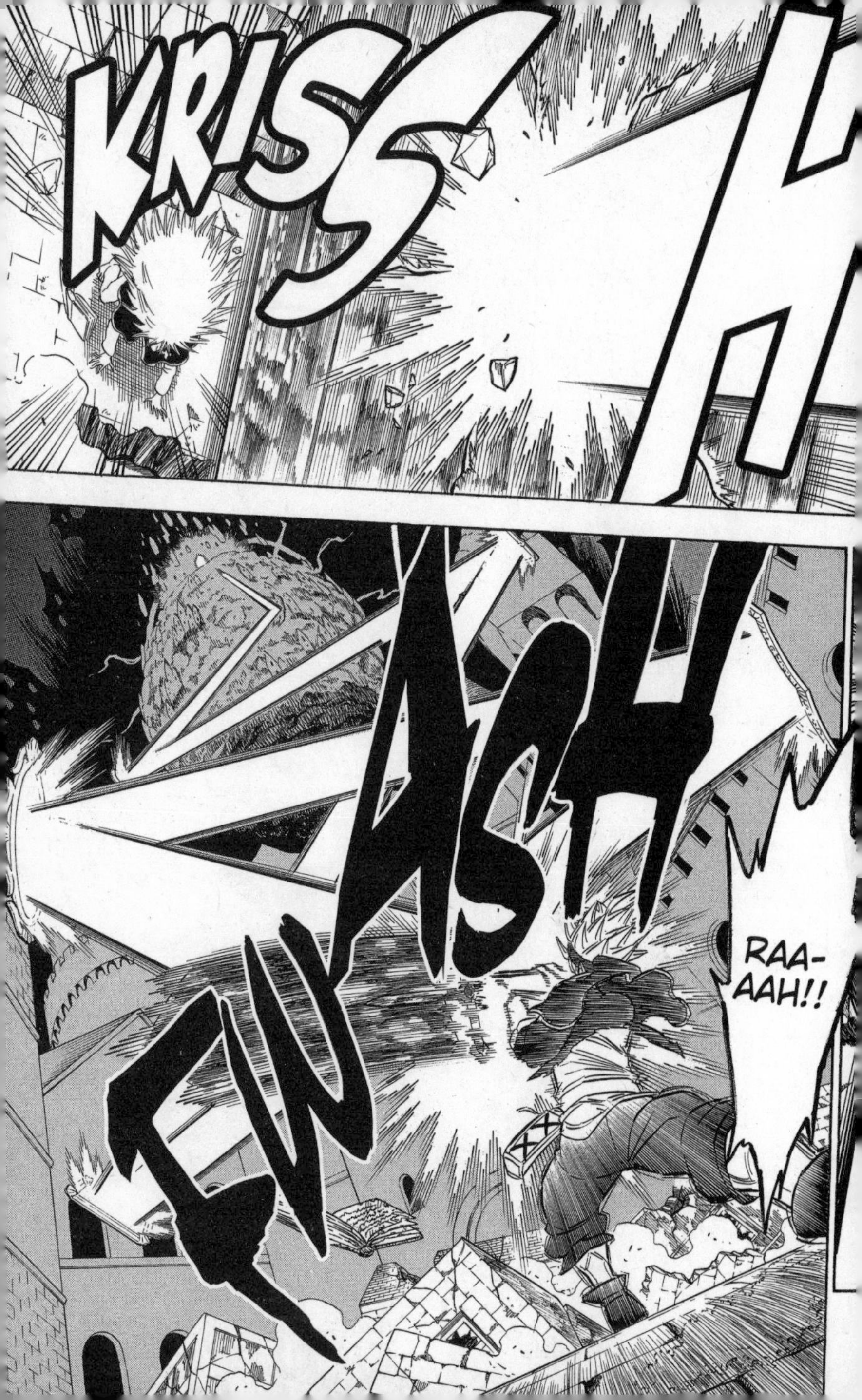
KRISSH
RAA-
AAH!!

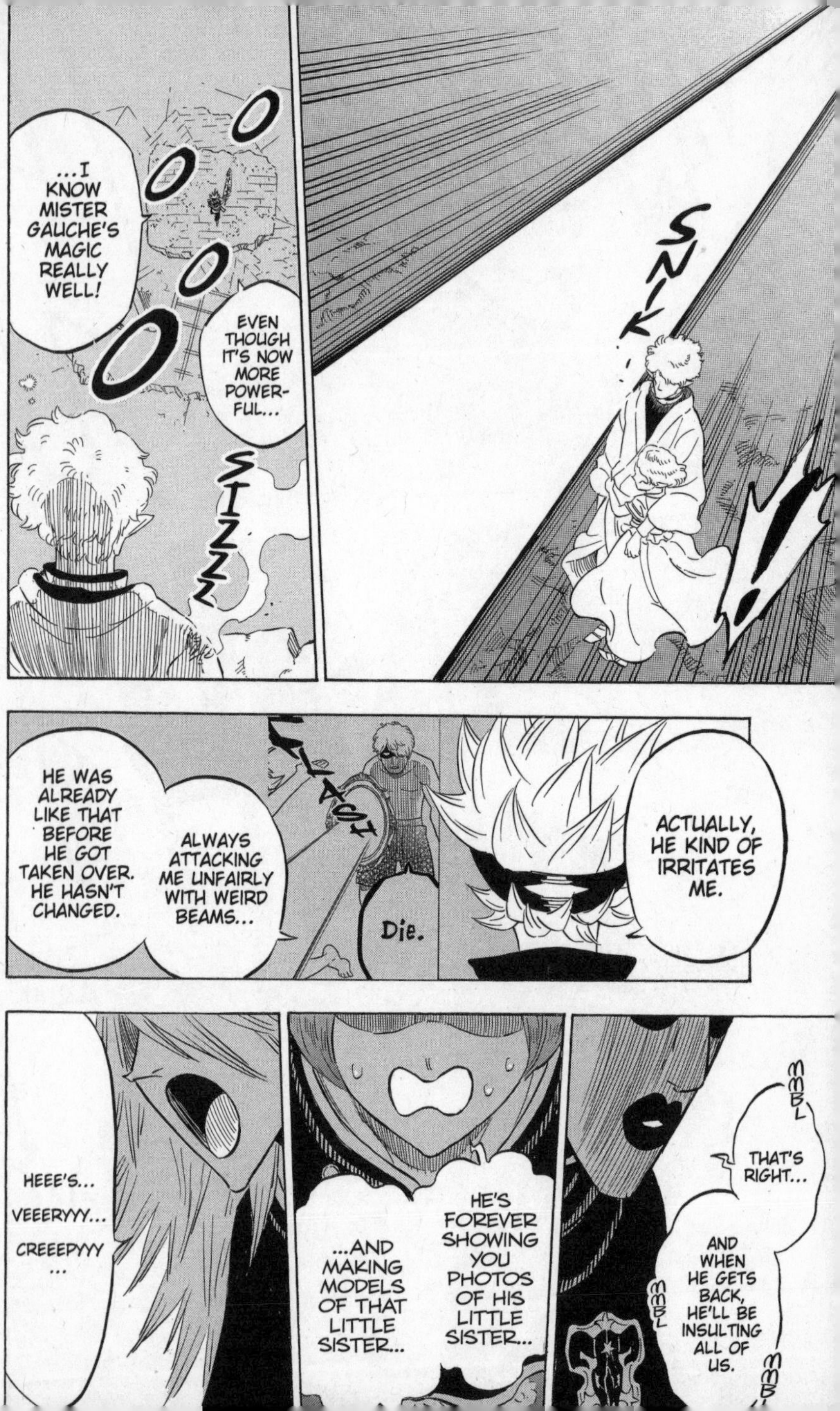
SNIK
!!
...I KNOW MISTER GAUCHE'S MAGIC REALLY WELL!
OOOO
EVEN THOUGH IT'S NOW MORE POWERFUL...
SIZZZZ
ACTUALLY, HE KIND OF IRRITATES ME.
LASH
Die.
ALWAYS ATTACKING ME UNFAIRLY WITH WEIRD BEAMS...
HE WAS ALREADY LIKE THAT BEFORE HE GOT TAKEN OVER. HE HASN'T CHANGED.
MMBL
THAT'S RIGHT...
AND WHEN HE GETS BACK, HE'LL BE INSULTING ALL OF US.
MMBL
MMBL
HE'S FOREVER SHOWING YOU PHOTOS OF HIS LITTLE SISTER...
...AND MAKING MODELS OF THAT LITTLE SISTER...
HEEE'S...
VEEERYYY...
CREEEPYYY...

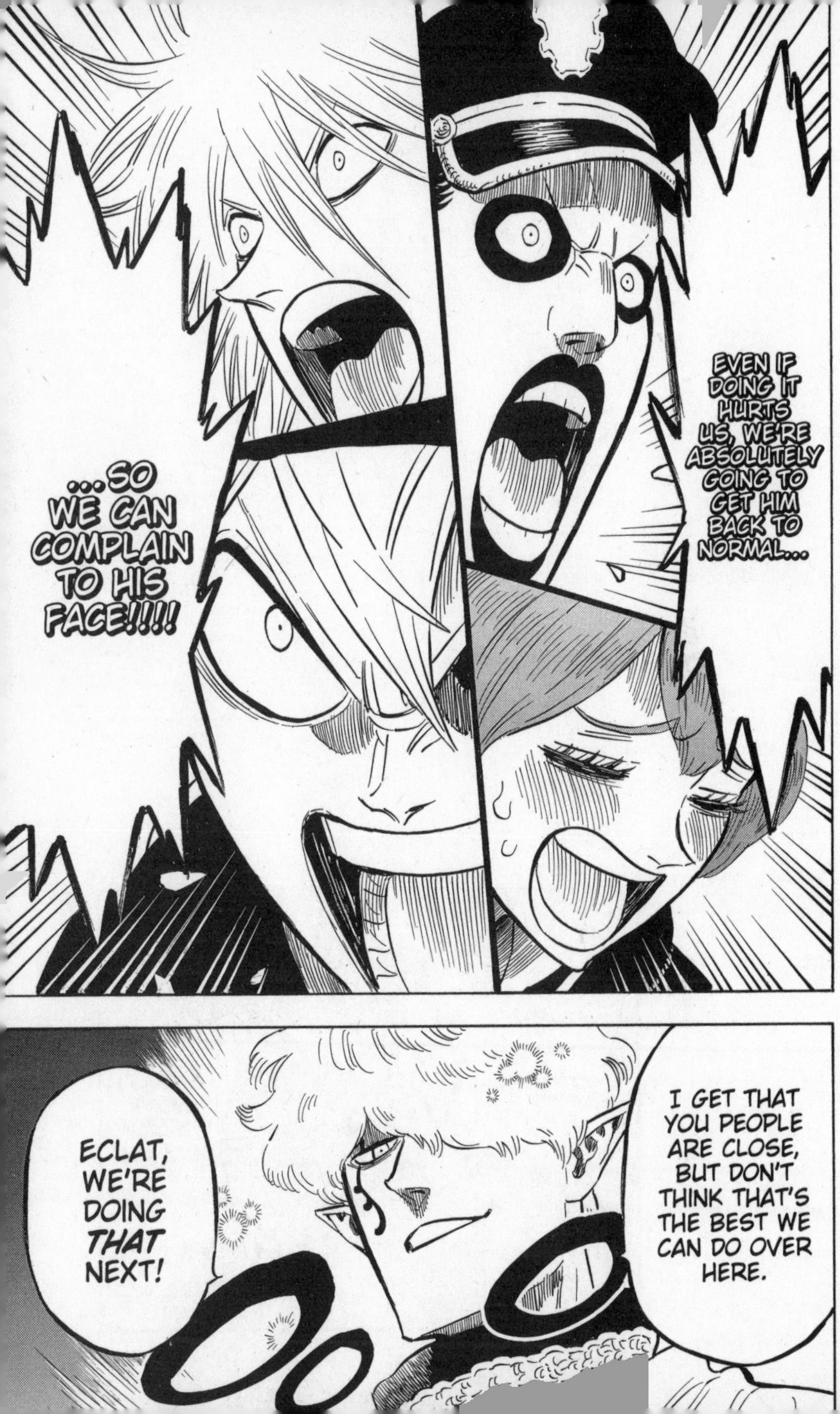
EVEN IF DOING IT HURTS US, WE'RE ABSOLUTELY GOING TO GET HIM BACK TO NORMAL...
...SO WE CAN COMPLAIN TO HIS FACE!!!!
I GET THAT YOU PEOPLE ARE CLOSE, BUT DON'T THINK THAT'S THE BEST WE CAN DO OVER HERE.
ECLAT, WE'RE DOING *THAT* NEXT!

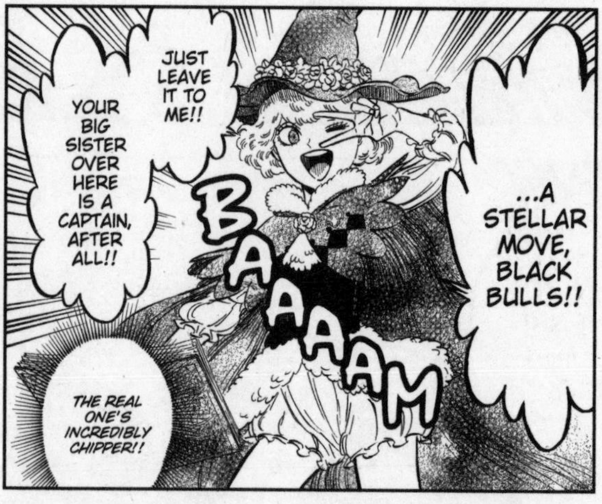
...A STELLAR MOVE, BLACK BULLS!!
JUST LEAVE IT TO ME!!
YOUR BIG SISTER OVER HERE IS A CAPTAIN, AFTER ALL!!
BAAAAAM
THE REAL ONE'S INCREDIBLY CHIPPER!!

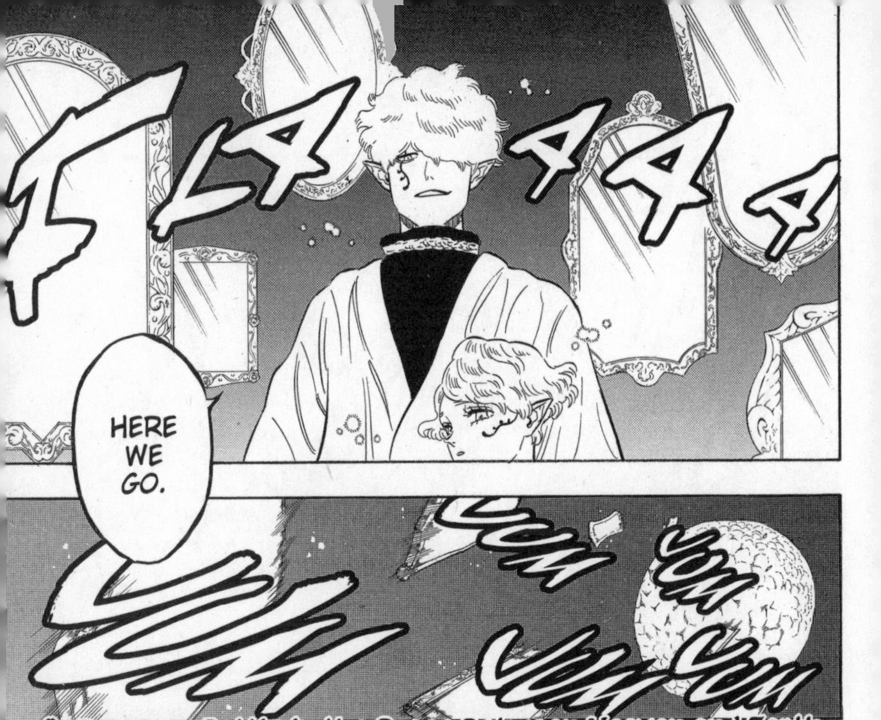
HERE WE GO.

Page 187: Battle in the Space Between Heaven and Earth

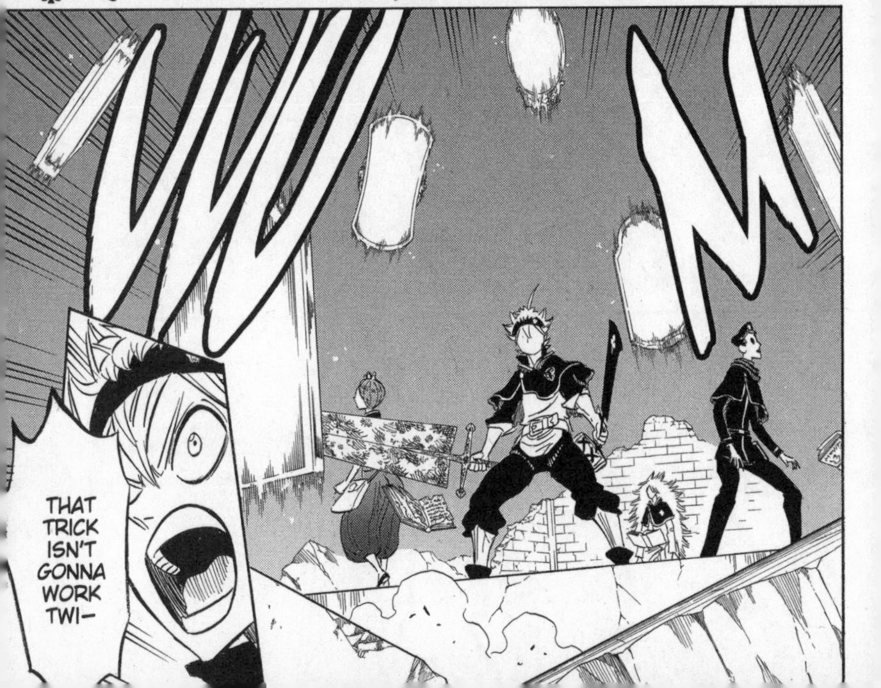
THAT TRICK ISN'T GONNA WORK TWI–

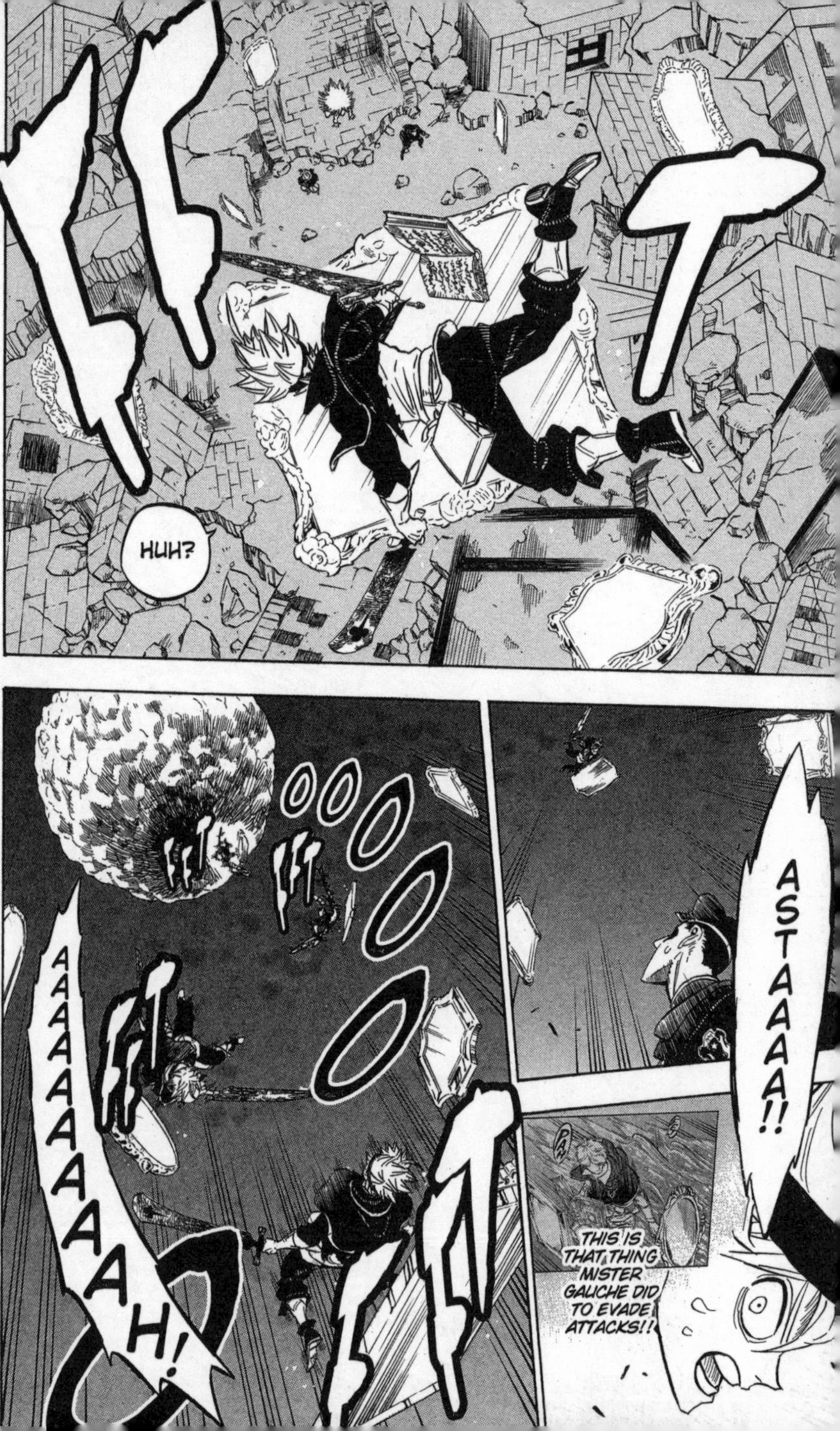
HUH?
ASTAAAAA!!
THIS IS THAT THING MISTER GAUCHE DID TO EVADE ATTACKS!!
AAAAAAAAAAH!

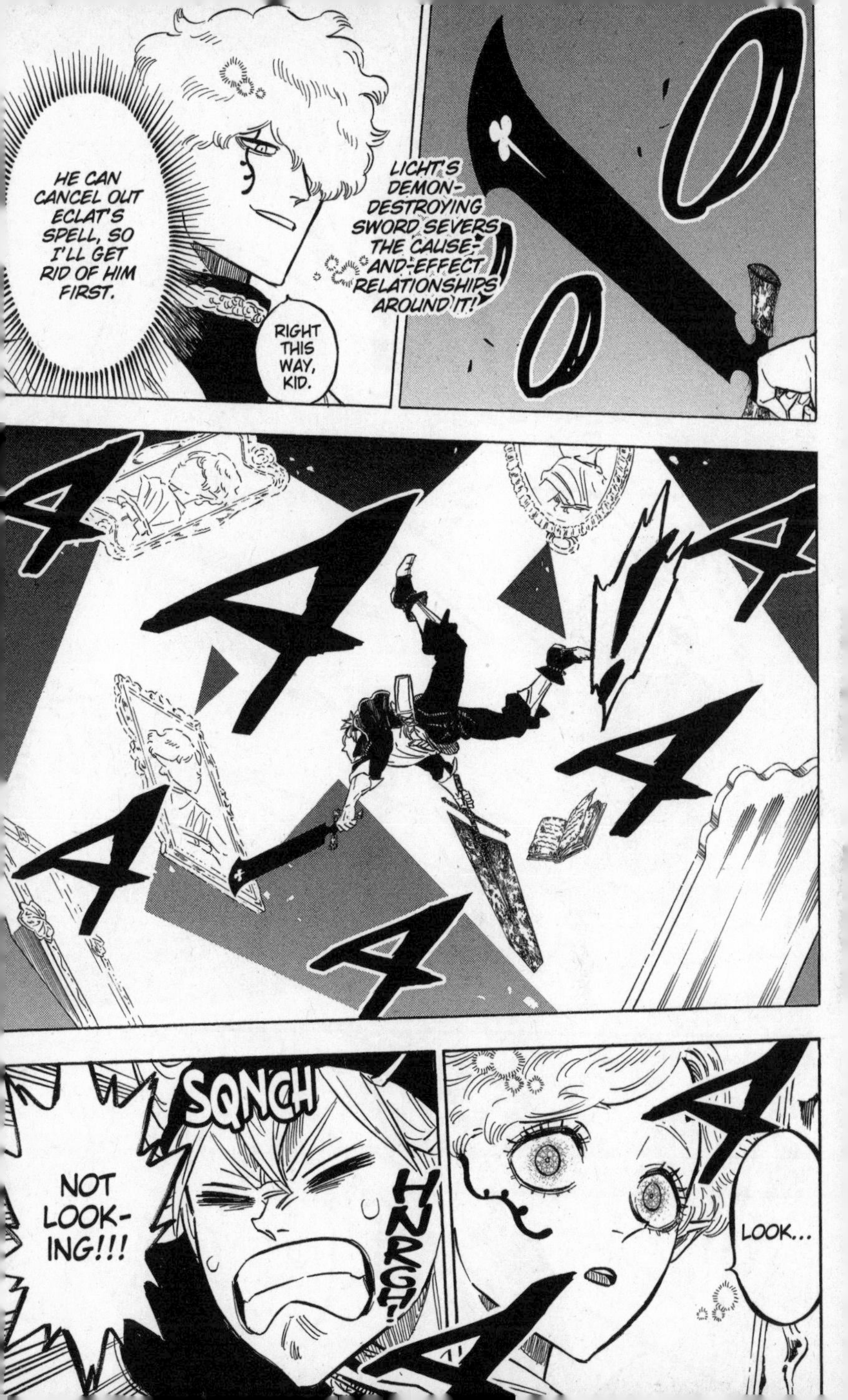
LICHT'S DEMON-DESTROYING SWORD SEVERS THE CAUSE-AND-EFFECT RELATIONSHIPS AROUND IT!
RIGHT THIS WAY, KID.
HE CAN CANCEL OUT ECLAT'S SPELL, SO I'LL GET RID OF HIM FIRST.
LOOK...
SQNCH
HNRGH!
NOT LOOK-ING!!!

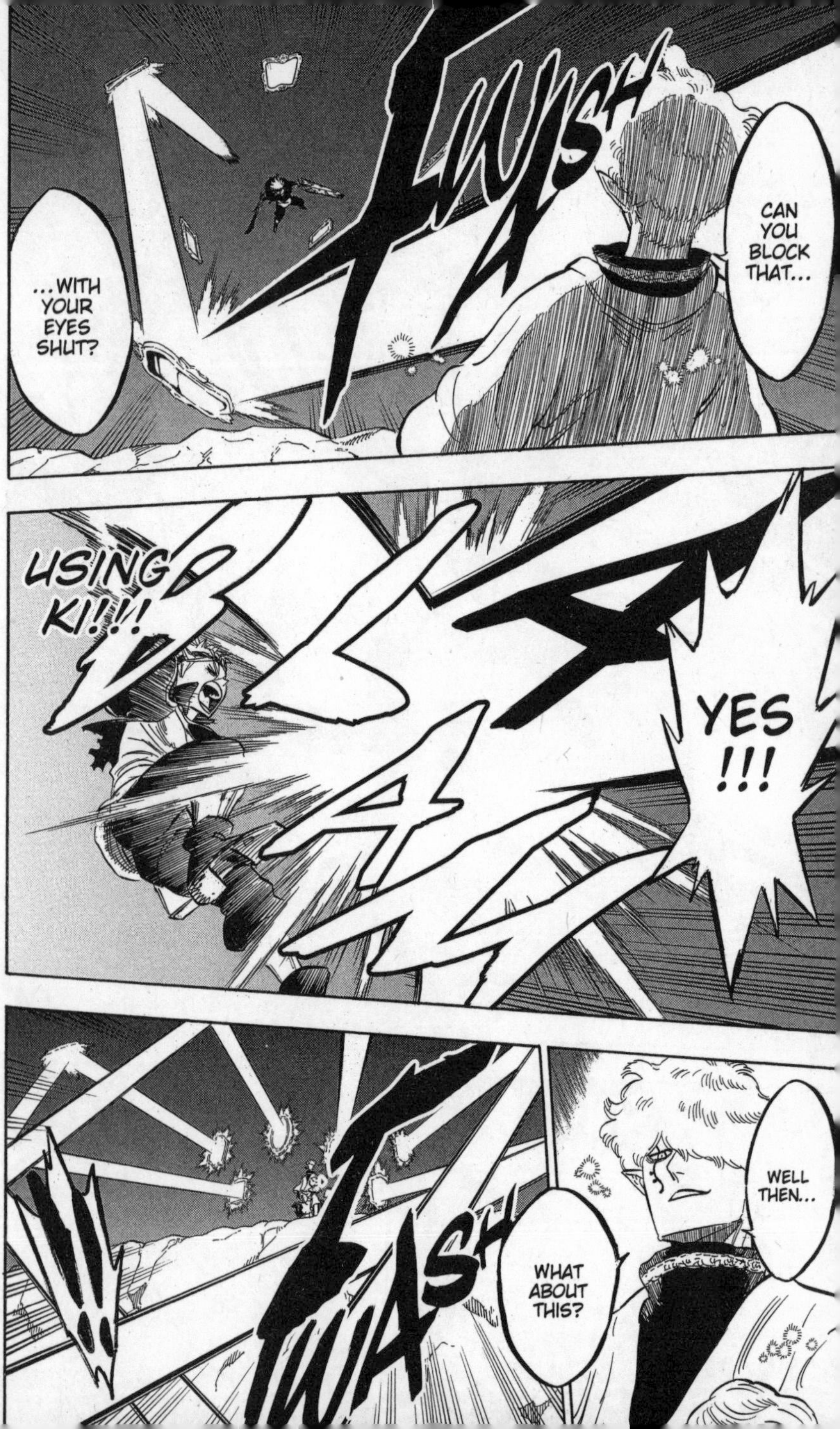
CAN YOU BLOCK THAT...
FWISH
...WITH YOUR EYES SHUT?
YES!!!
USING KI!!!
WELL THEN...
WHAT ABOUT THIS?
FWASH
!!

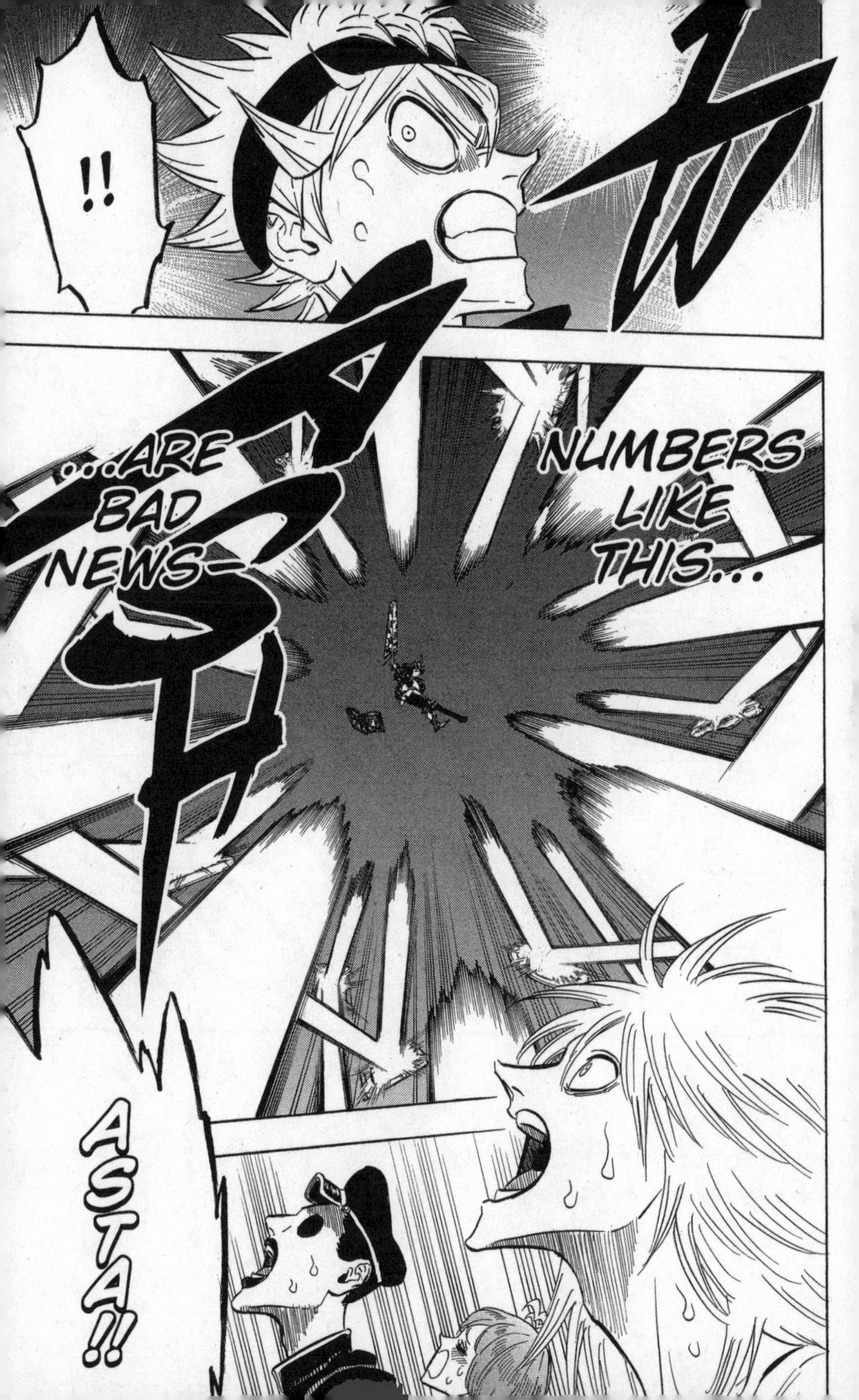
!!
NUMBERS LIKE THIS...
...ARE BAD NEWS—
ASTA!!

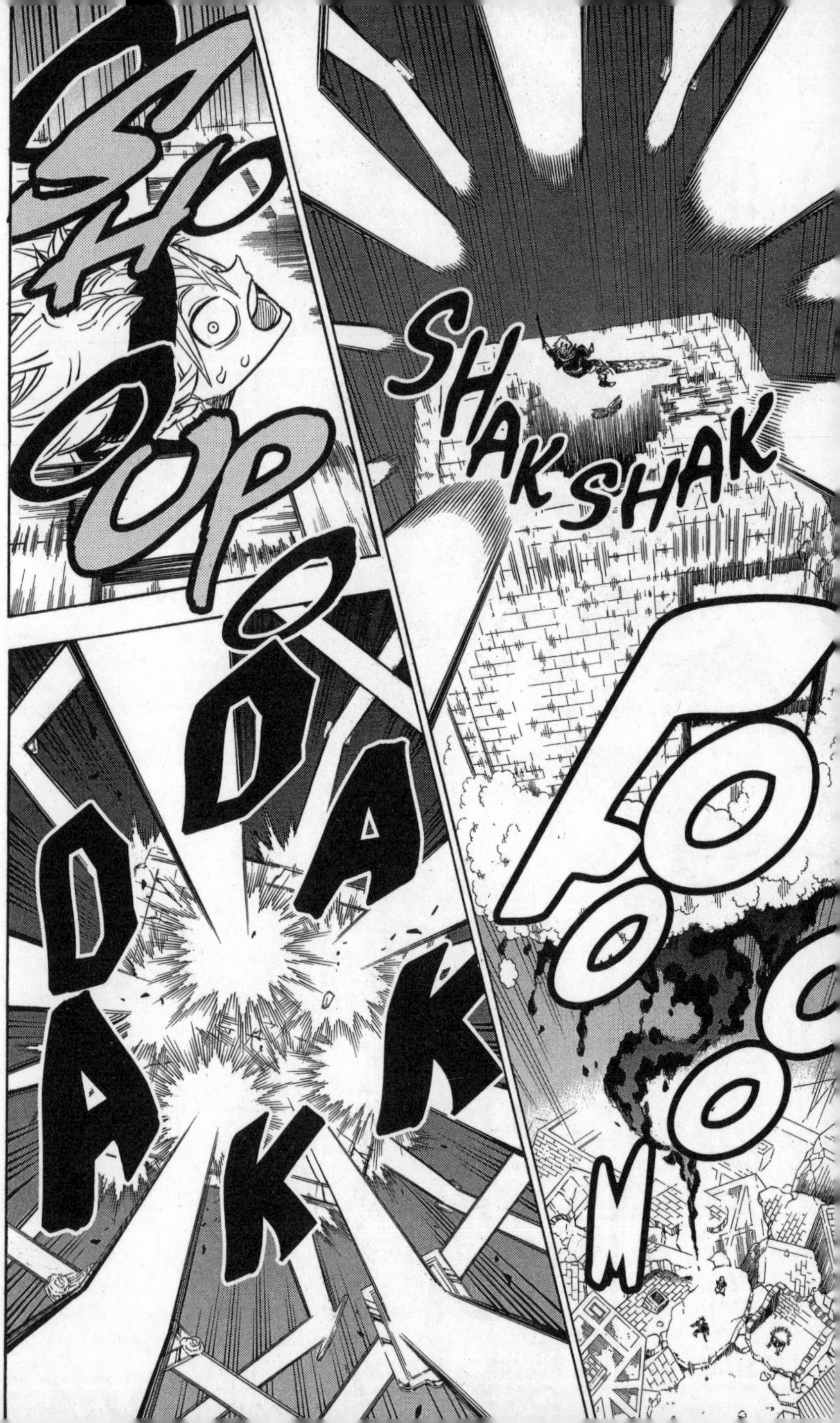
SHAK SHAK
SHOOP
FOOOOM
DAK
DAK

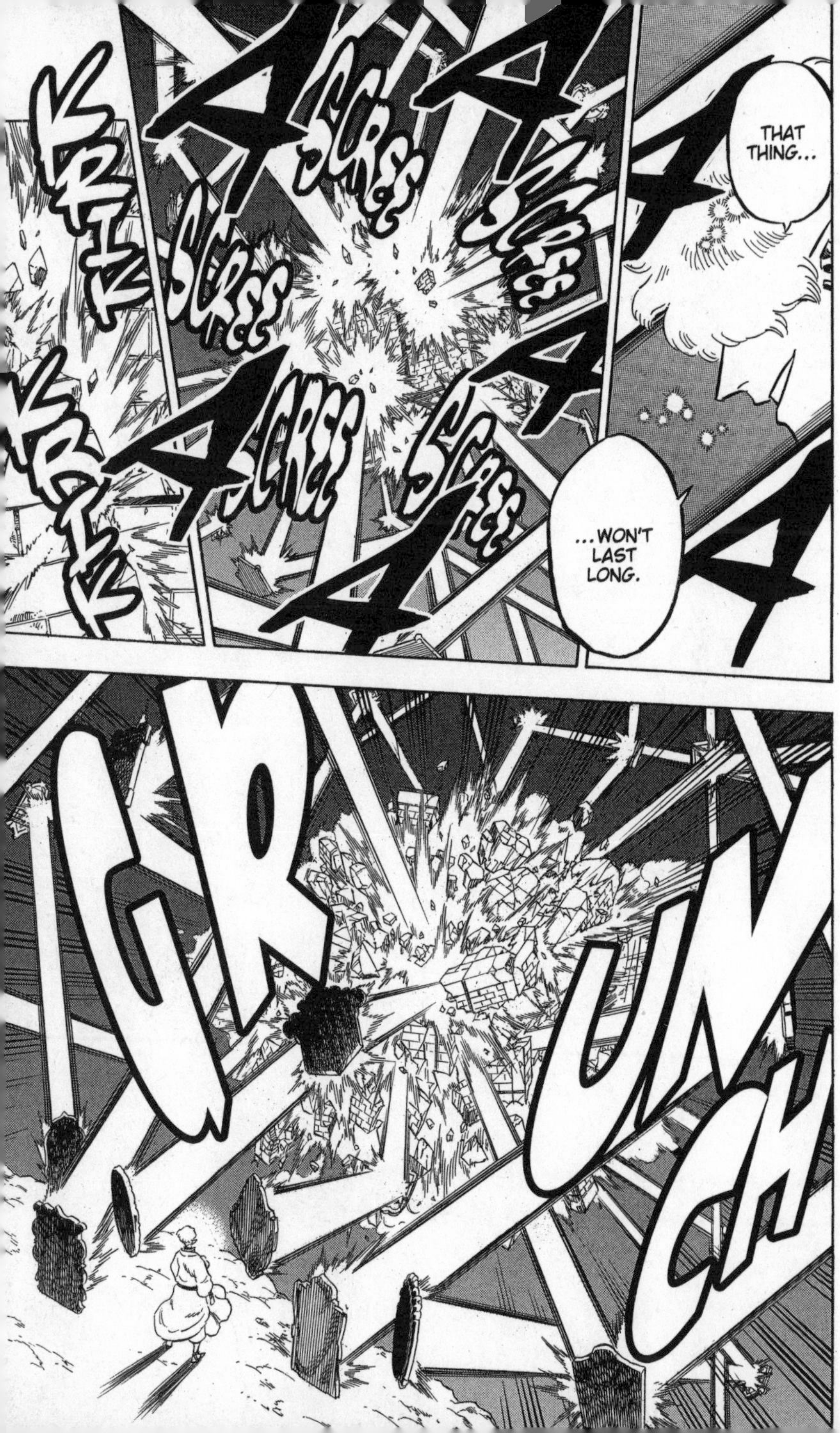
THAT THING...
...WON'T LAST LONG.
SCREE
SCREE
SCREE
SCREE
SCREE
CRUNCH

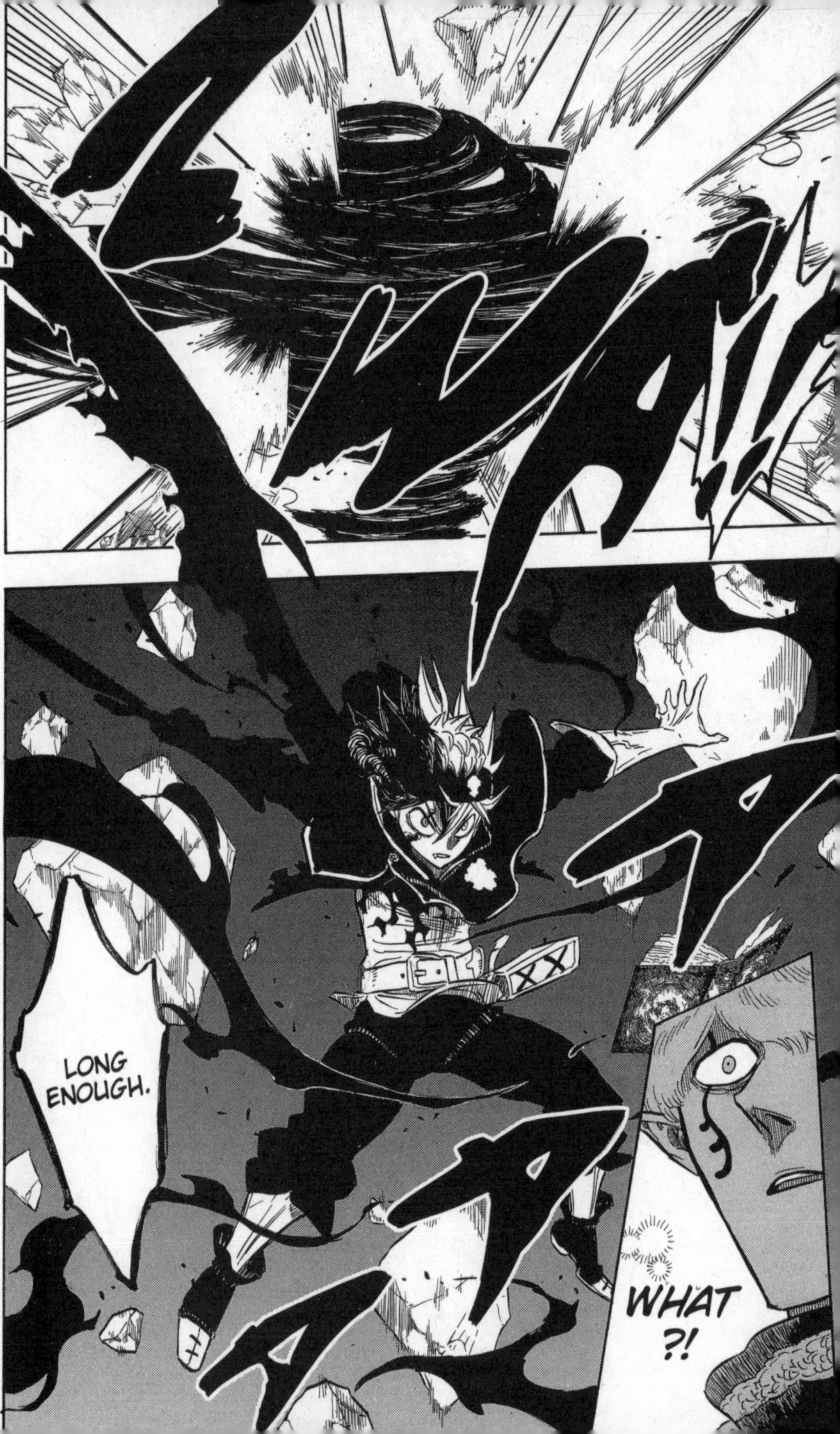
LONG ENOUGH.
WHAT ?!

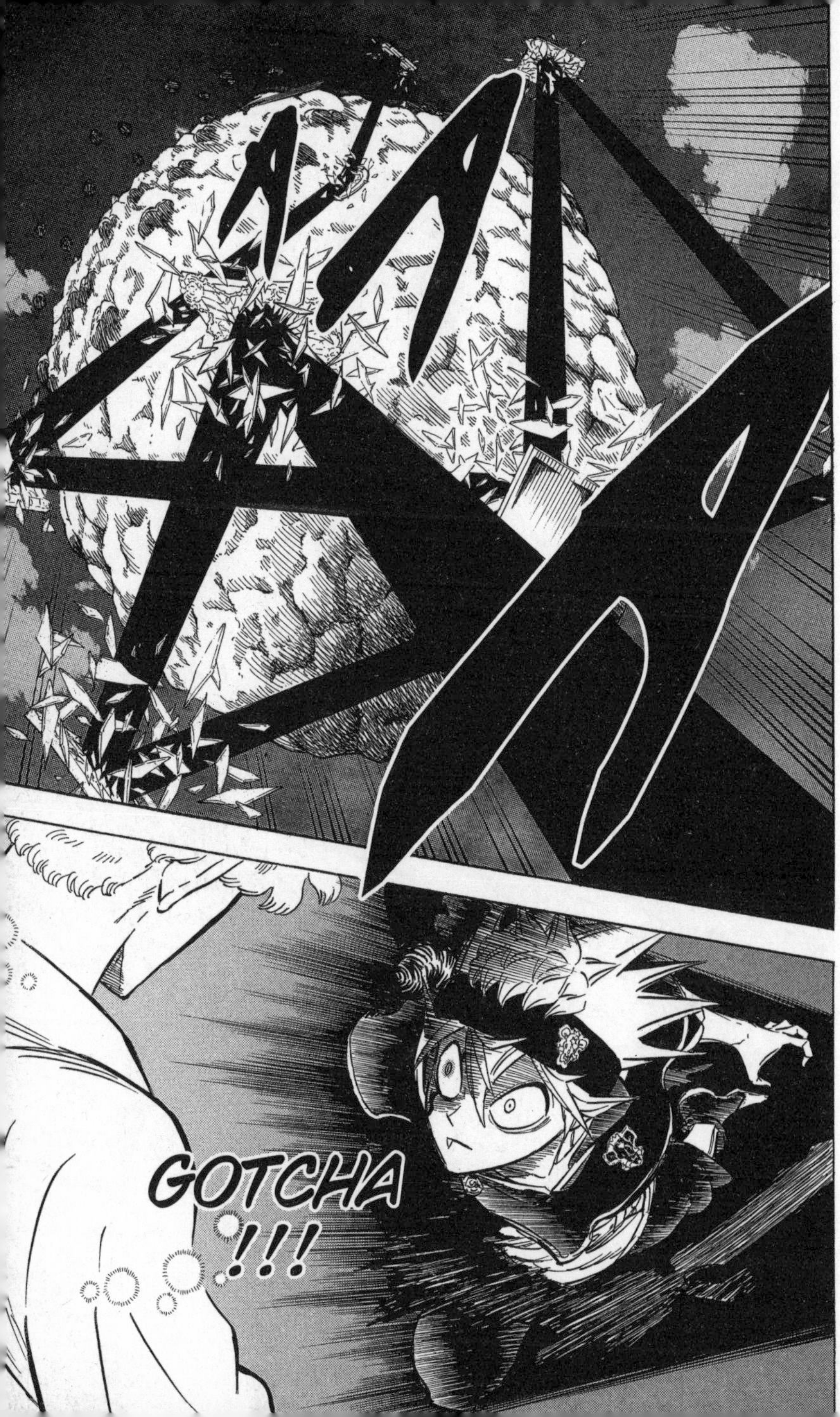
GOTCHA
!!!

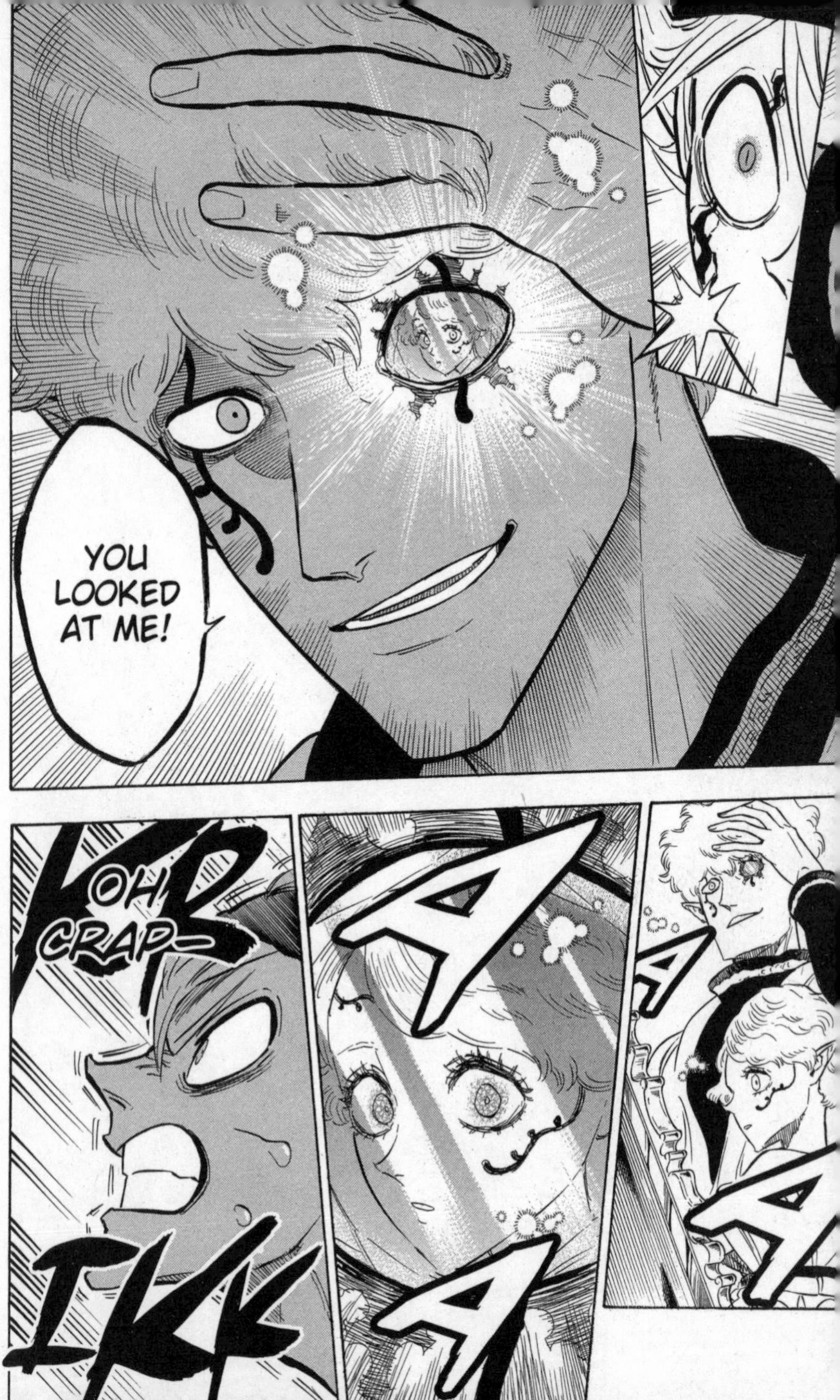
YOU LOOKED AT ME!
OH CRAP—

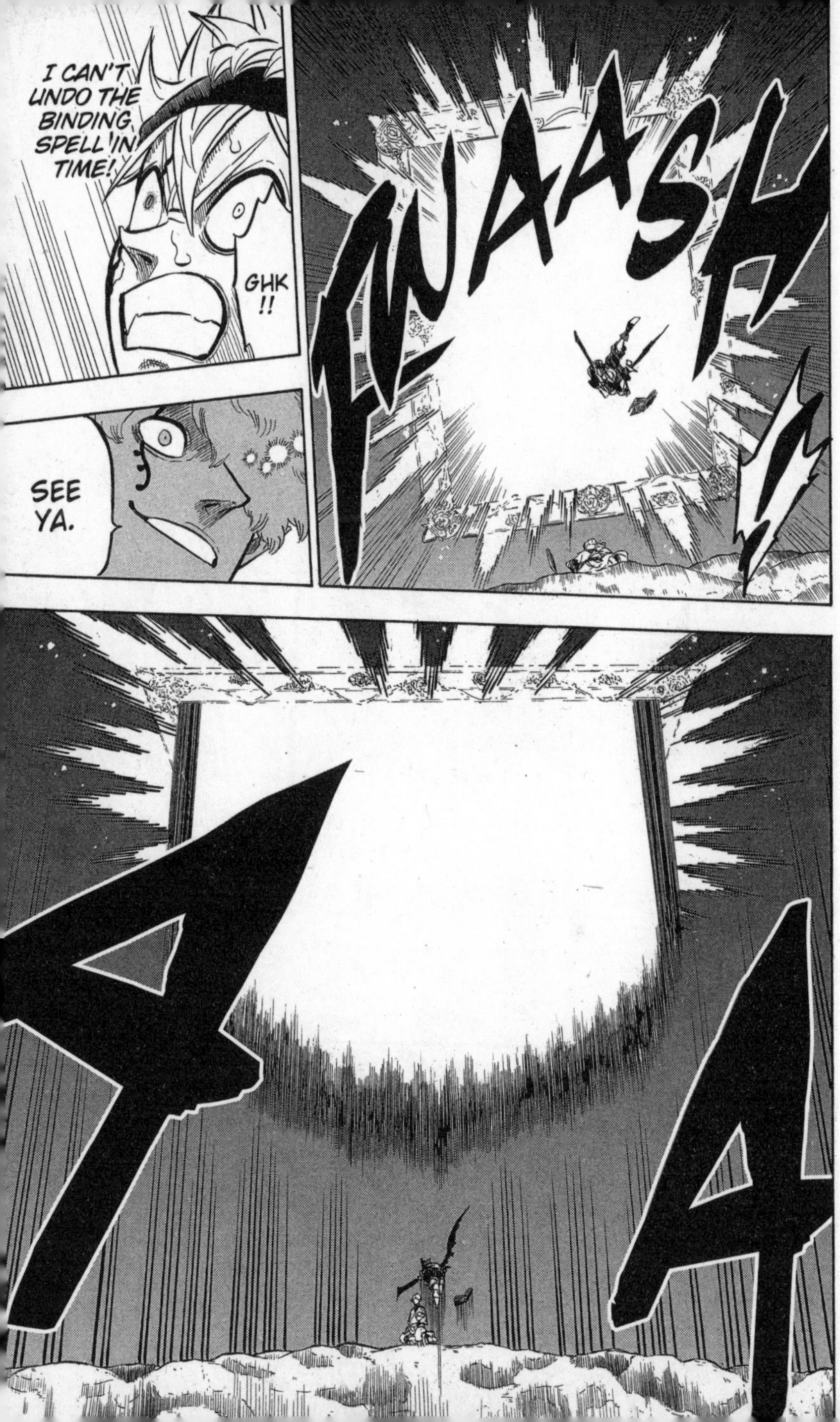
I CAN'T UNDO THE BINDING SPELL IN TIME!
GHK!!
SEE YA.
FWAASH!

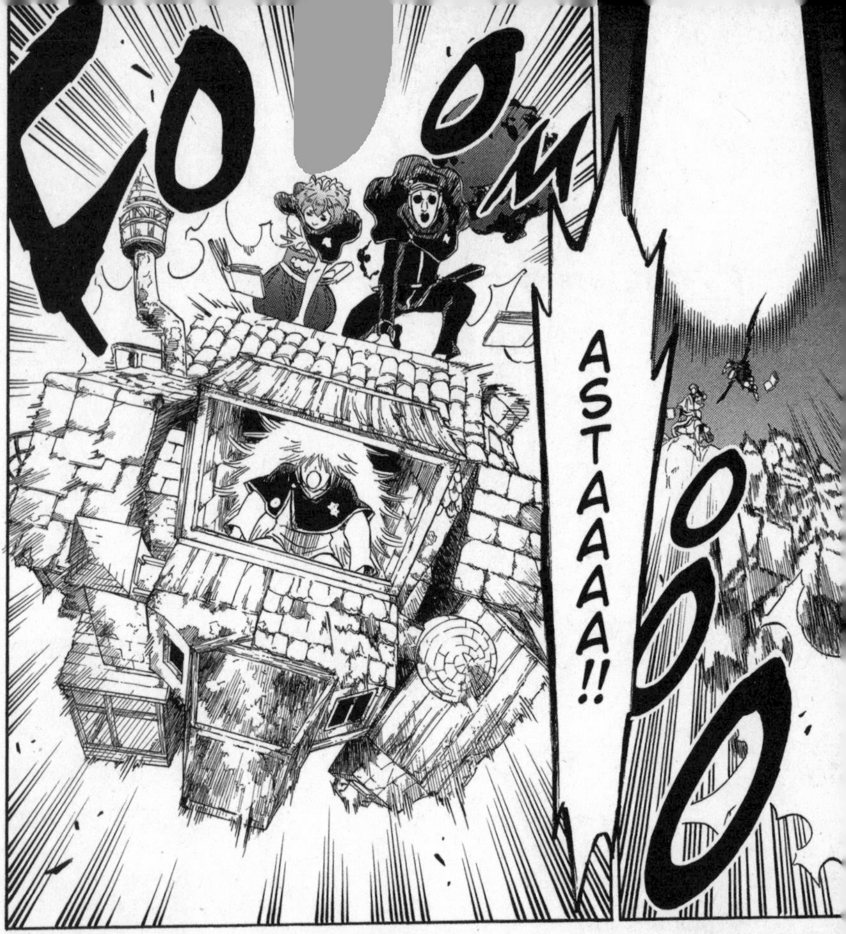
ASTAAAAA!!
KO OM

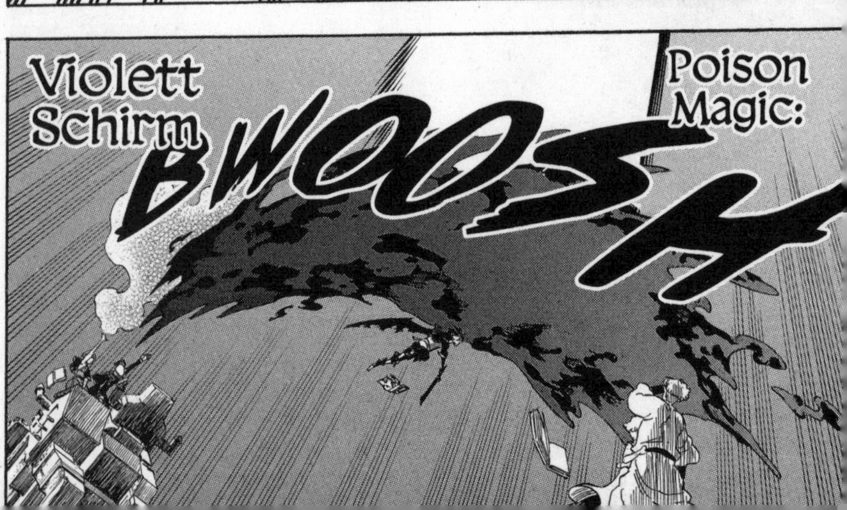
Poison Magic:
Violett Schirm
BWOOSH

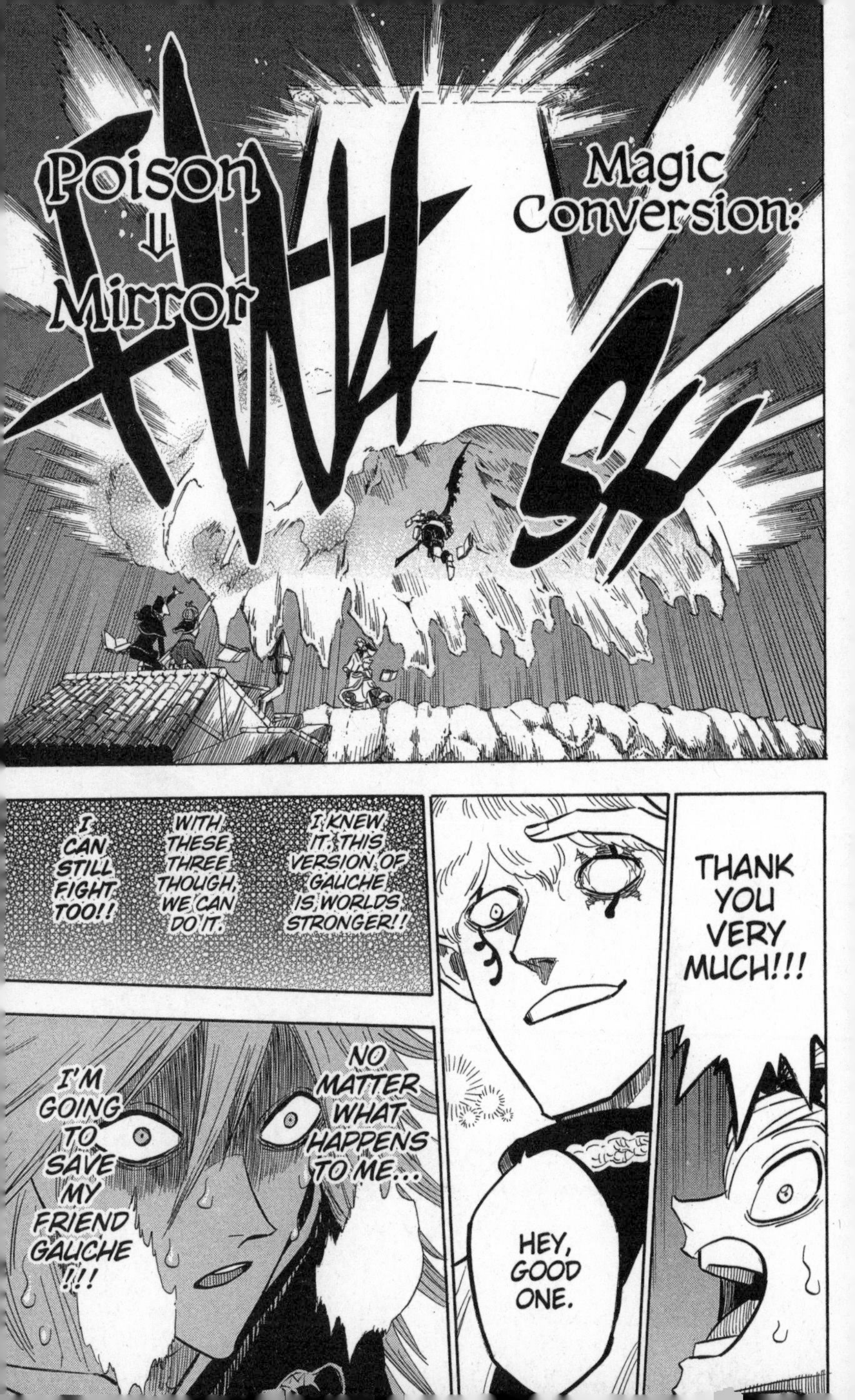
Magic Conversion:
Poison ⇓ Mirror
THANK YOU VERY MUCH!!!
HEY, GOOD ONE.
I KNEW IT. THIS VERSION OF GAUCHE IS WORLDS STRONGER!!
WITH THESE THREE THOUGH, WE CAN DO IT.
I CAN STILL FIGHT TOO!!
NO MATTER WHAT HAPPENS TO ME...
I'M GOING TO SAVE MY FRIEND GAUCHE!!!

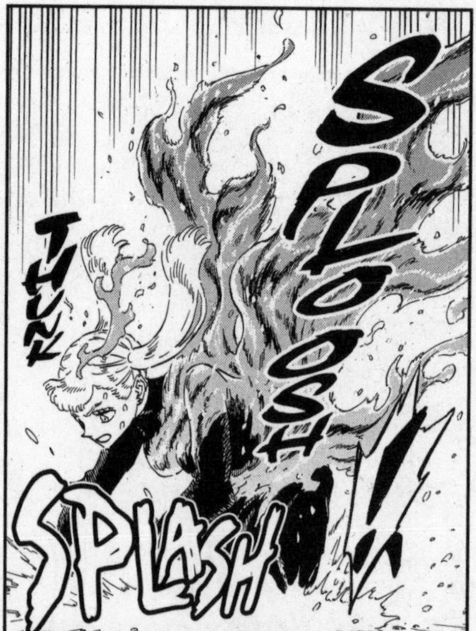
SPLOOSH
THUNK
SPLASH!!

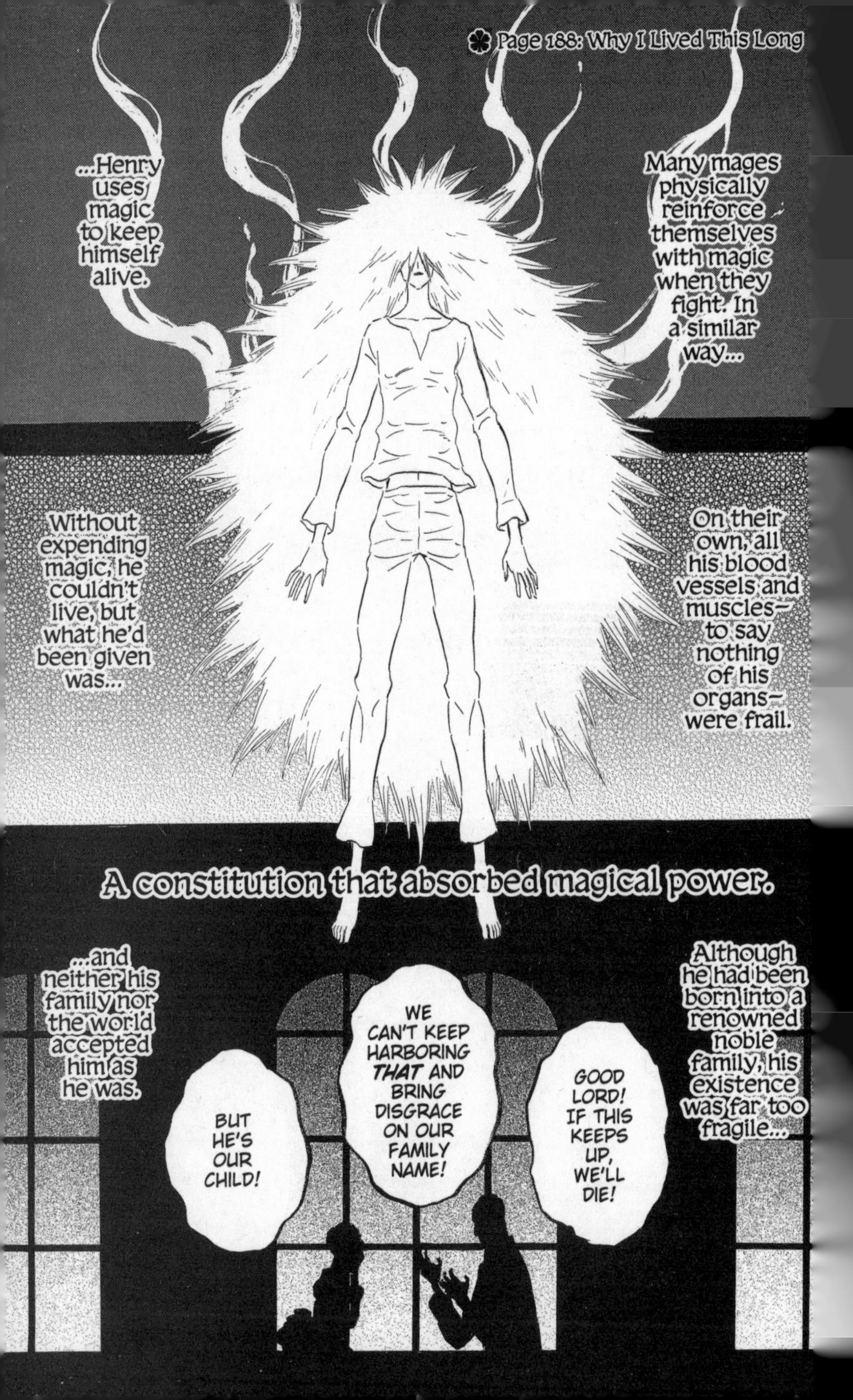
Page 188: Why I Lived This Long
Many mages physically reinforce themselves with magic when they fight. In a similar way...
...Henry uses magic to keep himself alive.
On their own, all his blood vessels and muscles—to say nothing of his organs—were frail.
Without expending magic, he couldn't live, but what he'd been given was...
A constitution that absorbed magical power.
Although he had been born into a renowned noble family, his existence was far too fragile...
GOOD LORD! IF THIS KEEPS UP, WE'LL DIE!
WE CAN'T KEEP HARBORING *THAT* AND BRING DISGRACE ON OUR FAMILY NAME!
BUT HE'S OUR CHILD!
...and neither his family nor the world accepted him as he was.

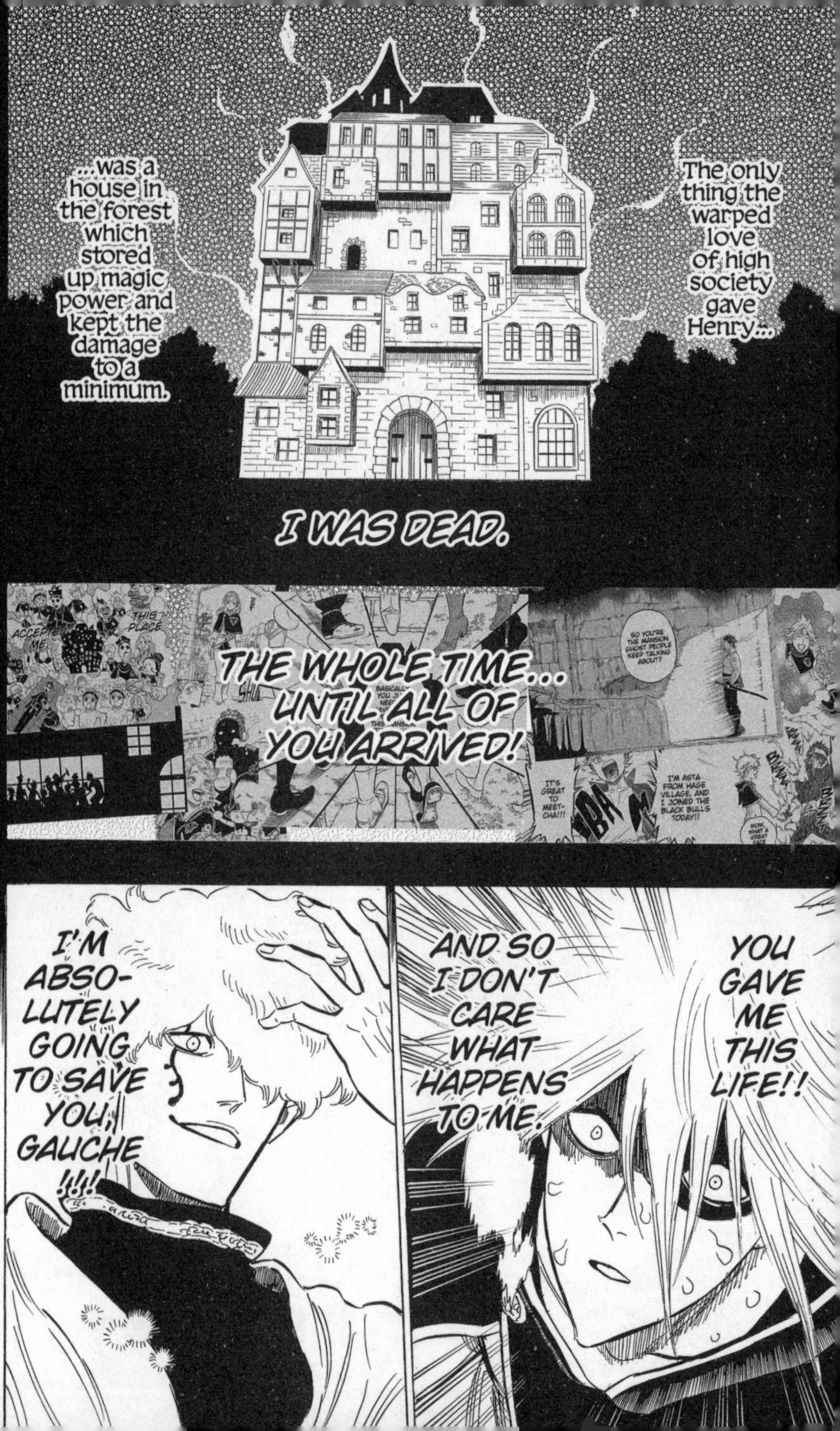
The only thing the warped love of high society gave Henry...
...was a house in the forest which stored up magic power and kept the damage to a minimum.
I WAS DEAD.
THE WHOLE TIME... UNTIL ALL OF YOU ARRIVED!
SO YOU'RE THE MANSION GHOST PEOPLE KEEP TALKING ABOUT?
I'M ASTA FROM HAGE VILLAGE, AND I JOINED THE BLACK BULLS TODAY!!
IT'S GREAT TO MEET-CHA!!!
THIS PLACE
ACCEPTED ME
YOU GAVE ME THIS LIFE!!
AND SO I DON'T CARE WHAT HAPPENS TO ME.
I'M ABSOLUTELY GOING TO SAVE YOU, GAUCHE!!!

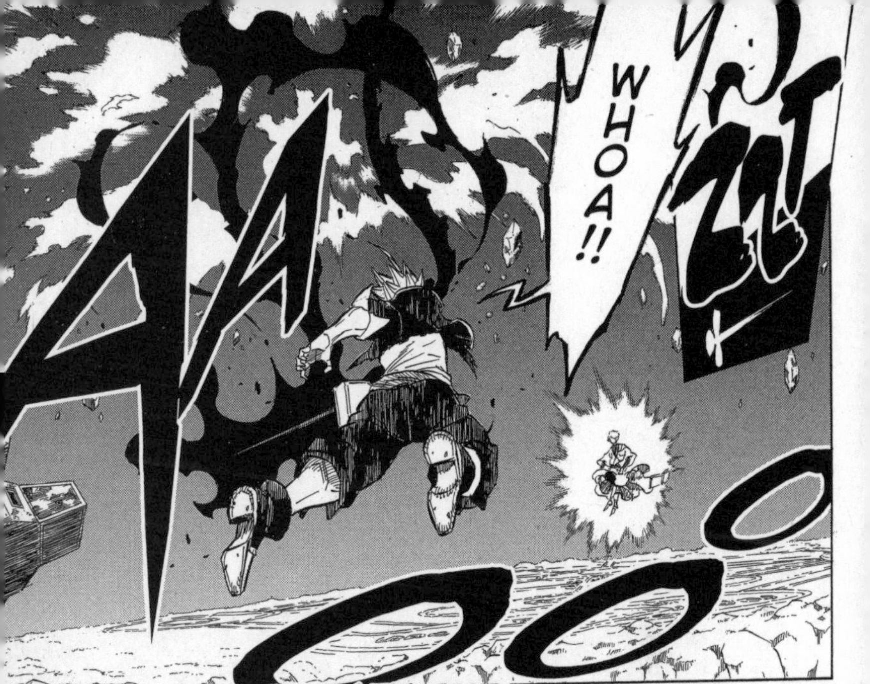
WHOA!!

Page 188: Why I Lived This Long

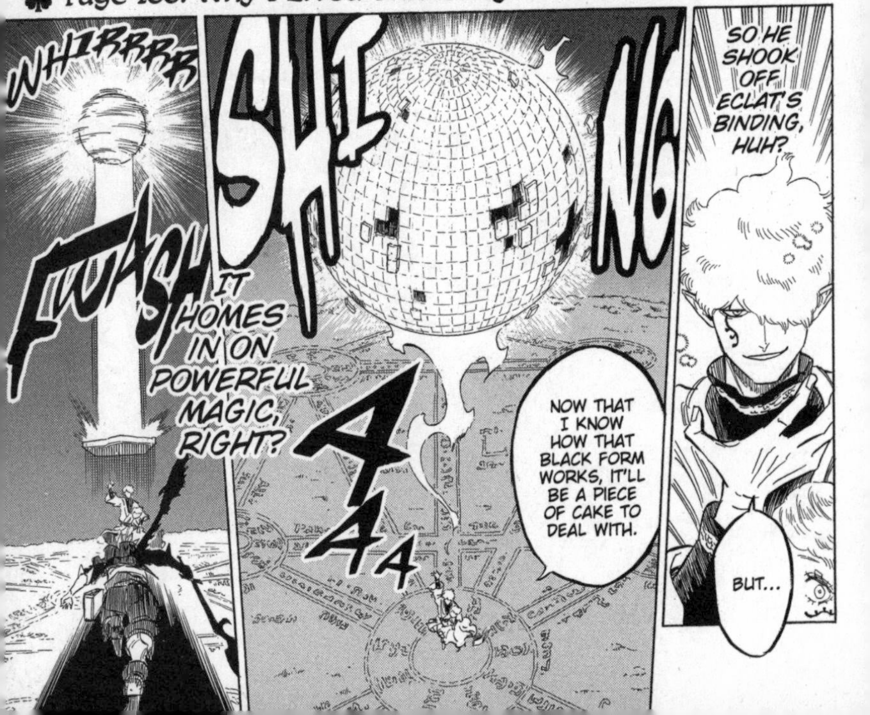
SO HE SHOOK OFF ECLAT'S BINDING, HUH?
NOW THAT I KNOW HOW THAT BLACK FORM WORKS, IT'LL BE A PIECE OF CAKE TO DEAL WITH.
BUT...
IT HOMES IN ON POWERFUL MAGIC, RIGHT?
WHIRRRR

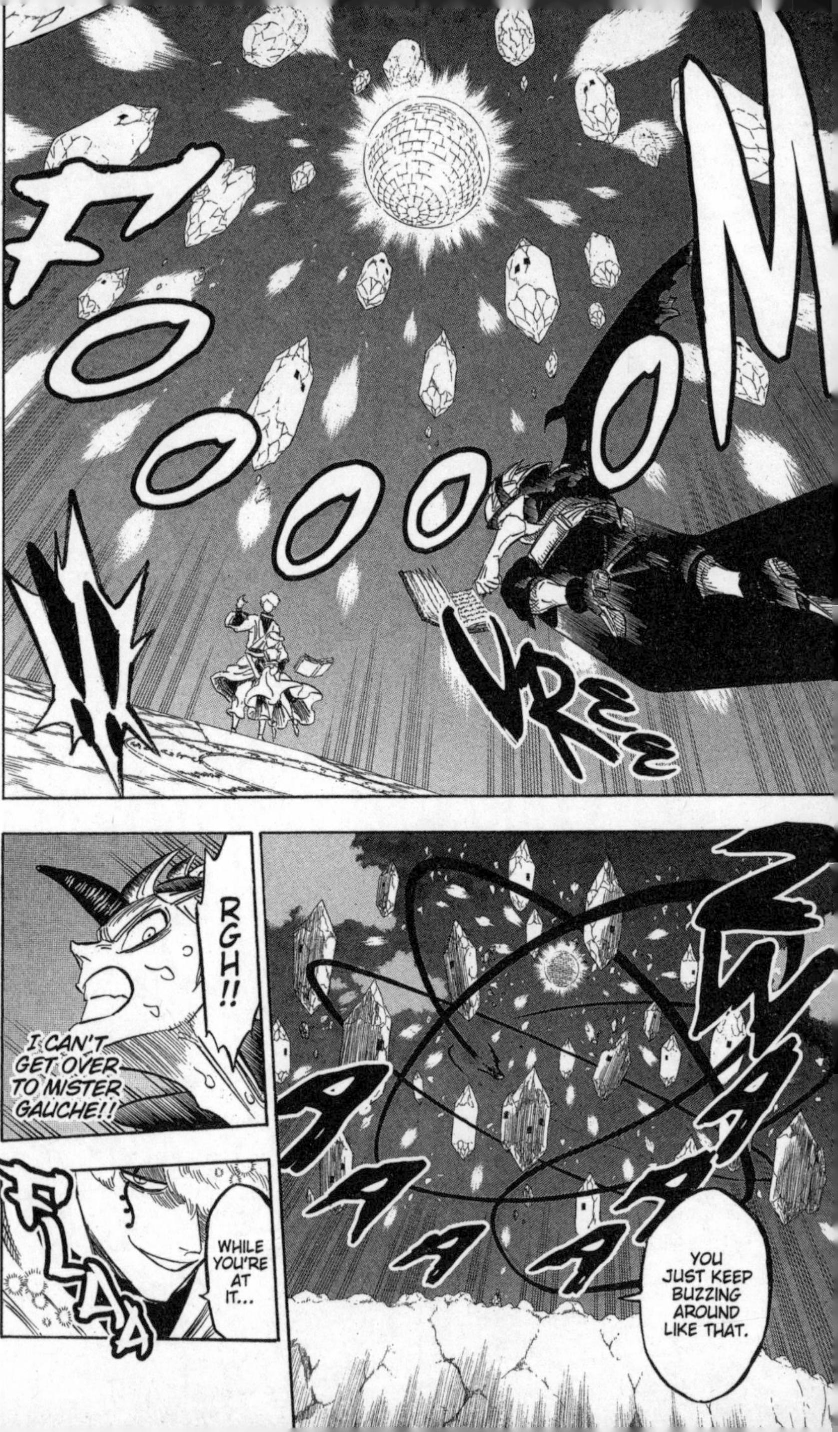
FOOOOOOM
!!
VREE
RGH!!
I CAN'T GET OVER TO MISTER GAUCHE!!
WHILE YOU'RE AT IT...
YOU JUST KEEP BUZZING AROUND LIKE THAT.

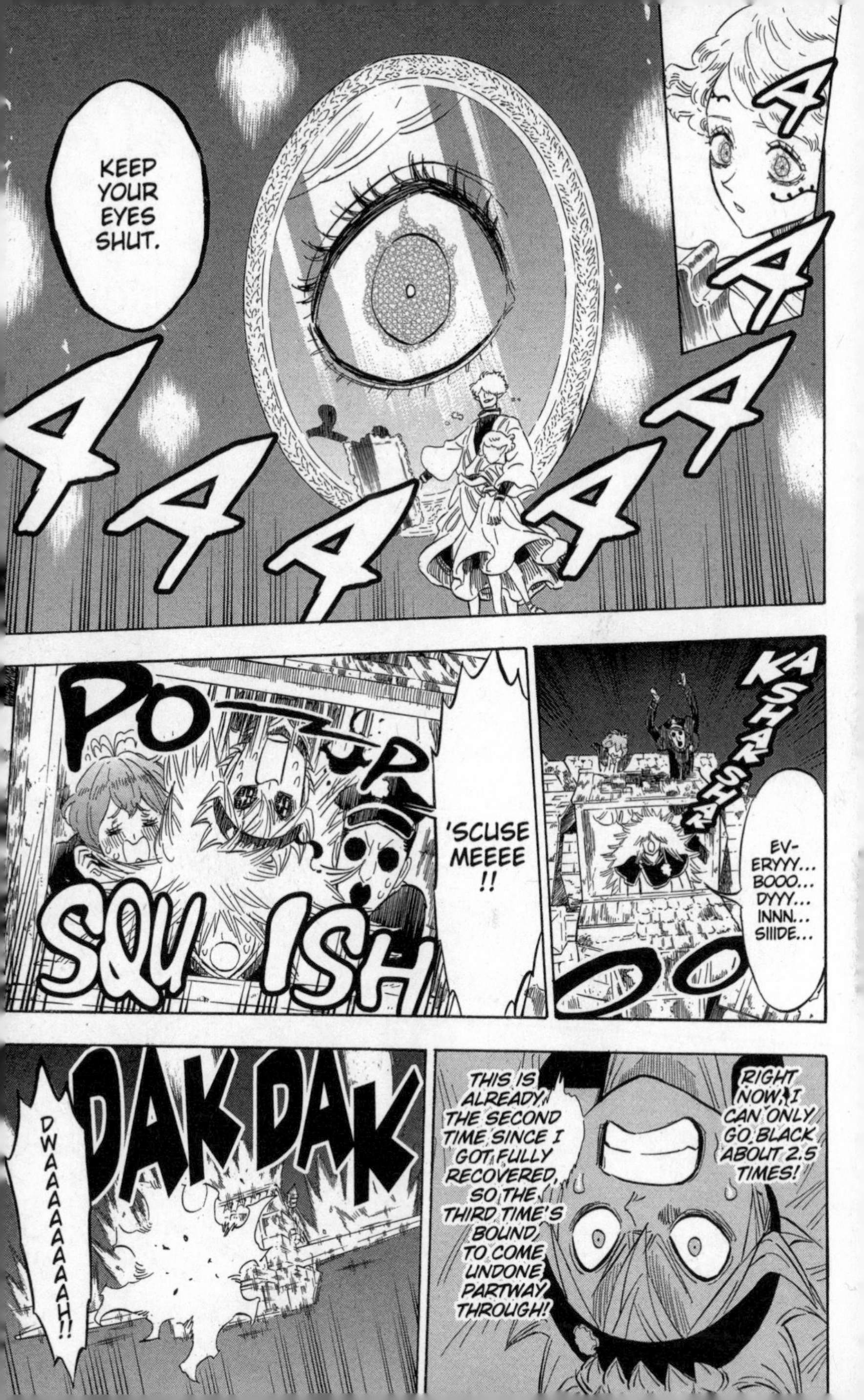
KEEP YOUR EYES SHUT.
AAAAAAAA
KASHASHASHA
EV-ERYYY... BOOO... DYYY... INNN... SIIIDE...
DOO
'SCUSE MEEEE!!
POZUP
SQUISH
RIGHT NOW, I CAN ONLY GO BLACK ABOUT 2.5 TIMES!
THIS IS ALREADY THE SECOND TIME SINCE I GOT FULLY RECOVERED, SO THE THIRD TIME'S BOUND TO COME UNDONE PARTWAY THROUGH!
DAK DAK
DWAAAAAAAAAH!!

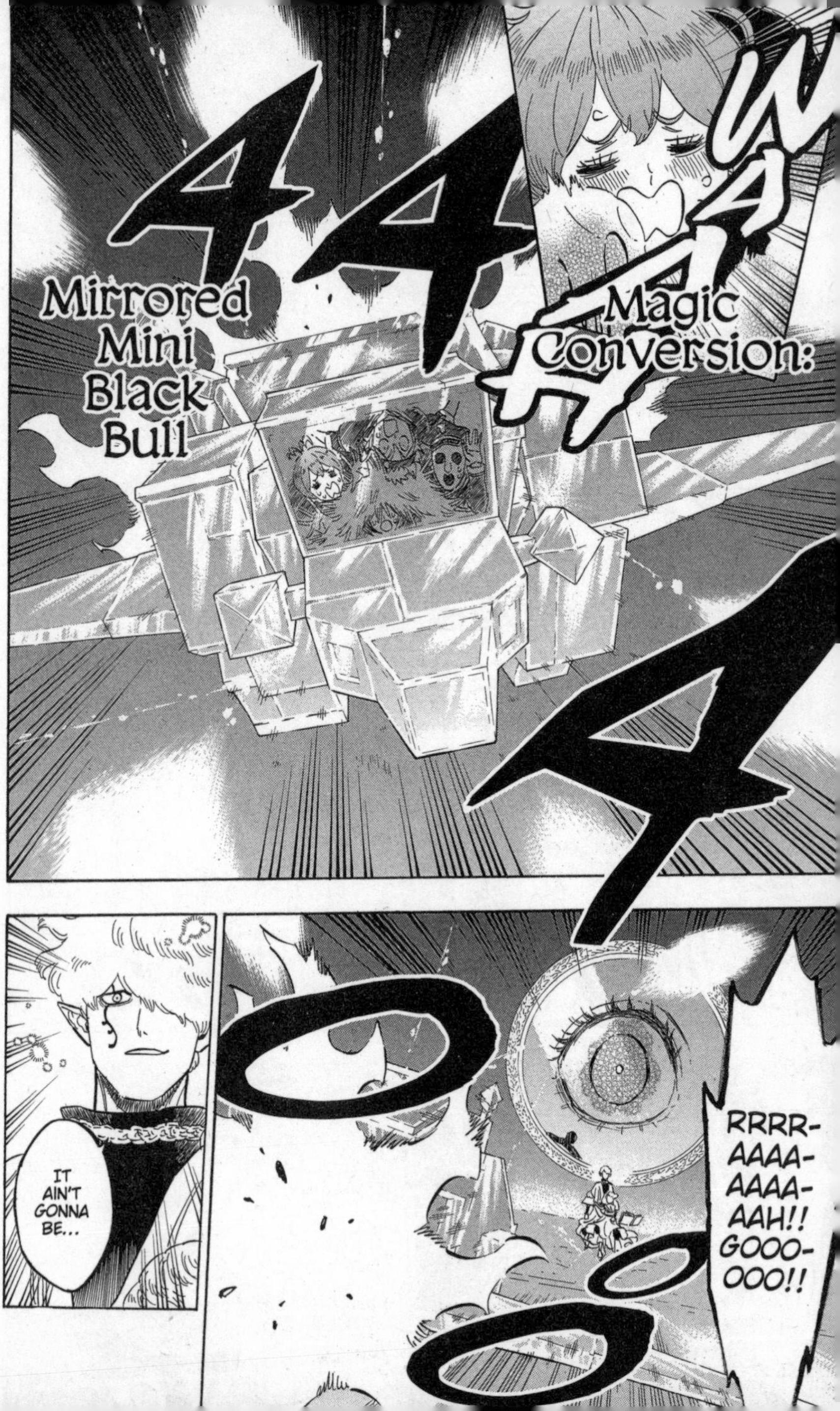
Magic Conversion:
Mirrored Mini Black Bull
RRRR-AAAA-AAAA-AAH!! GOOO-OOO!!
IT AIN'T GONNA BE...

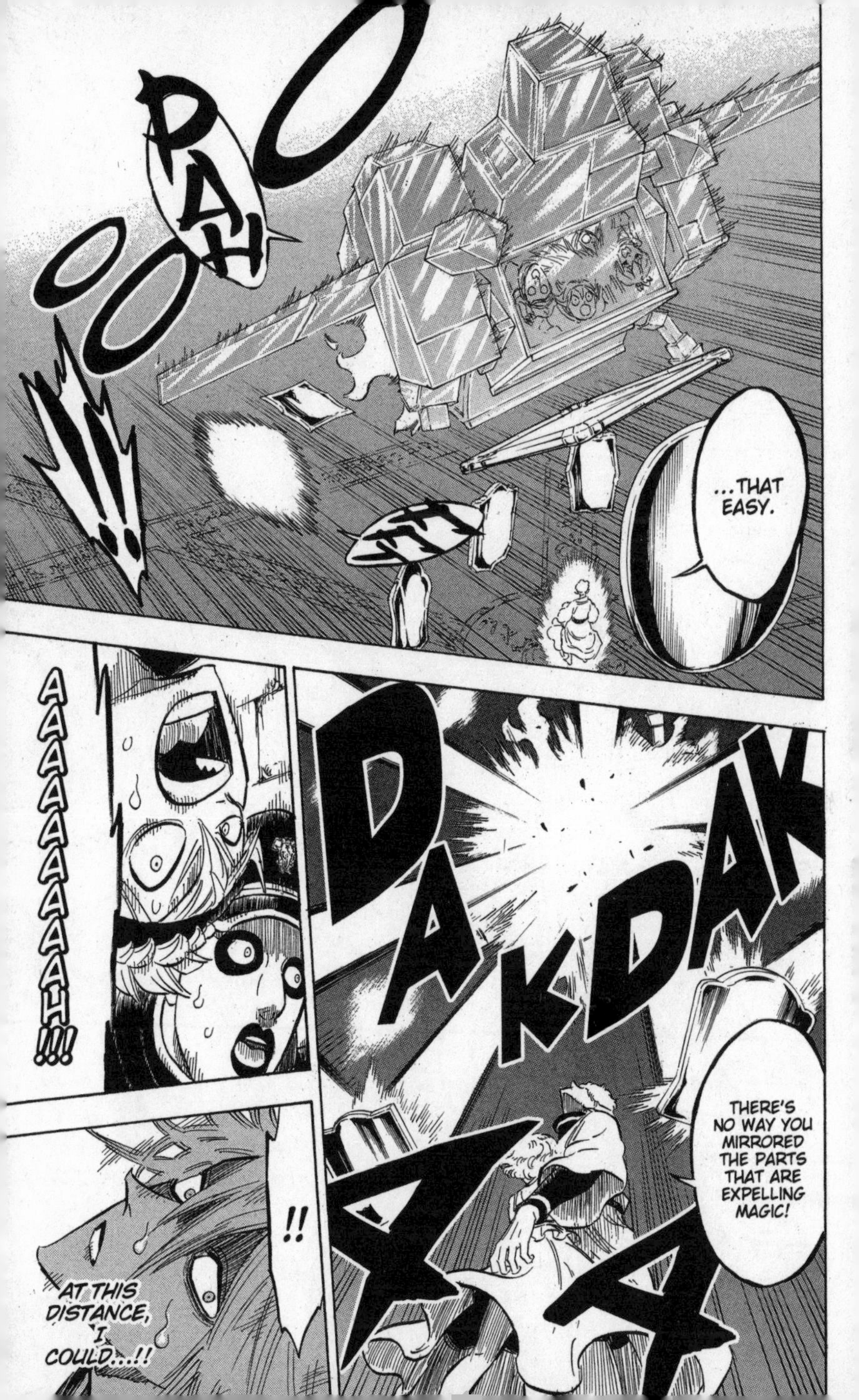
...THAT EASY.
PAH
!!!
THERE'S NO WAY YOU MIRRORED THE PARTS THAT ARE EXPELLING MAGIC!
DAKDAK
AAAAAAAAAAAAAH!!!
!!
AT THIS DISTANCE, I COULD...!!

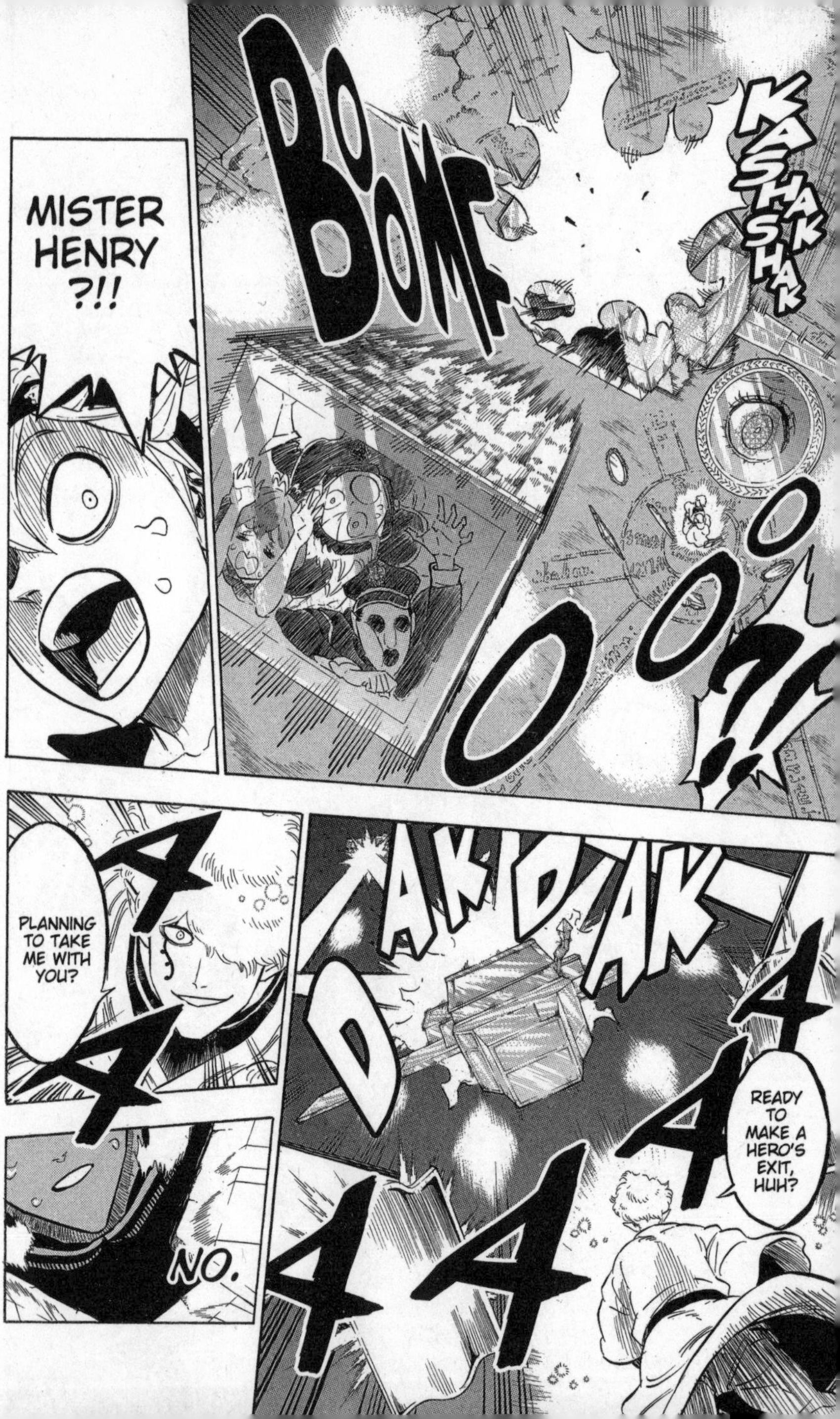
KASHAKSHAK
BOOMF
OOOO?!!
MISTER HENRY ?!!
DAK DAK
READY TO MAKE A HERO'S EXIT, HUH?
PLANNING TO TAKE ME WITH YOU?
NO.

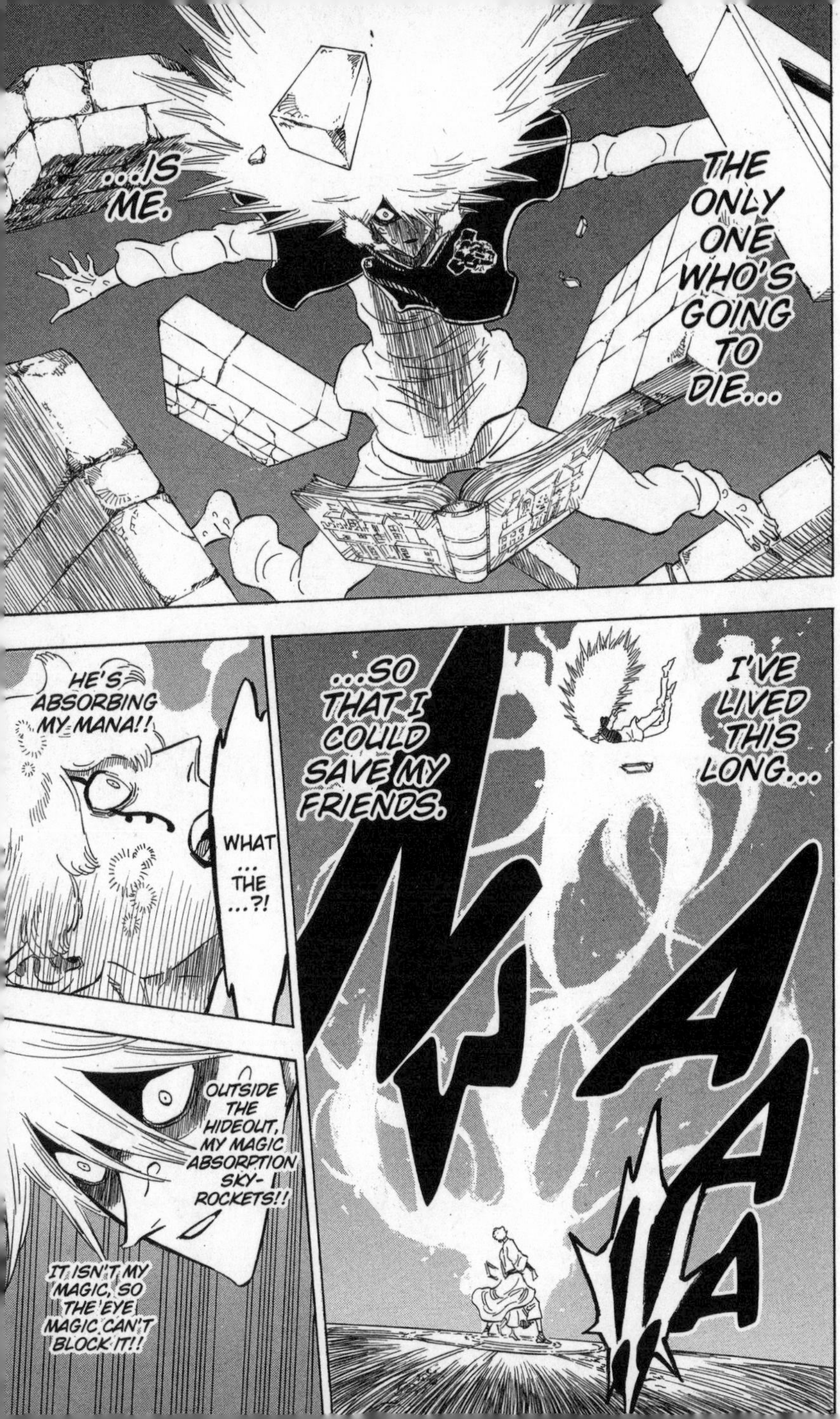
THE ONLY ONE WHO'S GOING TO DIE...
...IS ME.
I'VE LIVED THIS LONG...
...SO THAT I COULD SAVE MY FRIENDS.
WHAT ... THE ...?!
HE'S ABSORBING MY MANA!!
OUTSIDE THE HIDEOUT, MY MAGIC ABSORPTION SKY-ROCKETS!!
IT ISN'T MY MAGIC, SO THE EYE MAGIC CAN'T BLOCK IT!!

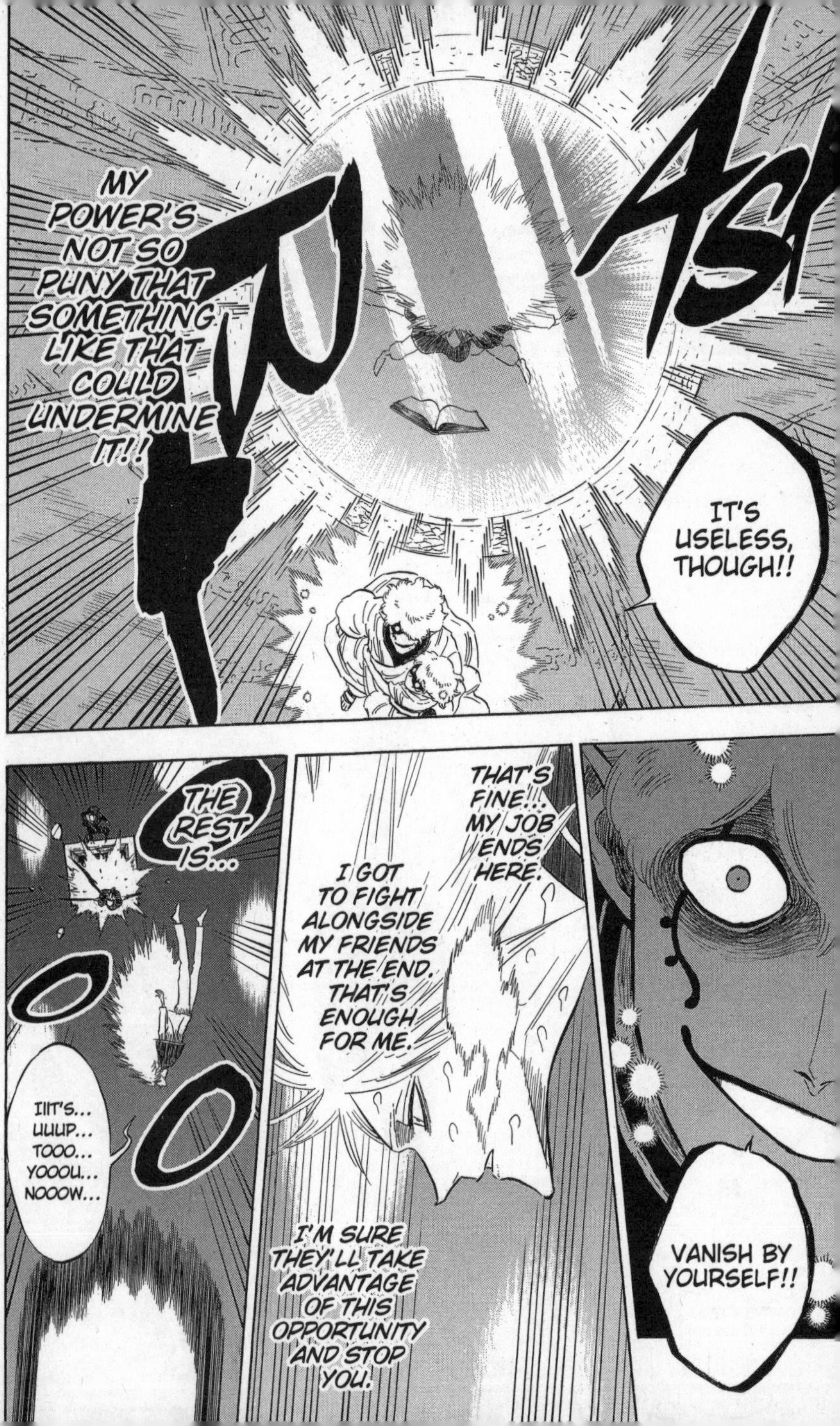
MY POWER'S NOT SO PUNY THAT SOMETHING LIKE THAT COULD UNDERMINE IT!!
IT'S USELESS, THOUGH!!
VANISH BY YOURSELF!!
THAT'S FINE... MY JOB ENDS HERE.
I GOT TO FIGHT ALONGSIDE MY FRIENDS AT THE END. THAT'S ENOUGH FOR ME.
I'M SURE THEY'LL TAKE ADVANTAGE OF THIS OPPORTUNITY AND STOP YOU.
THE REST IS...
IIIT'S... UUUP... TOOO... YOOOU... NOOOW...

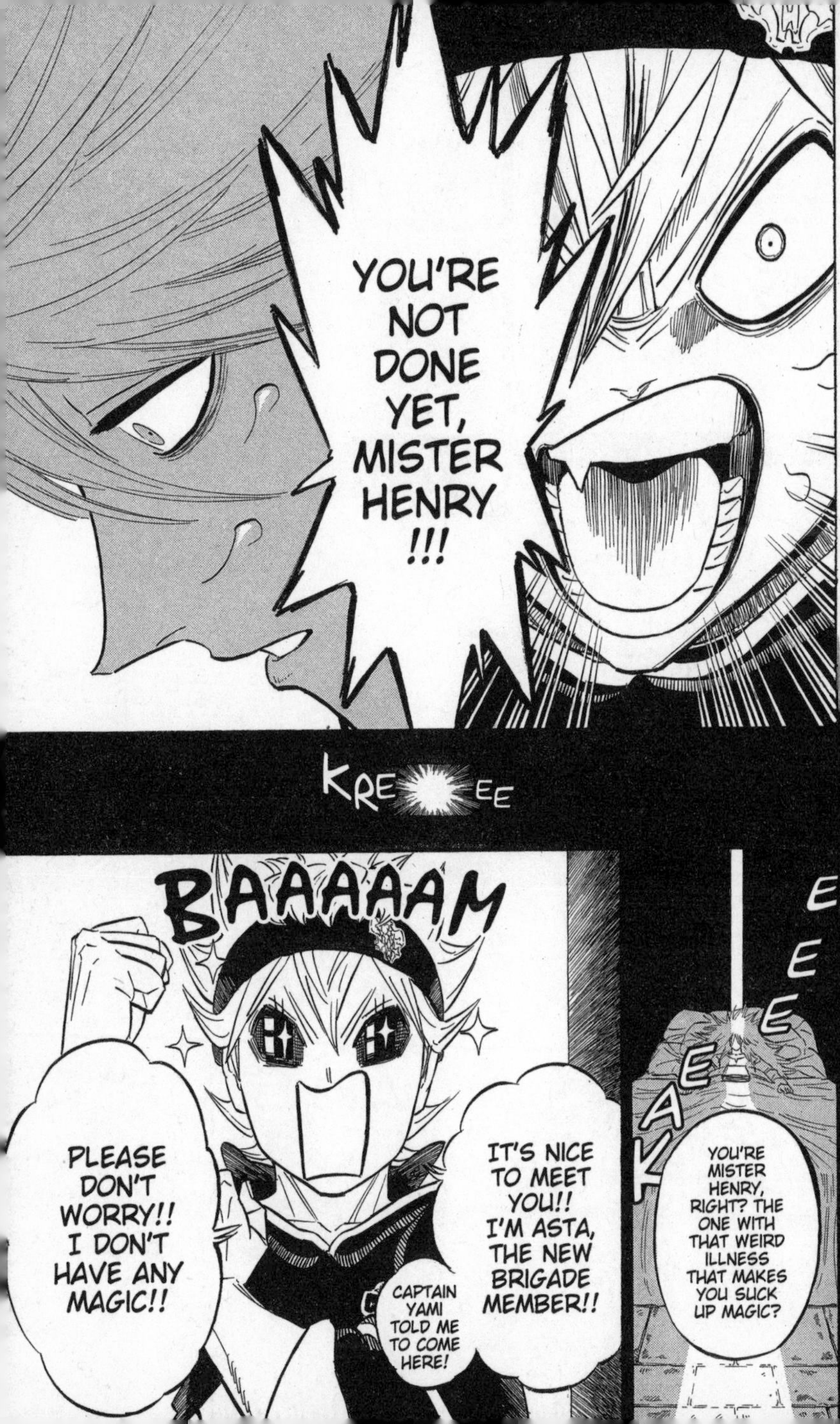
YOU'RE NOT DONE YET, MISTER HENRY!!!
KRE EE
KAEEEE
YOU'RE MISTER HENRY, RIGHT? THE ONE WITH THAT WEIRD ILLNESS THAT MAKES YOU SUCK UP MAGIC?
BAAAAAM
IT'S NICE TO MEET YOU!! I'M ASTA, THE NEW BRIGADE MEMBER!!
CAPTAIN YAMI TOLD ME TO COME HERE!
PLEASE DON'T WORRY!! I DON'T HAVE ANY MAGIC!!

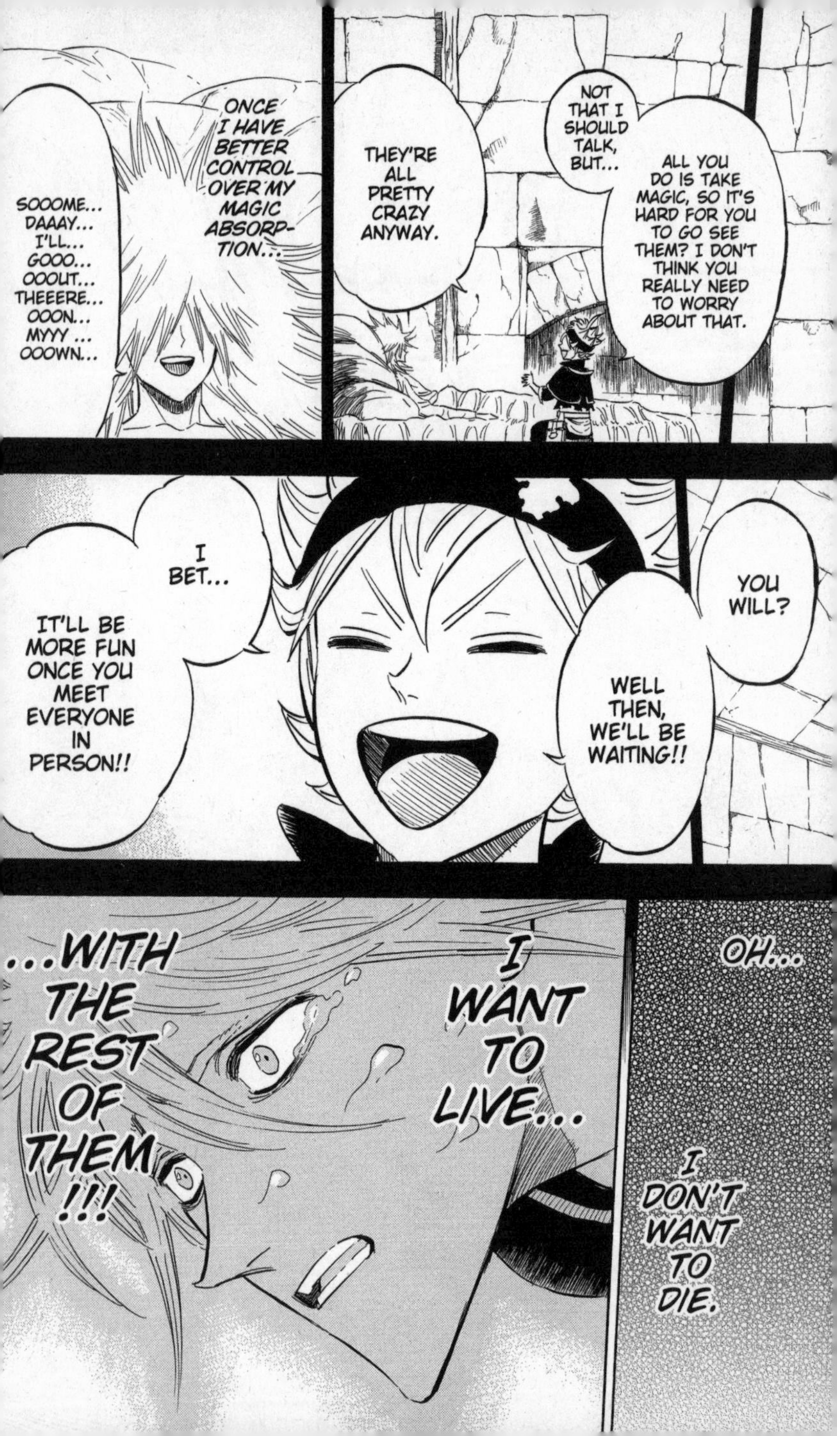
NOT THAT I SHOULD TALK, BUT...
ALL YOU DO IS TAKE MAGIC, SO IT'S HARD FOR YOU TO GO SEE THEM? I DON'T THINK YOU REALLY NEED TO WORRY ABOUT THAT.
THEY'RE ALL PRETTY CRAZY ANYWAY.
ONCE I HAVE BETTER CONTROL OVER MY MAGIC ABSORPTION...
SOOOME... DAAAY... I'LL... GOOO... OOOUT... THEEERE... OOON... MYYY ... OOOWN...
YOU WILL?
WELL THEN, WE'LL BE WAITING!!
I BET...
IT'LL BE MORE FUN ONCE YOU MEET EVERYONE IN PERSON!!
OH...
I DON'T WANT TO DIE.
I WANT TO LIVE...
...WITH THE REST OF THEM!!!

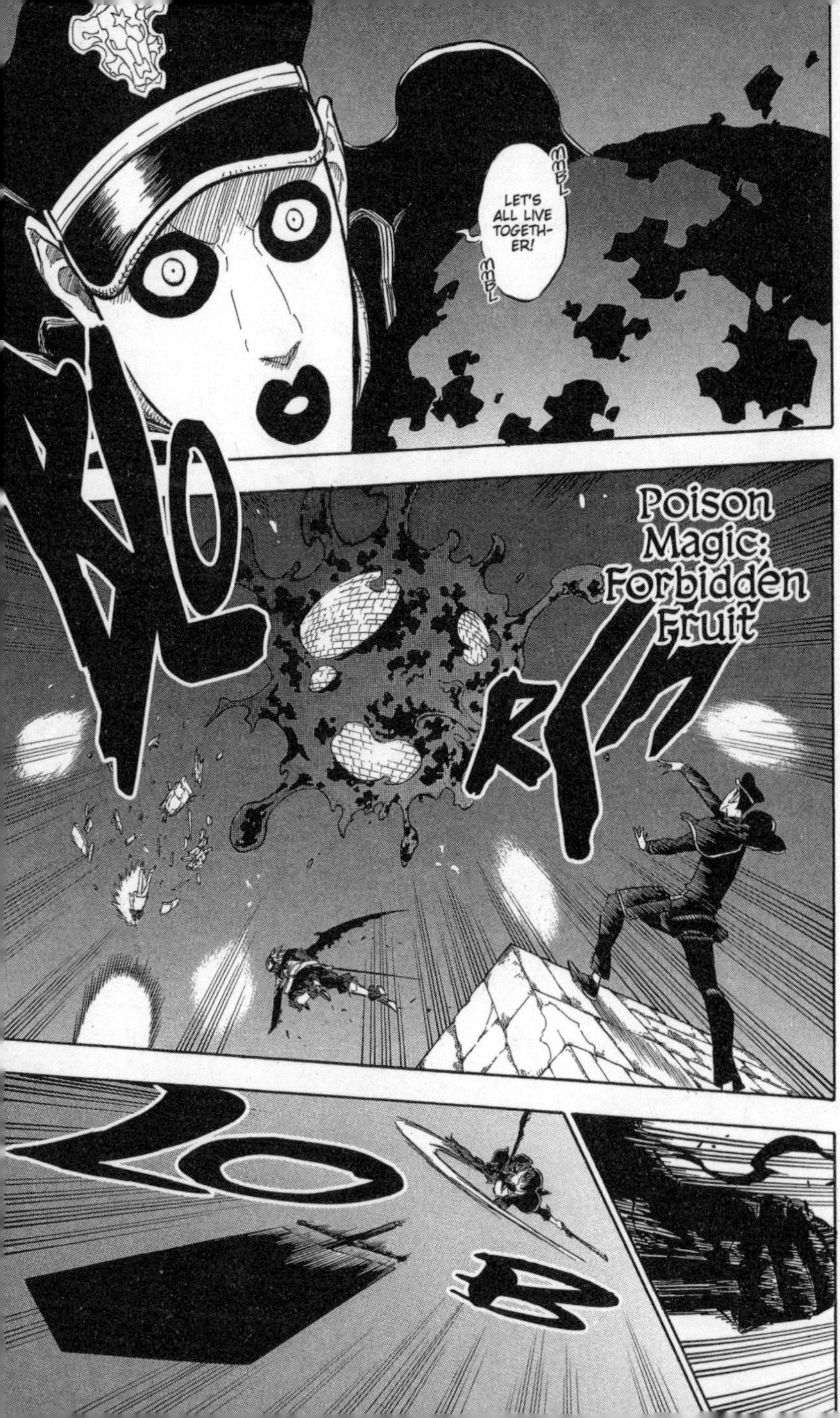
MMBL
LET'S ALL LIVE TOGETHER!
MMBL
Poison Magic: Forbidden Fruit

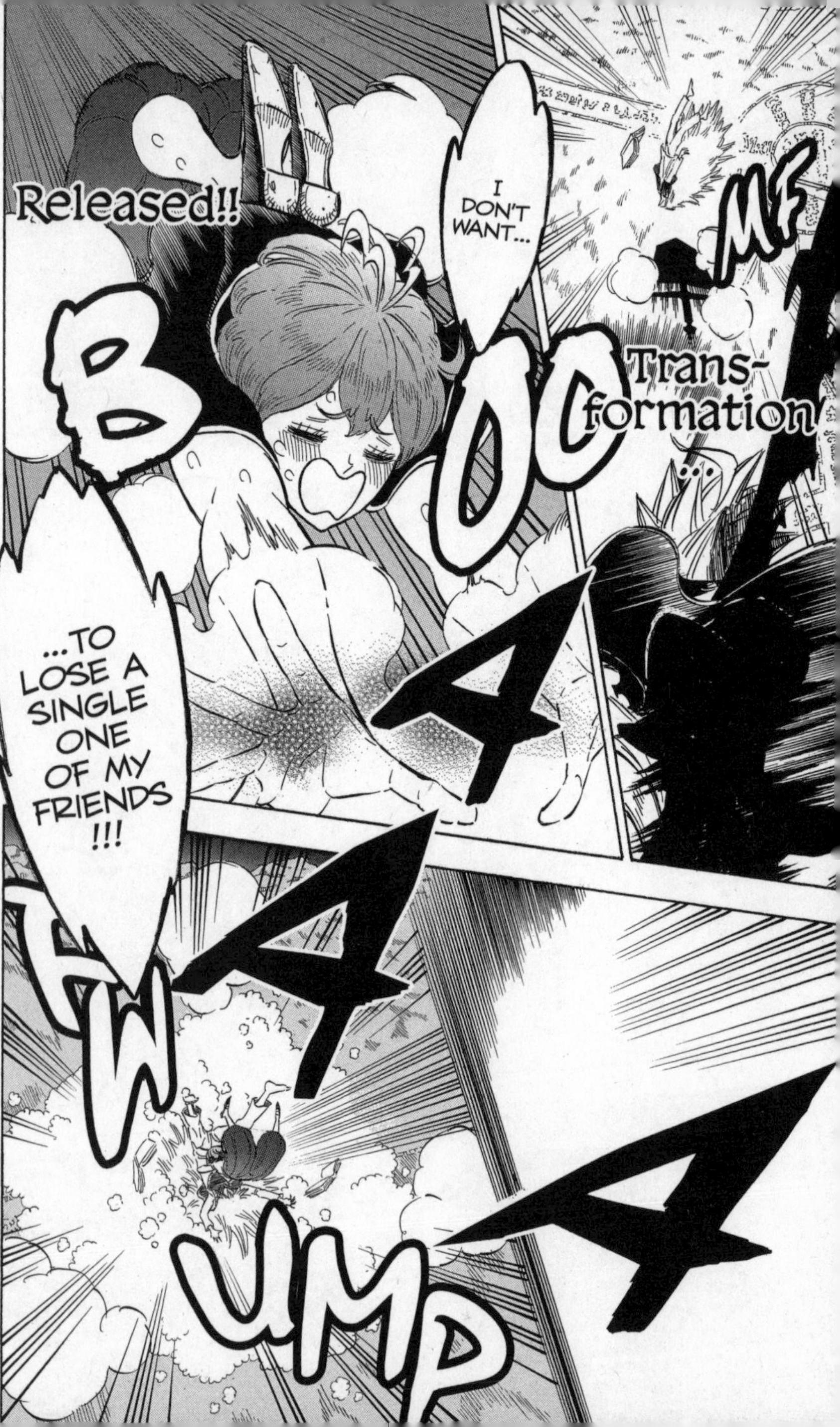
Trans-formation...
Released!!
I DON'T WANT...
...TO LOSE A SINGLE ONE OF MY FRIENDS!!!

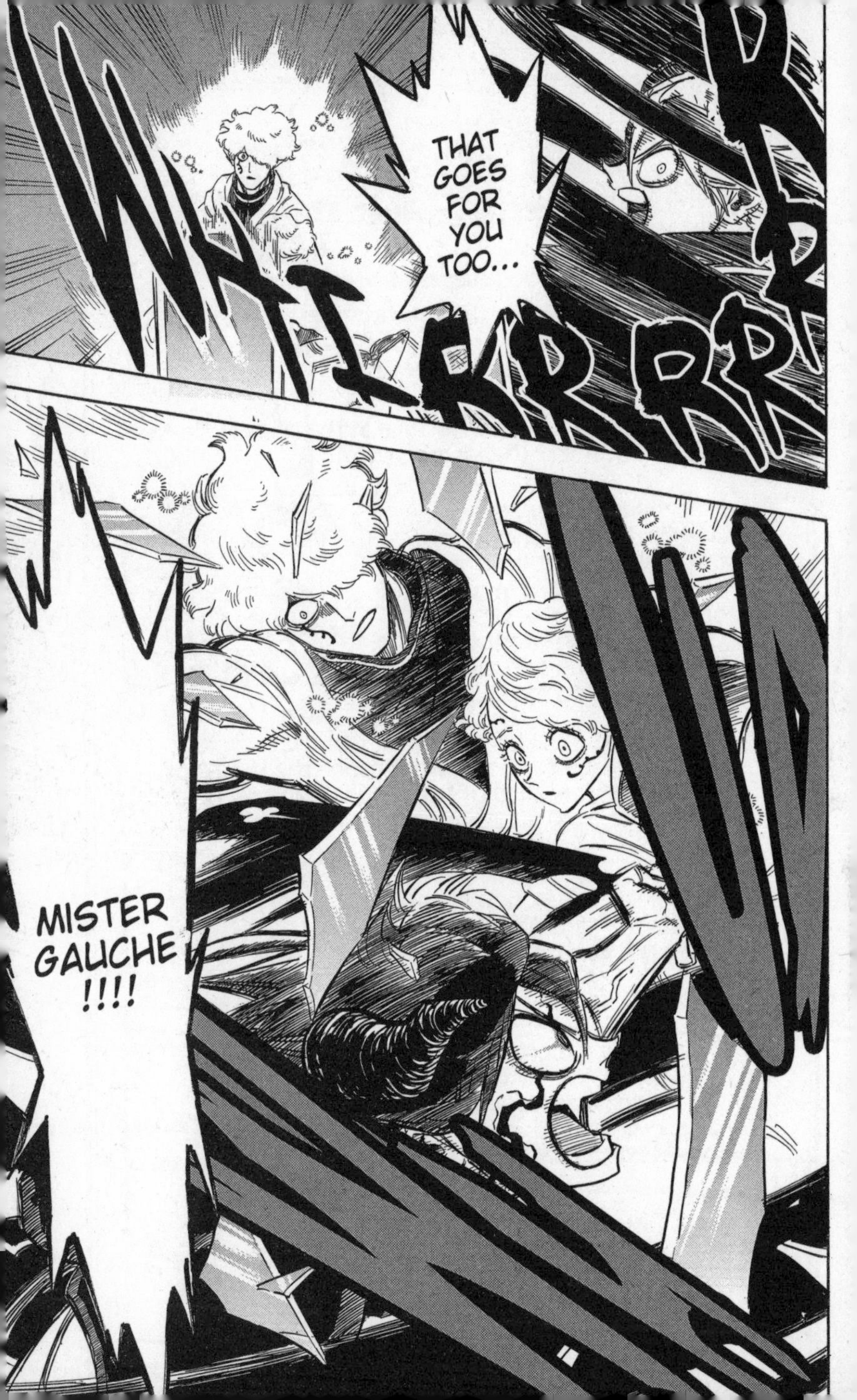
THAT GOES FOR YOU TOO...
MISTER GAUCHE !!!!

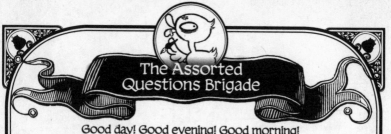

The Assorted Questions Brigade

Good day! Good evening! Good morning!

It's time for the letters corner.

This time, you just might learn some unexpected things about the captains!!

Q: At what point during their time in the brigade did Asta and Henry meet? (*Bluebar*, Kyoto)

A: It happened during the flashback scene shown in the chapter right before this one (Page 188), but in terms of the greater story, it was just before they went to the Underwater Temple, after Asta learned to read Ki.

KAEEEEE
YOU'RE MISTER HENRY, RIGHT? THE ONE WITH THAT WEIRD ILLNESS THAT MAKES YOU SUCK UP MAGIC?
BAAAAAM
IT'S NICE TO MEET YOU!! I'M ASTA, THE NEW BRIGADE MEMBER!!
CAPTAIN YAMI TOLD ME TO COME HERE!
PLEASE DON'T WORRY!! I DON'T HAVE ANY MAGIC!!

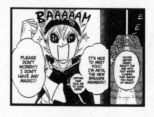

Q: Does Mereoleona have the "mark of the oath to oneself" that's passed down through the House of Vermillion? (Because of her bangs, I can't tell if she has one or not.) (*Oroshi Daikon*, Miyagi)

A: She doesn't have one, because she has no plans to become either the king or the Wizard King.

I'M PLANNING...
...TO KILL ALL OF YOU!!
KRAKL

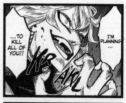

Q: If you were to compare Noelle's magic to other *Black Clover* characters, who else has about as much as she does? (*Maika Saito*, Chiba)

A: Umm... Her latent magic might be about the same as her mother Acier's or Wizard King Julius's.

Valkyrie Armor
WHROOSH

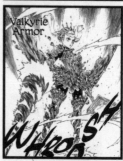

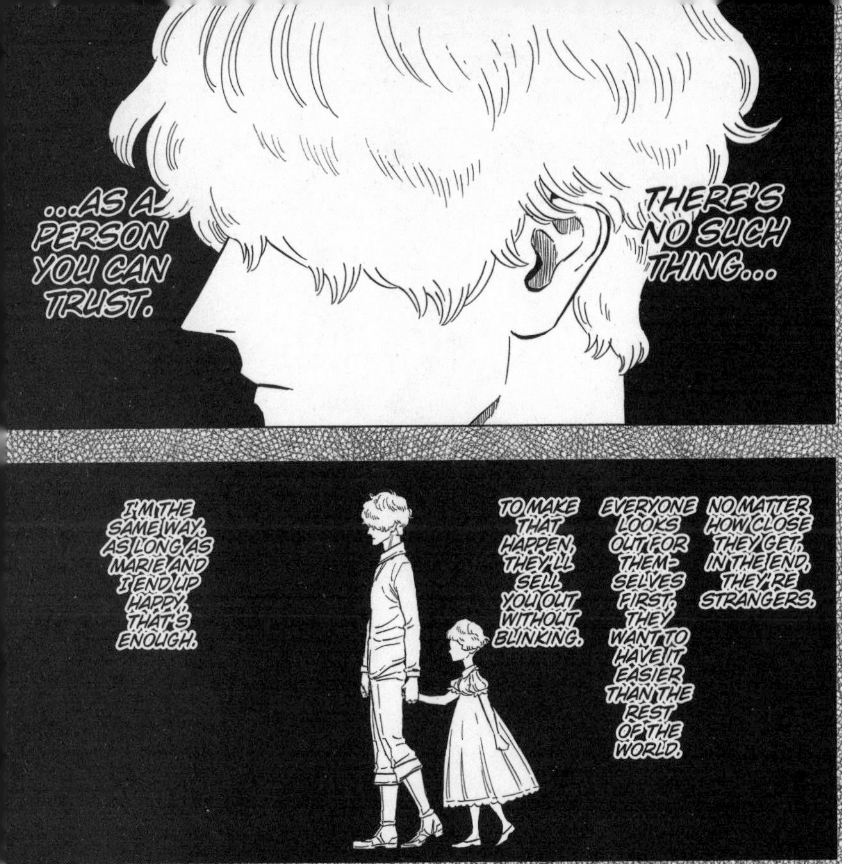
THERE'S NO SUCH THING...
...AS A PERSON YOU CAN TRUST.
NO MATTER HOW CLOSE THEY GET, IN THE END, THEY'RE STRANGERS.
EVERYONE LOOKS OUT FOR THEMSELVES FIRST. THEY WANT TO HAVE IT EASIER THAN THE REST OF THE WORLD.
TO MAKE THAT HAPPEN, THEY'LL SELL YOU OUT WITHOUT BLINKING.
I'M THE SAME WAY. AS LONG AS MARIE AND I END UP HAPPY, THAT'S ENOUGH.

Page 189: Humans Who Can Be Trusted

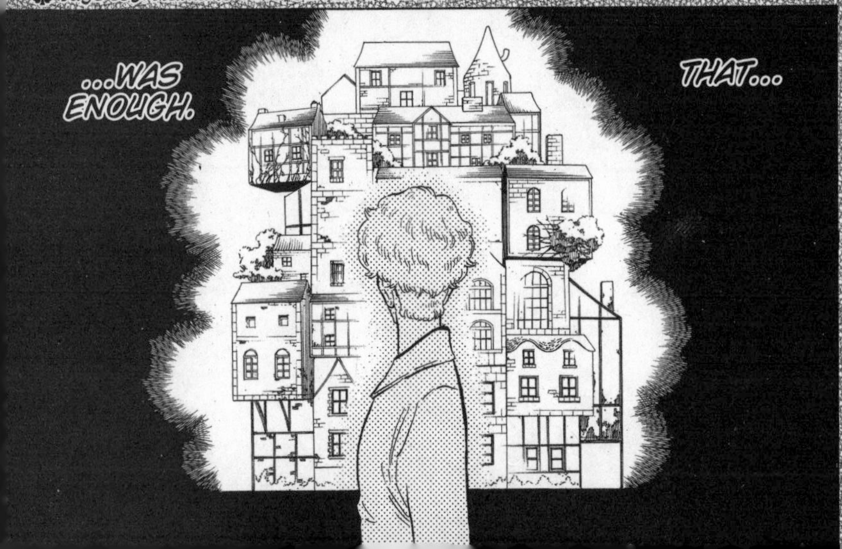
THAT...
...WAS ENOUGH.

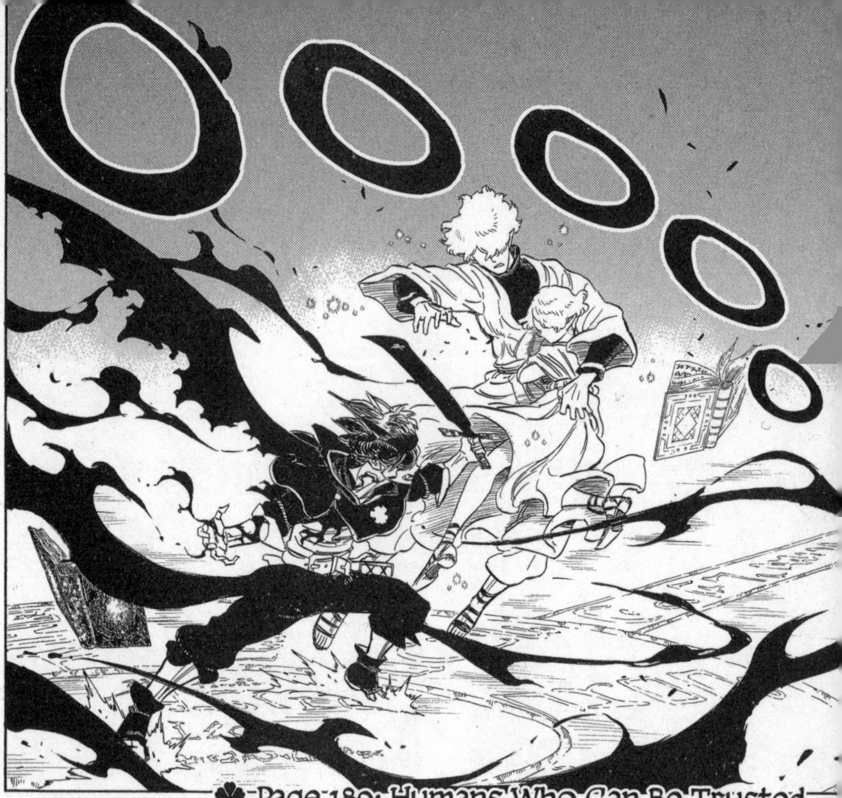

Page 189: Humans Who Can Be Trusted

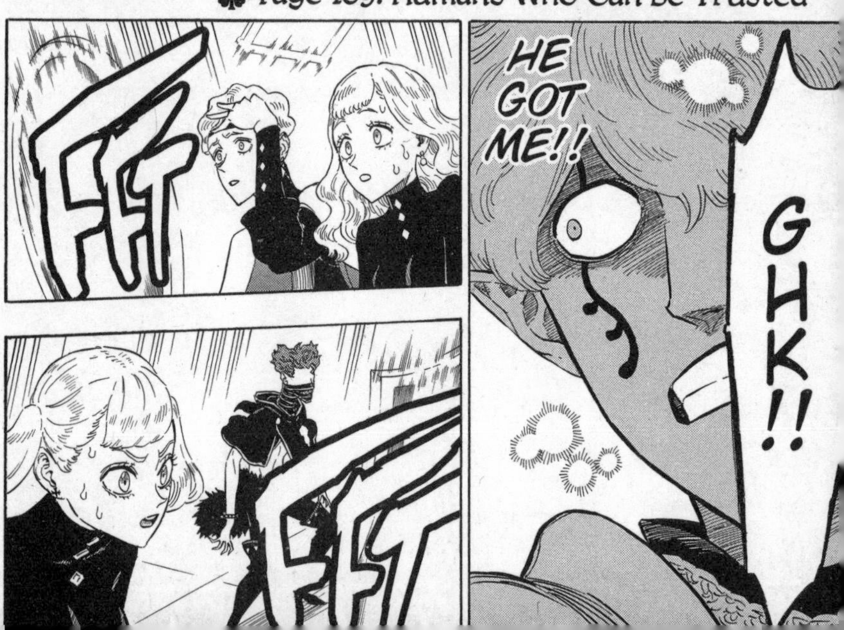
GHK!!
HE GOT ME!!
FFT
FFT

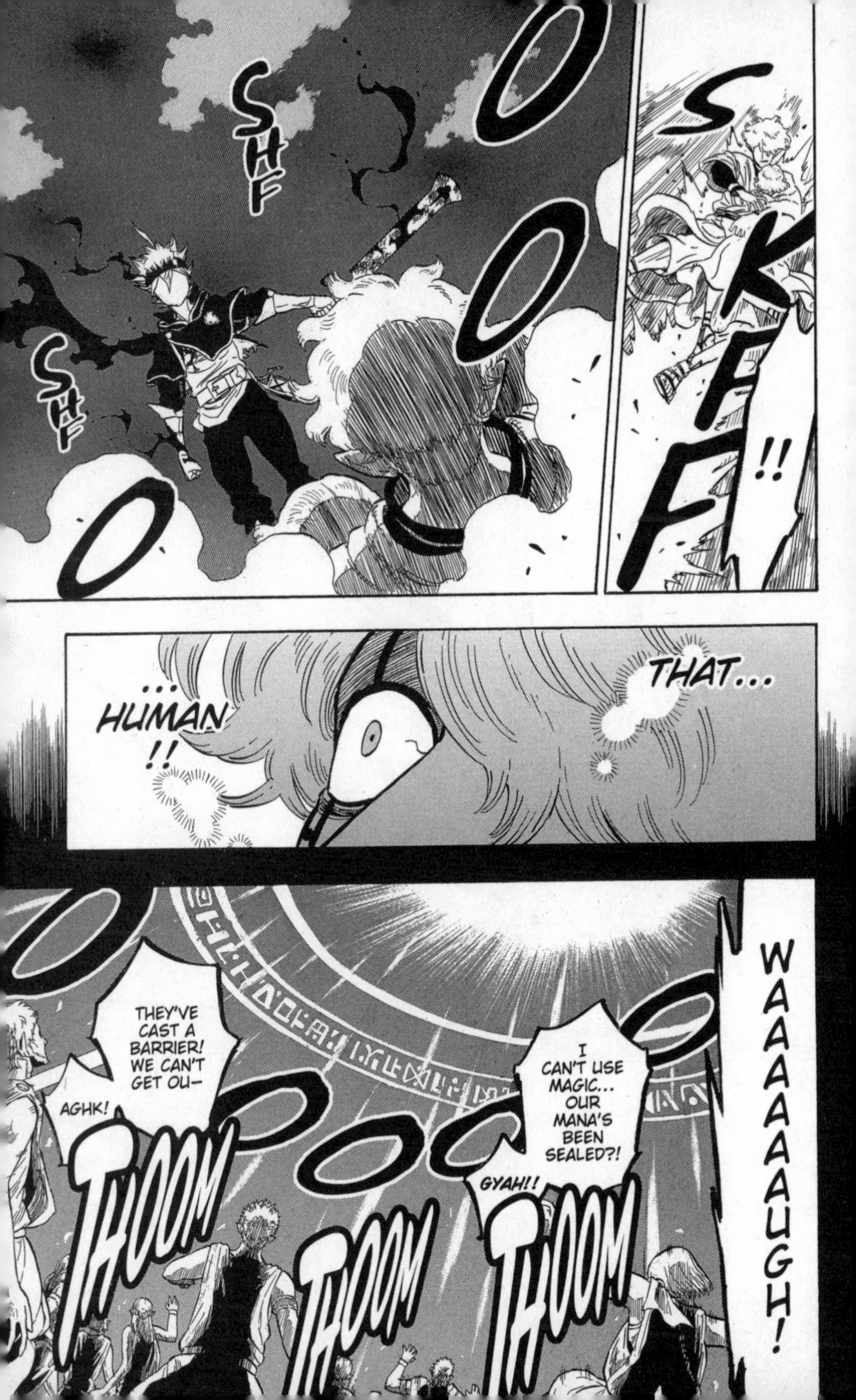
SKFF!!
SHF
SHF
THAT...
...HUMAN!!
WAAAAAAAUGH!
I CAN'T USE MAGIC... OUR MANA'S BEEN SEALED?!
GYAH!!
THOOM
THOOM
THEY'VE CAST A BARRIER! WE CAN'T GET OU–
AGHK!
THOOM

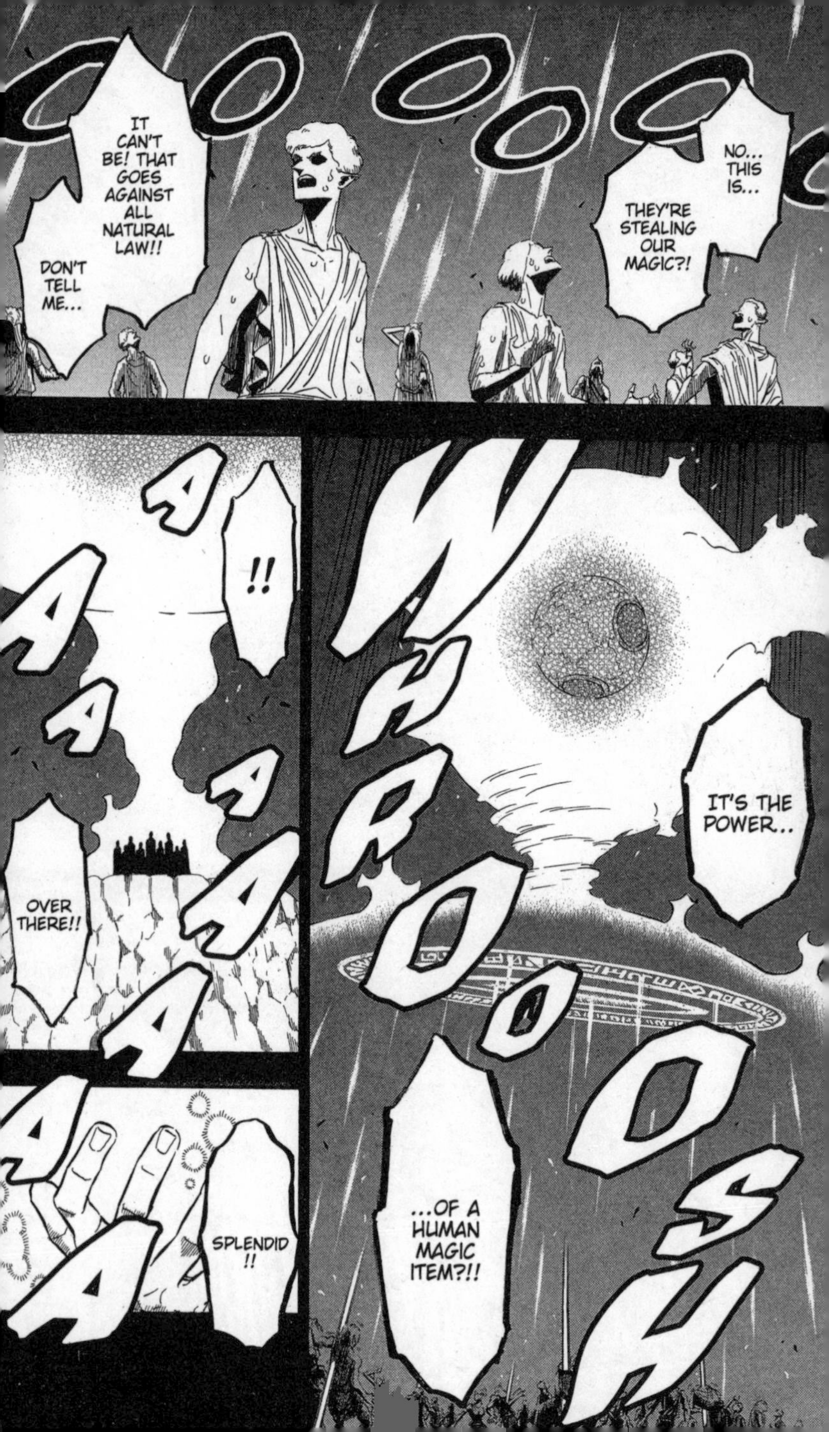
NO... THIS IS...
THEY'RE STEALING OUR MAGIC?!
IT CAN'T BE! THAT GOES AGAINST ALL NATURAL LAW!!
DON'T TELL ME...
WHROOOSH
IT'S THE POWER...
...OF A HUMAN MAGIC ITEM?!!
!!
OVER THERE!!
AAAAAAAAA
SPLENDID!!

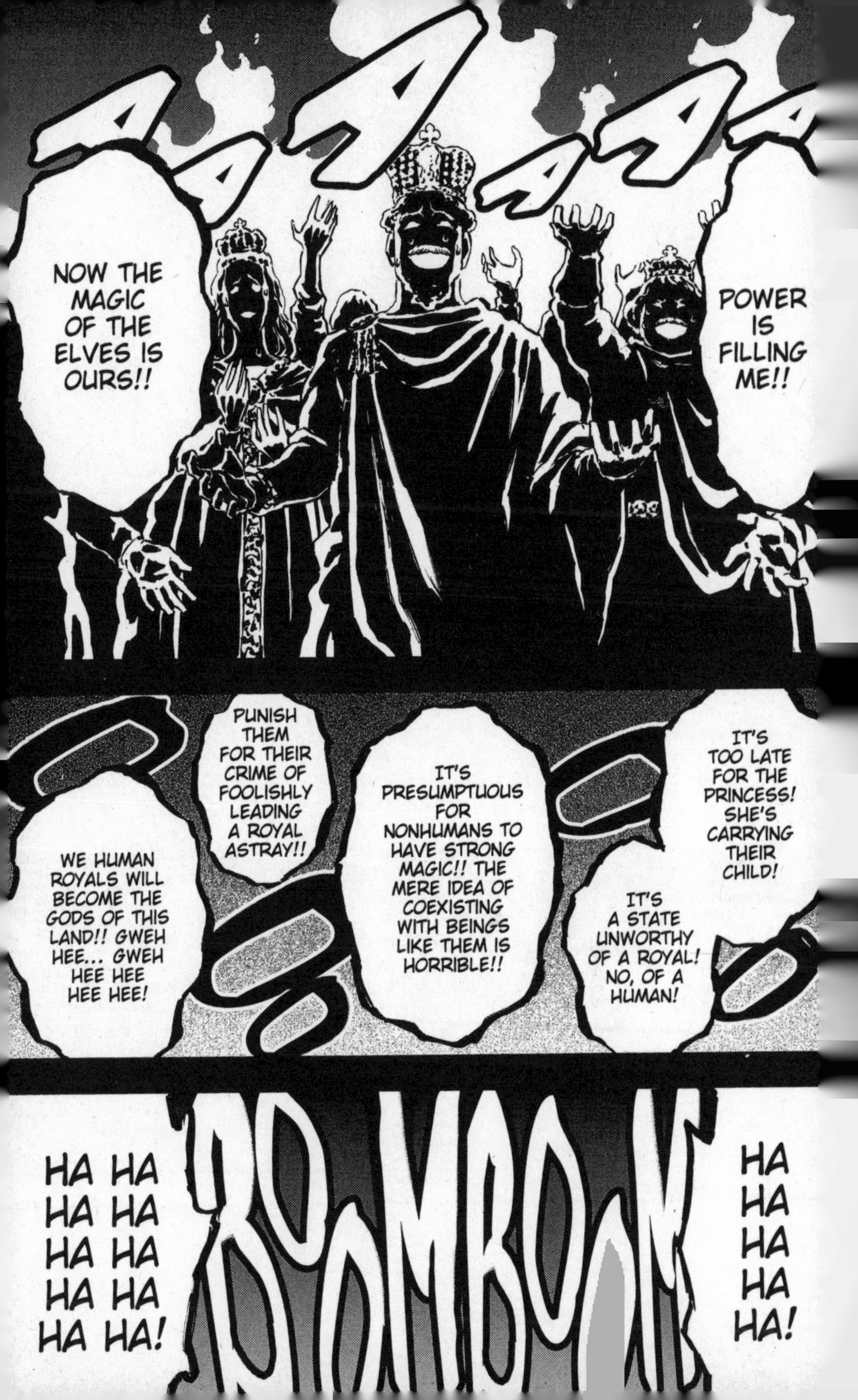
AAAAAAAA
POWER IS FILLING ME!!
NOW THE MAGIC OF THE ELVES IS OURS!!
IT'S TOO LATE FOR THE PRINCESS! SHE'S CARRYING THEIR CHILD!
IT'S A STATE UNWORTHY OF A ROYAL! NO, OF A HUMAN!
IT'S PRESUMPTUOUS FOR NONHUMANS TO HAVE STRONG MAGIC!! THE MERE IDEA OF COEXISTING WITH BEINGS LIKE THEM IS HORRIBLE!!
PUNISH THEM FOR THEIR CRIME OF FOOLISHLY LEADING A ROYAL ASTRAY!!
WE HUMAN ROYALS WILL BECOME THE GODS OF THIS LAND!! GWEH HEE... GWEH HEE HEE HEE HEE!
HA HA HA HA HA!
BOOMBOOM
HA HA HA HA HA HA HA HA HA HA!

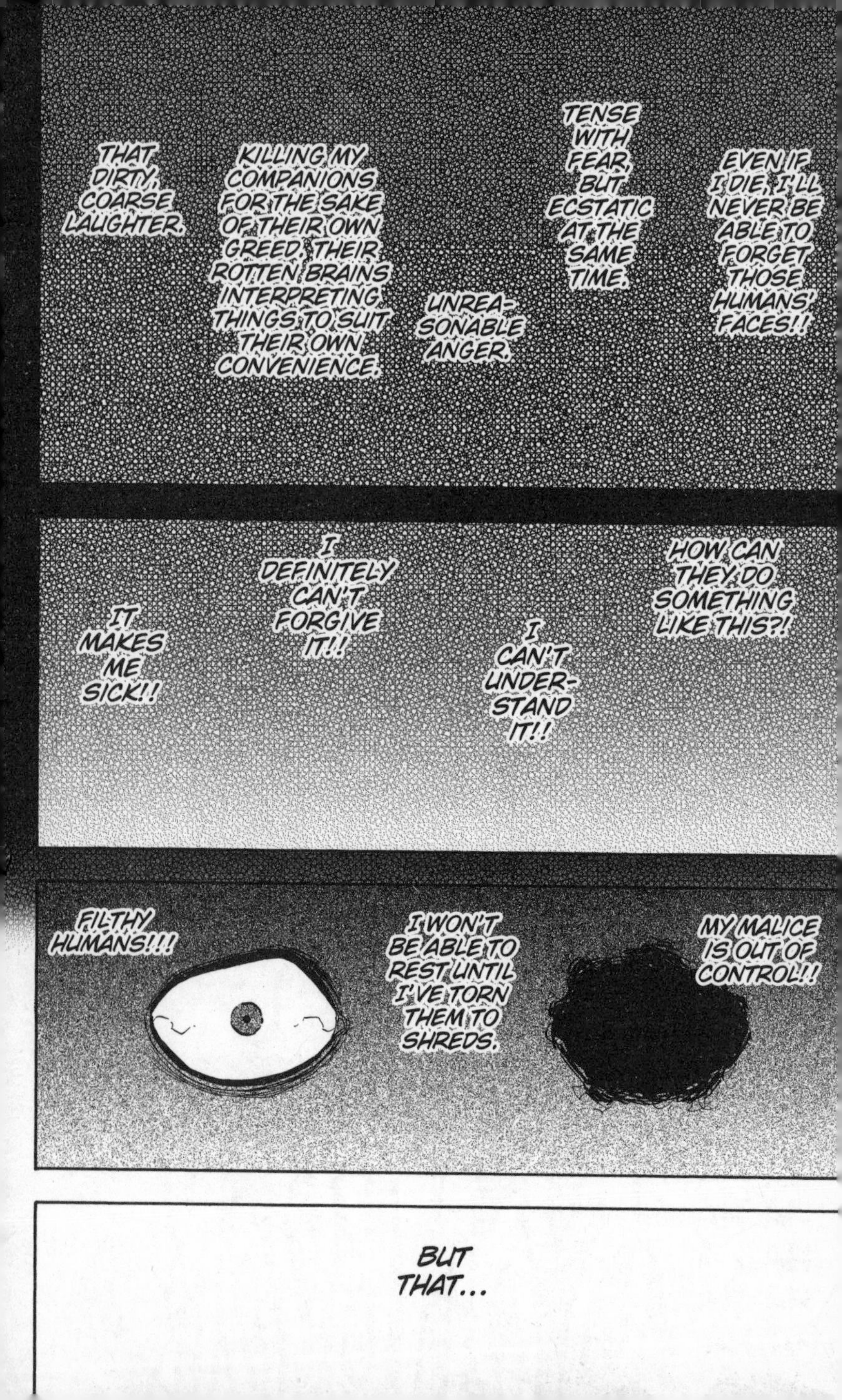
EVEN IF I DIE, I'LL NEVER BE ABLE TO FORGET THOSE HUMANS' FACES!!
TENSE WITH FEAR, BUT ECSTATIC AT THE SAME TIME.
UNREA-SONABLE ANGER.
KILLING MY COMPANIONS FOR THE SAKE OF THEIR OWN GREED, THEIR ROTTEN BRAINS INTERPRETING THINGS TO SUIT THEIR OWN CONVENIENCE.
THAT DIRTY, COARSE LAUGHTER.
HOW CAN THEY DO SOMETHING LIKE THIS?!
I CAN'T UNDER-STAND IT!!
I DEFINITELY CAN'T FORGIVE IT!!
IT MAKES ME SICK!!
MY MALICE IS OUT OF CONTROL!!
I WON'T BE ABLE TO REST UNTIL I'VE TORN THEM TO SHREDS.
FILTHY HUMANS!!!
BUT THAT...

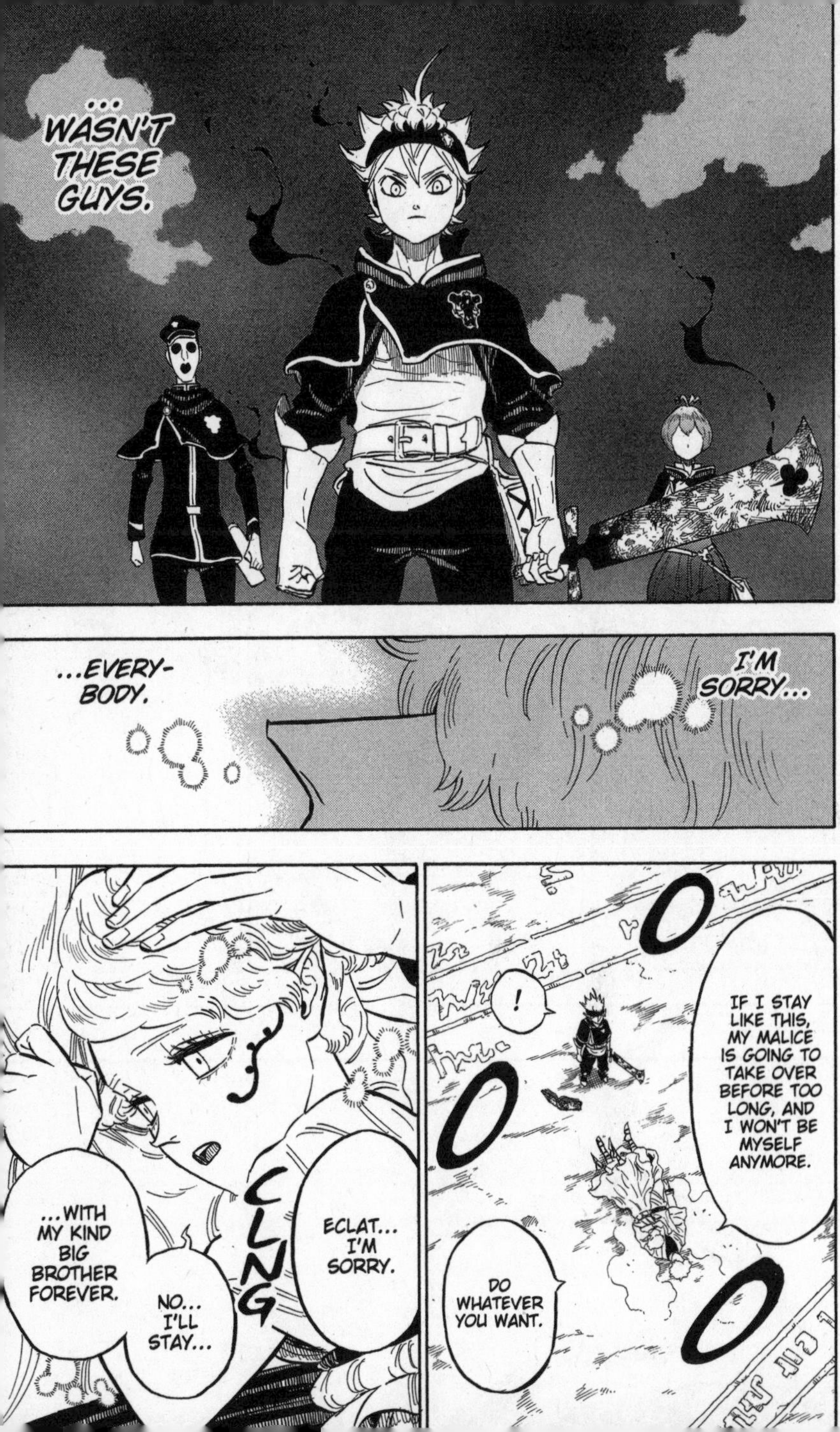
... WASN'T THESE GUYS.
I'M SORRY...
...EVERY-BODY.
!
IF I STAY LIKE THIS, MY MALICE IS GOING TO TAKE OVER BEFORE TOO LONG, AND I WON'T BE MYSELF ANYMORE.
DO WHATEVER YOU WANT.
ECLAT... I'M SORRY.
CLNG
NO... I'LL STAY...
...WITH MY KIND BIG BROTHER FOREVER.

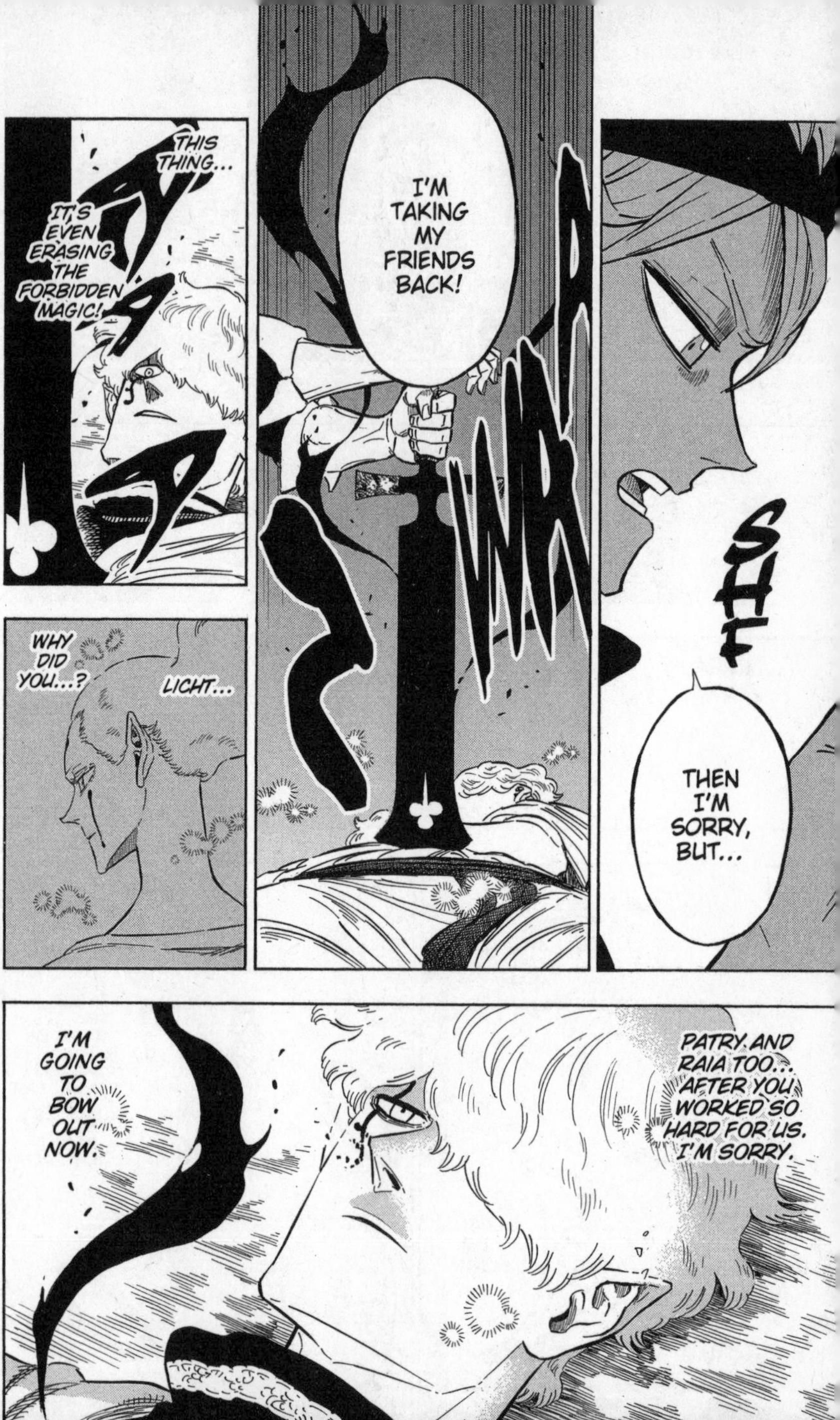
SHF
THEN I'M SORRY, BUT...
I'M TAKING MY FRIENDS BACK!
THIS THING...
IT'S EVEN ERASING THE FORBIDDEN MAGIC!
LICHT...
WHY DID YOU...?
PATRY AND RAIA TOO... AFTER YOU WORKED SO HARD FOR US. I'M SORRY.
I'M GOING TO BOW OUT NOW.

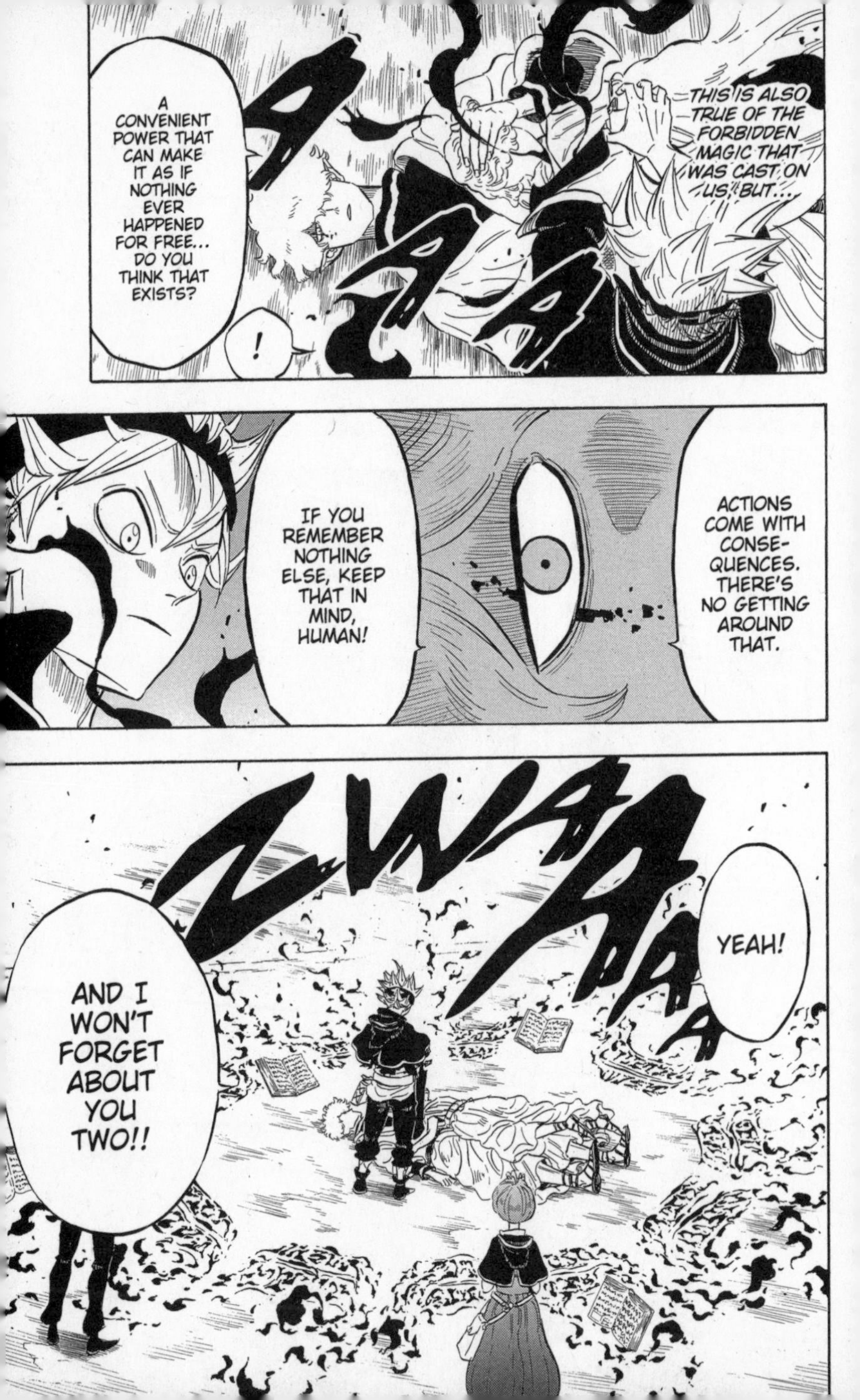
THIS IS ALSO TRUE OF THE FORBIDDEN MAGIC THAT WAS CAST ON US, BUT...
A CONVENIENT POWER THAT CAN MAKE IT AS IF NOTHING EVER HAPPENED FOR FREE... DO YOU THINK THAT EXISTS?
!
ACTIONS COME WITH CONSE-QUENCES. THERE'S NO GETTING AROUND THAT.
IF YOU REMEMBER NOTHING ELSE, KEEP THAT IN MIND, HUMAN!
YEAH!
AND I WON'T FORGET ABOUT YOU TWO!!

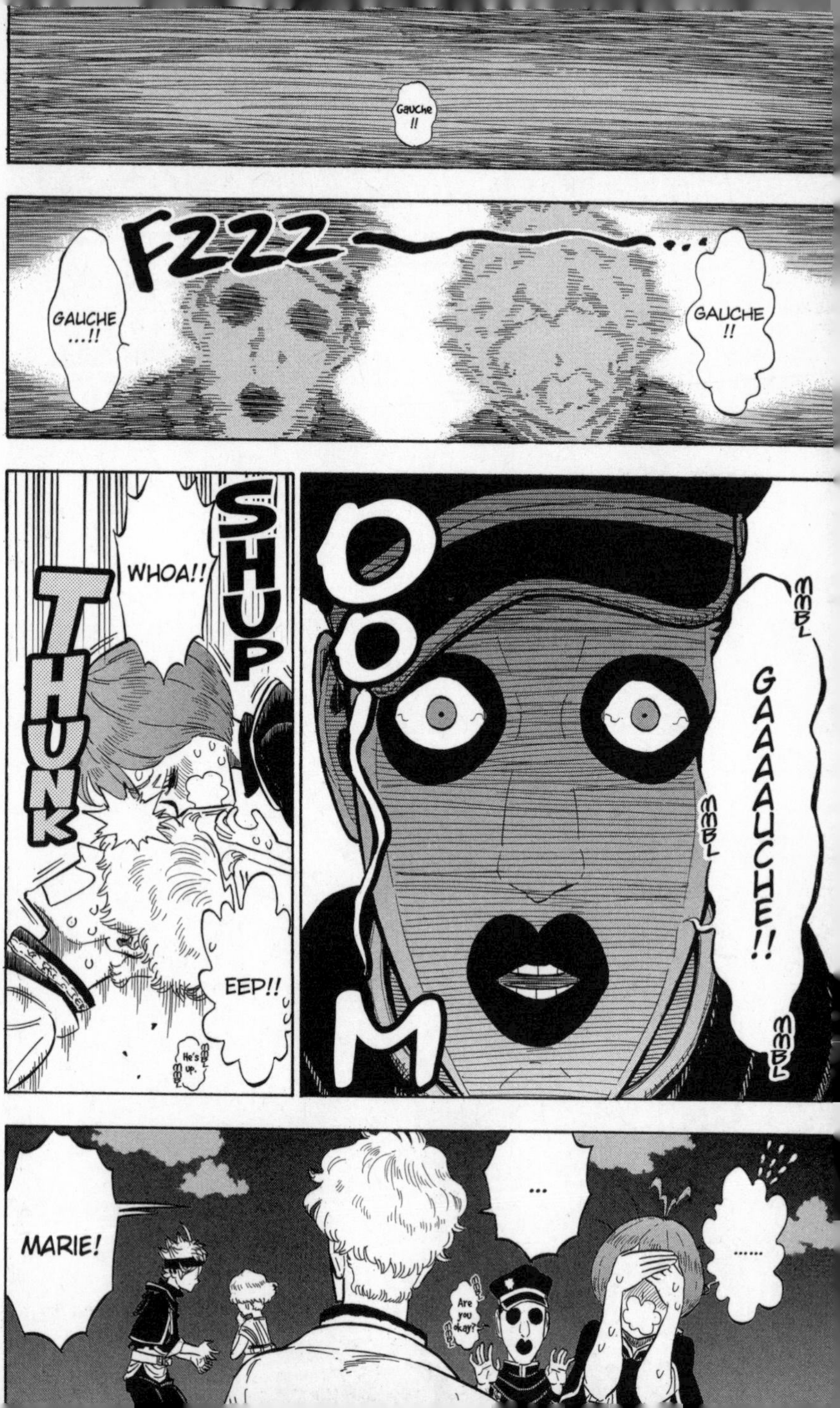
Gauche !!
GAUCHE !!
FZZZ...
GAUCHE ...!!
OOOM
MMBL
GAAAAUCHE!!
MMBL
MMBL
SHUP
WHOA!!
THUNK
EEP!!
MMBL He's up. MMBL
......
...
MMBL Are you okay? MMBL
MARIE!

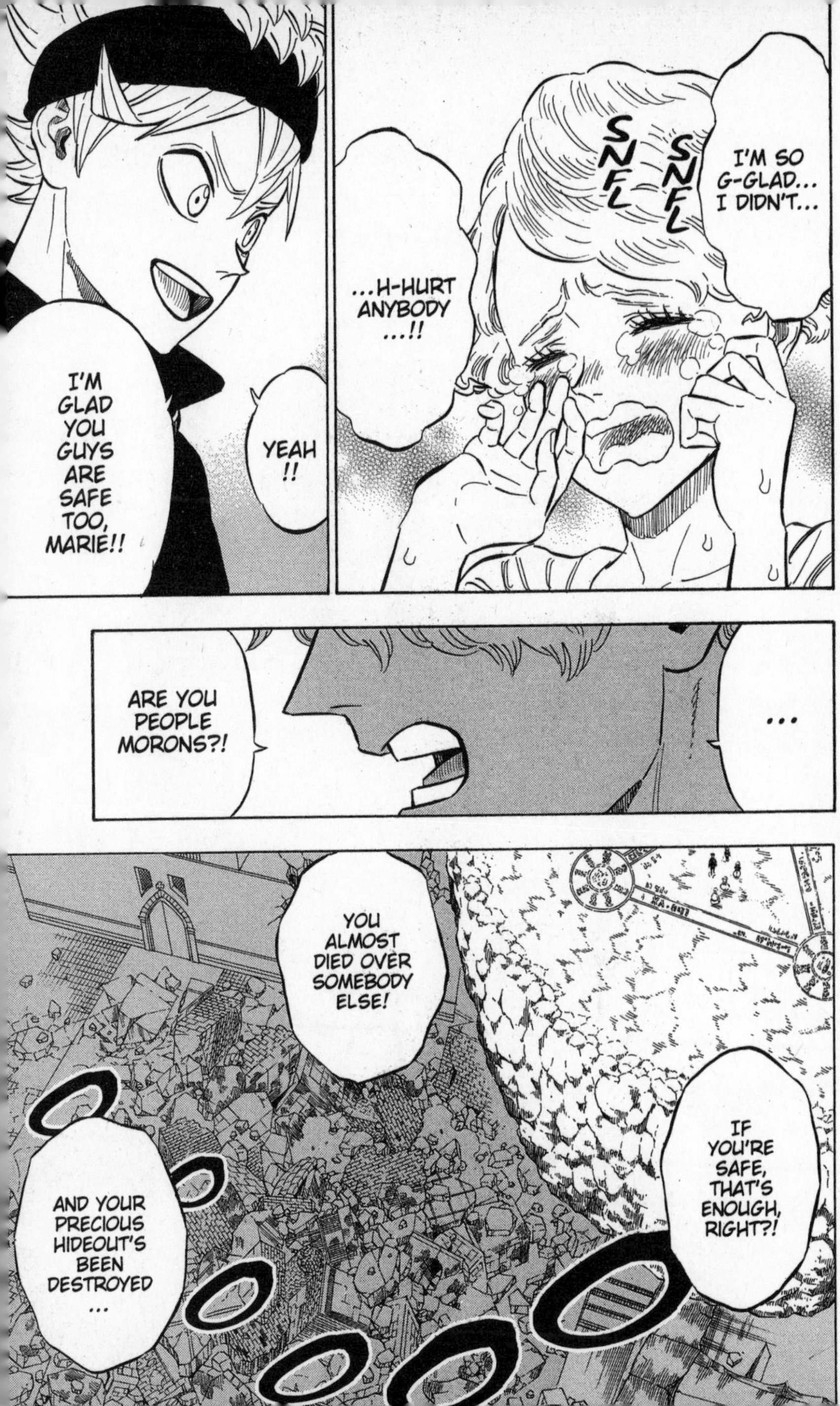
SNFL SNFL
I'M SO G-GLAD... I DIDN'T...
...H-HURT ANYBODY ...!!
I'M GLAD YOU GUYS ARE SAFE TOO, MARIE!!
YEAH !!
...
ARE YOU PEOPLE MORONS?!
YOU ALMOST DIED OVER SOMEBODY ELSE!
IF YOU'RE SAFE, THAT'S ENOUGH, RIGHT?!
AND YOUR PRECIOUS HIDEOUT'S BEEN DESTROYED ...

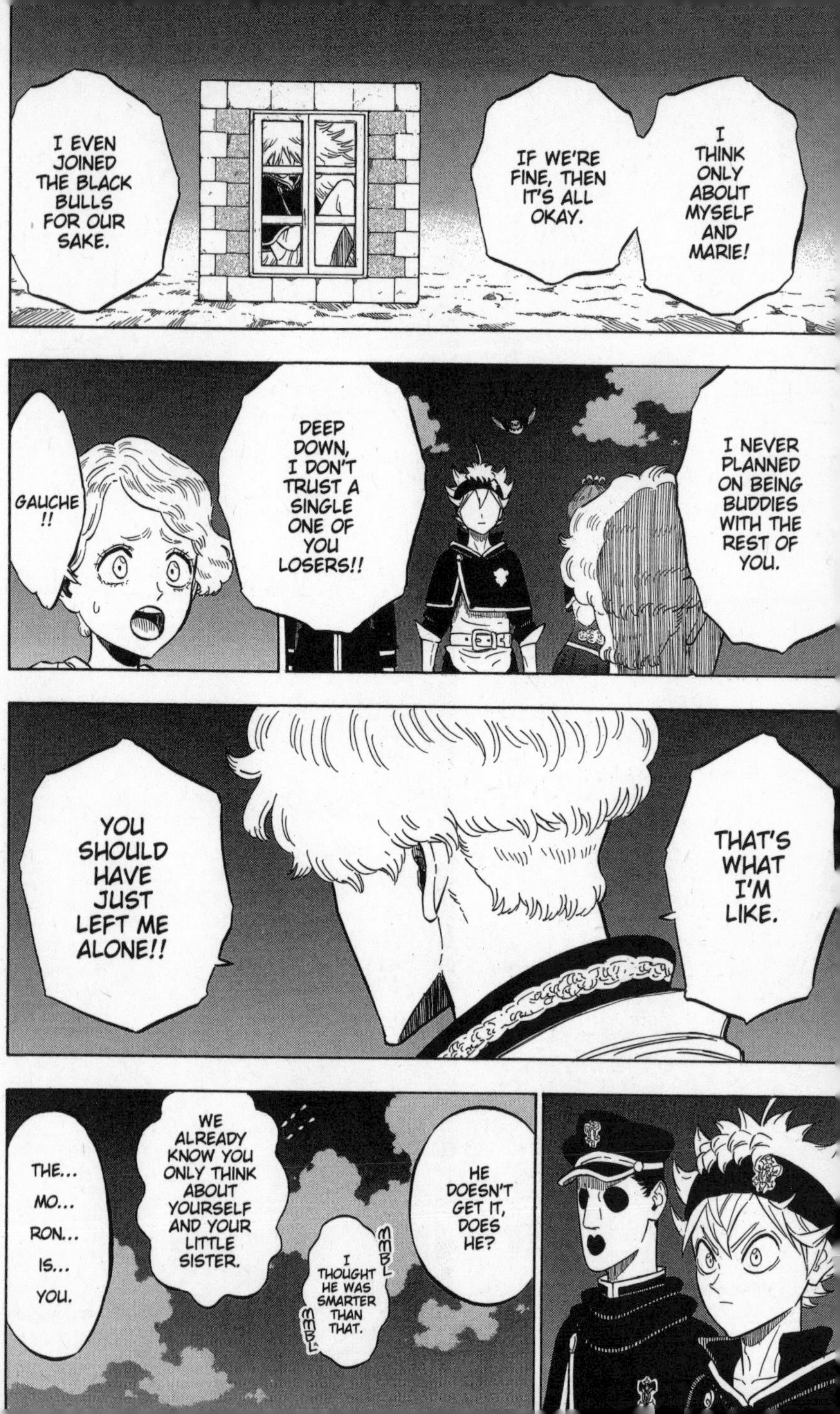
I THINK ONLY ABOUT MYSELF AND MARIE!
IF WE'RE FINE, THEN IT'S ALL OKAY.
I EVEN JOINED THE BLACK BULLS FOR OUR SAKE.
I NEVER PLANNED ON BEING BUDDIES WITH THE REST OF YOU.
DEEP DOWN, I DON'T TRUST A SINGLE ONE OF YOU LOSERS!!
GAUCHE!!
THAT'S WHAT I'M LIKE.
YOU SHOULD HAVE JUST LEFT ME ALONE!!
HE DOESN'T GET IT, DOES HE?
MMBL
I THOUGHT HE WAS SMARTER THAN THAT.
MMBL
WE ALREADY KNOW YOU ONLY THINK ABOUT YOURSELF AND YOUR LITTLE SISTER.
THE... MO... RON... IS... YOU.

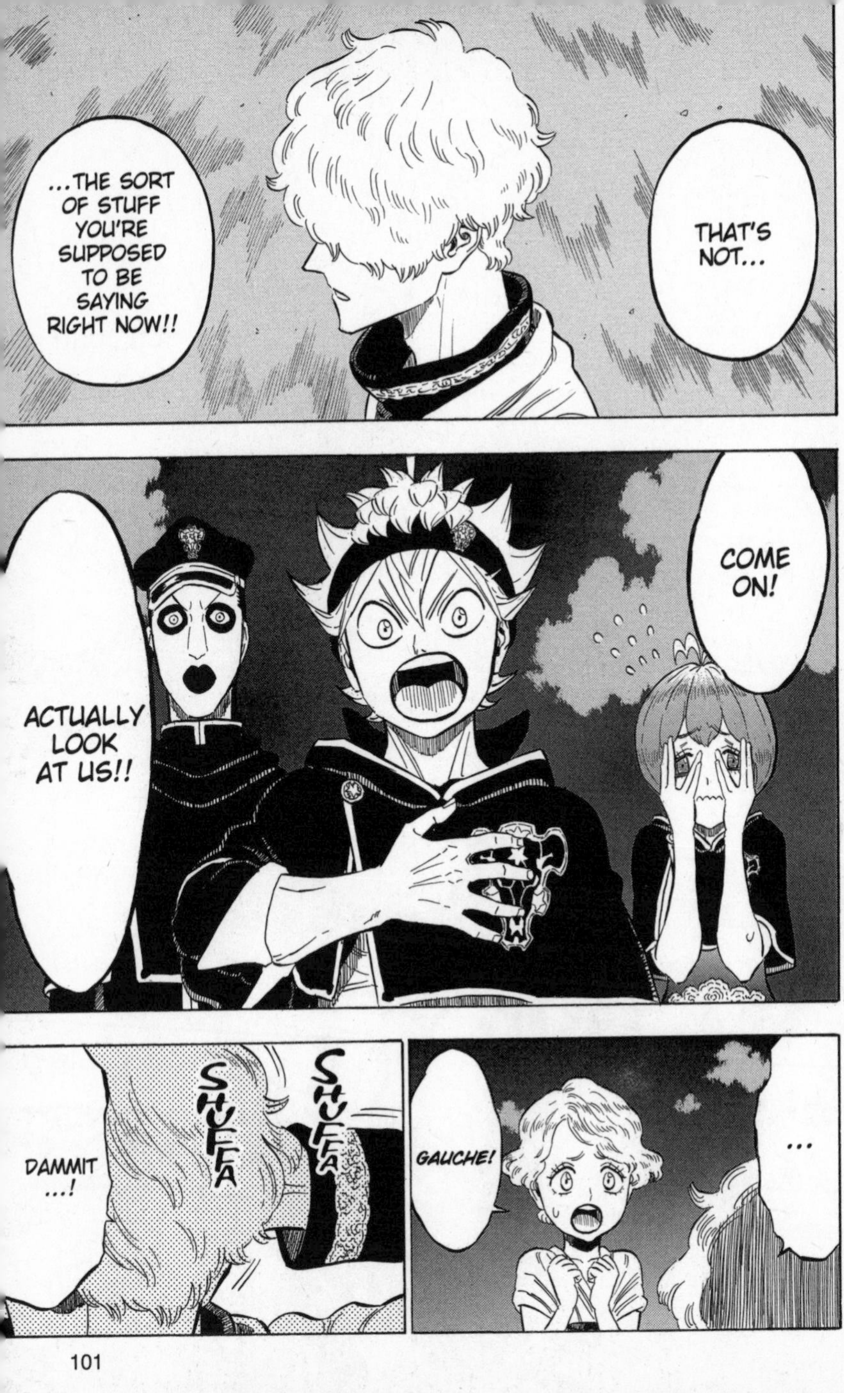
THAT'S NOT...
...THE SORT OF STUFF YOU'RE SUPPOSED TO BE SAYING RIGHT NOW!!
COME ON!
ACTUALLY LOOK AT US!!
...
GAUCHE!
SHUFFA
SHUFFA
DAMMIT ...!

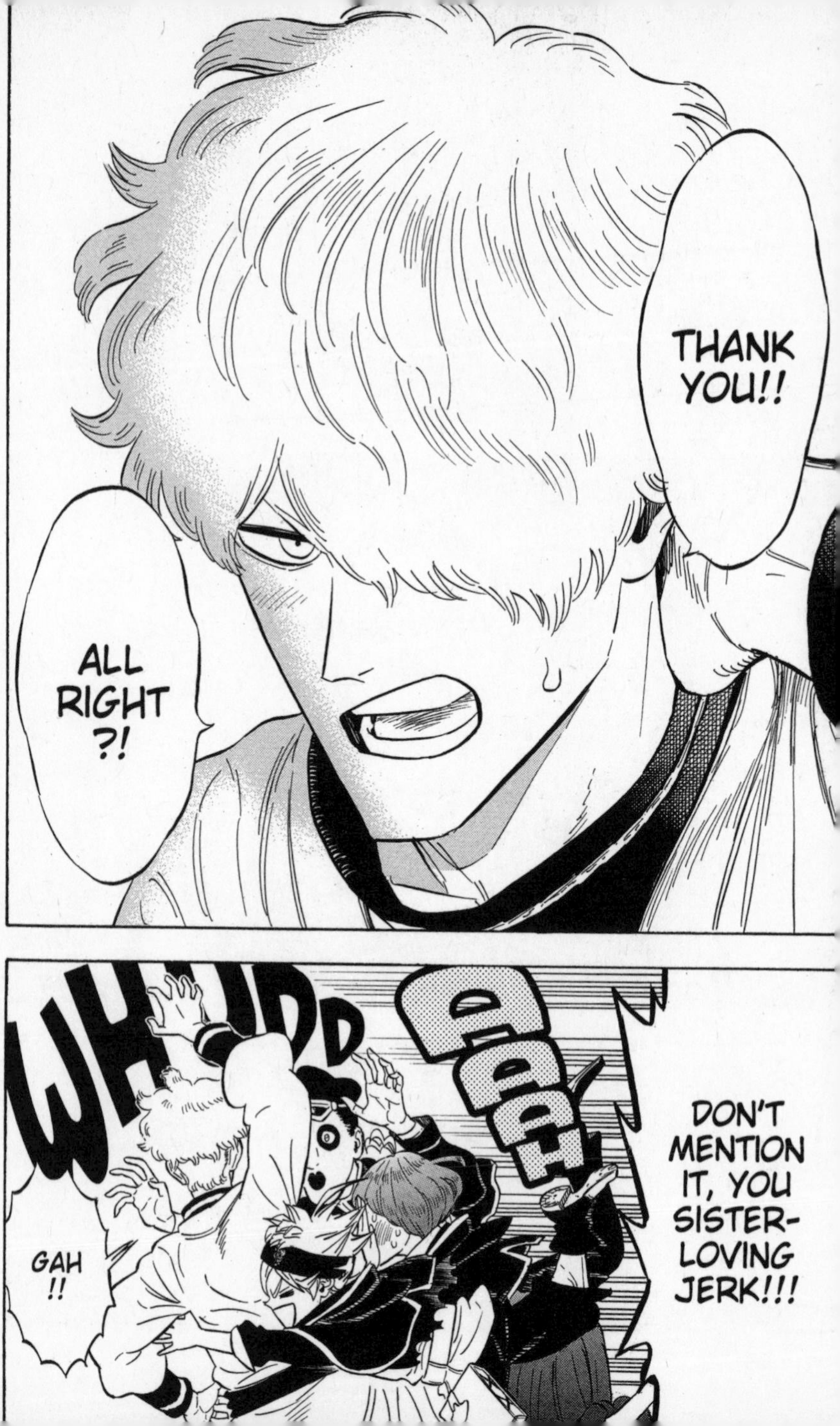
THANK YOU!!
ALL RIGHT ?!
DON'T MENTION IT, YOU SISTER-LOVING JERK!!!
AAAH!
GAH !!

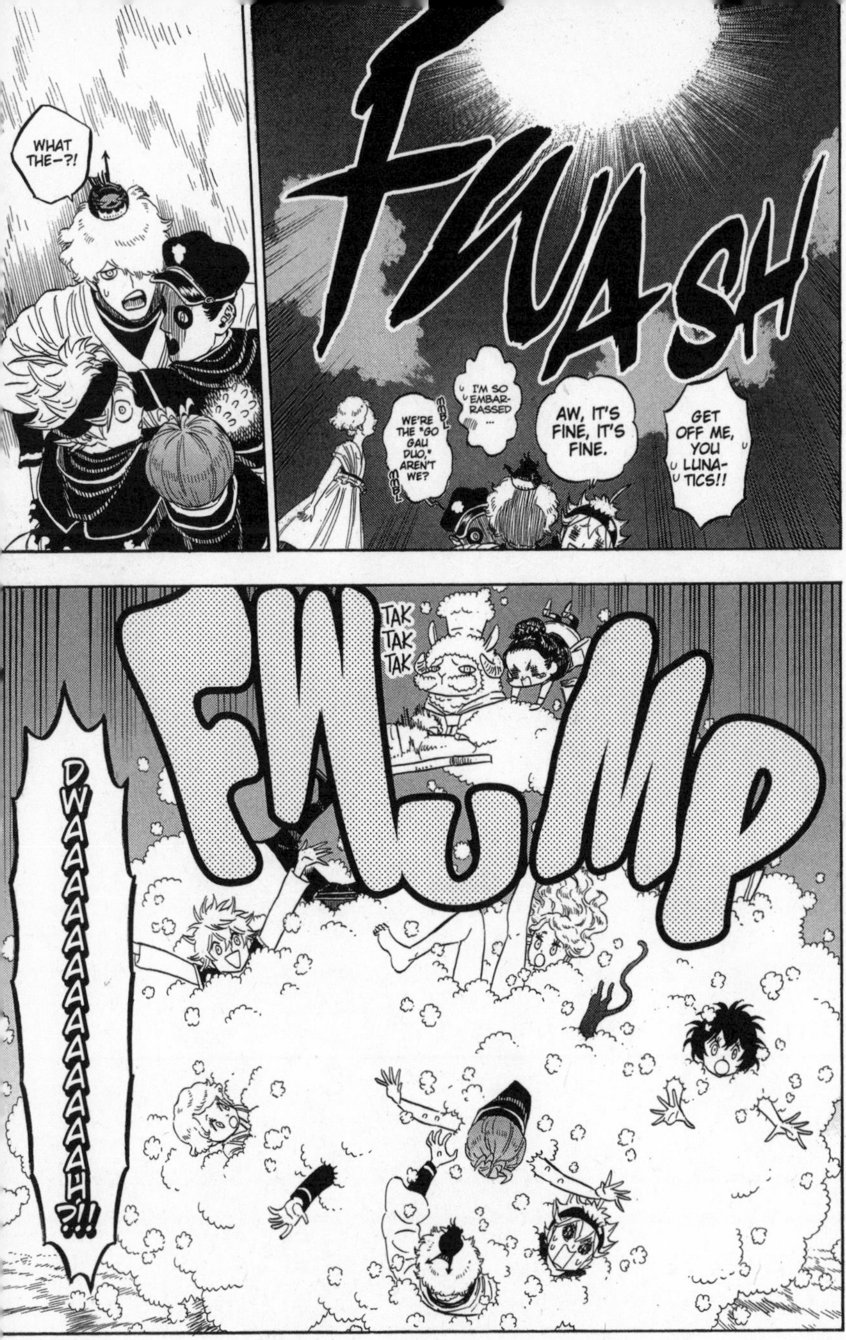
FLASH
GET OFF ME, YOU LUNATICS!!
AW, IT'S FINE, IT'S FINE.
I'M SO EMBARRASSED...
WE'RE THE "GO GAU DUO," AREN'T WE?
MMBL
MMBL
WHAT THE-?!
TAK TAK TAK
FWUMP
DWAAAAAAAAAAAAAAAAH?!!

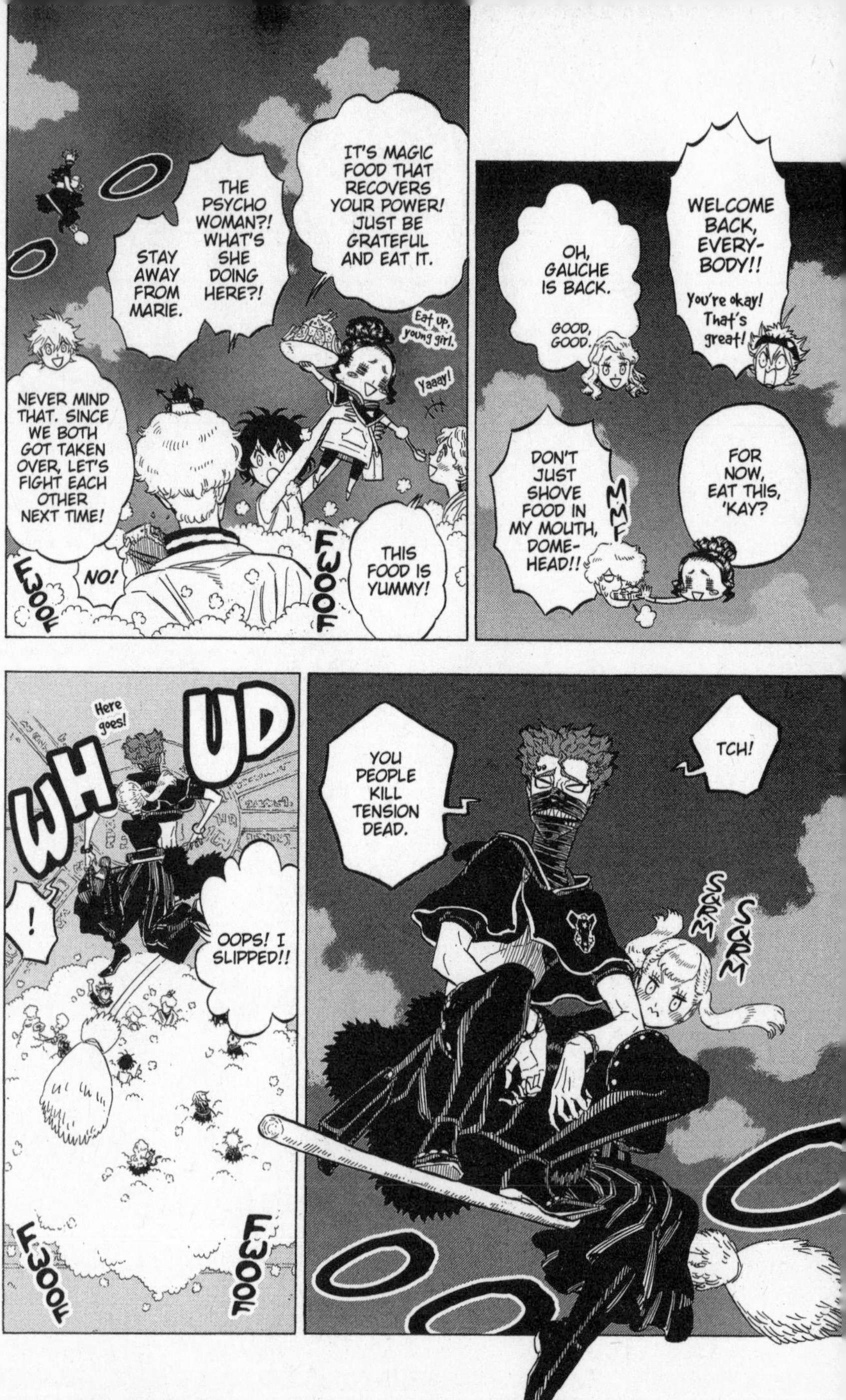
WELCOME BACK, EVERY-BODY!!
You're okay! That's great!
OH, GAUCHE IS BACK.
GOOD, GOOD.
FOR NOW, EAT THIS, 'KAY?
MMMF
DON'T JUST SHOVE FOOD IN MY MOUTH, DOME-HEAD!!
IT'S MAGIC FOOD THAT RECOVERS YOUR POWER! JUST BE GRATEFUL AND EAT IT.
THE PSYCHO WOMAN?! WHAT'S SHE DOING HERE?!
STAY AWAY FROM MARIE.
Eat up, young girl.
Yaaay!
NEVER MIND THAT. SINCE WE BOTH GOT TAKEN OVER, LET'S FIGHT EACH OTHER NEXT TIME!
FWOOF
THIS FOOD IS YUMMY!
NO!
FWOOF
TCH!
YOU PEOPLE KILL TENSION DEAD.
SQRM SQRM
Here goes!
WHUD
OOPS! I SLIPPED!!
!
FWOOF
FWOOF

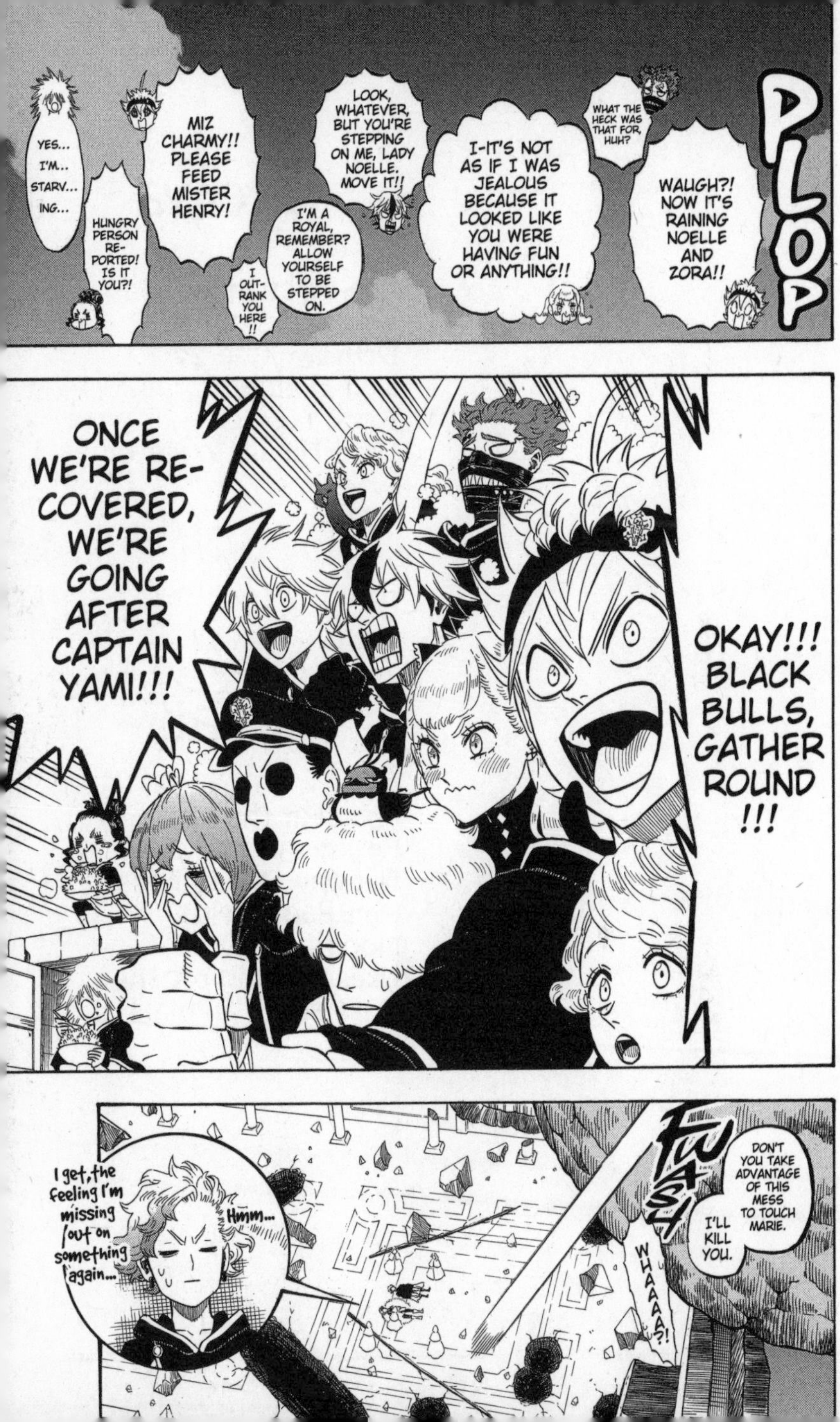
PLOP
WAUGH?! NOW IT'S RAINING NOELLE AND ZORA!!
WHAT THE HECK WAS THAT FOR, HUH?
I-IT'S NOT AS IF I WAS JEALOUS BECAUSE IT LOOKED LIKE YOU WERE HAVING FUN OR ANYTHING!!
LOOK, WHATEVER, BUT YOU'RE STEPPING ON ME, LADY NOELLE. MOVE IT!!
I'M A ROYAL, REMEMBER? ALLOW YOURSELF TO BE STEPPED ON.
I OUT-RANK YOU HERE!!
MIZ CHARMY!! PLEASE FEED MISTER HENRY!
HUNGRY PERSON RE-PORTED! IS IT YOU?!
YES... I'M... STARV... ING...
OKAY!!! BLACK BULLS, GATHER ROUND!!!
ONCE WE'RE RE-COVERED, WE'RE GOING AFTER CAPTAIN YAMI!!!
FWASH
DON'T YOU TAKE ADVANTAGE OF THIS MESS TO TOUCH MARIE.
I'LL KILL YOU.
WHAAAAA?!
Hmm...
I get the feeling I'm missing out on something again...

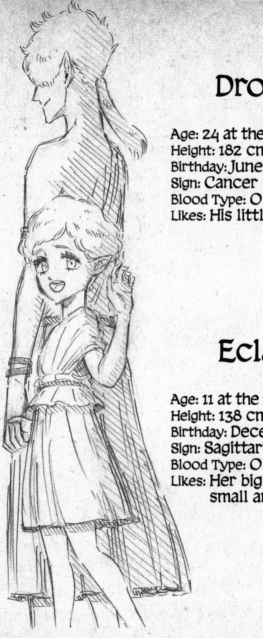

Drowa

Age: 24 at the time
Height: 182 cm
Birthday: June 27
Sign: Cancer
Blood Type: O
Likes: His little sister

Eclat

Age: 11 at the time
Height: 138 cm
Birthday: December 21
Sign: Sagittarius
Blood Type: O
Likes: Her big brother,
small animals

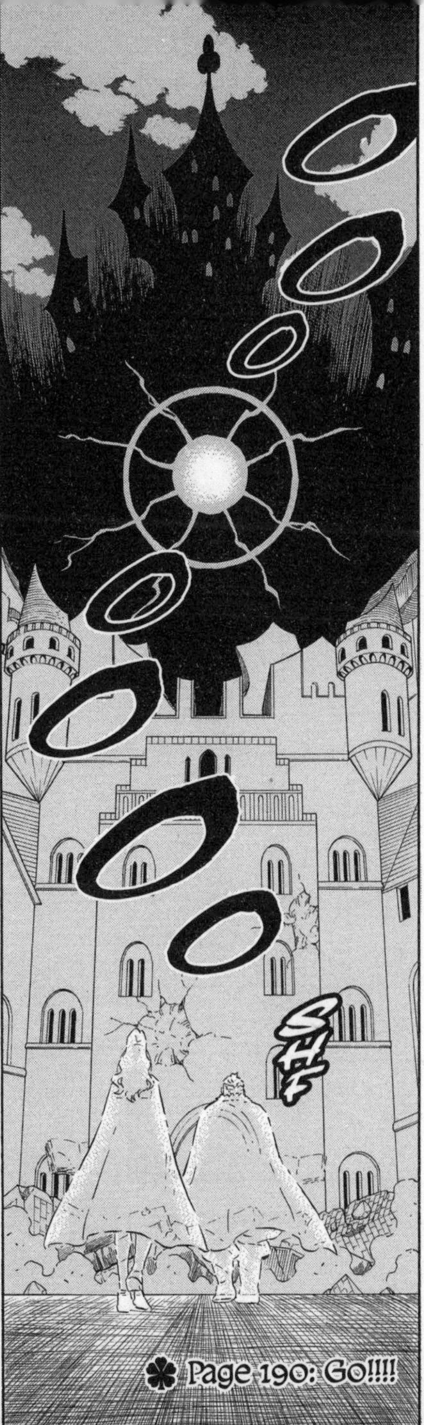
SHH

Page 190: Go!!!!

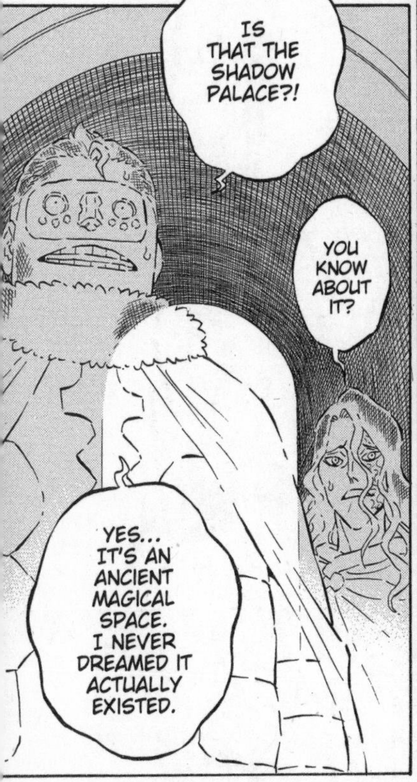
IS THAT THE SHADOW PALACE?!
YOU KNOW ABOUT IT?
YES... IT'S AN ANCIENT MAGICAL SPACE. I NEVER DREAMED IT ACTUALLY EXISTED.

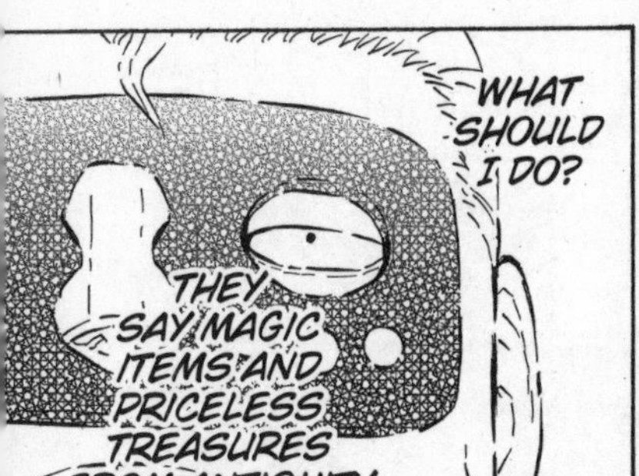
WHAT SHOULD I DO?
THEY SAY MAGIC ITEMS AND PRICELESS TREASURES FROM ANTIQUITY LIE WITHIN IT, BUT...

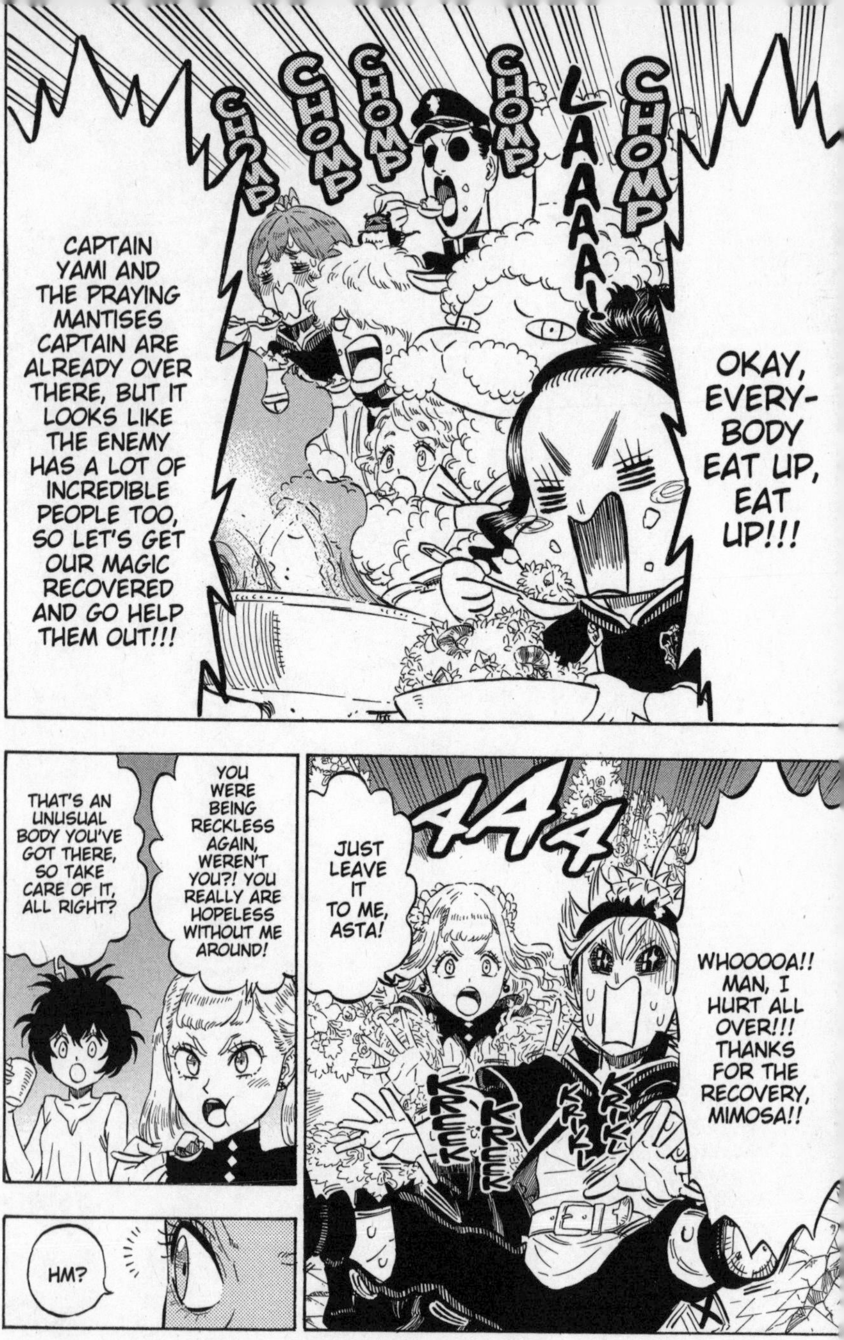
CHOMP
LAAAAA!
CHOMP
CHOMP
CHOMP
CHOMP
OKAY, EVERYBODY EAT UP, EAT UP!!!
CAPTAIN YAMI AND THE PRAYING MANTISES CAPTAIN ARE ALREADY OVER THERE, BUT IT LOOKS LIKE THE ENEMY HAS A LOT OF INCREDIBLE PEOPLE TOO, SO LET'S GET OUR MAGIC RECOVERED AND GO HELP THEM OUT!!!
444
WHOOOOA!! MAN, I HURT ALL OVER!!! THANKS FOR THE RECOVERY, MIMOSA!!
KRIKL
KRIKL
KREEK
KREEK
JUST LEAVE IT TO ME, ASTA!
YOU WERE BEING RECKLESS AGAIN, WEREN'T YOU?! YOU REALLY ARE HOPELESS WITHOUT ME AROUND!
THAT'S AN UNUSUAL BODY YOU'VE GOT THERE, SO TAKE CARE OF IT, ALL RIGHT?
HM?

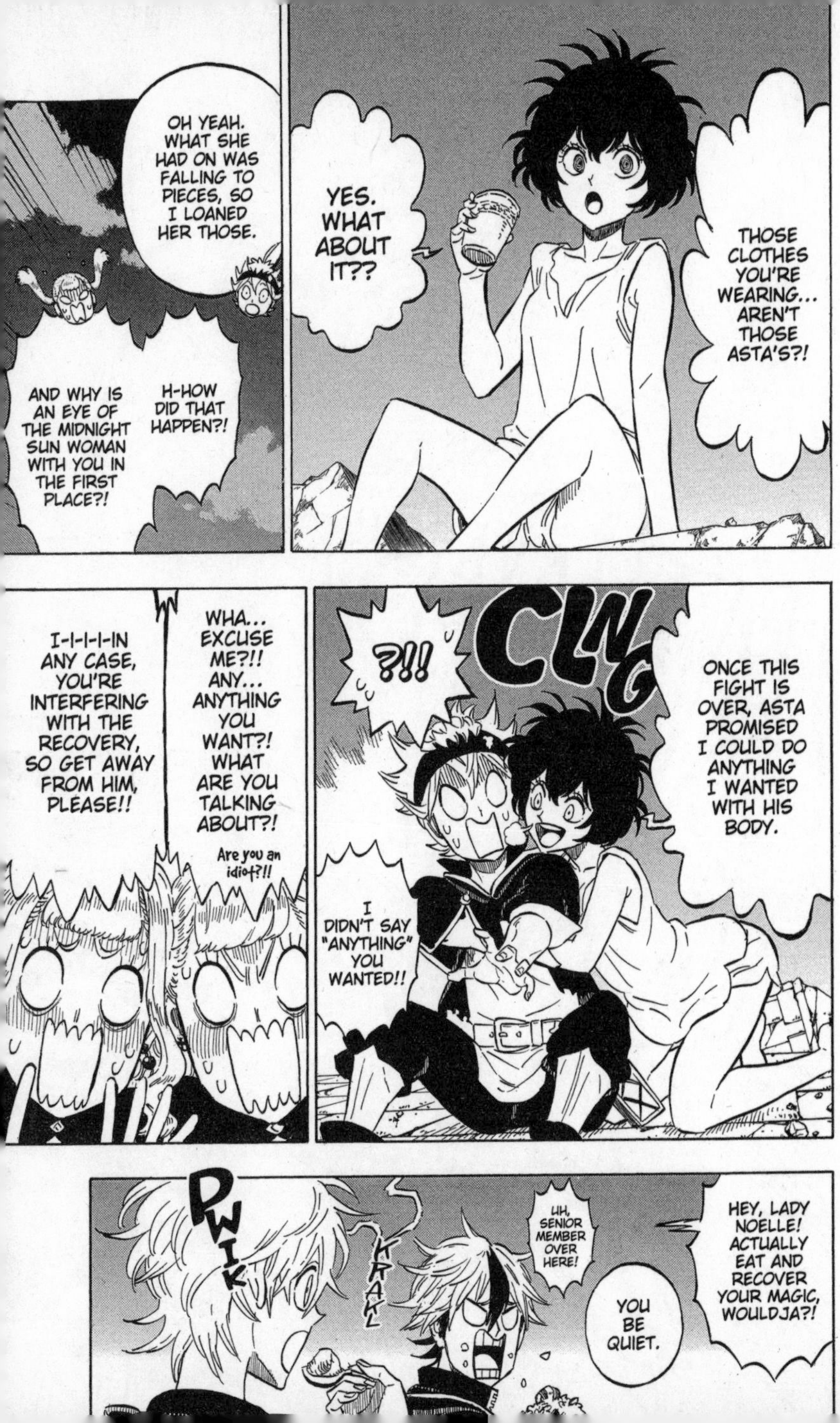
THOSE CLOTHES YOU'RE WEARING... AREN'T THOSE ASTA'S?!
YES. WHAT ABOUT IT??
OH YEAH. WHAT SHE HAD ON WAS FALLING TO PIECES, SO I LOANED HER THOSE.
H-HOW DID THAT HAPPEN?!
AND WHY IS AN EYE OF THE MIDNIGHT SUN WOMAN WITH YOU IN THE FIRST PLACE?!
ONCE THIS FIGHT IS OVER, ASTA PROMISED I COULD DO ANYTHING I WANTED WITH HIS BODY.
CLING
?!!
I DIDN'T SAY "ANYTHING" YOU WANTED!!
WHA... EXCUSE ME?!! ANY... ANYTHING YOU WANT?! WHAT ARE YOU TALKING ABOUT?!
Are you an idiot?!!
I-I-I-I-IN ANY CASE, YOU'RE INTERFERING WITH THE RECOVERY, SO GET AWAY FROM HIM, PLEASE!!
HEY, LADY NOELLE! ACTUALLY EAT AND RECOVER YOUR MAGIC, WOULDJA?!
UH, SENIOR MEMBER OVER HERE!
YOU BE QUIET.
KRAK
PWIK

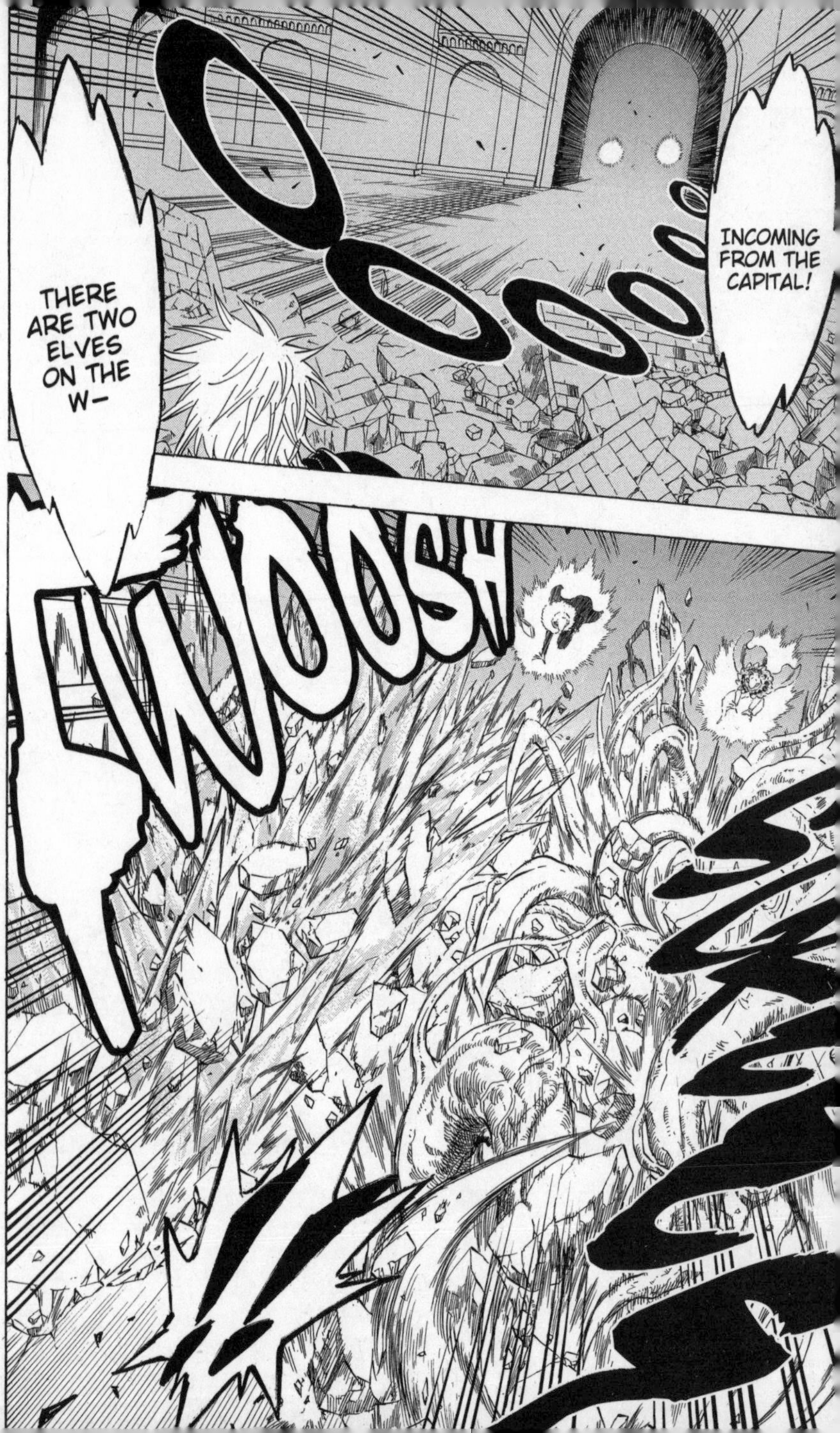
INCOMING FROM THE CAPITAL!
THERE ARE TWO ELVES ON THE W-
WOOSH

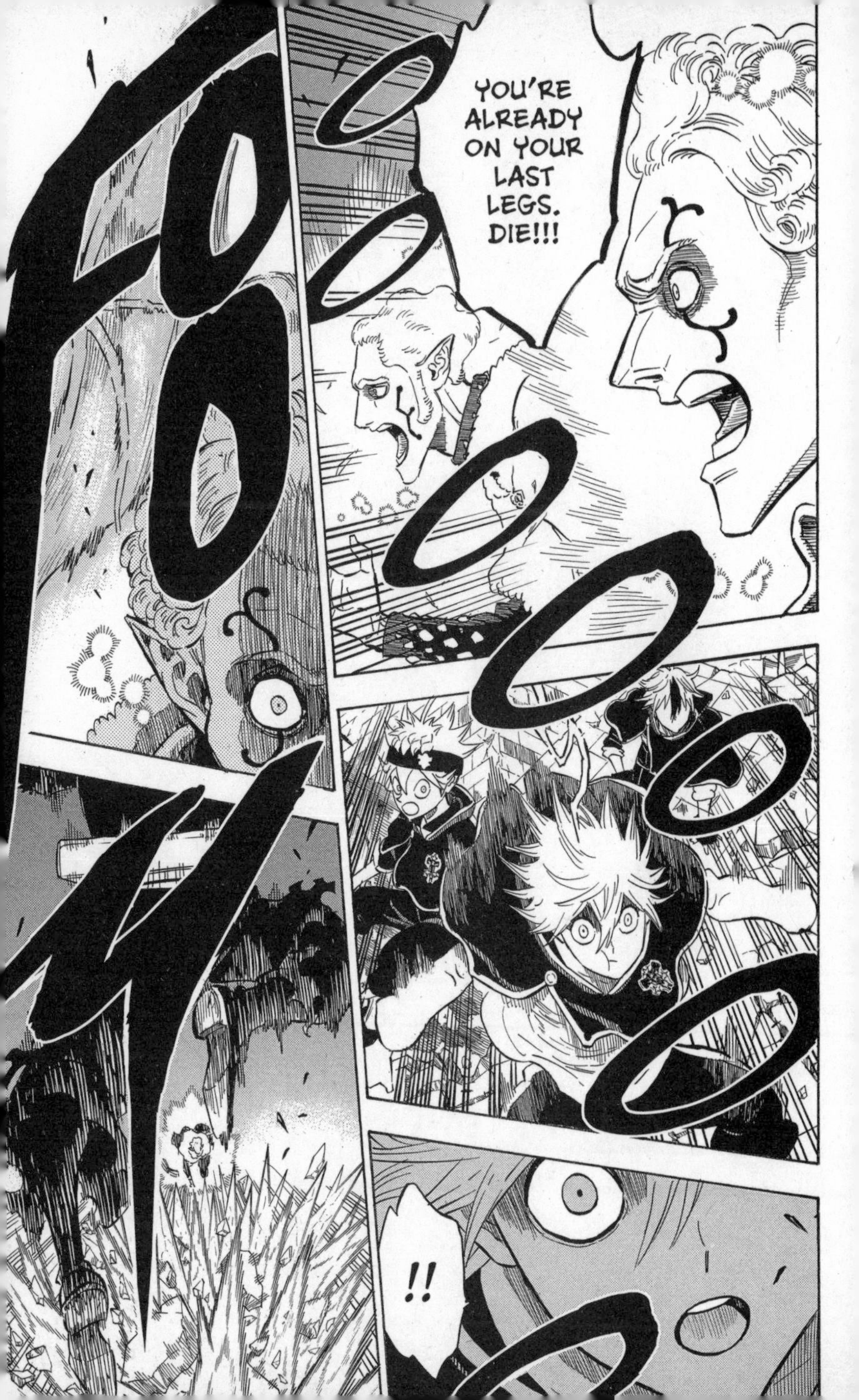
YOU'RE ALREADY ON YOUR LAST LEGS. DIE!!!
!!

SO YOU FINALLY WOKE UP, DID YOU?

BIG FOOL!!

I'M SORRY TO HAVE MADE EXTRA WORK FOR YOU...

...SISTER!!

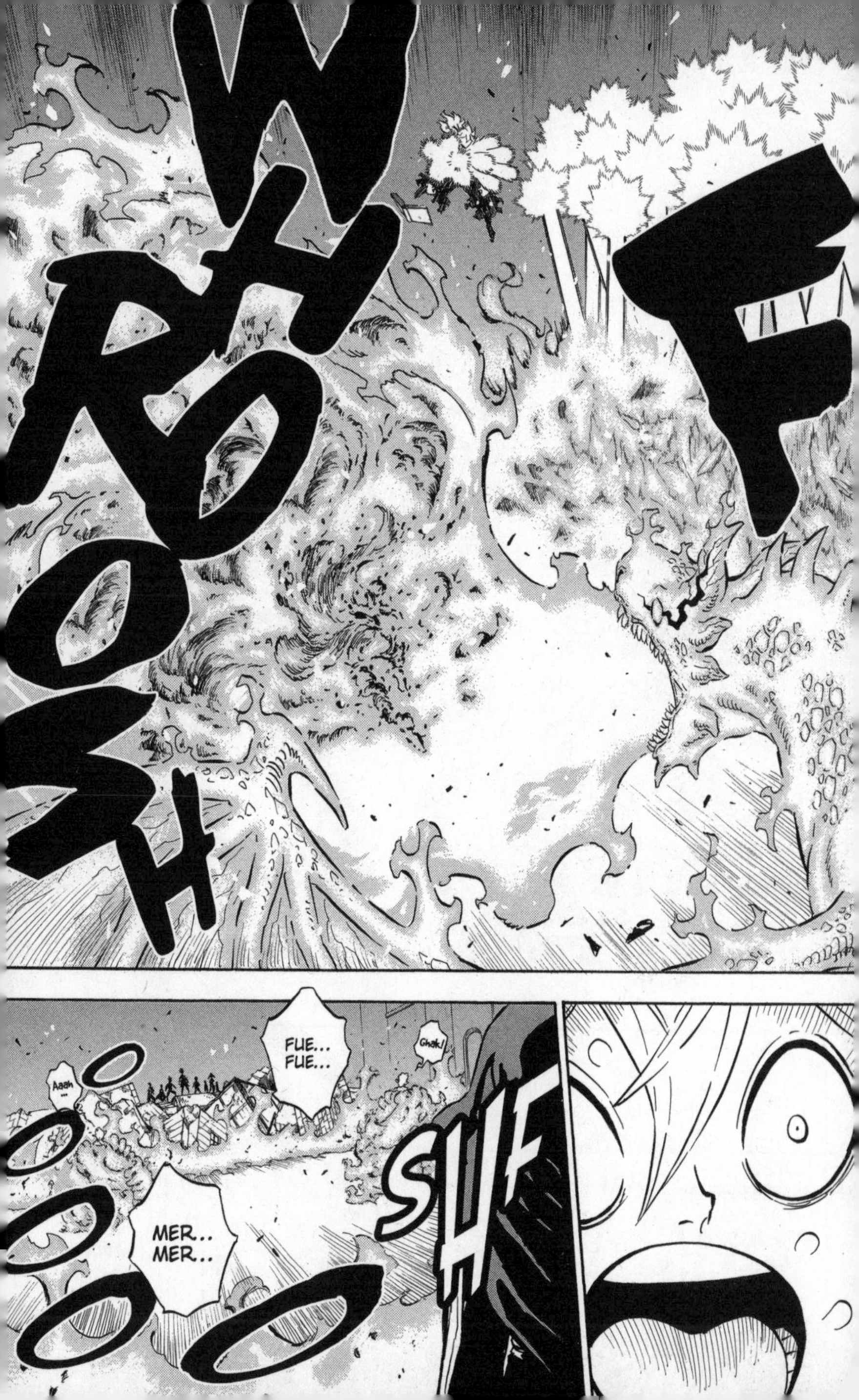
SHF
Ghak!
FUE... FUE...
Aaah...
MER... MER...

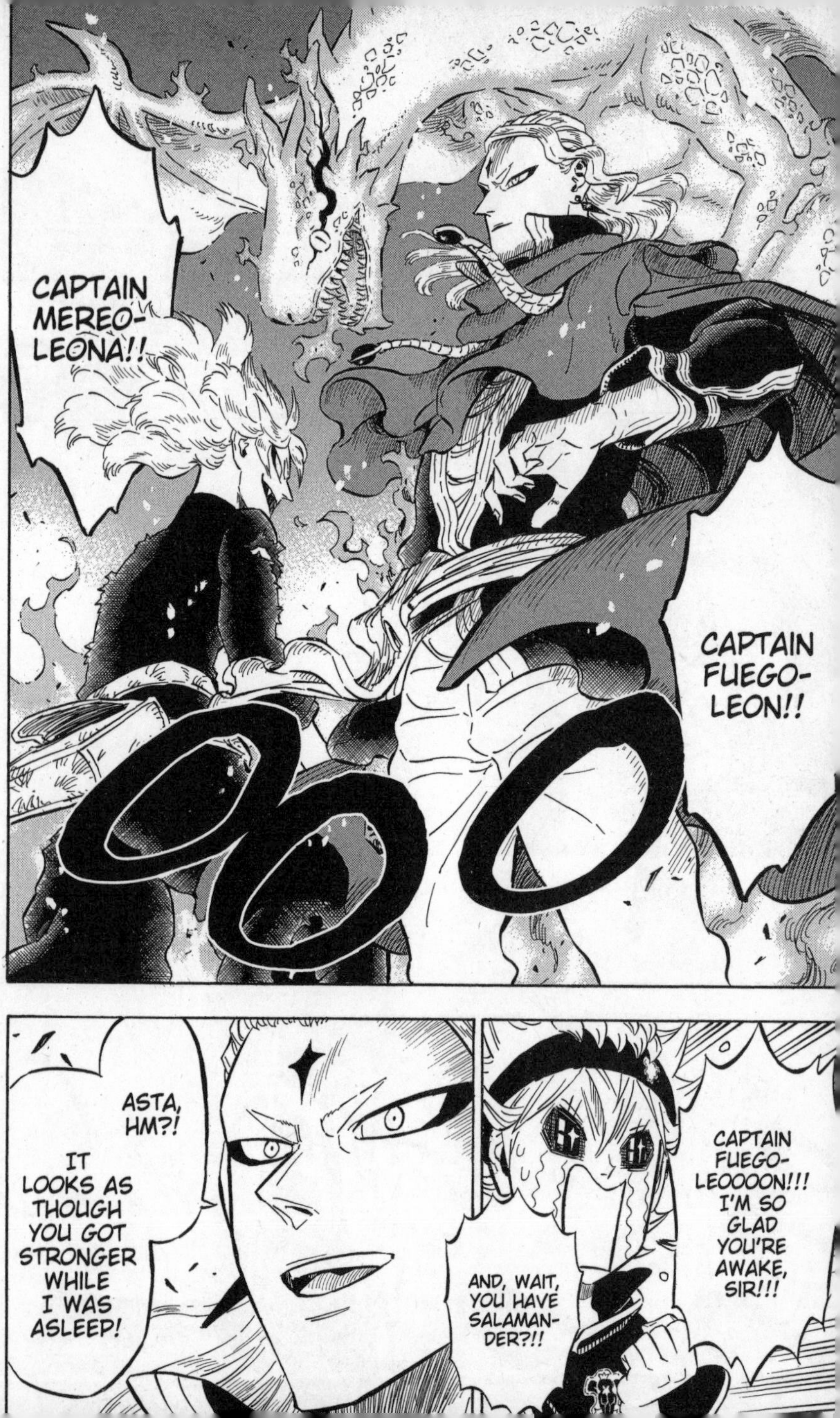
CAPTAIN MEREO-LEONA!!
CAPTAIN FUEGO-LEON!!
CAPTAIN FUEGO-LEOOOON!!! I'M SO GLAD YOU'RE AWAKE, SIR!!!
AND, WAIT, YOU HAVE SALAMANDER?!!
ASTA, HM?!
IT LOOKS AS THOUGH YOU GOT STRONGER WHILE I WAS ASLEEP!

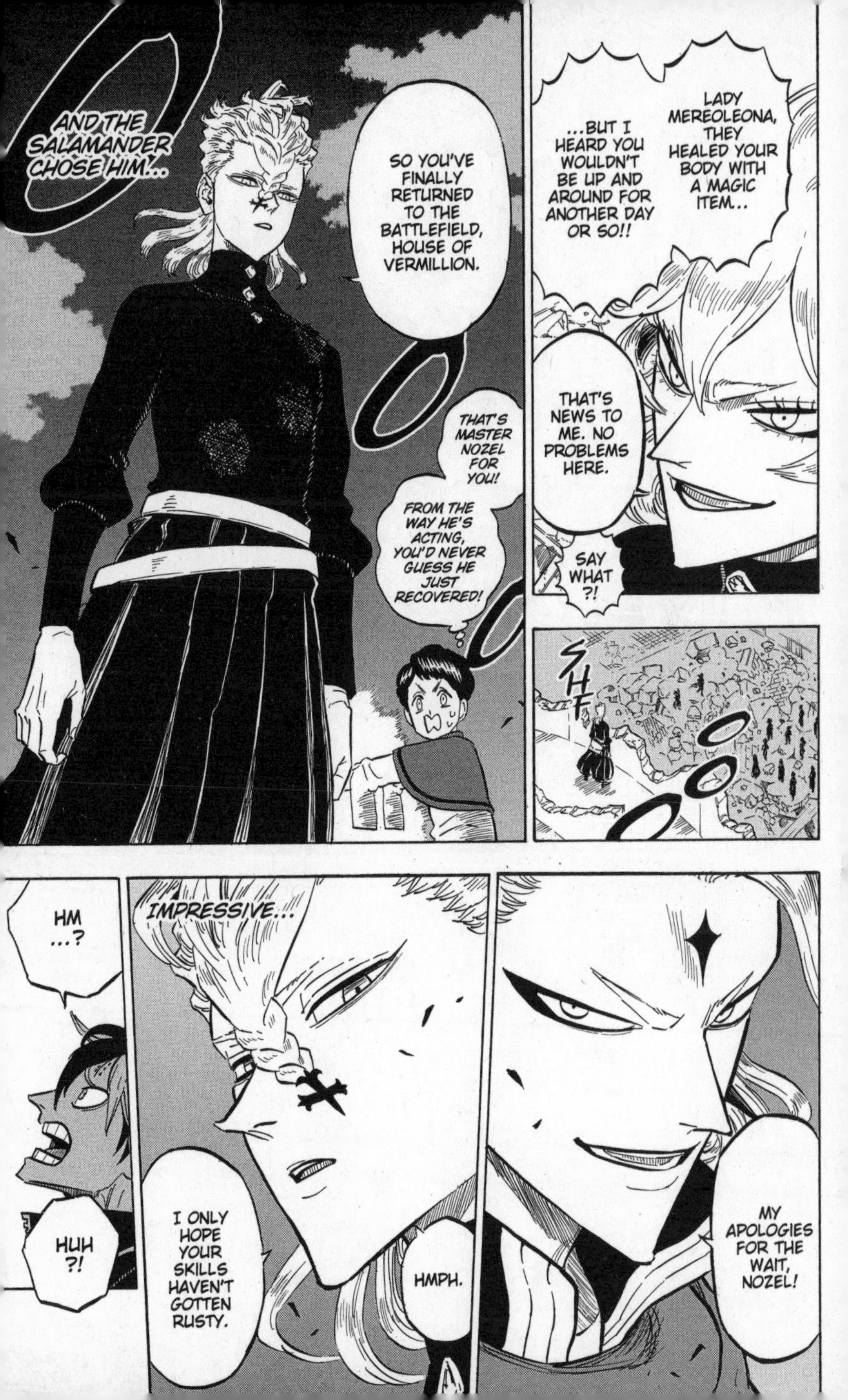
LADY MEREOLEONA, THEY HEALED YOUR BODY WITH A MAGIC ITEM...
...BUT I HEARD YOU WOULDN'T BE UP AND AROUND FOR ANOTHER DAY OR SO!!
THAT'S NEWS TO ME. NO PROBLEMS HERE.
SAY WHAT ?!
SHF
SO YOU'VE FINALLY RETURNED TO THE BATTLEFIELD, HOUSE OF VERMILLION.
AND THE SALAMANDER CHOSE HIM...
THAT'S MASTER NOZEL FOR YOU!
FROM THE WAY HE'S ACTING, YOU'D NEVER GUESS HE JUST RECOVERED!
MY APOLOGIES FOR THE WAIT, NOZEL!
IMPRESSIVE...
HMPH.
I ONLY HOPE YOUR SKILLS HAVEN'T GOTTEN RUSTY.
HM ...?
HUH ?!

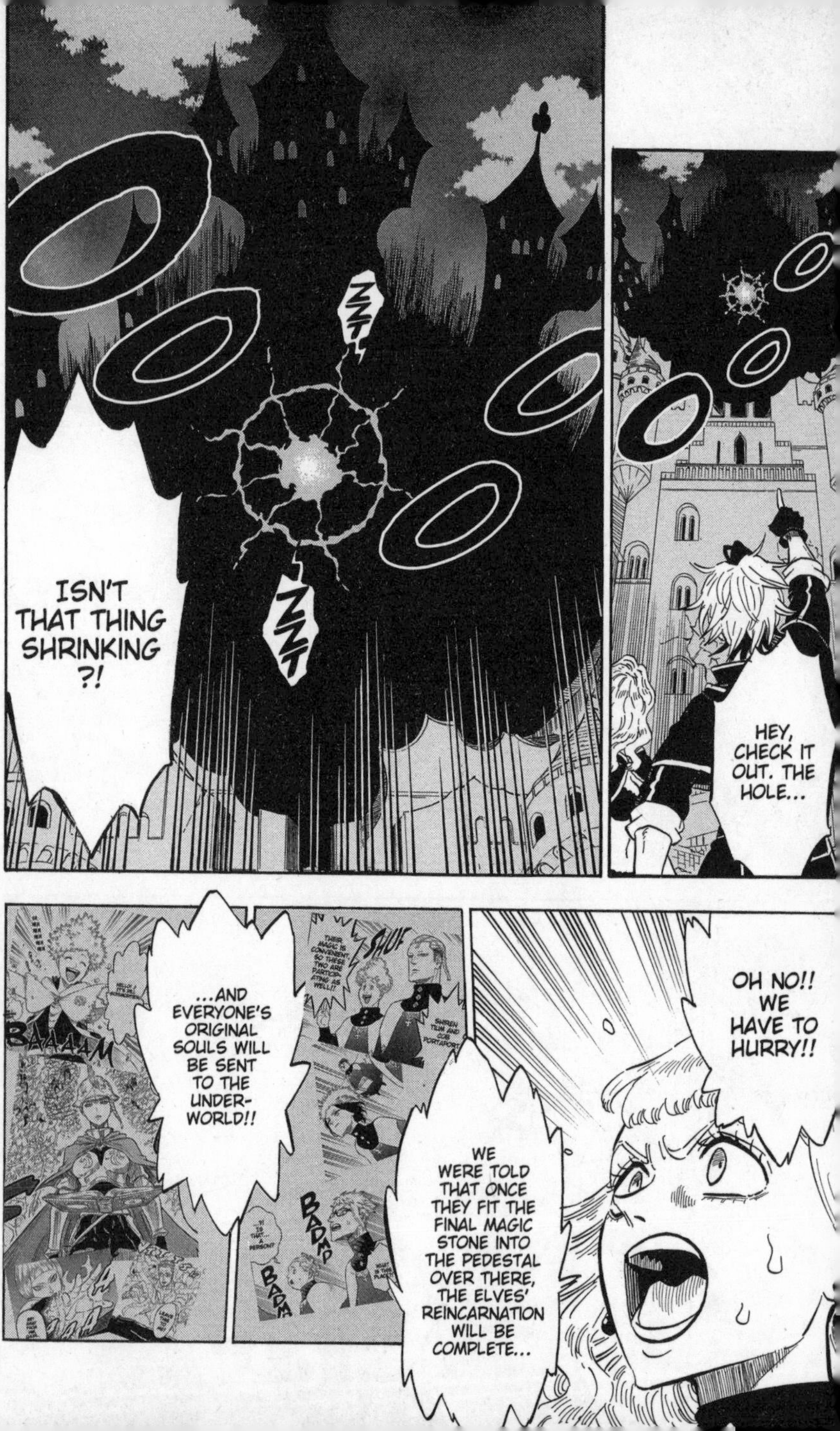
HEY, CHECK IT OUT. THE HOLE...
ZZZT
ZZZT
ISN'T THAT THING SHRINKING?!
OH NO!! WE HAVE TO HURRY!!
WE WERE TOLD THAT ONCE THEY FIT THE FINAL MAGIC STONE INTO THE PEDESTAL OVER THERE, THE ELVES' REINCARNATION WILL BE COMPLETE...
...AND EVERYONE'S ORIGINAL SOULS WILL BE SENT TO THE UNDER-WORLD!!

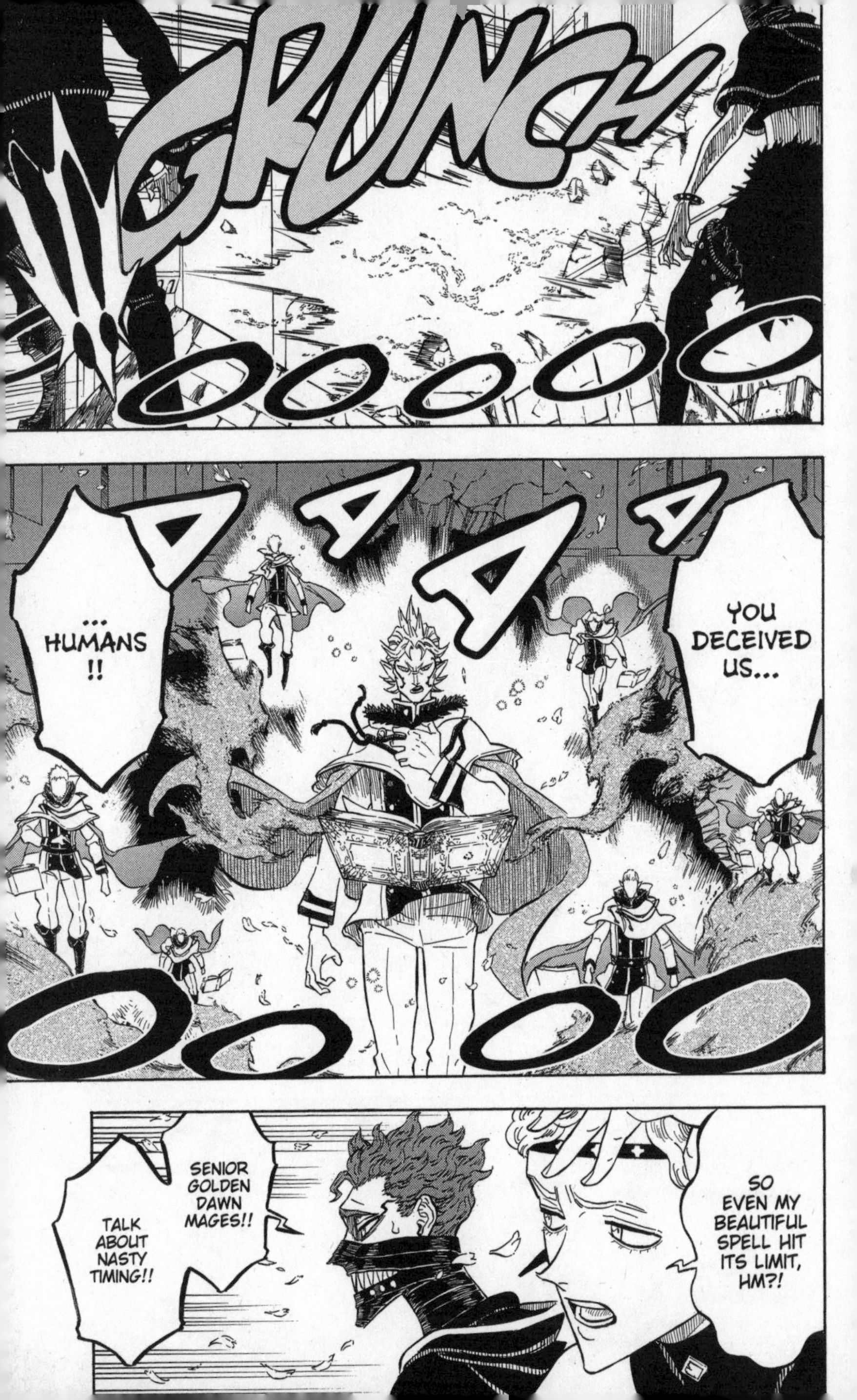
CRUNCH
OOOOOO
YOU DECEIVED US...
... HUMANS !!
AAAA
OOOOO
SO EVEN MY BEAUTIFUL SPELL HIT ITS LIMIT, HM?!
SENIOR GOLDEN DAWN MAGES!!
TALK ABOUT NASTY TIMING!!

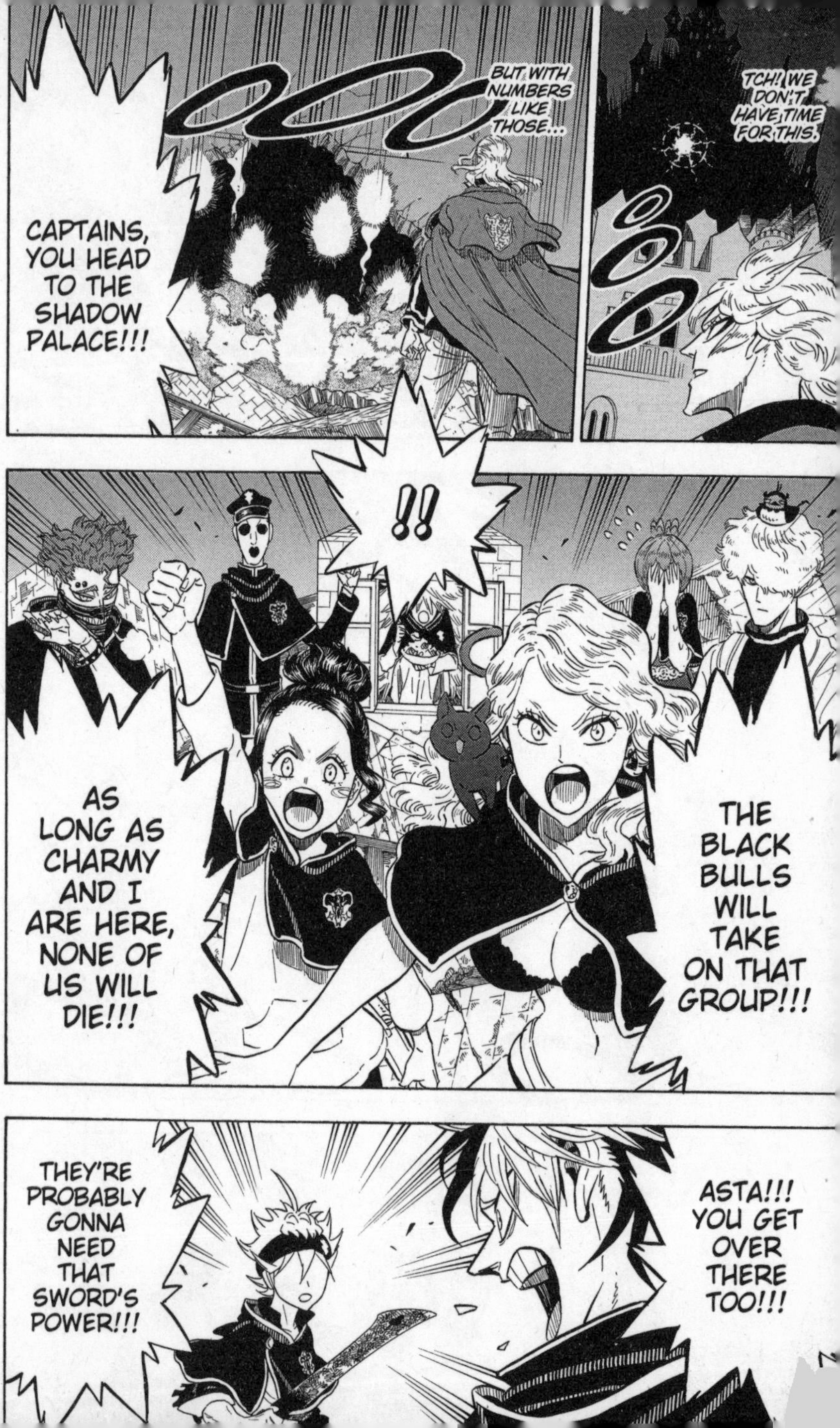
TCH! WE DON'T HAVE TIME FOR THIS.
BUT WITH NUMBERS LIKE THOSE...
CAPTAINS, YOU HEAD TO THE SHADOW PALACE!!!
!!
THE BLACK BULLS WILL TAKE ON THAT GROUP!!!
AS LONG AS CHARMY AND I ARE HERE, NONE OF US WILL DIE!!!
ASTA!!! YOU GET OVER THERE TOO!!!
THEY'RE PROBABLY GONNA NEED THAT SWORD'S POWER!!!

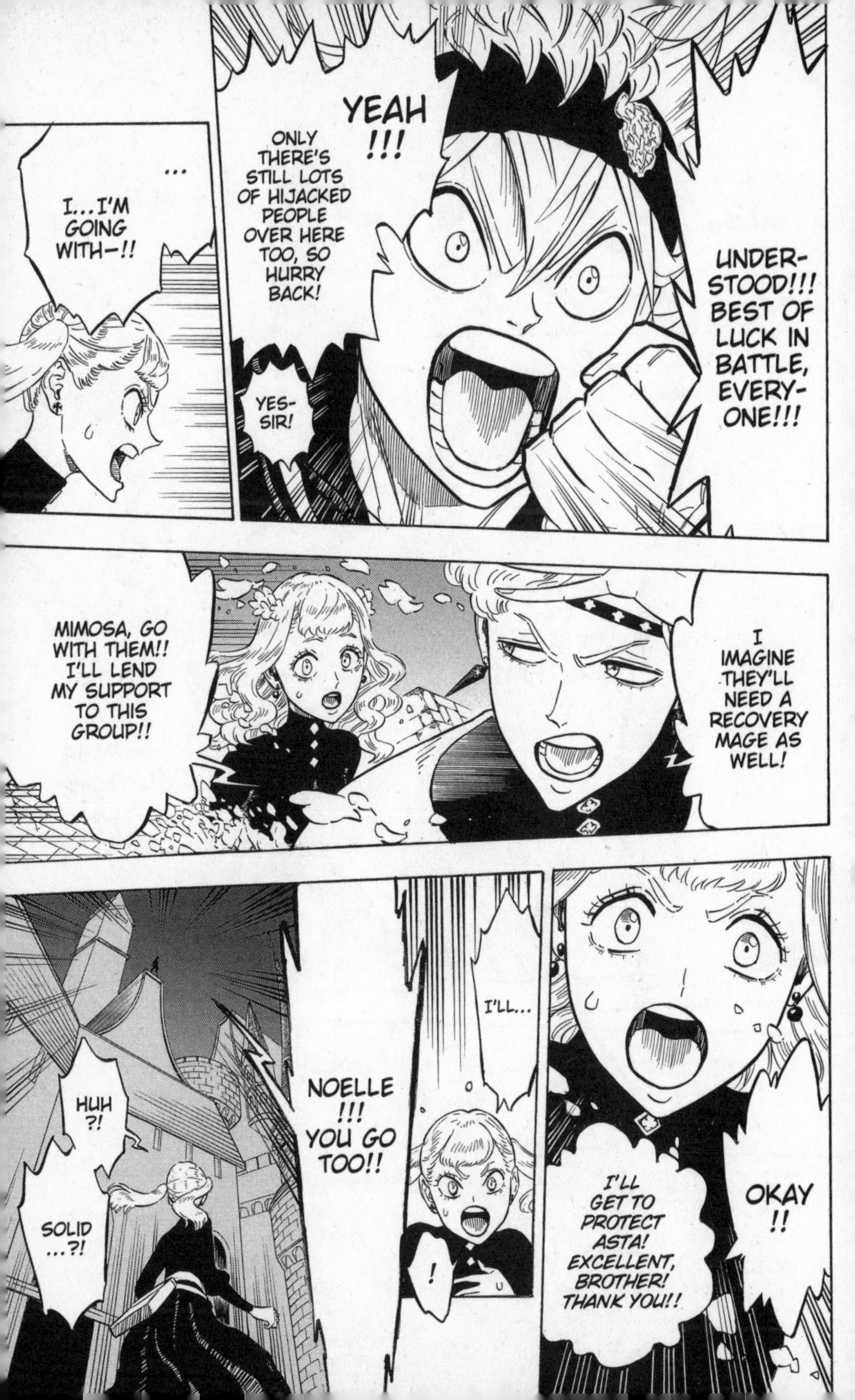
UNDERSTOOD!!! BEST OF LUCK IN BATTLE, EVERYONE!!!
YEAH!!!
ONLY THERE'S STILL LOTS OF HIJACKED PEOPLE OVER HERE TOO, SO HURRY BACK!
YES-SIR!
...
I...I'M GOING WITH—!!
I IMAGINE THEY'LL NEED A RECOVERY MAGE AS WELL!
MIMOSA, GO WITH THEM!! I'LL LEND MY SUPPORT TO THIS GROUP!!
OKAY!!
I'LL GET TO PROTECT ASTA! EXCELLENT, BROTHER! THANK YOU!!
I'LL...
NOELLE!!! YOU GO TOO!!
!
HUH?!
SOLID...?!

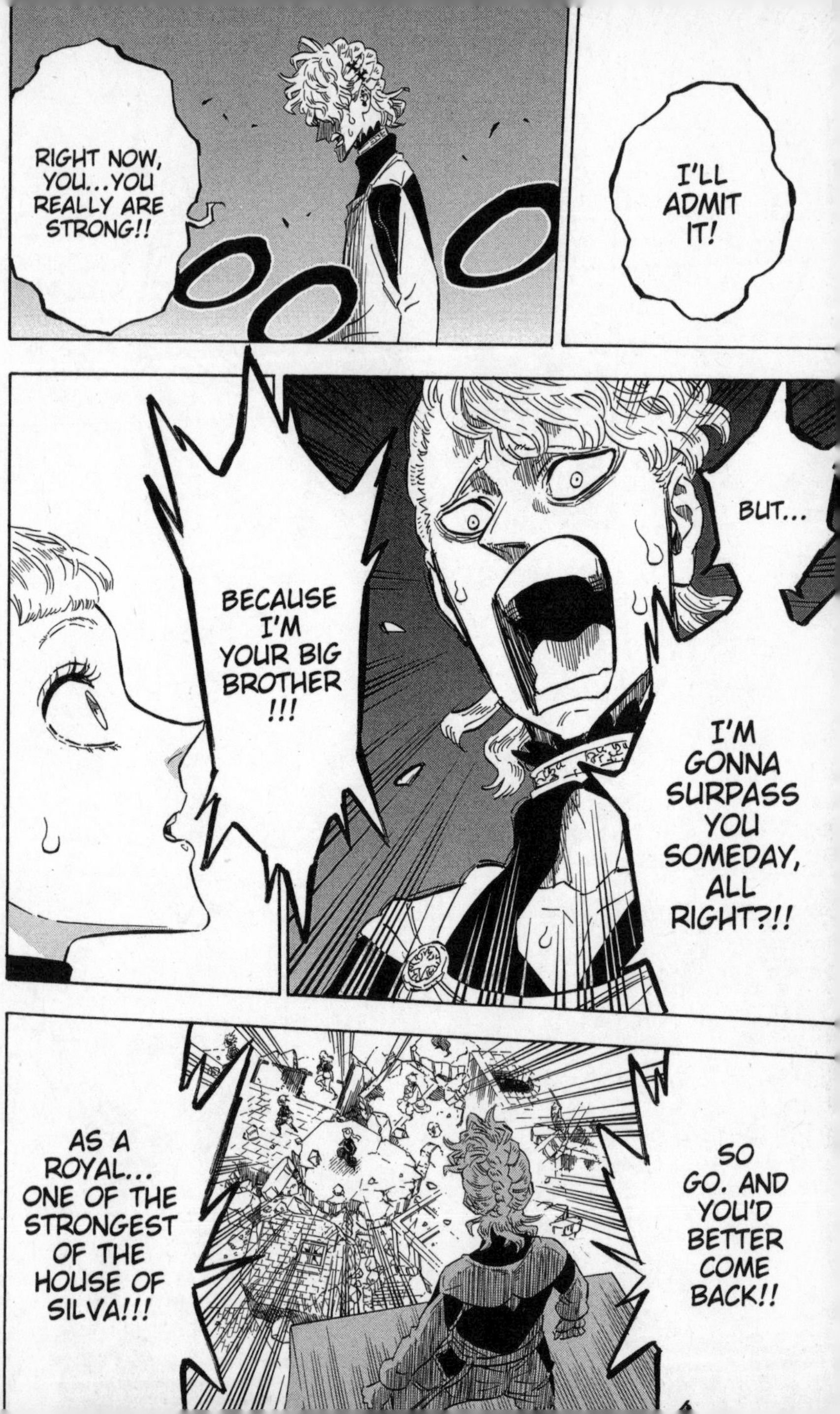
I'LL ADMIT IT!
RIGHT NOW, YOU...YOU REALLY ARE STRONG!!
BUT...
I'M GONNA SURPASS YOU SOMEDAY, ALL RIGHT?!!
BECAUSE I'M YOUR BIG BROTHER!!!
SO GO. AND YOU'D BETTER COME BACK!!
AS A ROYAL... ONE OF THE STRONGEST OF THE HOUSE OF SILVA!!!

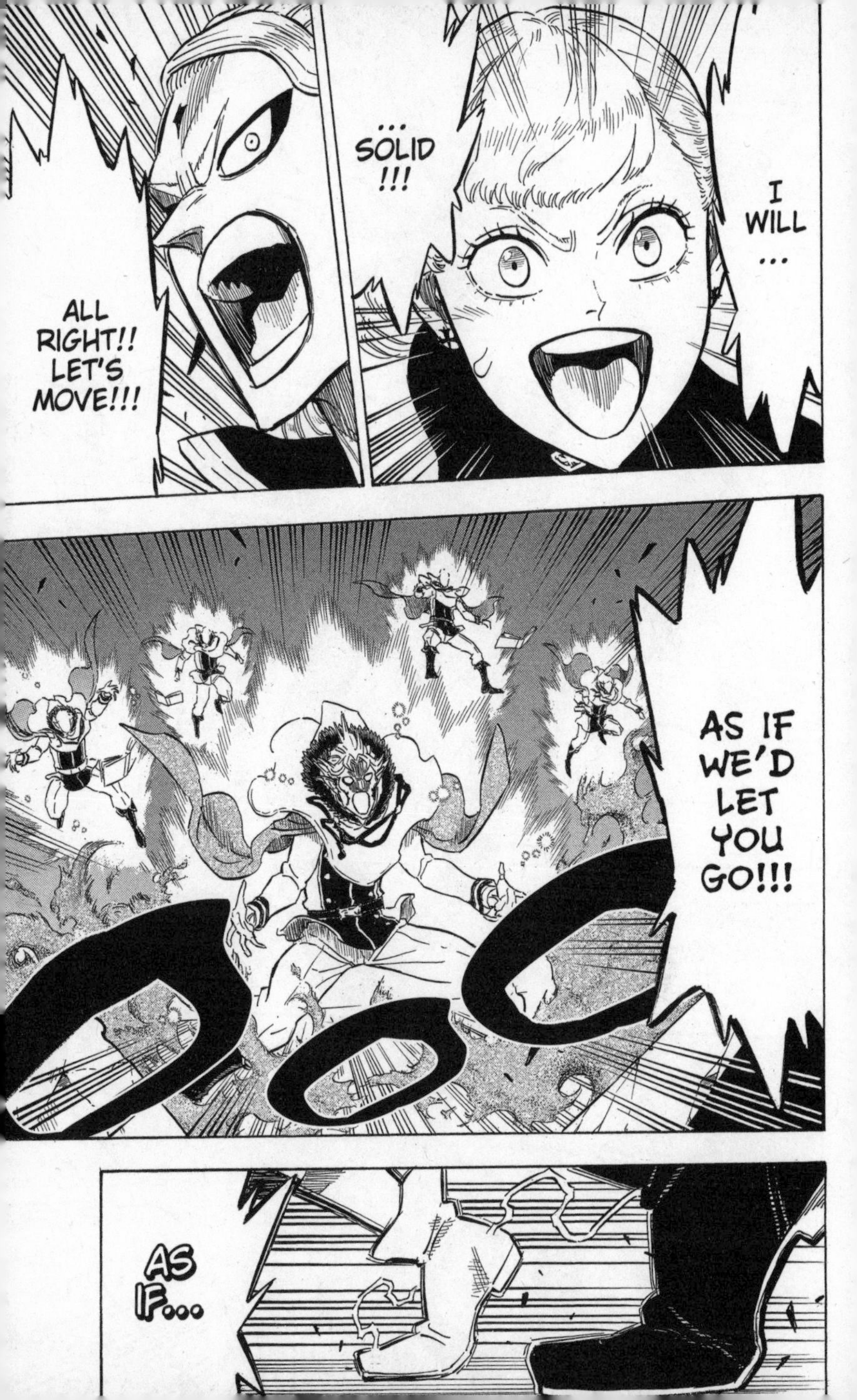
I WILL ...
... SOLID !!!
ALL RIGHT!! LET'S MOVE!!!
AS IF WE'D LET YOU GO!!!
AS IF...

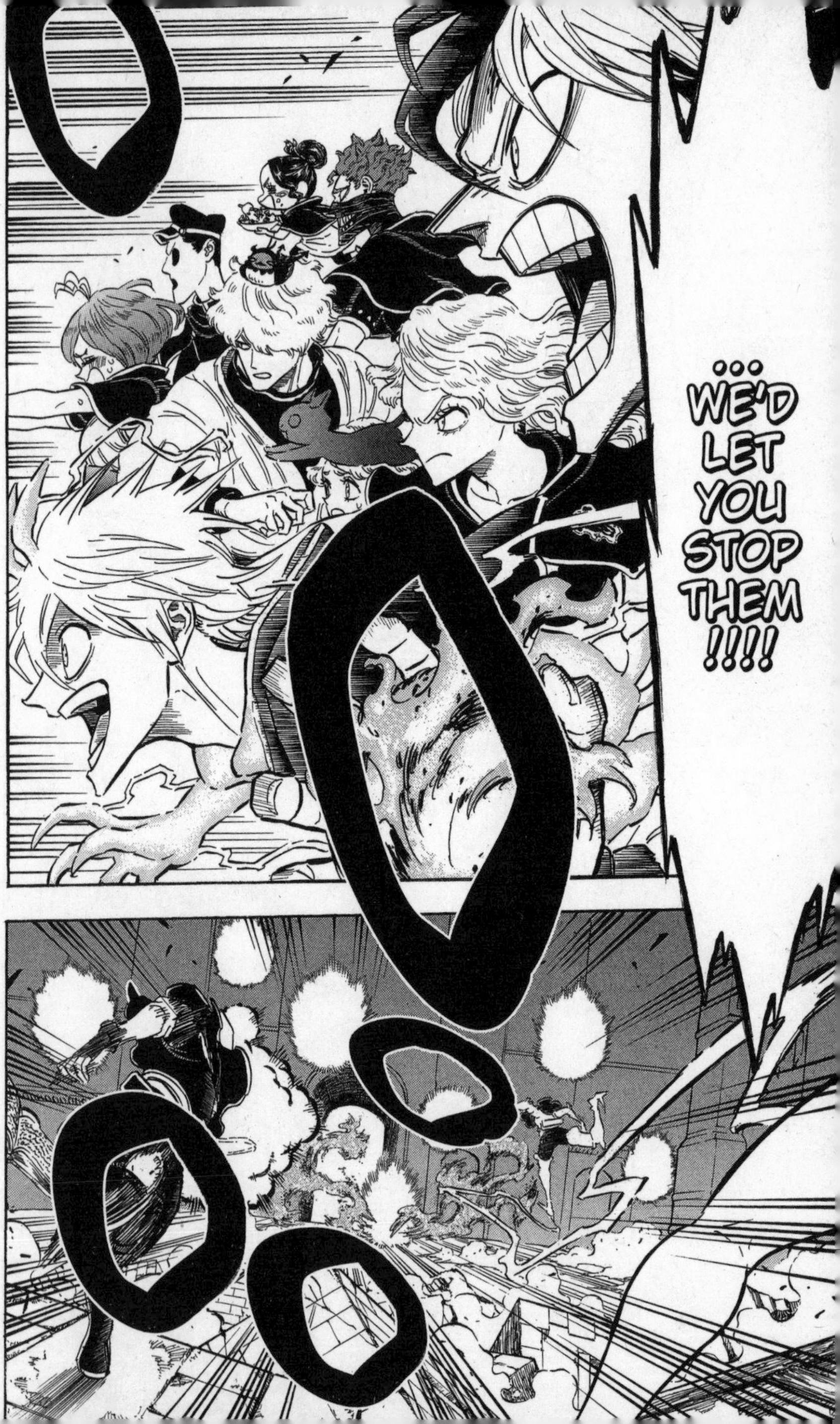
...WE'D LET YOU STOP THEM!!!!

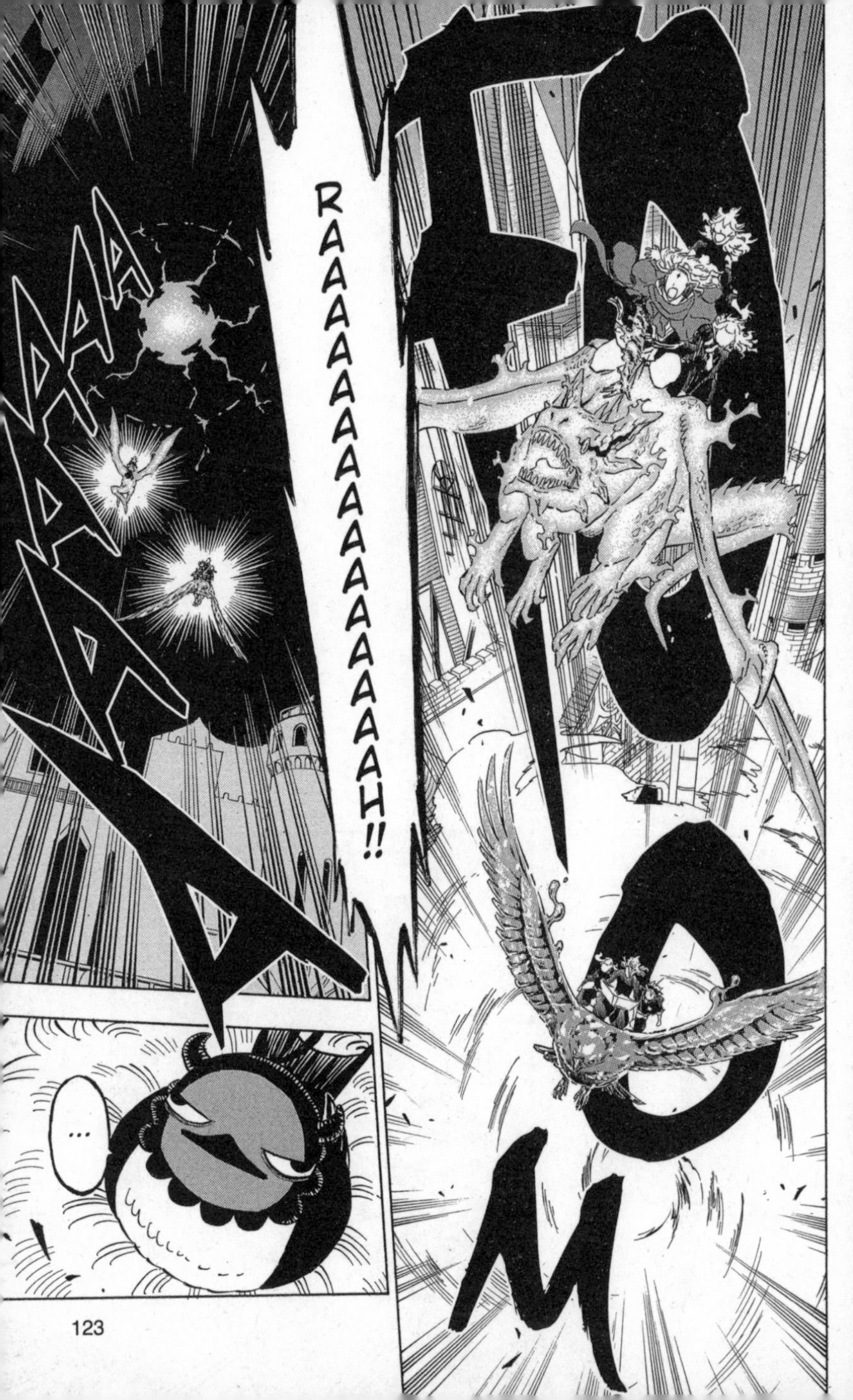
FOOM
RAAAAAAAAAAAAAAAAAAAAH!!
AAAAAAA
...

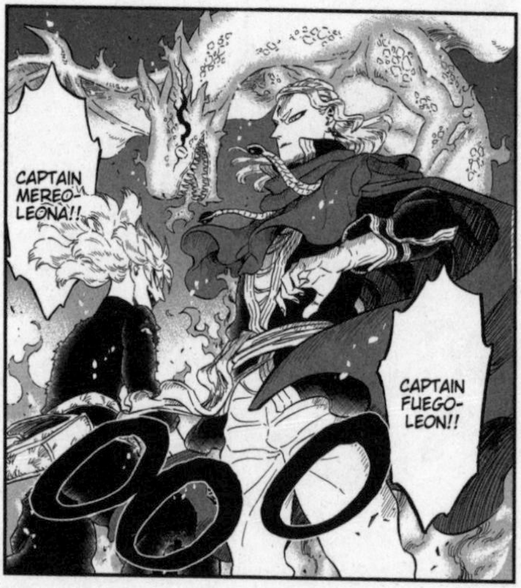
CAPTAIN FUEGO-LEON!!
CAPTAIN MEREO-LEONA!!

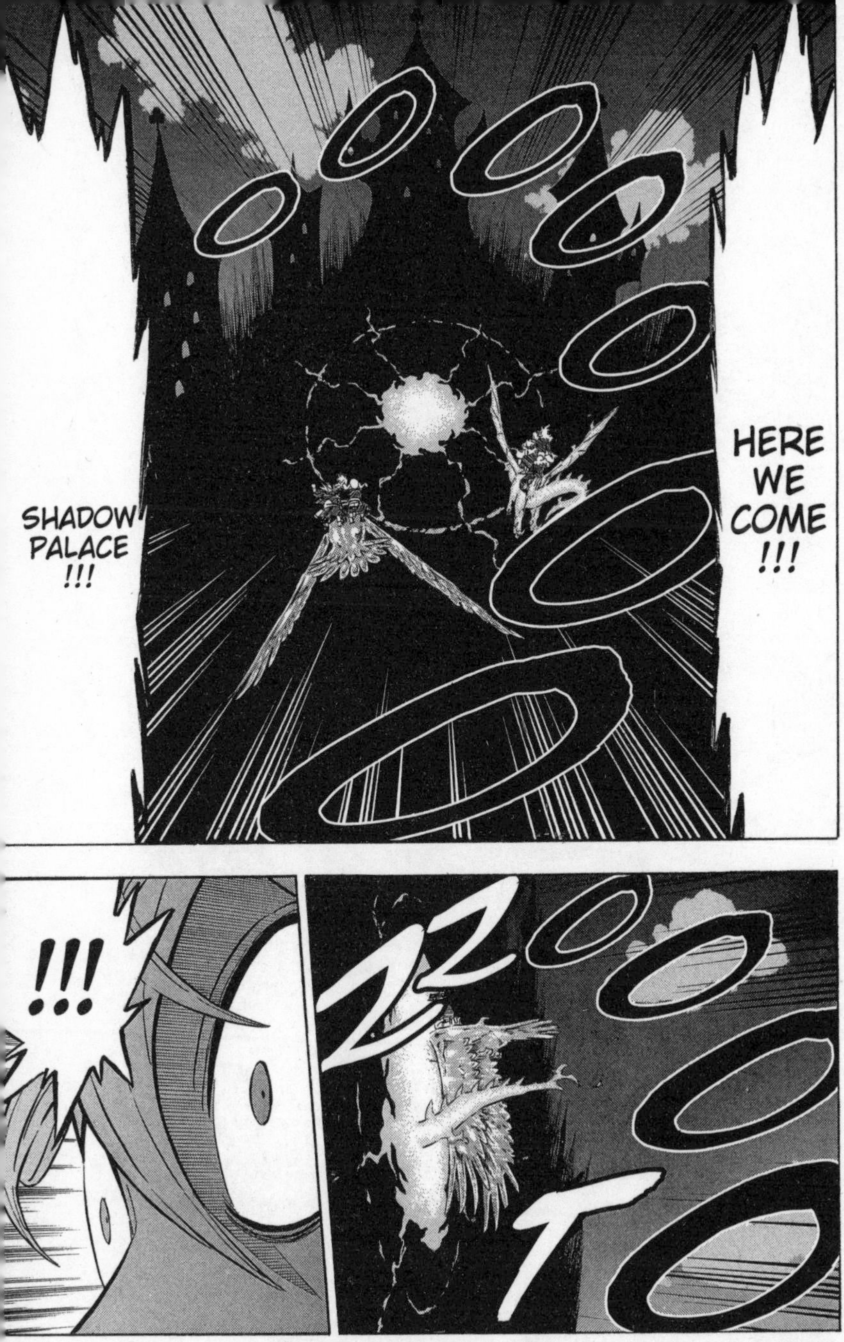
HERE WE COME!!!
SHADOW PALACE!!!
!!!

Page 191: Storming the Shadow Palace

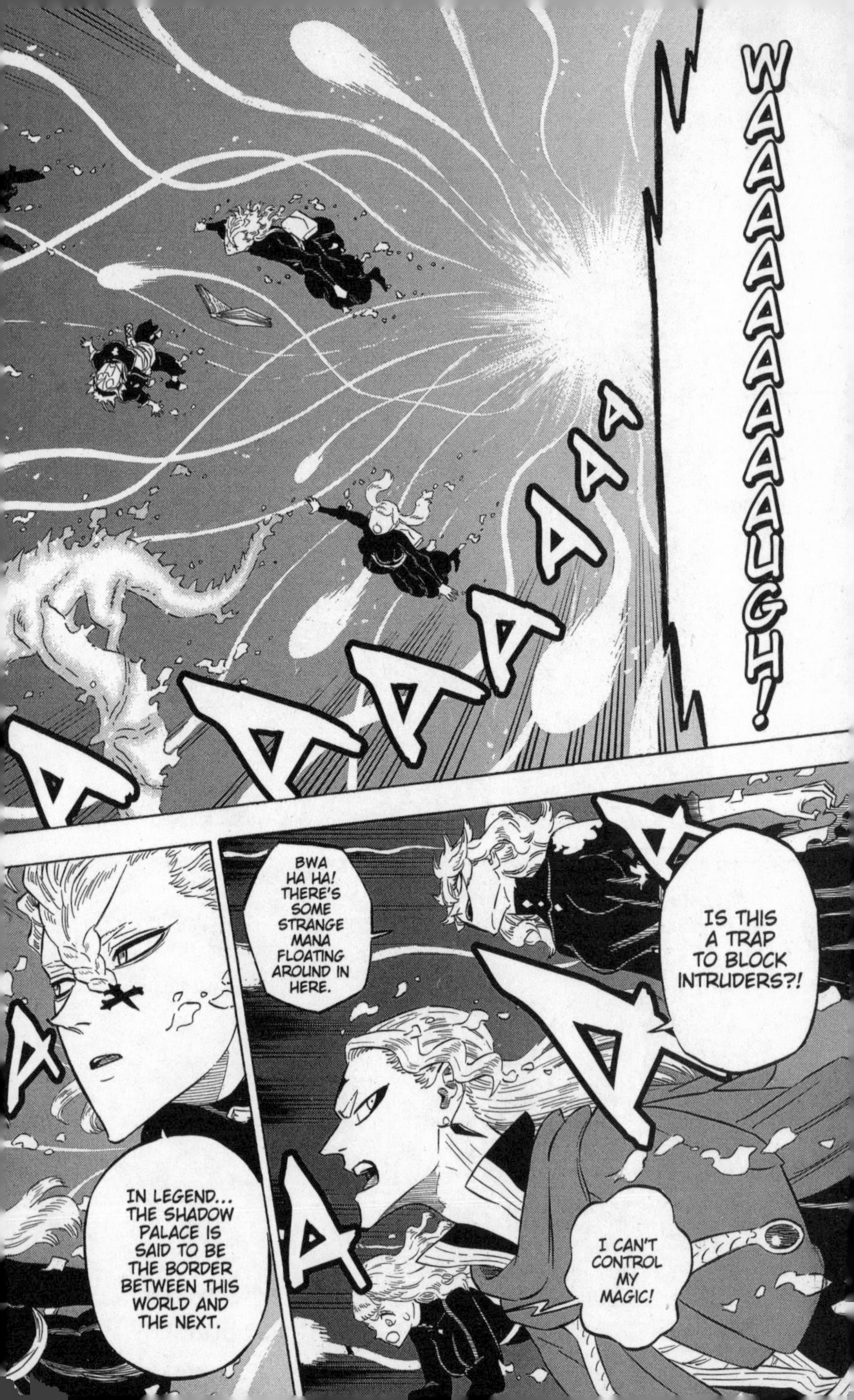
WAAAAAAAAAAAUGH!
IS THIS A TRAP TO BLOCK INTRUDERS?!
BWA HA HA! THERE'S SOME STRANGE MANA FLOATING AROUND IN HERE.
I CAN'T CONTROL MY MAGIC!
IN LEGEND... THE SHADOW PALACE IS SAID TO BE THE BORDER BETWEEN THIS WORLD AND THE NEXT.

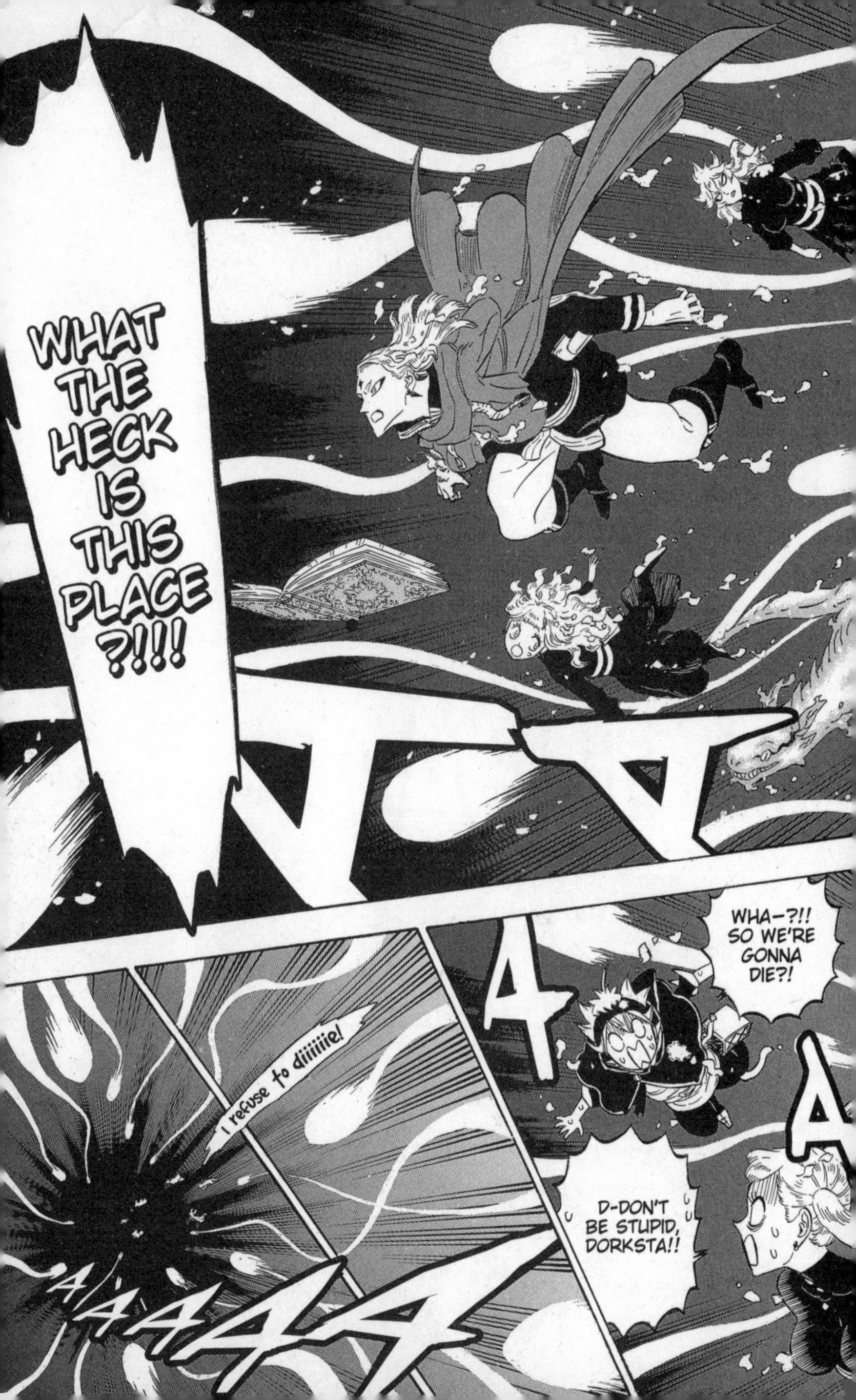
WHAT THE HECK IS THIS PLACE?!!!
WHA-?!! SO WE'RE GONNA DIE?!
D-DON'T BE STUPID, DORKSTA!!
I refuse to diiiiiie!
AAAAAA

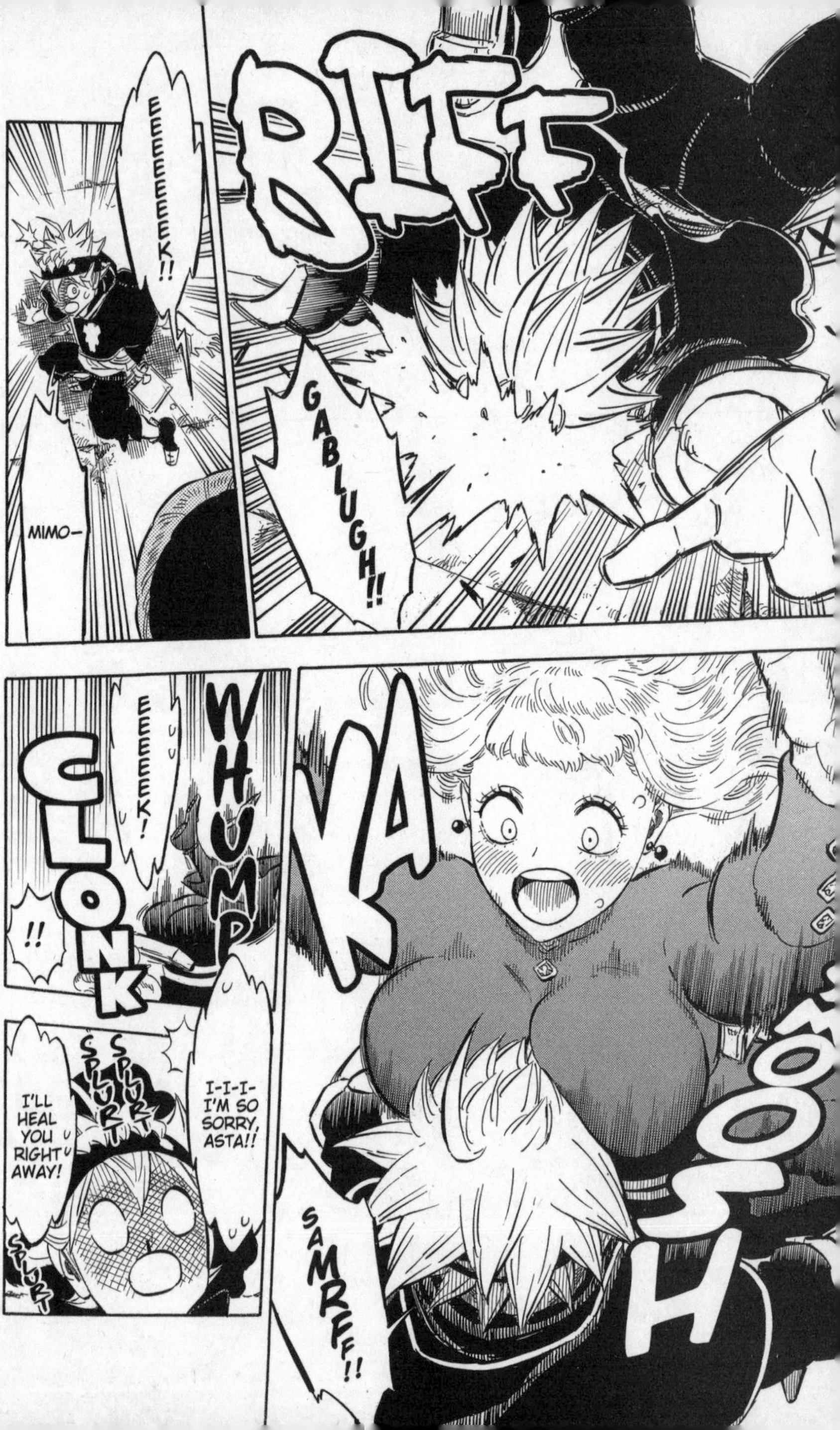

BIFF
GABLUGH!!
EEEEEEEEK!!
MIMO—
KA
WHOOSH
SAMRFF!!
EEEEEEK!
WHUMP
CLONK
!!
I-I-I- I'M SO SORRY, ASTA!!
I'LL HEAL YOU RIGHT AWAY!
SPLURT
SPLURT
SPLURT

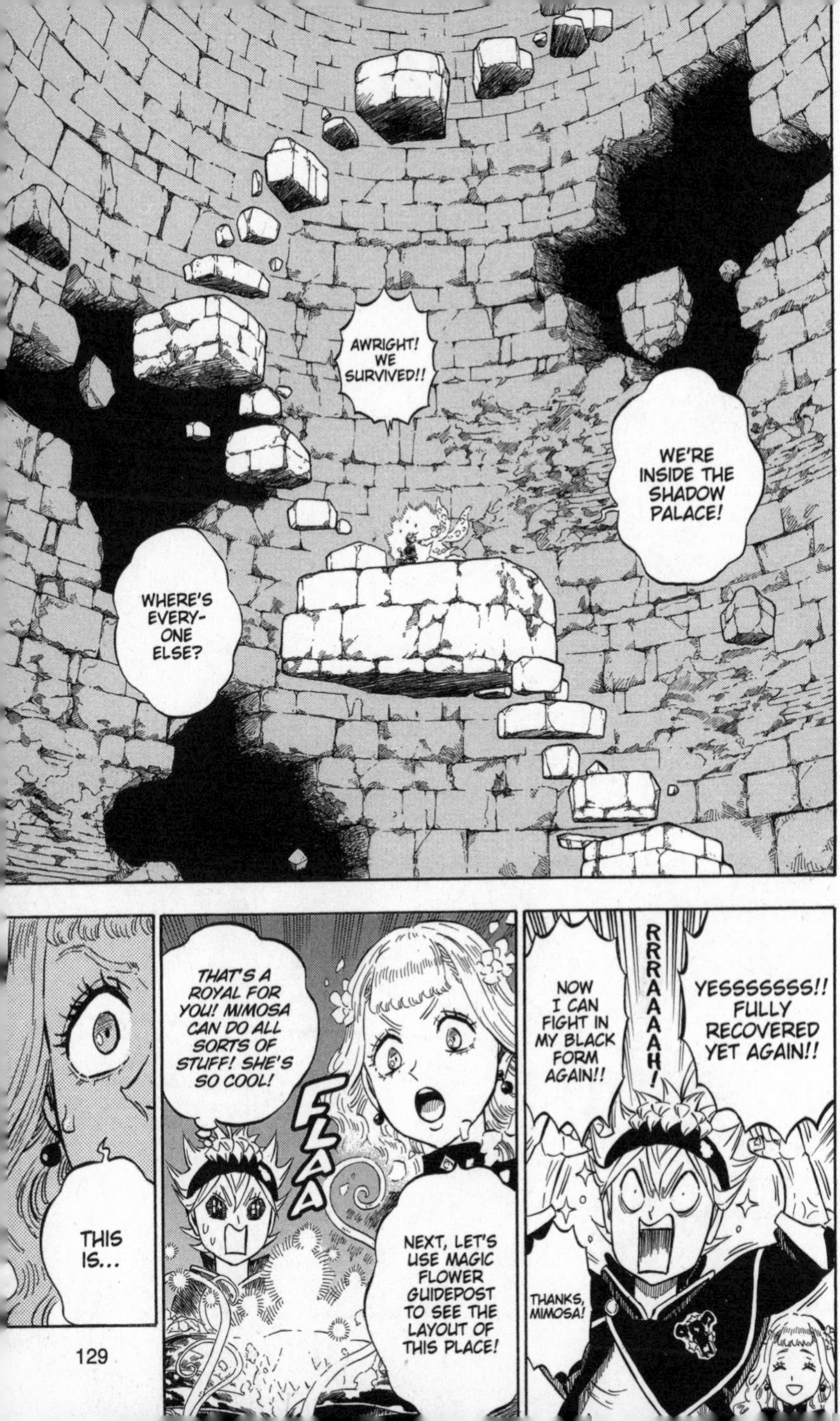
AWRIGHT! WE SURVIVED!!
WE'RE INSIDE THE SHADOW PALACE!
WHERE'S EVERY-ONE ELSE?
RRRAAAAAH!
YESSSSSSS!! FULLY RECOVERED YET AGAIN!!
NOW I CAN FIGHT IN MY BLACK FORM AGAIN!!
THANKS, MIMOSA!
THAT'S A ROYAL FOR YOU! MIMOSA CAN DO ALL SORTS OF STUFF! SHE'S SO COOL!
FLAA
NEXT, LET'S USE MAGIC FLOWER GUIDEPOST TO SEE THE LAYOUT OF THIS PLACE!
THIS IS...

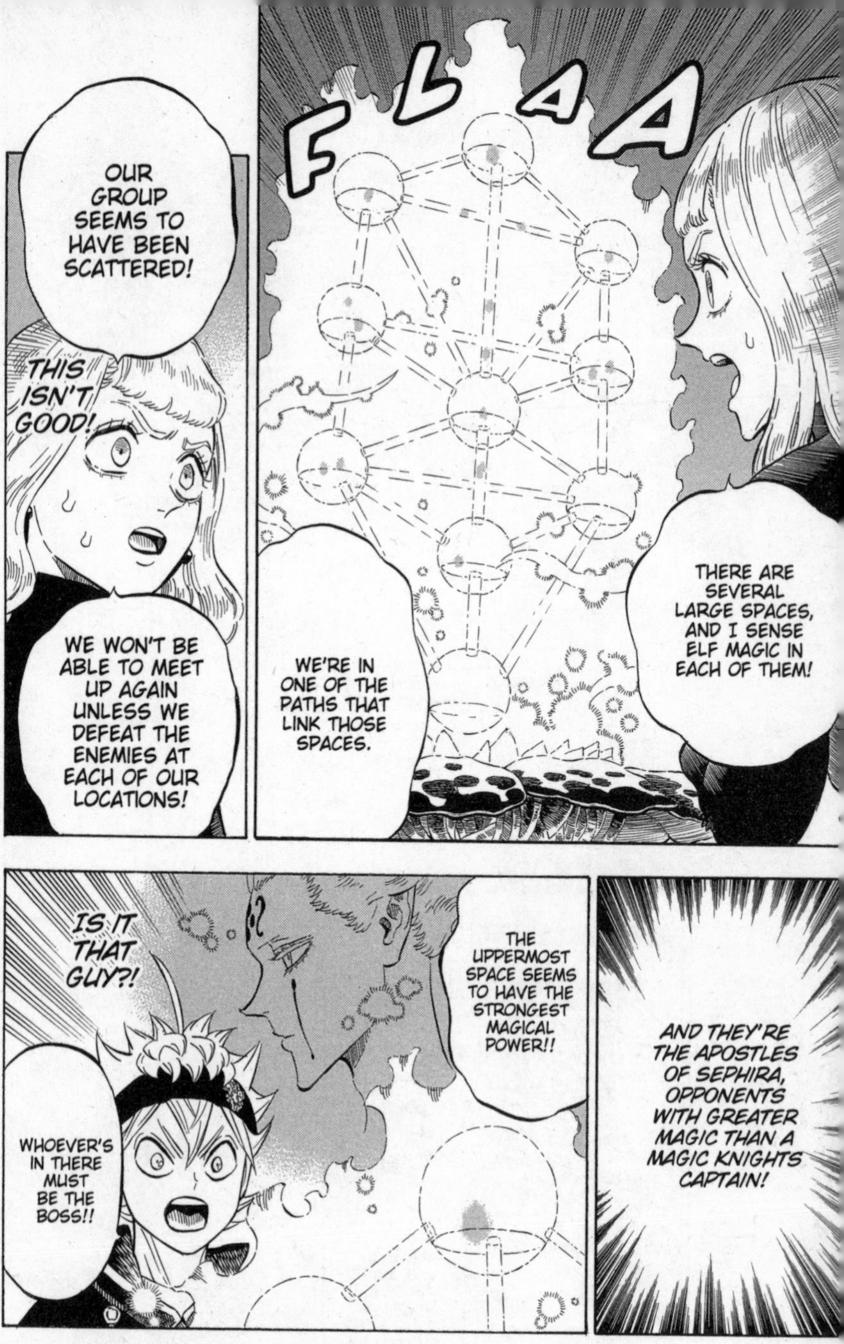
FLAA
THERE ARE SEVERAL LARGE SPACES, AND I SENSE ELF MAGIC IN EACH OF THEM!
WE'RE IN ONE OF THE PATHS THAT LINK THOSE SPACES.
OUR GROUP SEEMS TO HAVE BEEN SCATTERED!
THIS ISN'T GOOD!
WE WON'T BE ABLE TO MEET UP AGAIN UNLESS WE DEFEAT THE ENEMIES AT EACH OF OUR LOCATIONS!
AND THEY'RE THE APOSTLES OF SEPHIRA, OPPONENTS WITH GREATER MAGIC THAN A MAGIC KNIGHTS CAPTAIN!
THE UPPERMOST SPACE SEEMS TO HAVE THE STRONGEST MAGICAL POWER!!
IS IT THAT GUY?!
WHOEVER'S IN THERE MUST BE THE BOSS!!

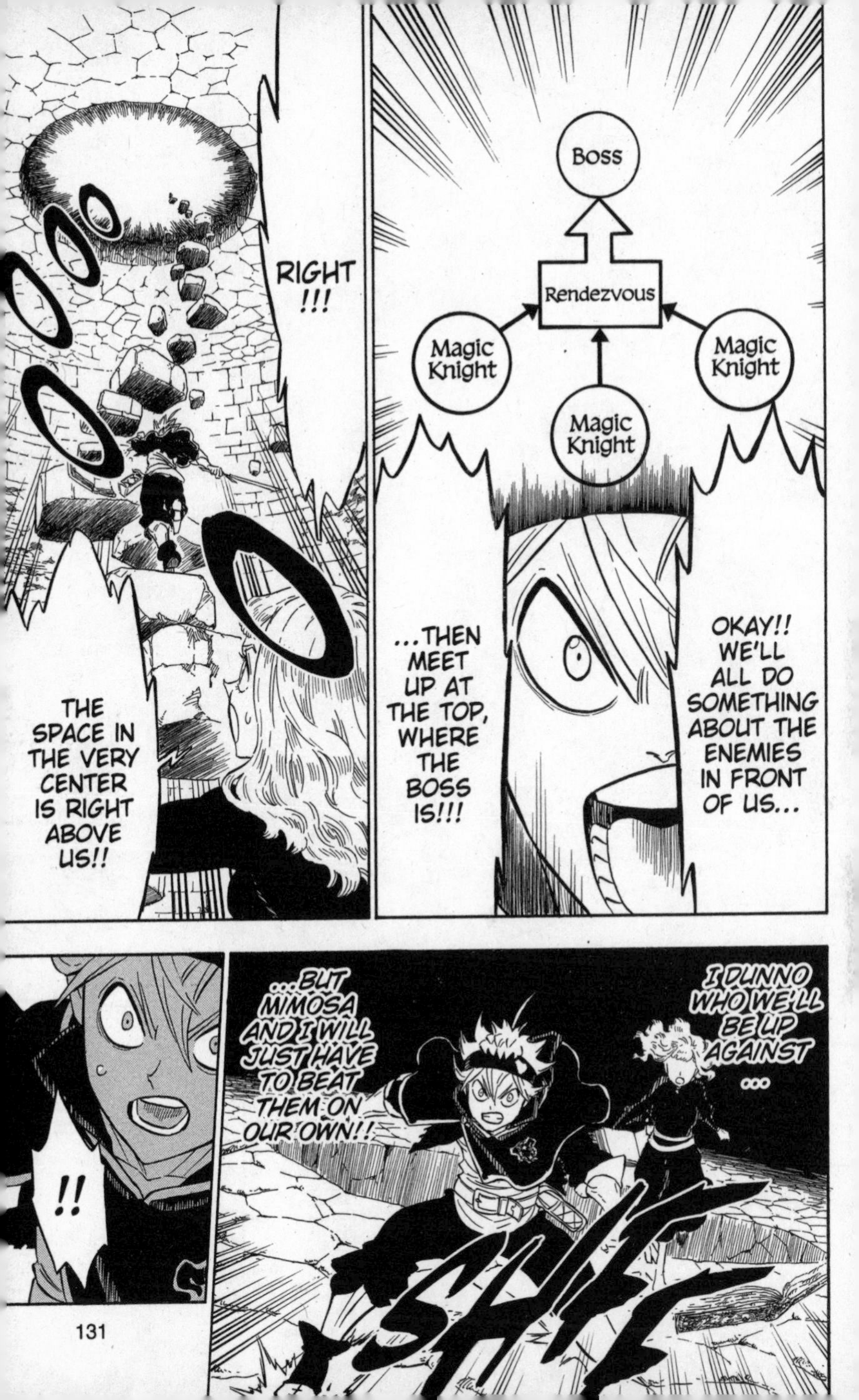
Boss
Rendezvous
Magic Knight
Magic Knight
Magic Knight
OKAY!! WE'LL ALL DO SOMETHING ABOUT THE ENEMIES IN FRONT OF US...
...THEN MEET UP AT THE TOP, WHERE THE BOSS IS!!!
RIGHT !!!
THE SPACE IN THE VERY CENTER IS RIGHT ABOVE US!!
I DUNNO WHO WE'LL BE UP AGAINST...
...BUT MIMOSA AND I WILL JUST HAVE TO BEAT THEM ON OUR OWN!!
SHF
!!

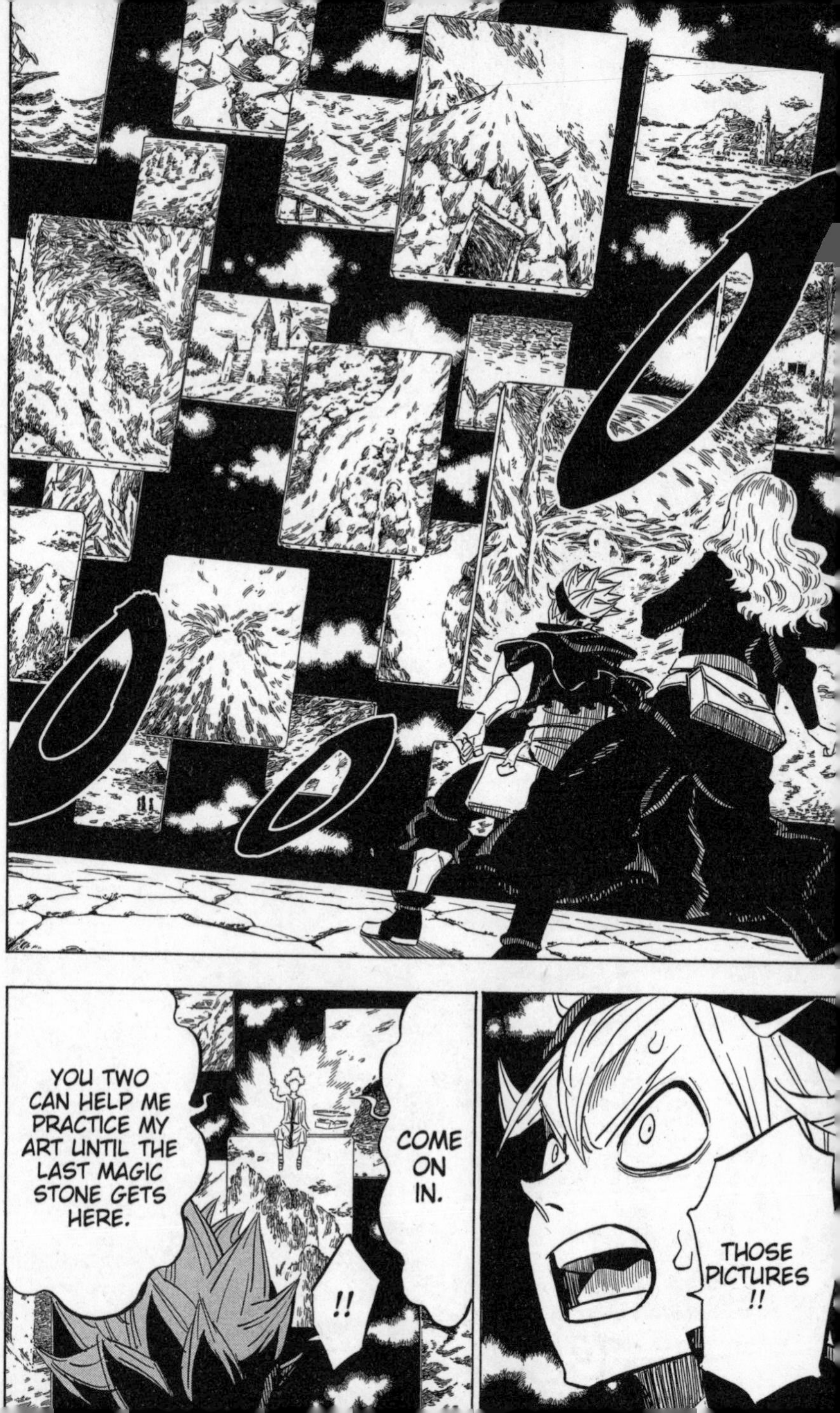
THOSE PICTURES!!
COME ON IN.
YOU TWO CAN HELP ME PRACTICE MY ART UNTIL THE LAST MAGIC STONE GETS HERE.
!!

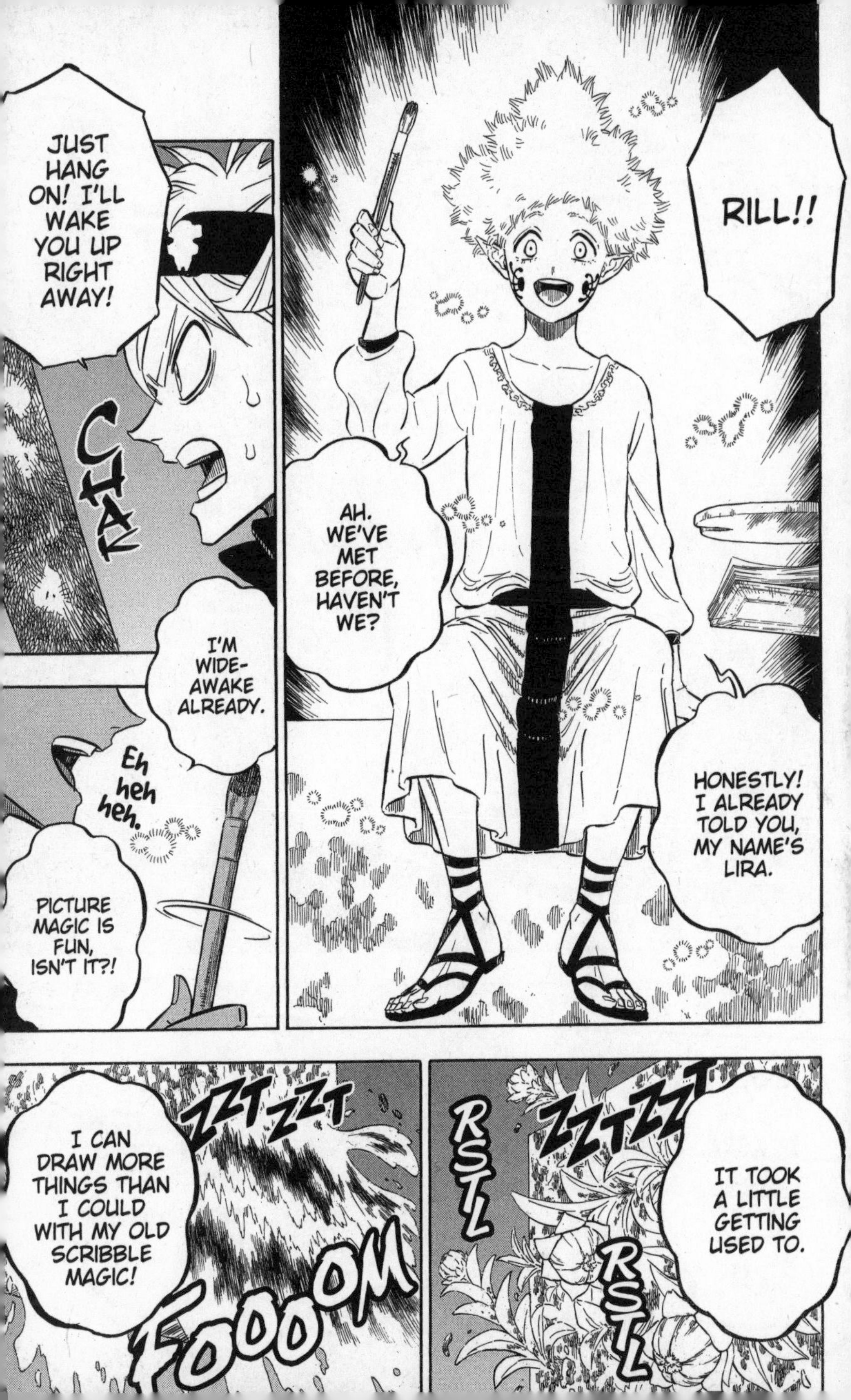
RILL!!
AH. WE'VE MET BEFORE, HAVEN'T WE?
HONESTLY! I ALREADY TOLD YOU, MY NAME'S LIRA.
JUST HANG ON! I'LL WAKE YOU UP RIGHT AWAY!
CHAK
I'M WIDE-AWAKE ALREADY.
Eh heh heh.
PICTURE MAGIC IS FUN, ISN'T IT?!
ZZZTZZT
RSTL
IT TOOK A LITTLE GETTING USED TO.
RSTL
ZZT ZZT
I CAN DRAW MORE THINGS THAN I COULD WITH MY OLD SCRIBBLE MAGIC!
FOOOOM

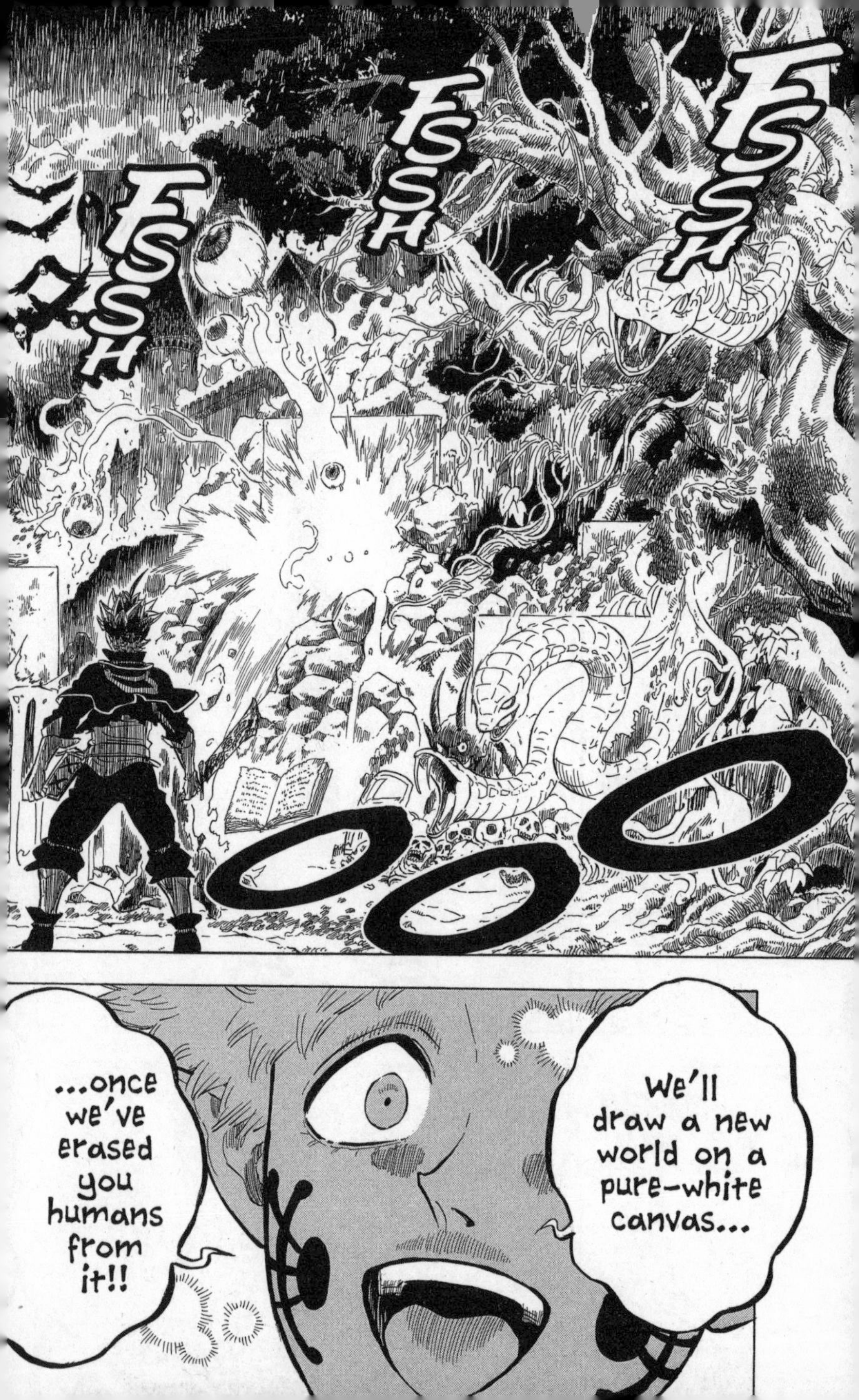
FSSH
FSSH
FSSH
OOO
We'll draw a new world on a pure-white canvas...
...once we've erased you humans from it!!

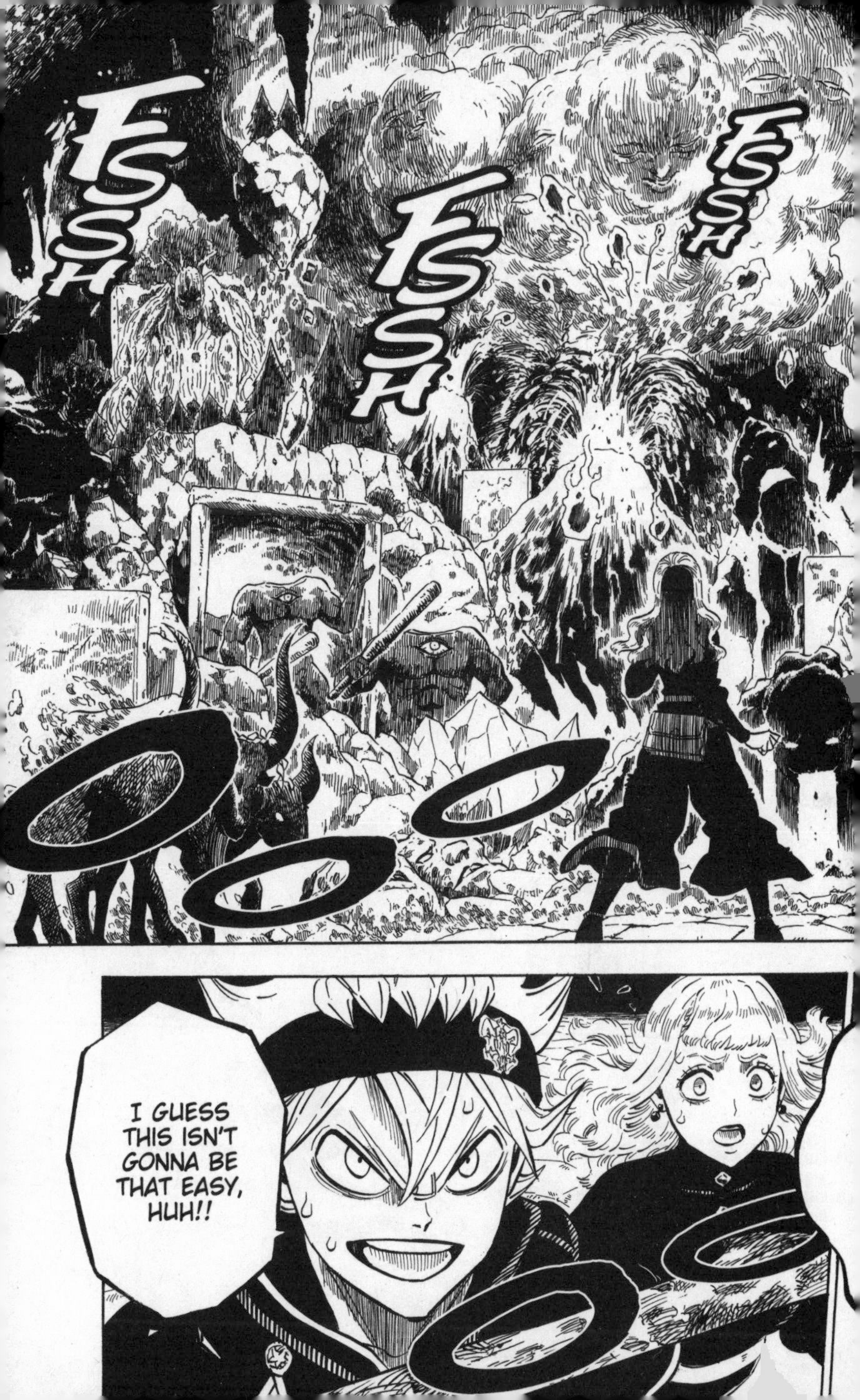
FSSH
FSSH
FSSH
I GUESS THIS ISN'T GONNA BE THAT EASY, HUH!!

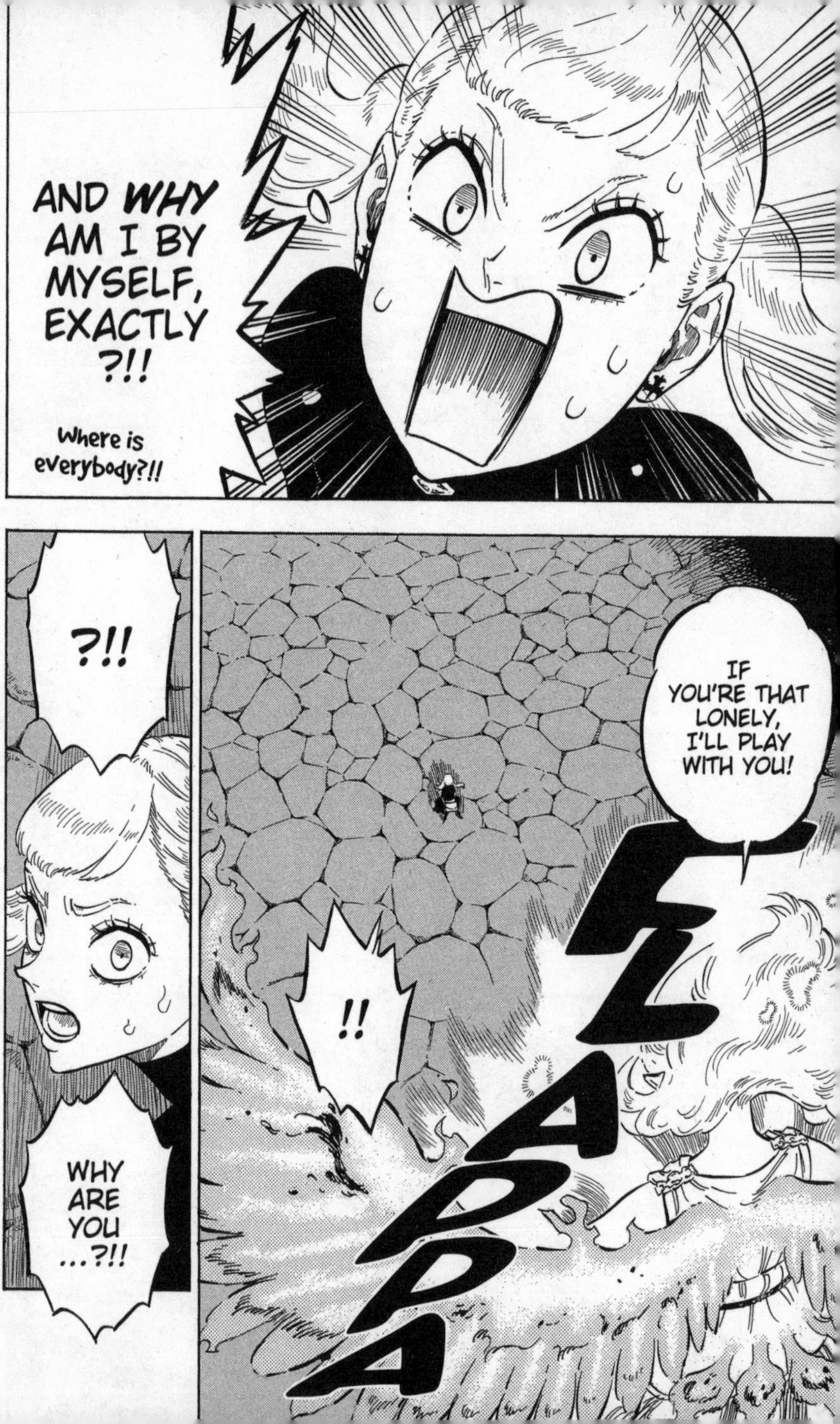
AND WHY AM I BY MYSELF, EXACTLY ?!!
Where is everybody?!!
IF YOU'RE THAT LONELY, I'LL PLAY WITH YOU!
!!
?!!
WHY ARE YOU ...?!!

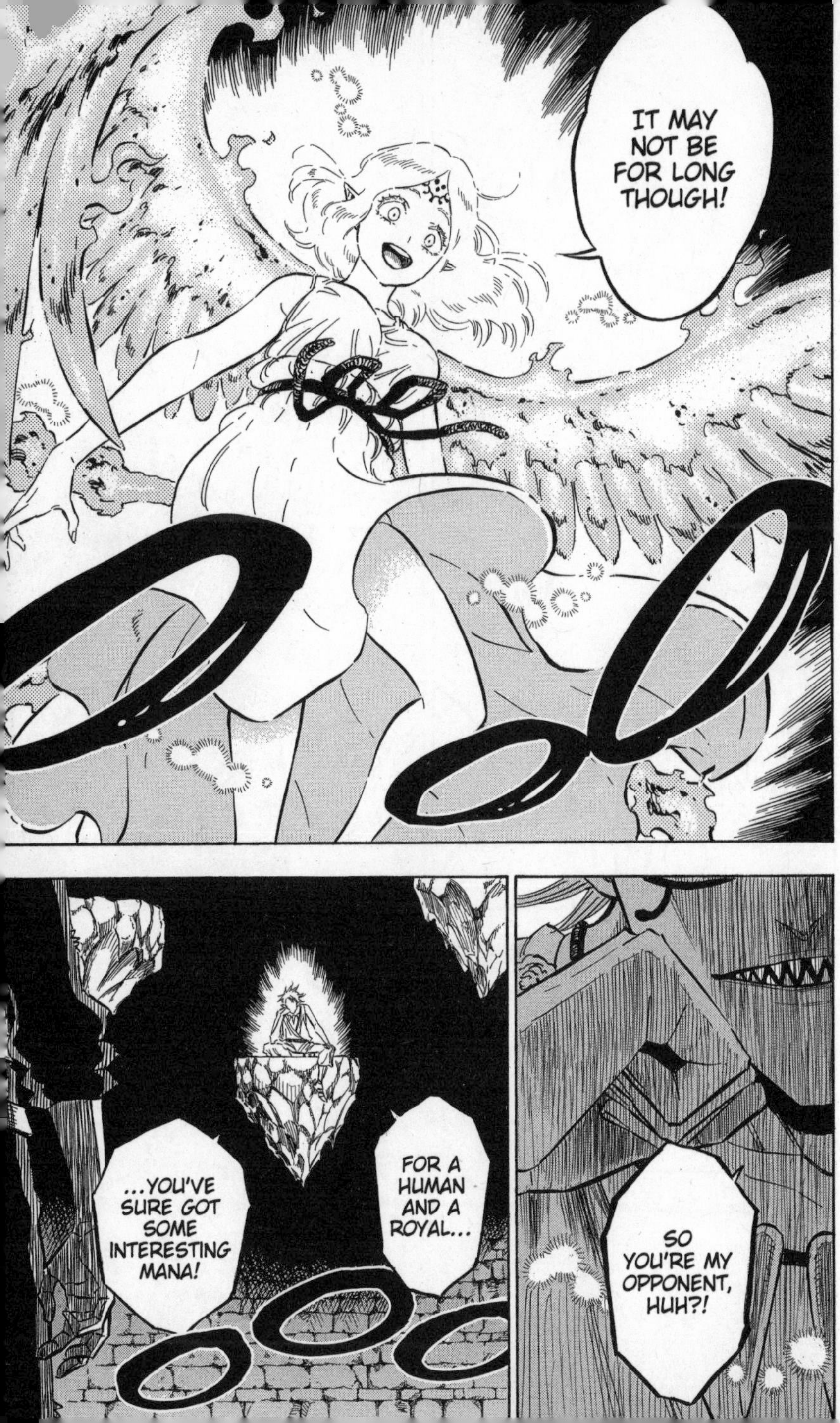
IT MAY NOT BE FOR LONG THOUGH!
SO YOU'RE MY OPPONENT, HUH?!
FOR A HUMAN AND A ROYAL...
...YOU'VE SURE GOT SOME INTERESTING MANA!

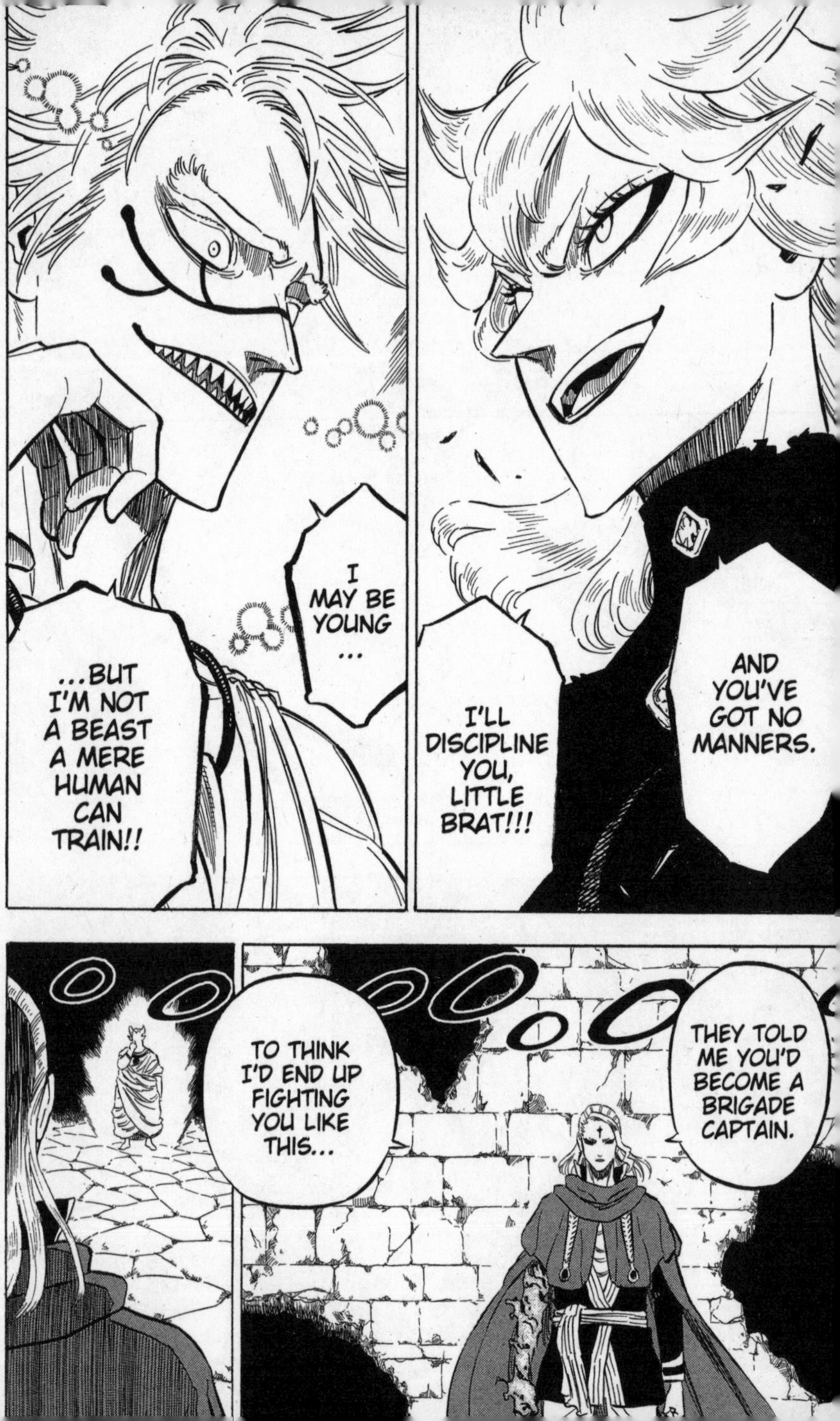
AND YOU'VE GOT NO MANNERS.
I'LL DISCIPLINE YOU, LITTLE BRAT!!!
I MAY BE YOUNG...
...BUT I'M NOT A BEAST A MERE HUMAN CAN TRAIN!!
THEY TOLD ME YOU'D BECOME A BRIGADE CAPTAIN.
TO THINK I'D END UP FIGHTING YOU LIKE THIS...

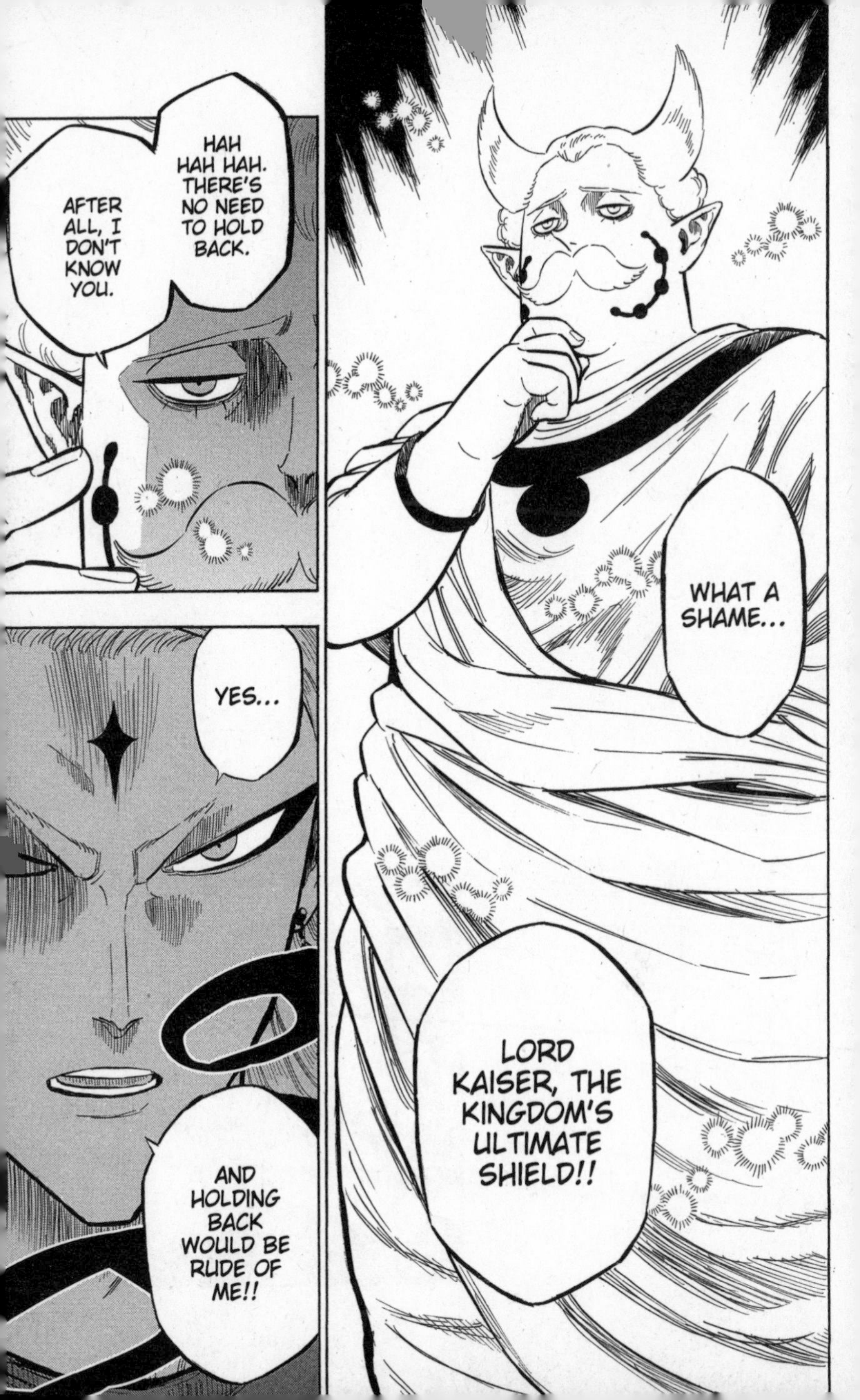
WHAT A SHAME...
LORD KAISER, THE KINGDOM'S ULTIMATE SHIELD!!
HAH HAH HAH. THERE'S NO NEED TO HOLD BACK.
AFTER ALL, I DON'T KNOW YOU.
YES...
AND HOLDING BACK WOULD BE RUDE OF ME!!

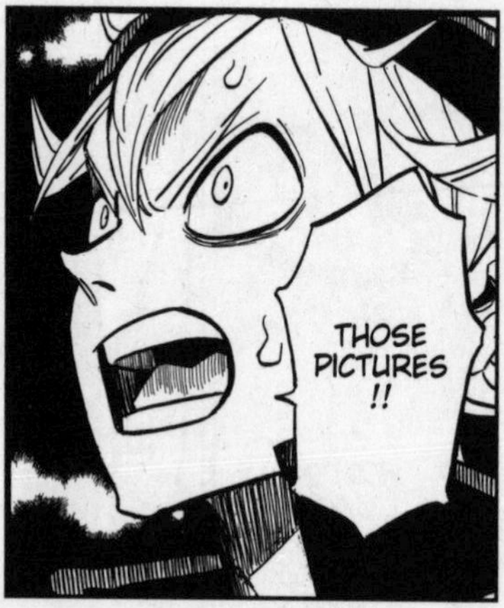
THOSE PICTURES !!

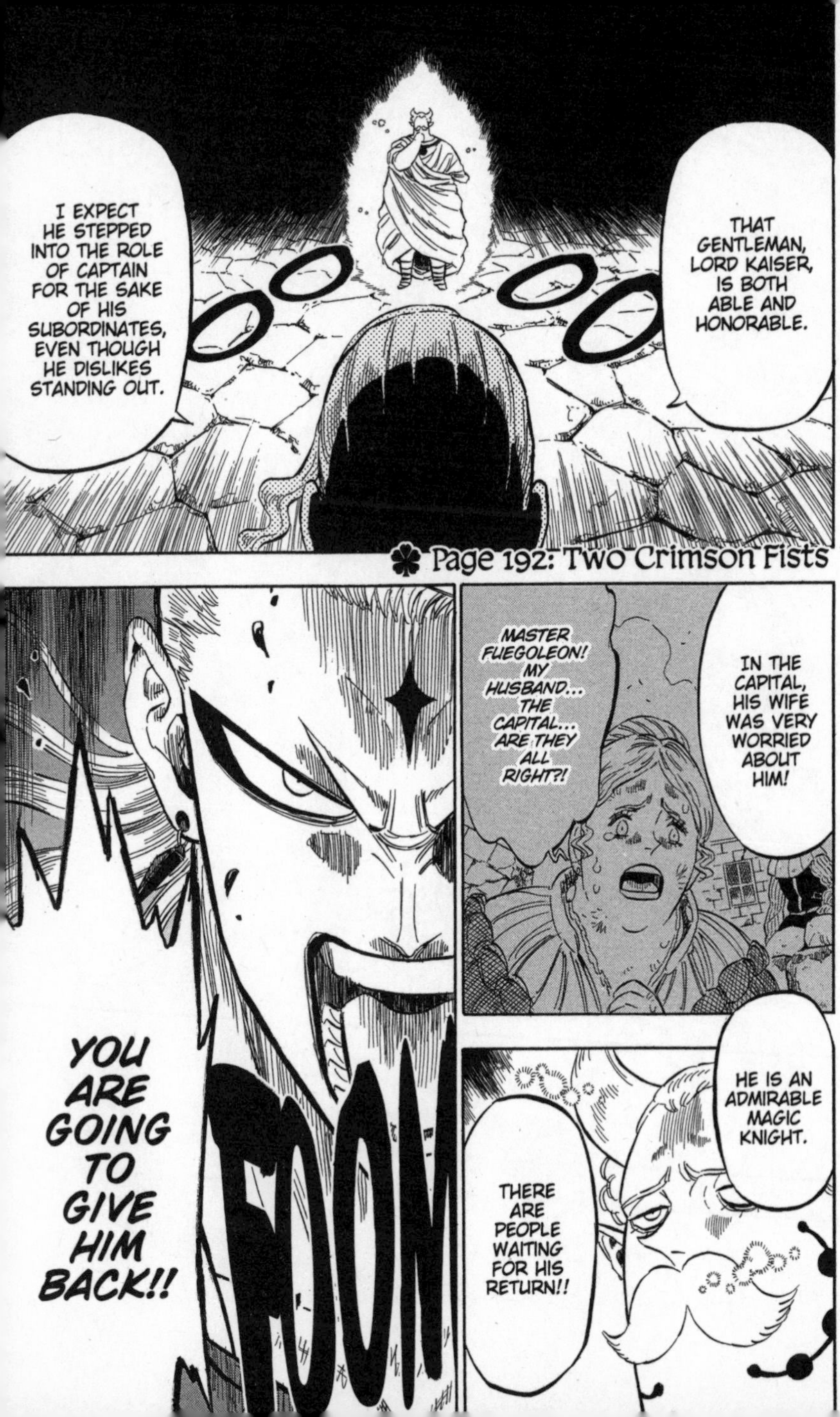
THAT GENTLEMAN, LORD KAISER, IS BOTH ABLE AND HONORABLE.
I EXPECT HE STEPPED INTO THE ROLE OF CAPTAIN FOR THE SAKE OF HIS SUBORDINATES, EVEN THOUGH HE DISLIKES STANDING OUT.
Page 192: Two Crimson Fists
IN THE CAPITAL, HIS WIFE WAS VERY WORRIED ABOUT HIM!
MASTER FUEGOLEON! MY HUSBAND... THE CAPITAL... ARE THEY ALL RIGHT?!
HE IS AN ADMIRABLE MAGIC KNIGHT.
THERE ARE PEOPLE WAITING FOR HIS RETURN!!
YOU ARE GOING TO GIVE HIM BACK!!
FOOM

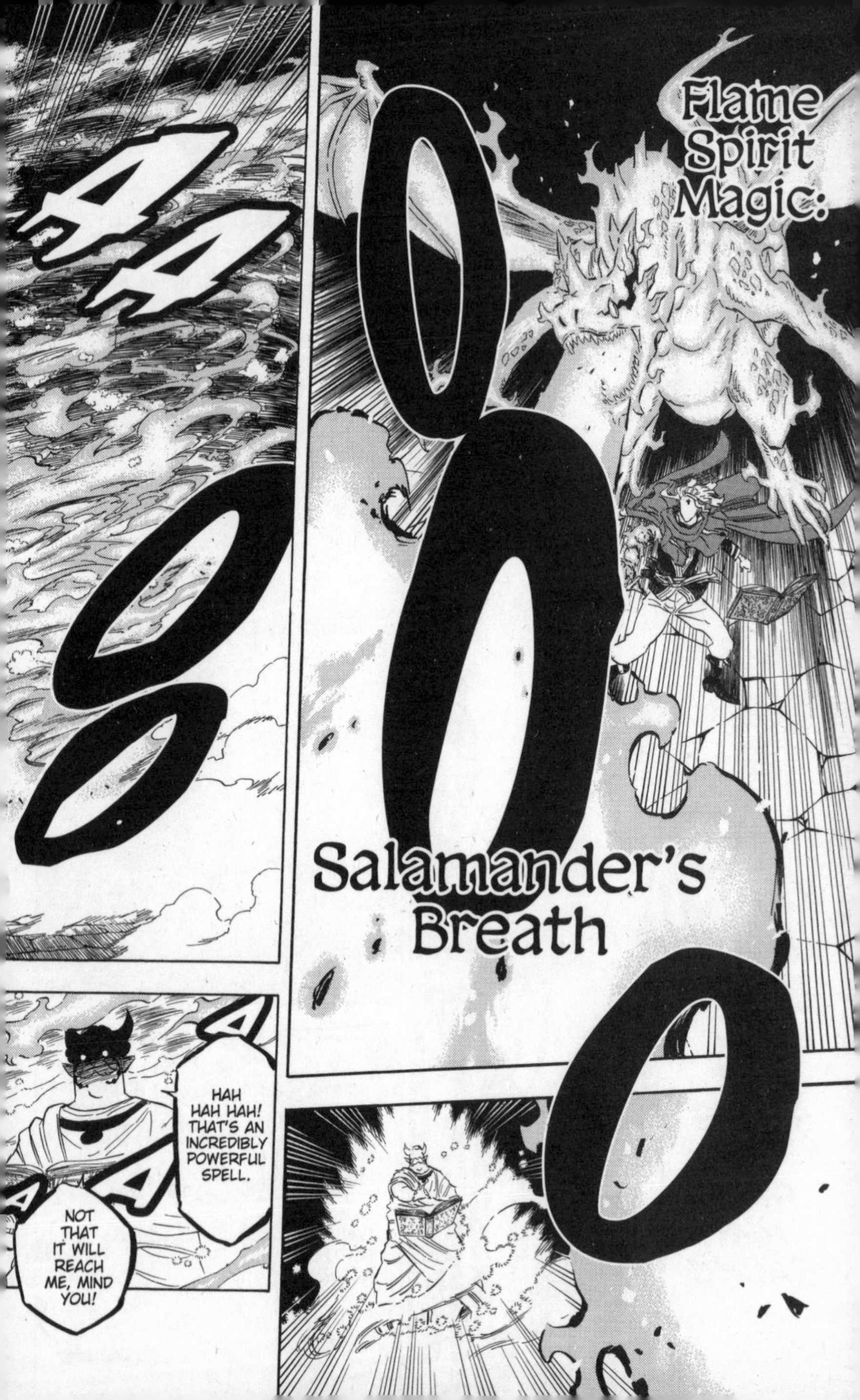
Flame Spirit Magic:
Salamander's Breath
HAH HAH HAH! THAT'S AN INCREDIBLY POWERFUL SPELL.
NOT THAT IT WILL REACH ME, MIND YOU!

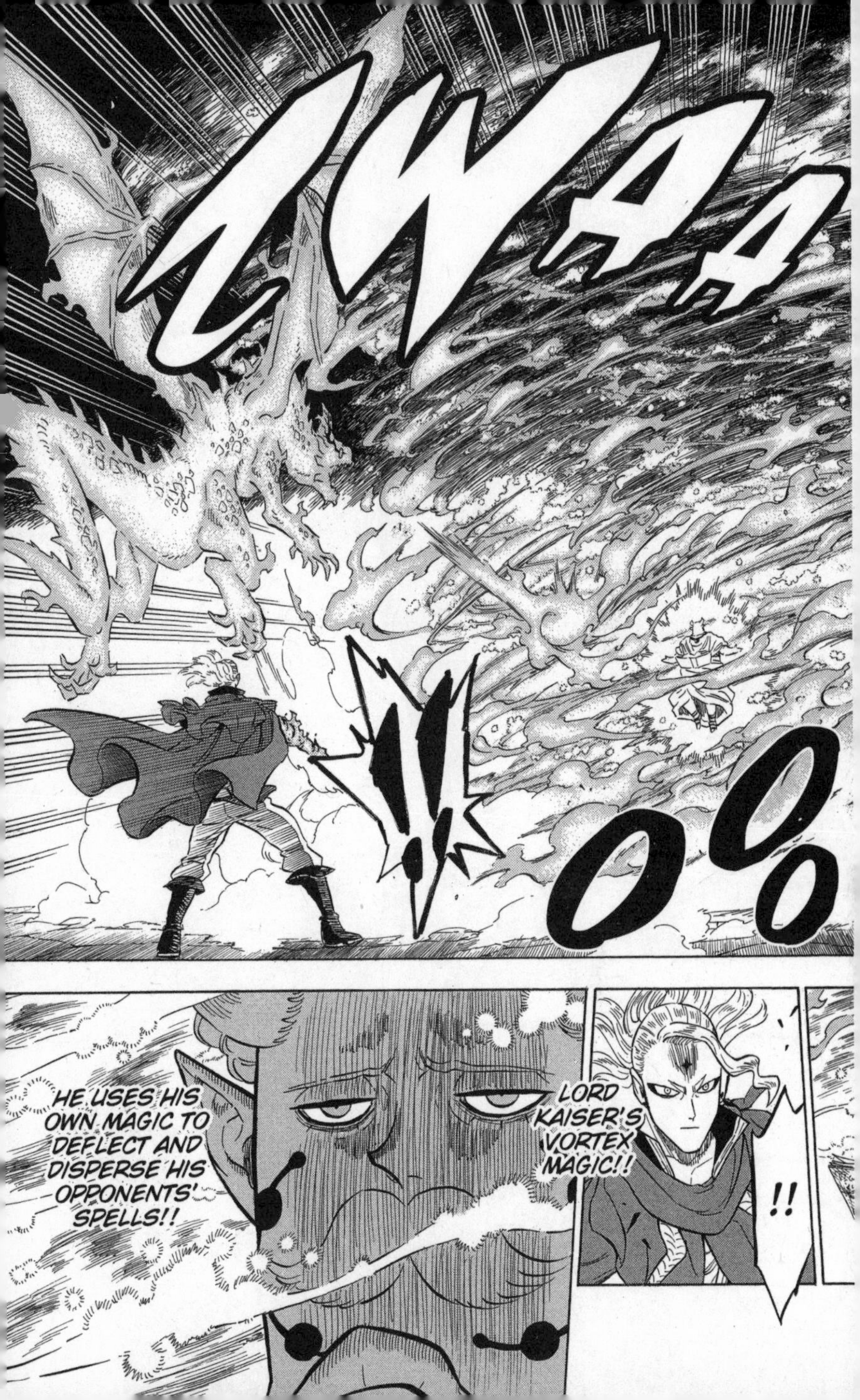

ZWAA
LORD KAISER'S VORTEX MAGIC!!
!!
HE USES HIS OWN MAGIC TO DEFLECT AND DISPERSE HIS OPPONENTS' SPELLS!!

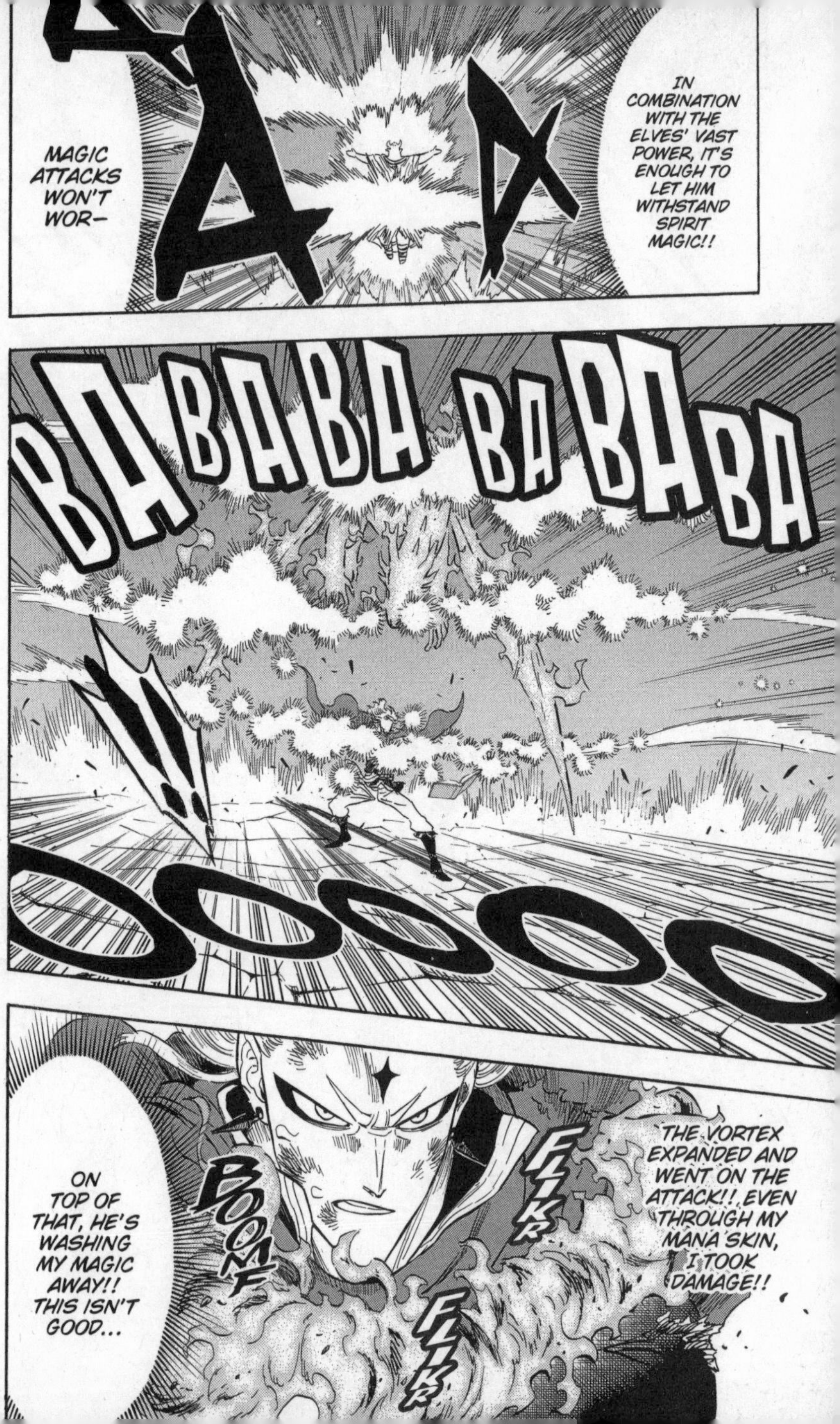
IN COMBINATION WITH THE ELVES' VAST POWER, IT'S ENOUGH TO LET HIM WITHSTAND SPIRIT MAGIC!!
MAGIC ATTACKS WON'T WOR—
BA BA BA BA BA BA BA
!!
THE VORTEX EXPANDED AND WENT ON THE ATTACK!! EVEN THROUGH MY MANA SKIN, I TOOK DAMAGE!!
FLIKR
FLIKR
BOOMF
ON TOP OF THAT, HE'S WASHING MY MAGIC AWAY!! THIS ISN'T GOOD...

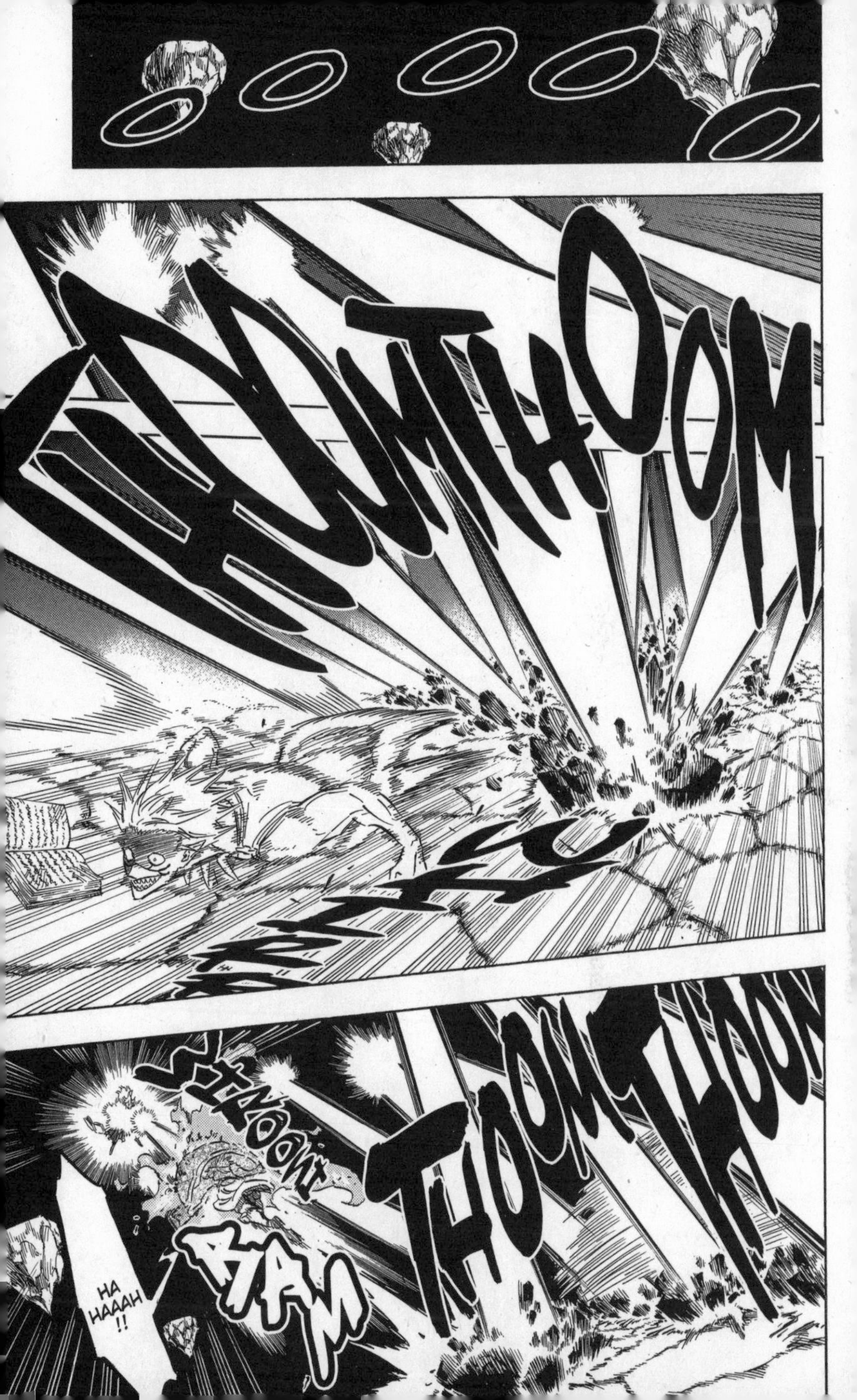
THOOM THOOM
BAM
HA HAAAH !!

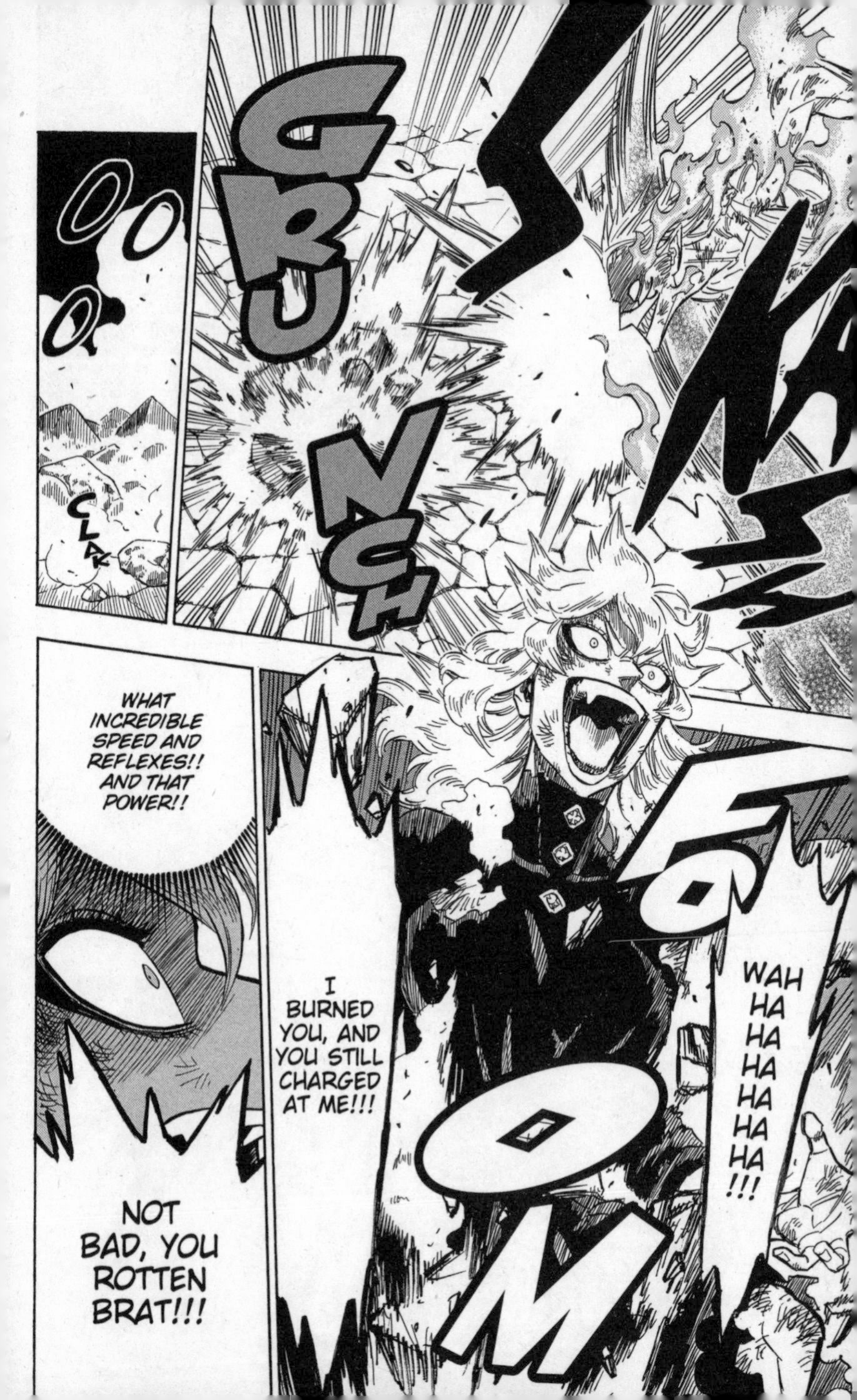
GRUNCH
OOOO
CLAK
WAH HA HA HA HA HA HA HA!!!
I BURNED YOU, AND YOU STILL CHARGED AT ME!!!
FOOM
WHAT INCREDIBLE SPEED AND REFLEXES!! AND THAT POWER!!
NOT BAD, YOU ROTTEN BRAT!!!

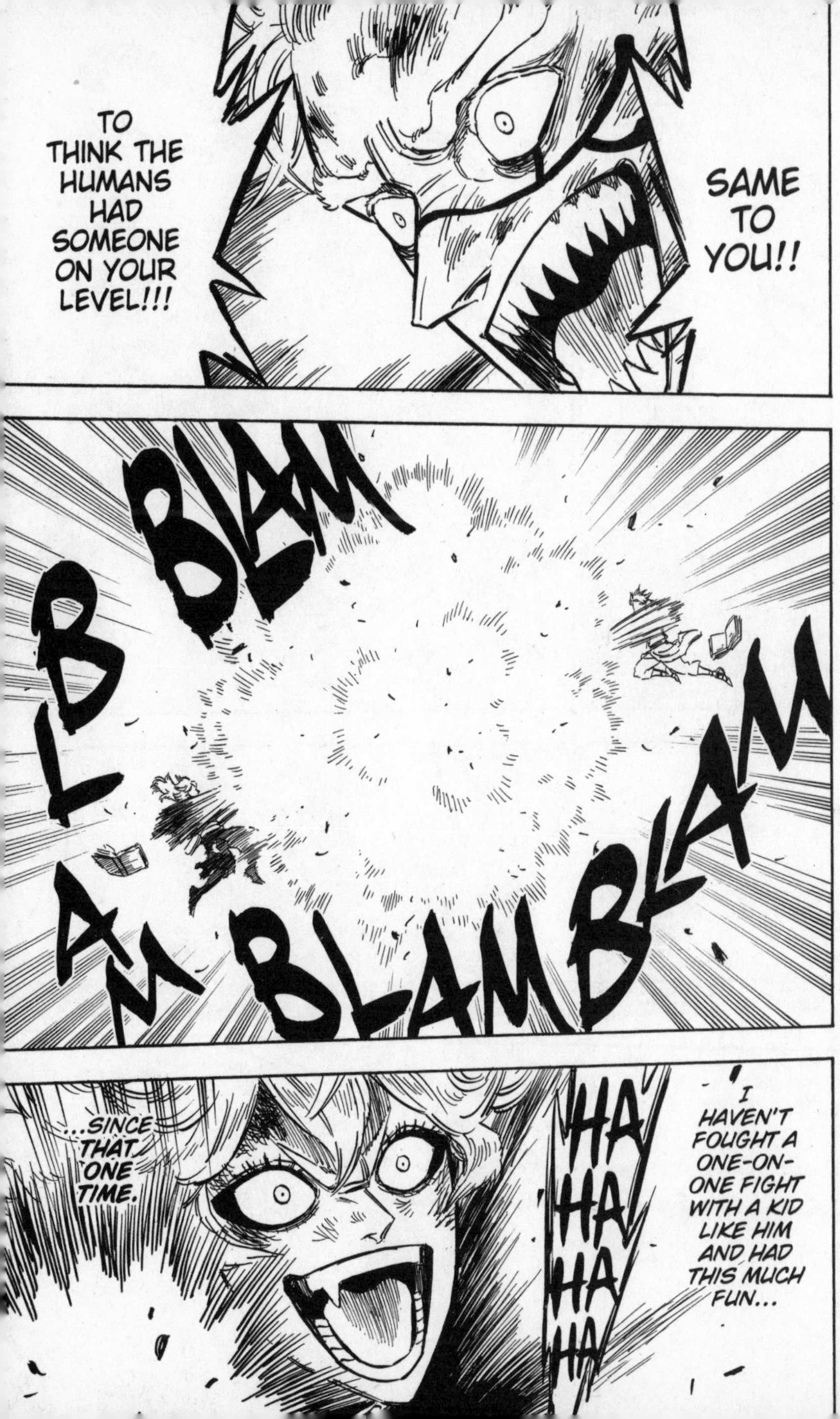
TO THINK THE HUMANS HAD SOMEONE ON YOUR LEVEL!!!
SAME TO YOU!!
BLAM
BLAM
BLAM
BLAM
I HAVEN'T FOUGHT A ONE-ON-ONE FIGHT WITH A KID LIKE HIM AND HAD THIS MUCH FUN...
HA HA HA HA HA
...SINCE THAT ONE TIME.

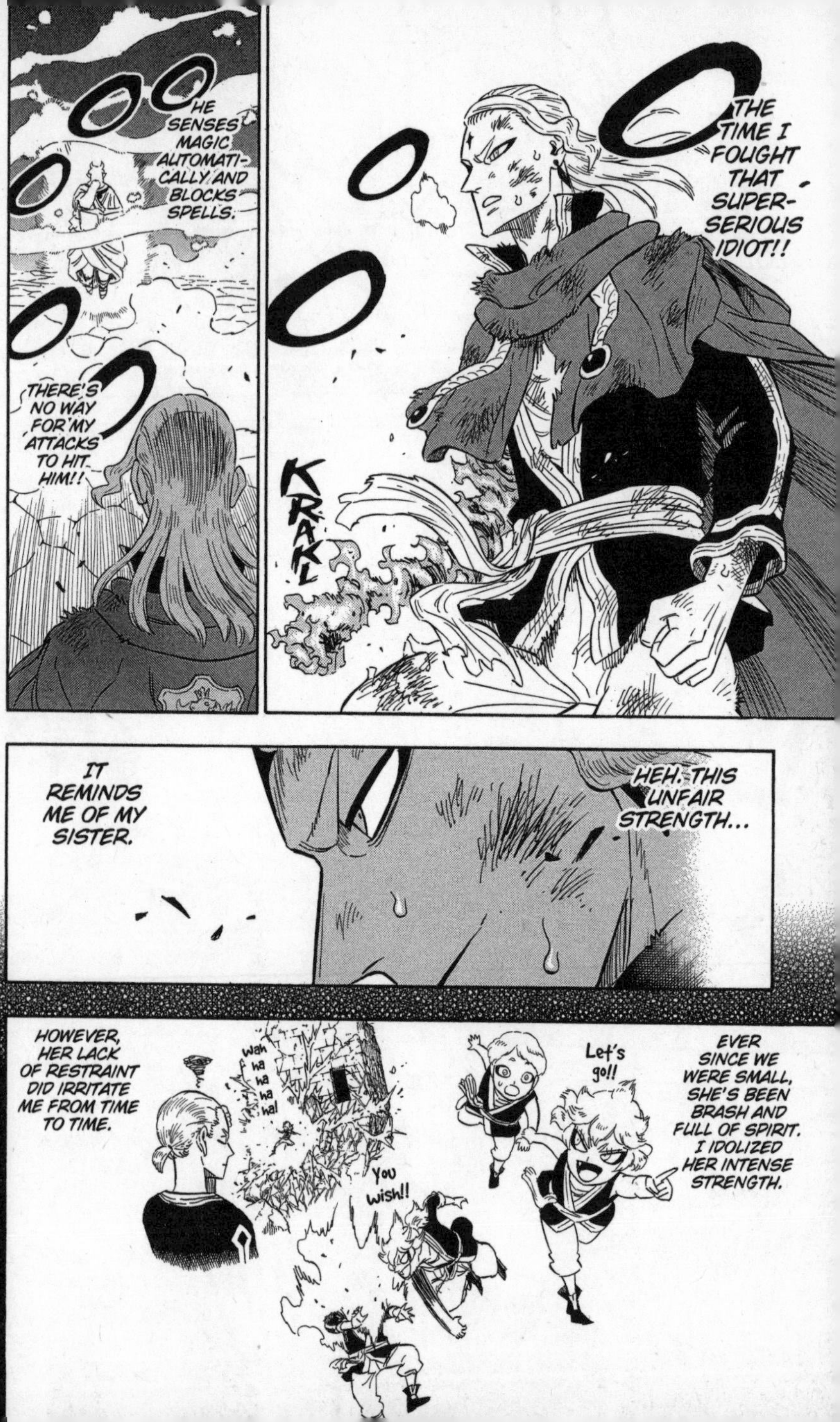
THE TIME I FOUGHT THAT SUPER-SERIOUS IDIOT!!
KRAKL
HE SENSES MAGIC AUTOMATICALLY AND BLOCKS SPELLS.
THERE'S NO WAY FOR MY ATTACKS TO HIT HIM!!
HEH. THIS UNFAIR STRENGTH...
IT REMINDS ME OF MY SISTER.
EVER SINCE WE WERE SMALL, SHE'S BEEN BRASH AND FULL OF SPIRIT. I IDOLIZED HER INTENSE STRENGTH.
Let's go!!
You wish!!
Wah ha ha ha ha!
HOWEVER, HER LACK OF RESTRAINT DID IRRITATE ME FROM TIME TO TIME.

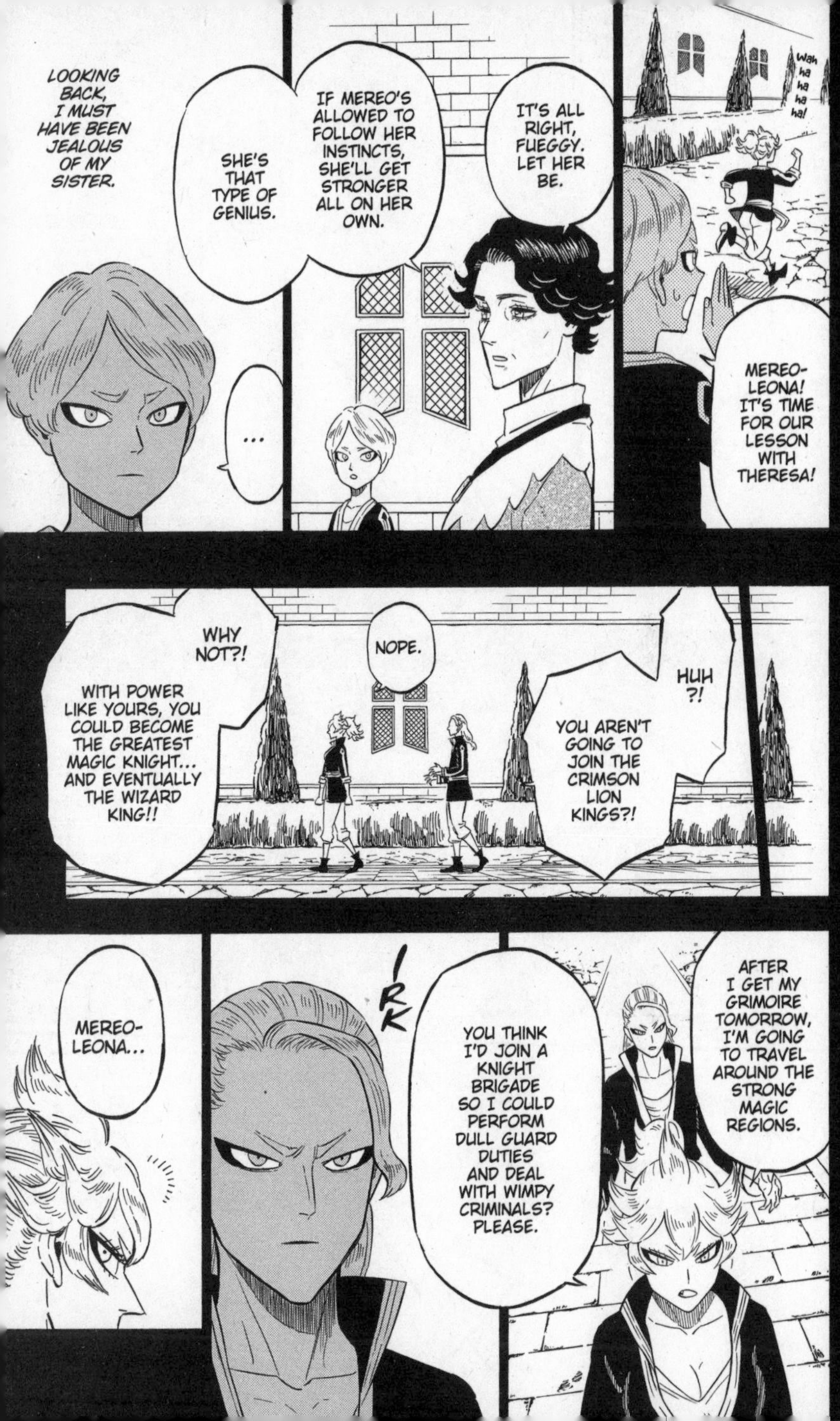
Wah ha ha ha ha!
MEREO-LEONA! IT'S TIME FOR OUR LESSON WITH THERESA!
IT'S ALL RIGHT, FUEGGY. LET HER BE.
IF MEREO'S ALLOWED TO FOLLOW HER INSTINCTS, SHE'LL GET STRONGER ALL ON HER OWN.
SHE'S THAT TYPE OF GENIUS.
...
LOOKING BACK, I MUST HAVE BEEN JEALOUS OF MY SISTER.
HUH?!
YOU AREN'T GOING TO JOIN THE CRIMSON LION KINGS?!
NOPE.
WHY NOT?!
WITH POWER LIKE YOURS, YOU COULD BECOME THE GREATEST MAGIC KNIGHT... AND EVENTUALLY THE WIZARD KING!!
AFTER I GET MY GRIMOIRE TOMORROW, I'M GOING TO TRAVEL AROUND THE STRONG MAGIC REGIONS.
YOU THINK I'D JOIN A KNIGHT BRIGADE SO I COULD PERFORM DULL GUARD DUTIES AND DEAL WITH WIMPY CRIMINALS? PLEASE.
IRK
MEREO-LEONA...

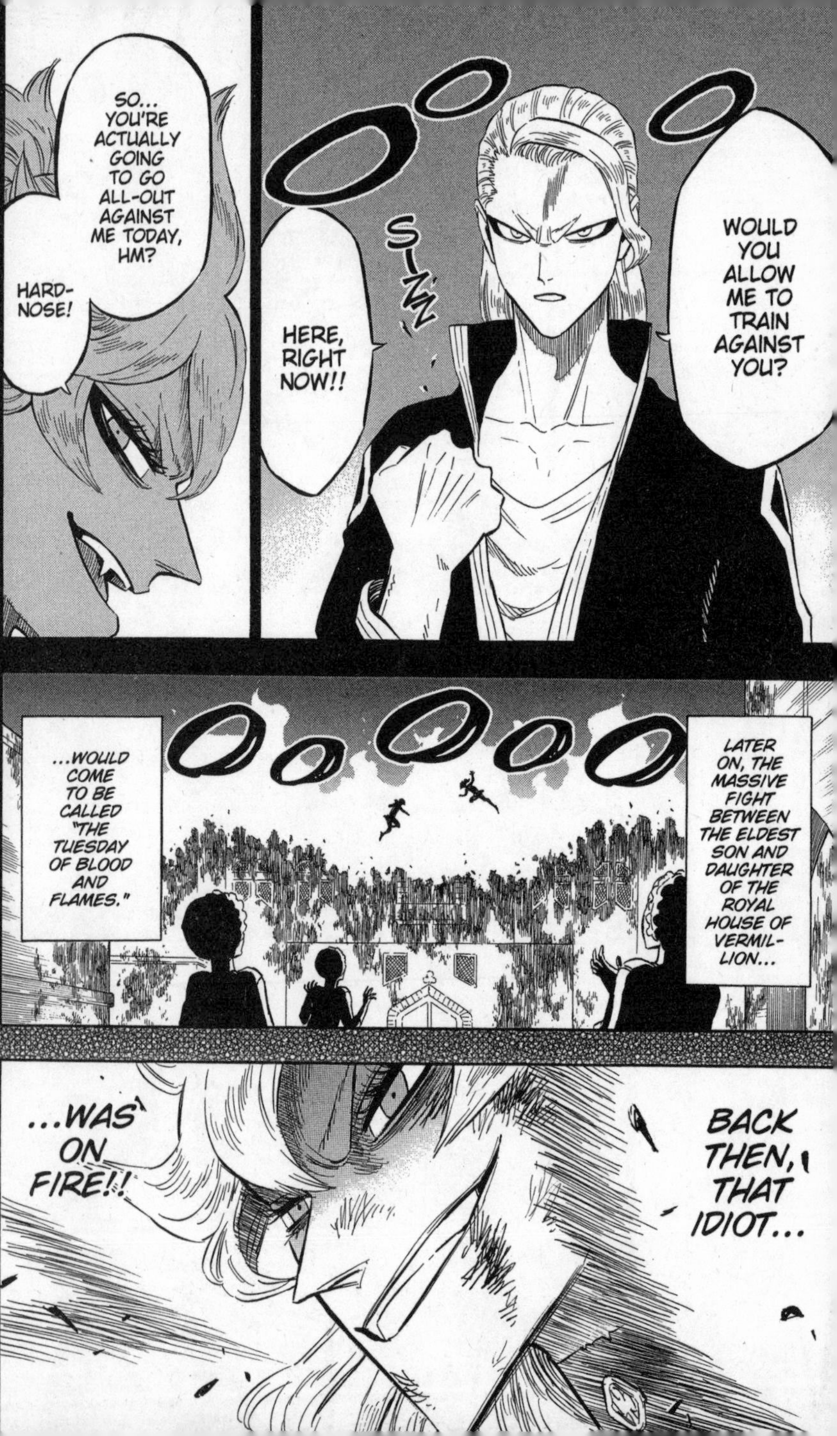
WOULD YOU ALLOW ME TO TRAIN AGAINST YOU?
SIZZ
HERE, RIGHT NOW!!
SO... YOU'RE ACTUALLY GOING TO GO ALL-OUT AGAINST ME TODAY, HM?
HARD-NOSE!
LATER ON, THE MASSIVE FIGHT BETWEEN THE ELDEST SON AND DAUGHTER OF THE ROYAL HOUSE OF VERMIL-LION...
...WOULD COME TO BE CALLED "THE TUESDAY OF BLOOD AND FLAMES."
BACK THEN, THAT IDIOT...
...WAS ON FIRE!!

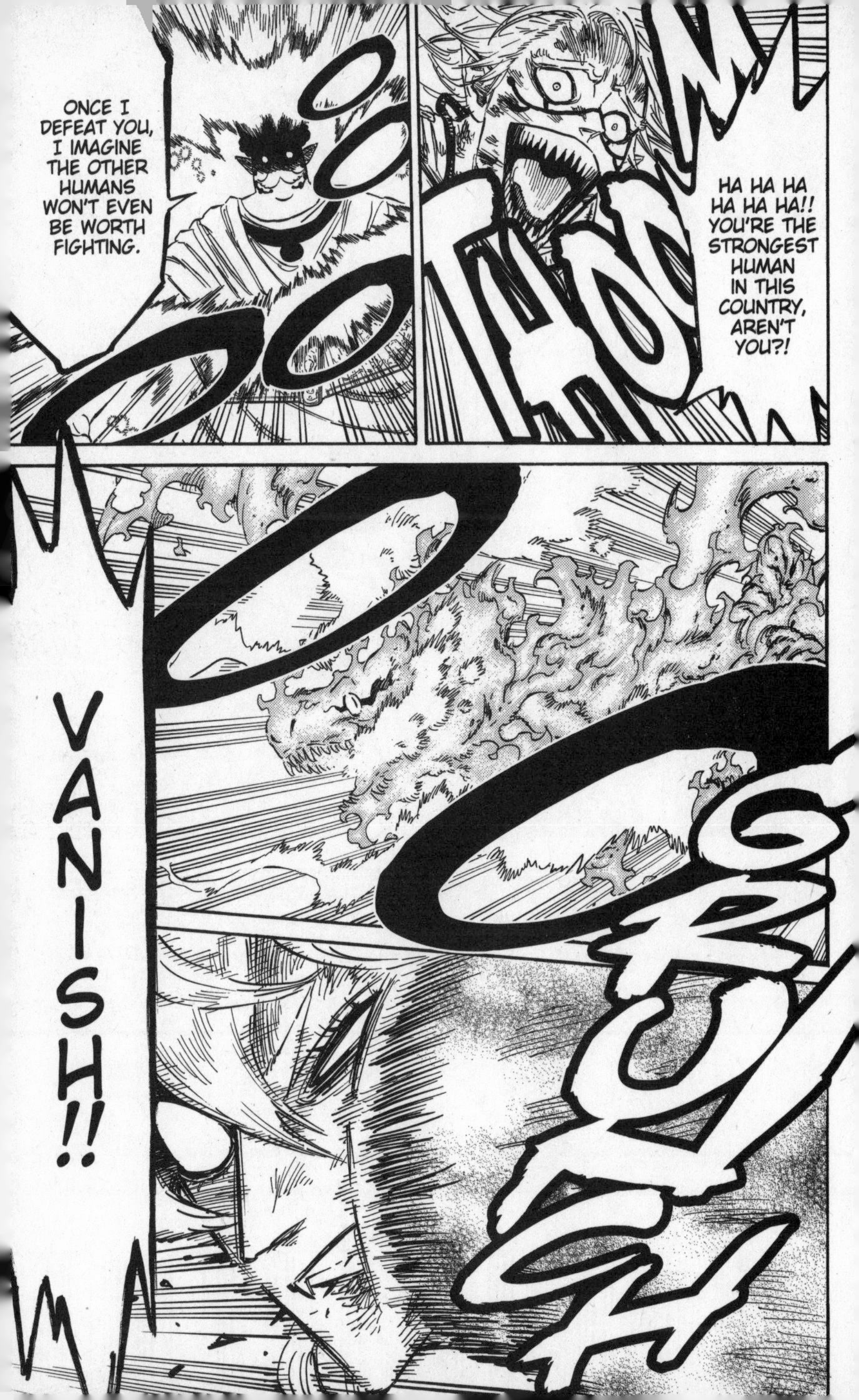
HA HA HA HA HA HA!! YOU'RE THE STRONGEST HUMAN IN THIS COUNTRY, AREN'T YOU?!
ONCE I DEFEAT YOU, I IMAGINE THE OTHER HUMANS WON'T EVEN BE WORTH FIGHTING.
VANISH!!

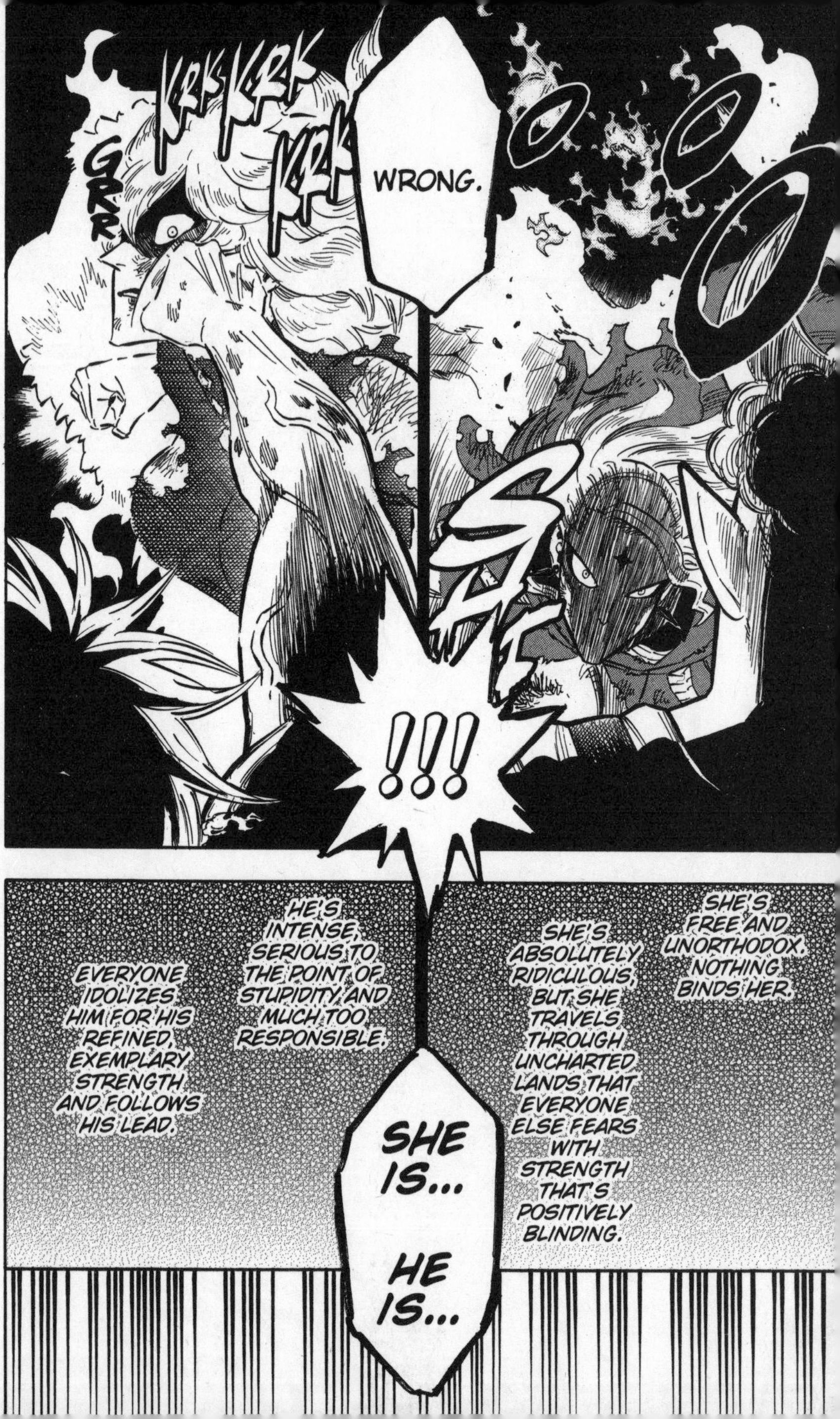
WRONG.
KRK KRK
KRK
GRRR
!!!
SHE'S FREE AND UNORTHODOX. NOTHING BINDS HER.
SHE'S ABSOLUTELY RIDICULOUS, BUT SHE TRAVELS THROUGH UNCHARTED LANDS THAT EVERYONE ELSE FEARS WITH STRENGTH THAT'S POSITIVELY BLINDING.
SHE IS...
HE'S INTENSE, SERIOUS TO THE POINT OF STUPIDITY AND MUCH TOO RESPONSIBLE.
EVERYONE IDOLIZES HIM FOR HIS REFINED, EXEMPLARY STRENGTH AND FOLLOWS HIS LEAD.
HE IS...

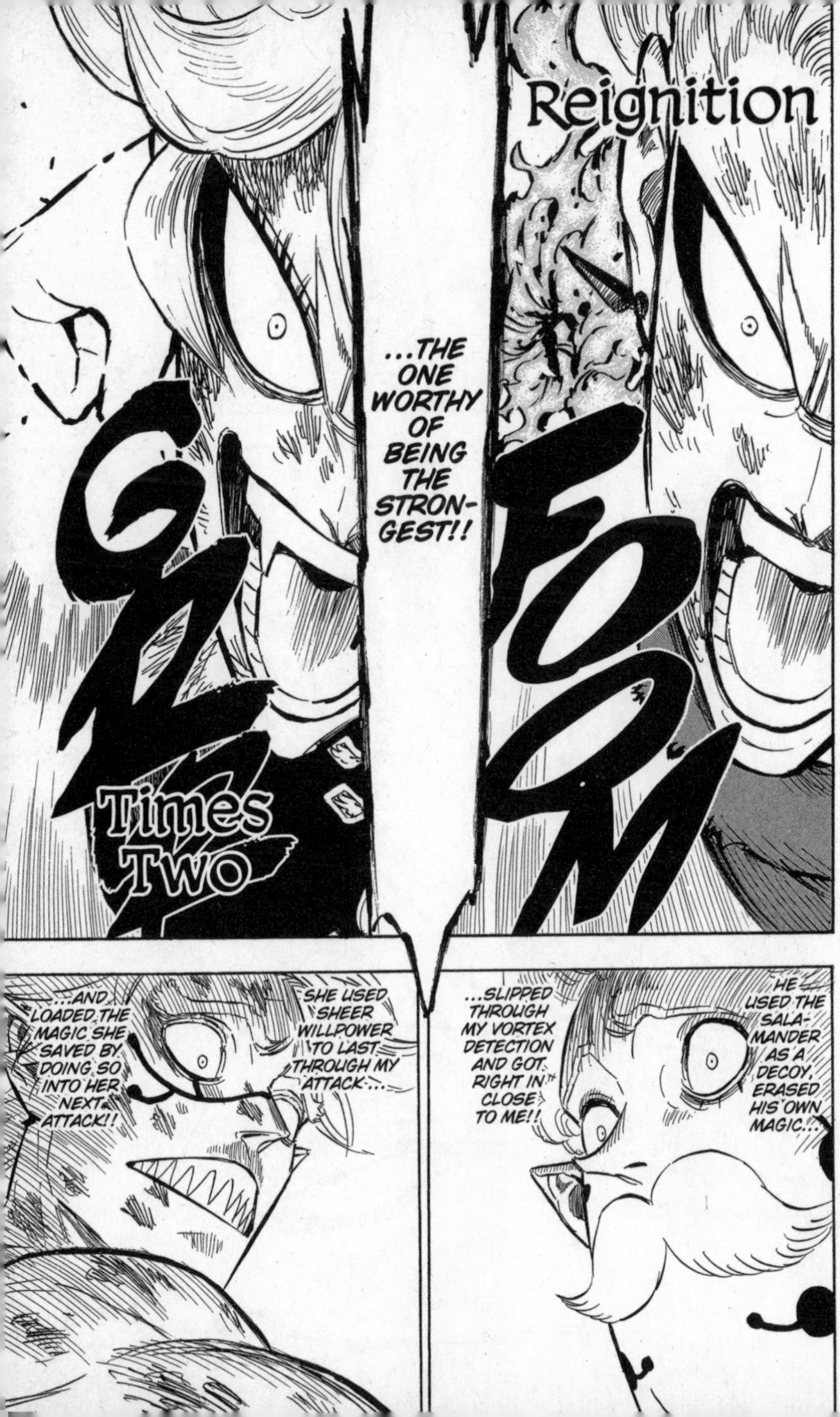
Reignition
...THE ONE WORTHY OF BEING THE STRONGEST!!
Times Two
HE USED THE SALAMANDER AS A DECOY, ERASED HIS OWN MAGIC...
...SLIPPED THROUGH MY VORTEX DETECTION AND GOT RIGHT IN CLOSE TO ME!!
SHE USED SHEER WILLPOWER TO LAST THROUGH MY ATTACK...
...AND LOADED THE MAGIC SHE SAVED BY DOING SO INTO HER NEXT ATTACK!!

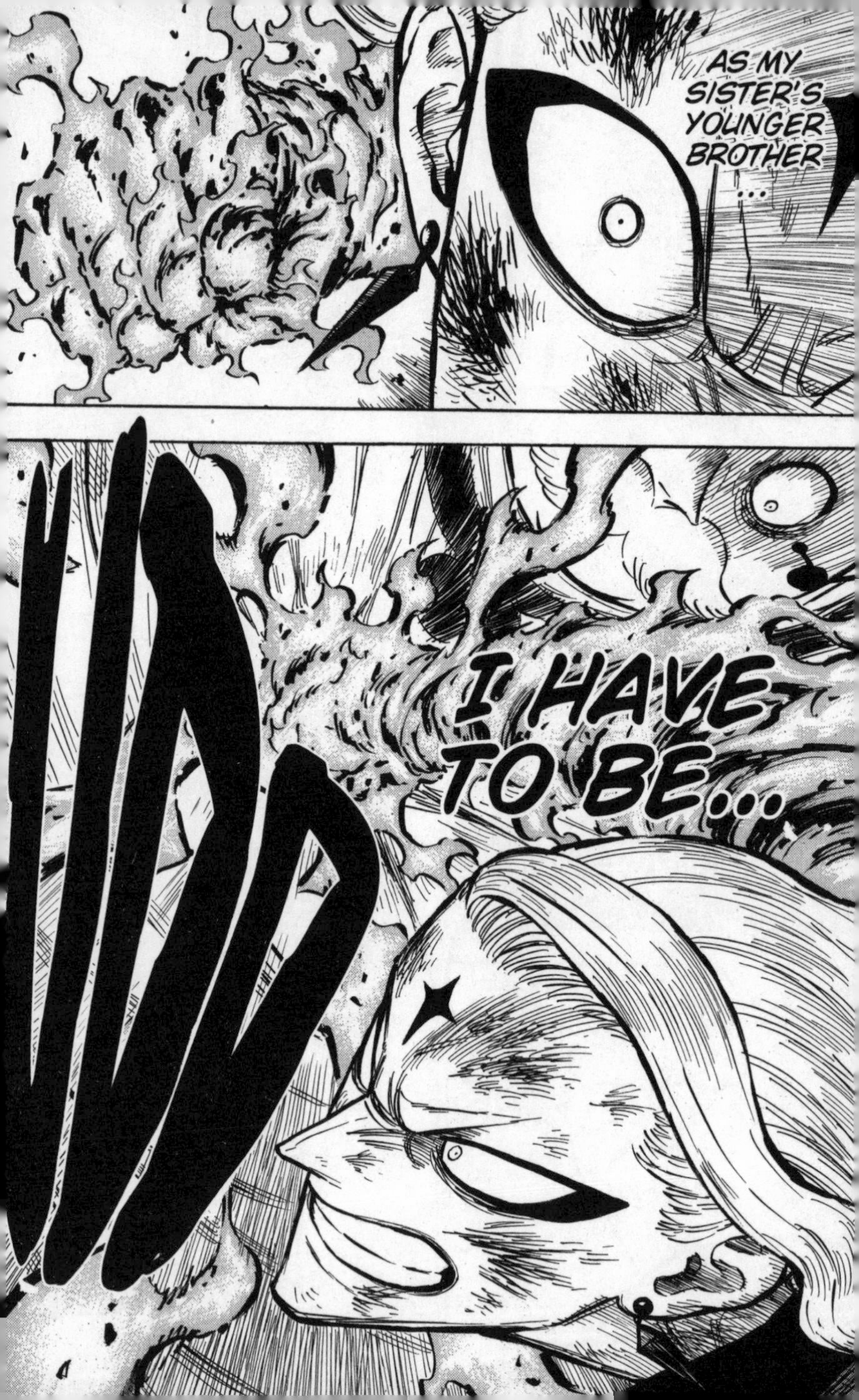
AS MY SISTER'S YOUNGER BROTHER...
I HAVE TO BE...

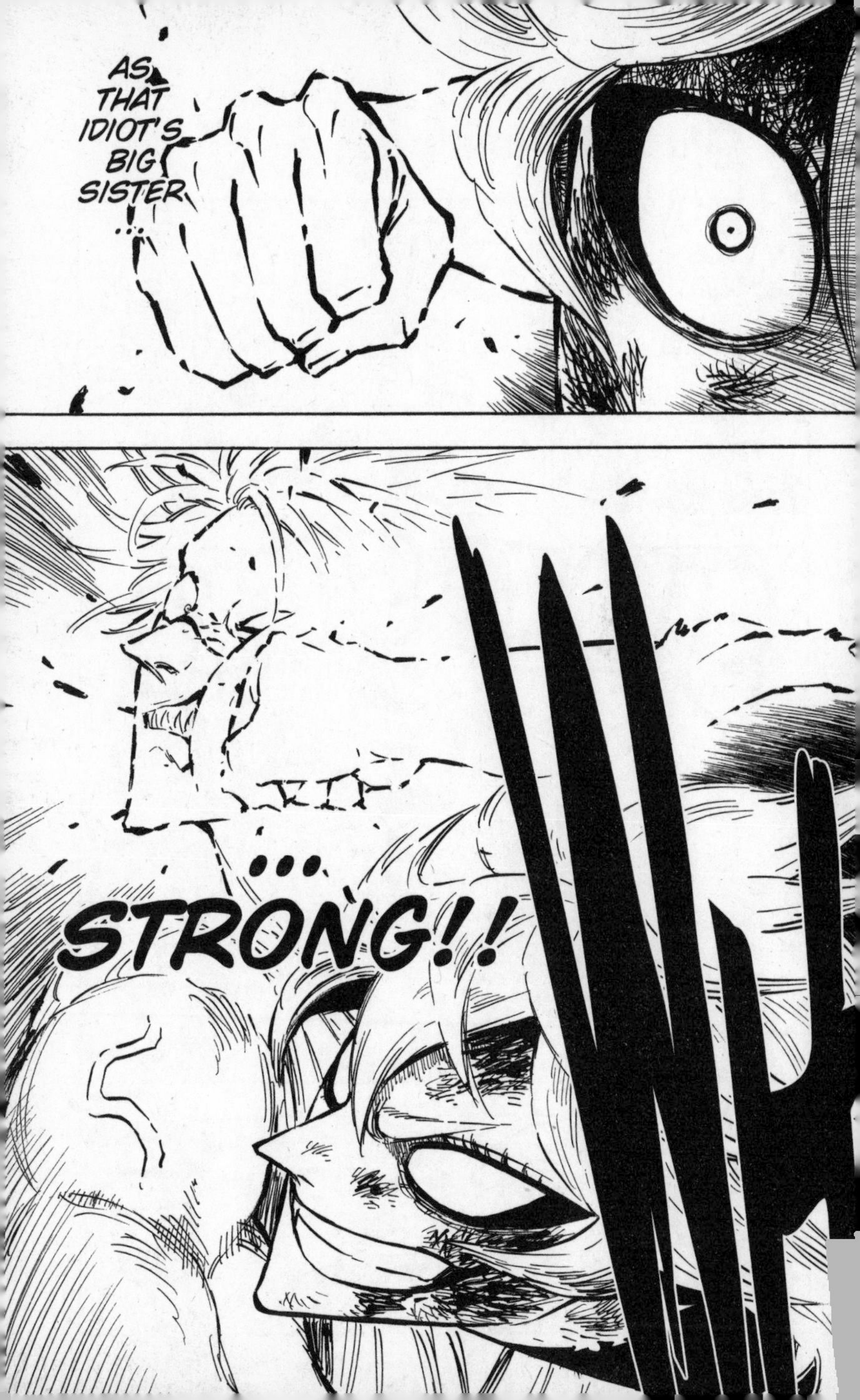
AS THAT IDIOT'S BIG SISTER ...
...STRONG!!

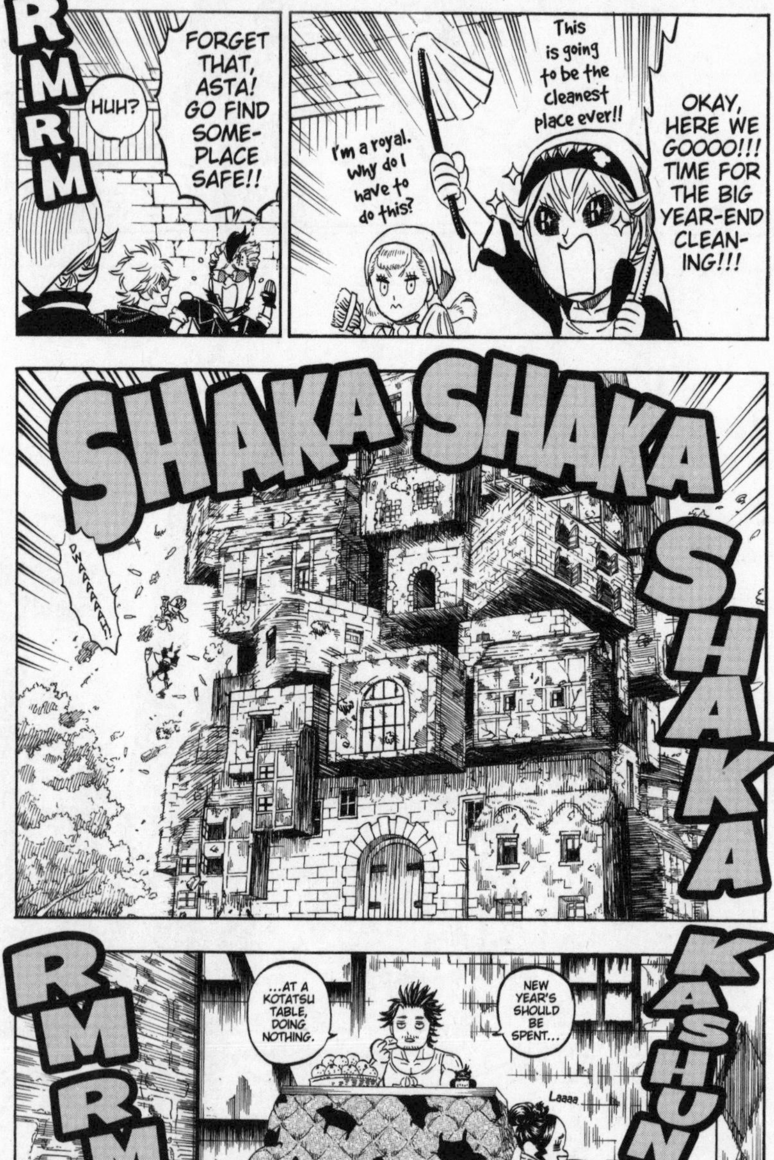
OKAY, HERE WE GOOOO!!! TIME FOR THE BIG YEAR-END CLEAN-ING!!!
This is going to be the cleanest place ever!!
I'm a royal. why do I have to do this?
FORGET THAT, ASTA! GO FIND SOME-PLACE SAFE!!
HUH?
RMRM
SHAKA SHAKA
SHAKA
DWAAAAAAH!!
KASHUNK
NEW YEAR'S SHOULD BE SPENT...
...AT A KOTATSU TABLE, DOING NOTHING.
Laaaa
RMRM

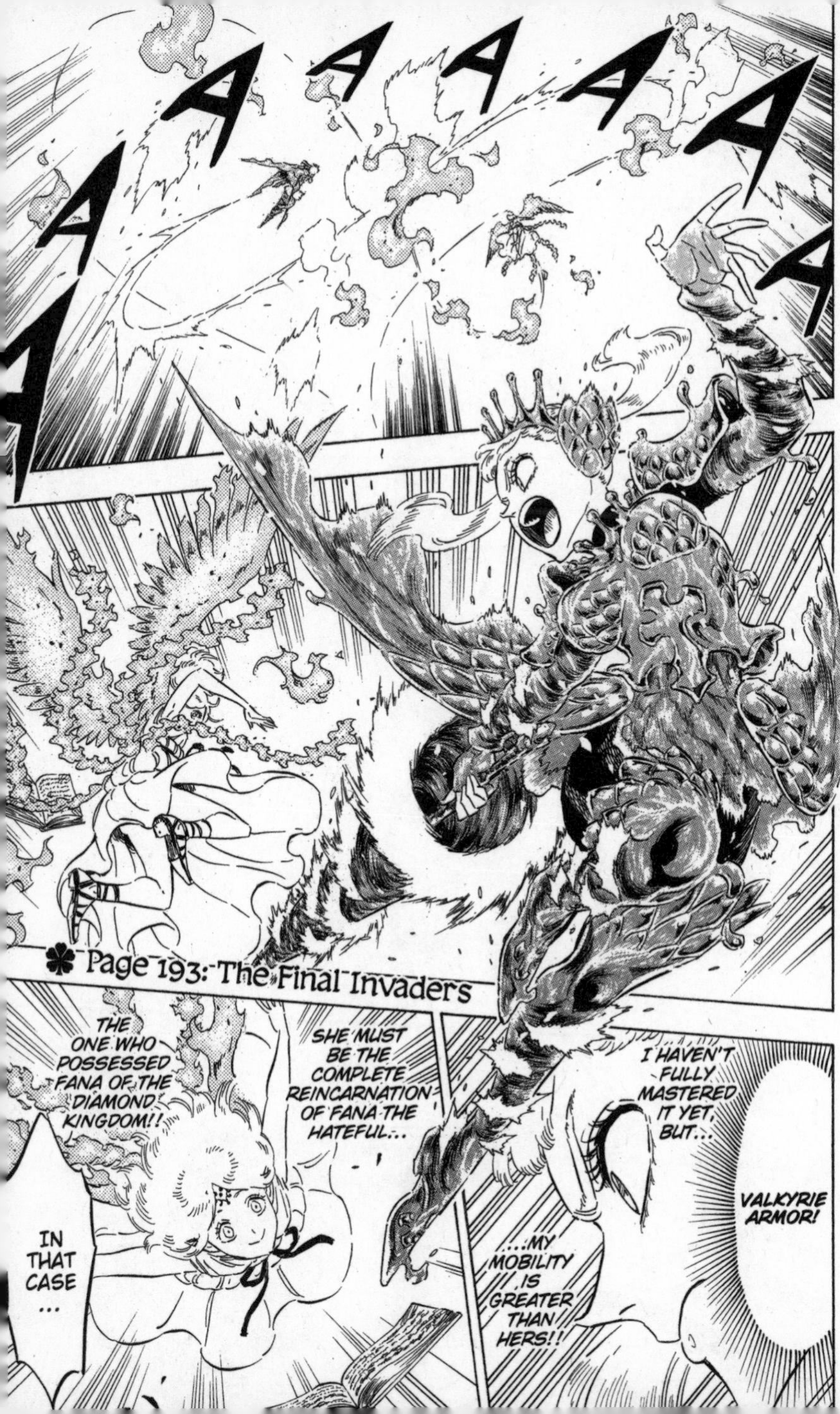
AAAAAAAAAA
Page 193: The Final Invaders
I HAVEN'T FULLY MASTERED IT YET, BUT...
VALKYRIE ARMOR!
SHE MUST BE THE COMPLETE REINCARNATION OF FANA THE HATEFUL...
...MY MOBILITY IS GREATER THAN HERS!!
THE ONE WHO POSSESSED FANA OF THE DIAMOND KINGDOM!!
IN THAT CASE...

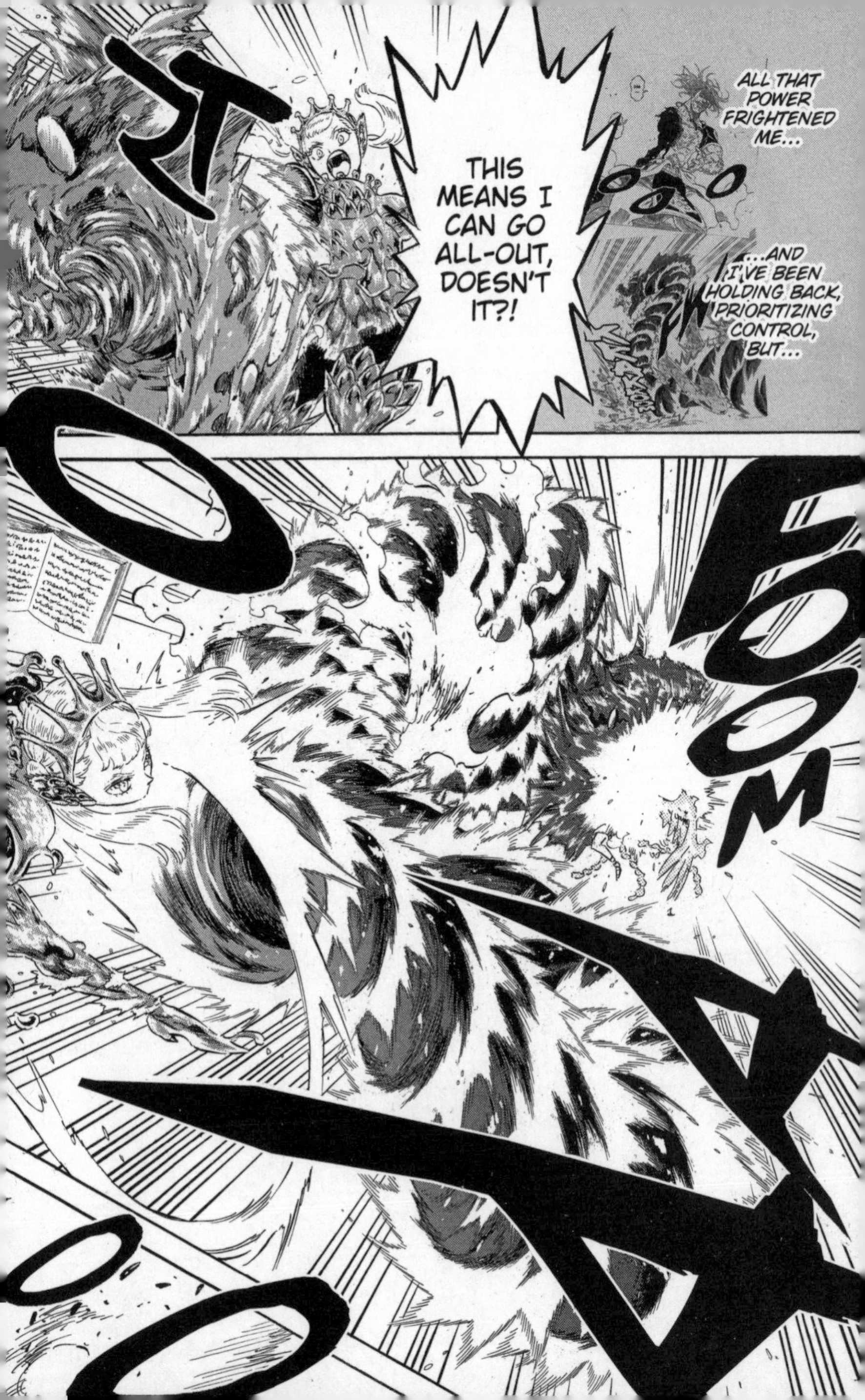
ALL THAT POWER FRIGHTENED ME...
...AND I'VE BEEN HOLDING BACK, PRIORITIZING CONTROL, BUT...
THIS MEANS I CAN GO ALL-OUT, DOESN'T IT?!

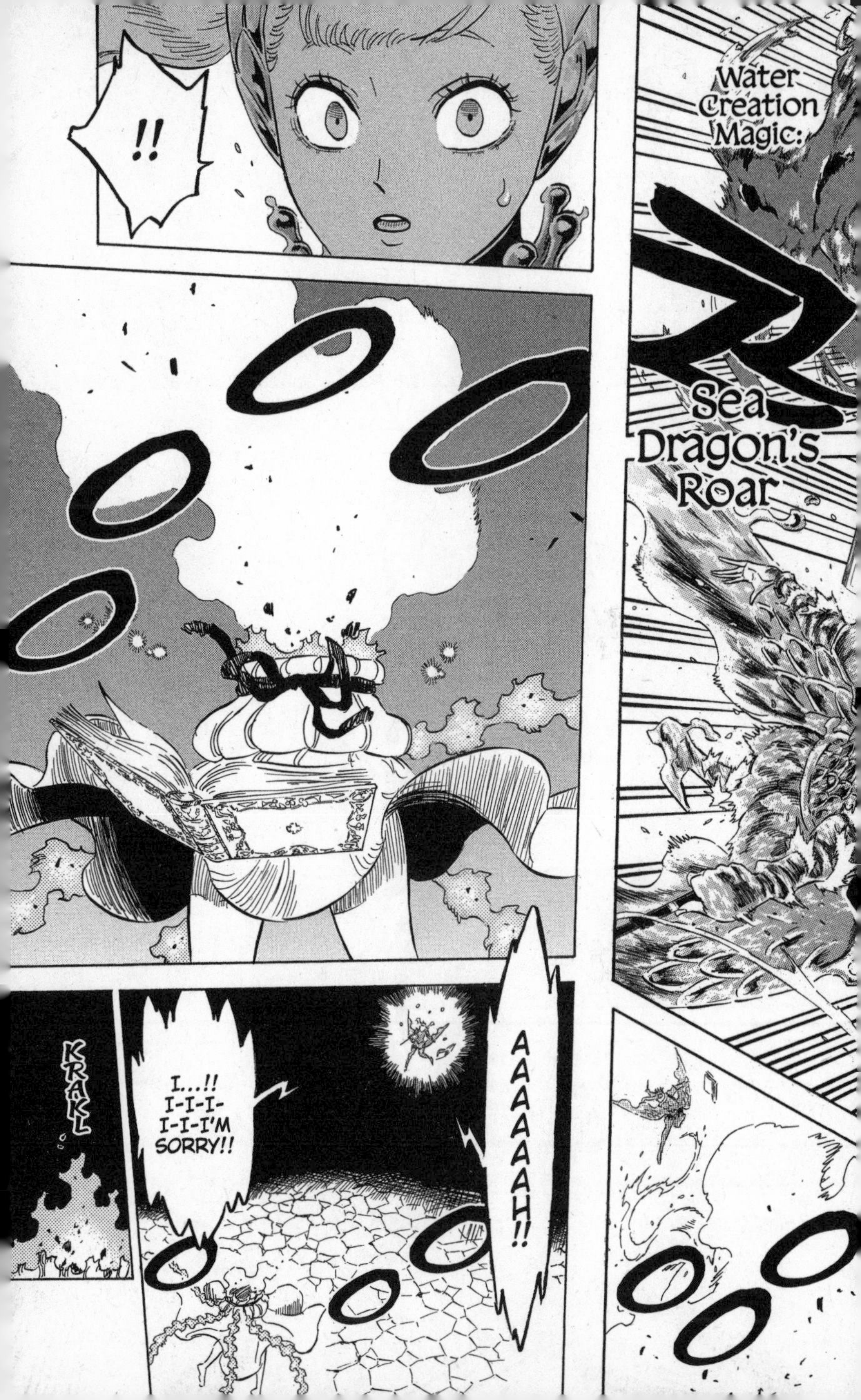
Water Creation Magic:
Sea Dragon's Roar
!!
AAAAAAAH!!
I...!! I-I-I- I-I-I'M SORRY!!
KRAKL

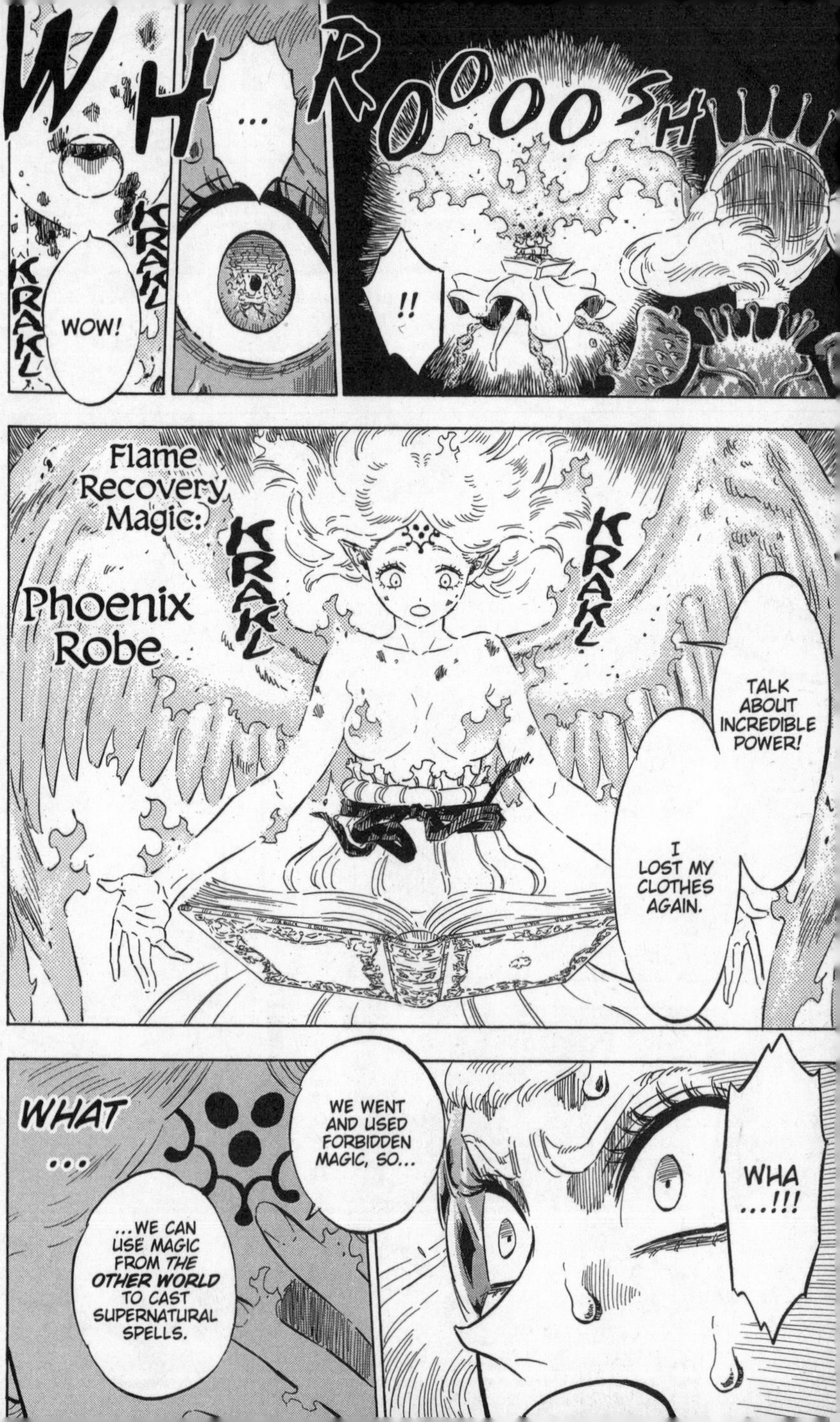
WHROOOOSH
!!
...
KRAKL
KRAKL
WOW!
TALK ABOUT INCREDIBLE POWER!
I LOST MY CLOTHES AGAIN.
KRAKL
KRAKL
Flame Recovery Magic:
Phoenix Robe
WHA ...!!!
WE WENT AND USED FORBIDDEN MAGIC, SO...
...WE CAN USE MAGIC FROM *THE OTHER WORLD* TO CAST SUPERNATURAL SPELLS.
WHAT ...

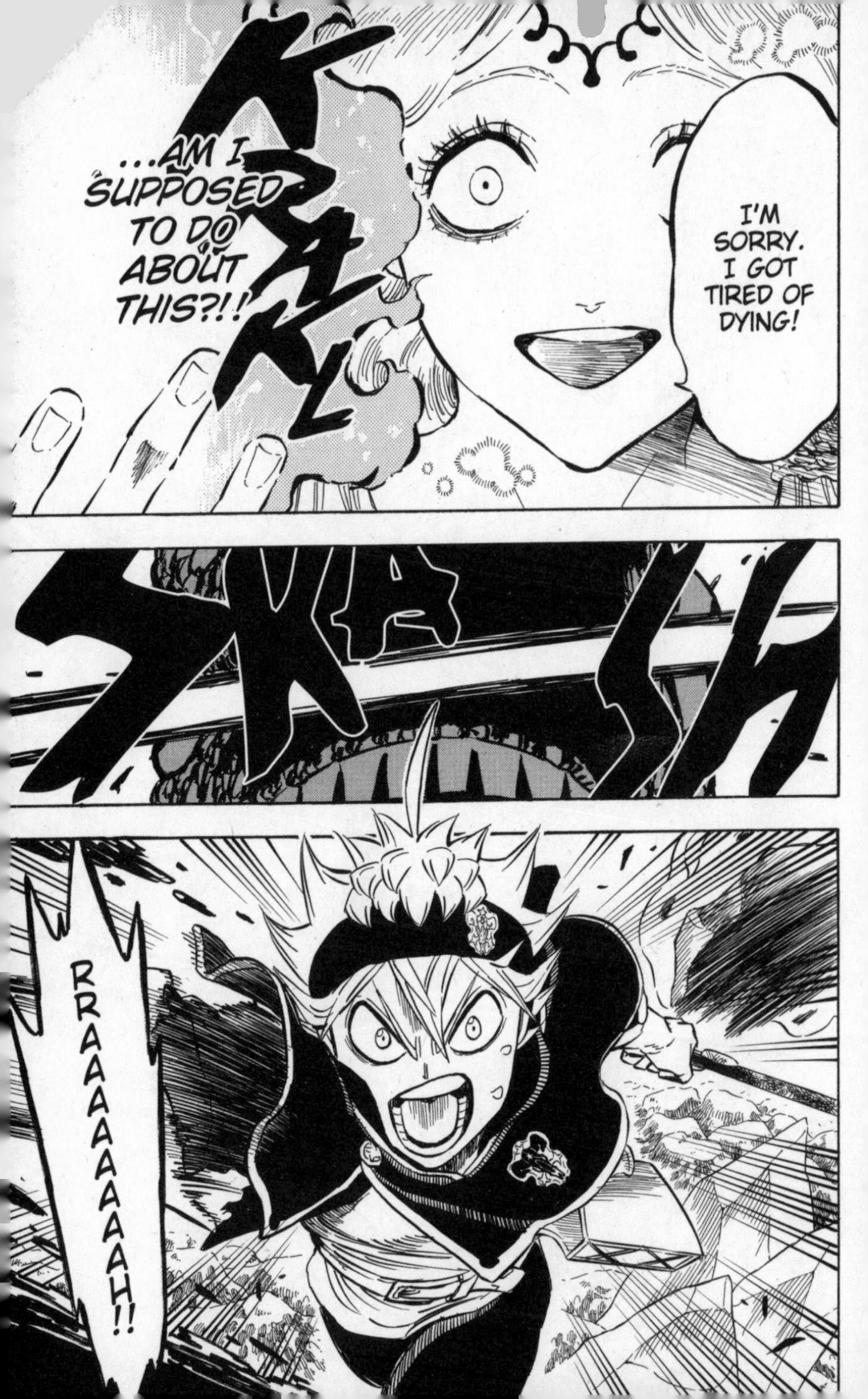
I'M SORRY. I GOT TIRED OF DYING!
...AM I SUPPOSED TO DO ABOUT THIS?!!
RRAAAAAAAAH!!

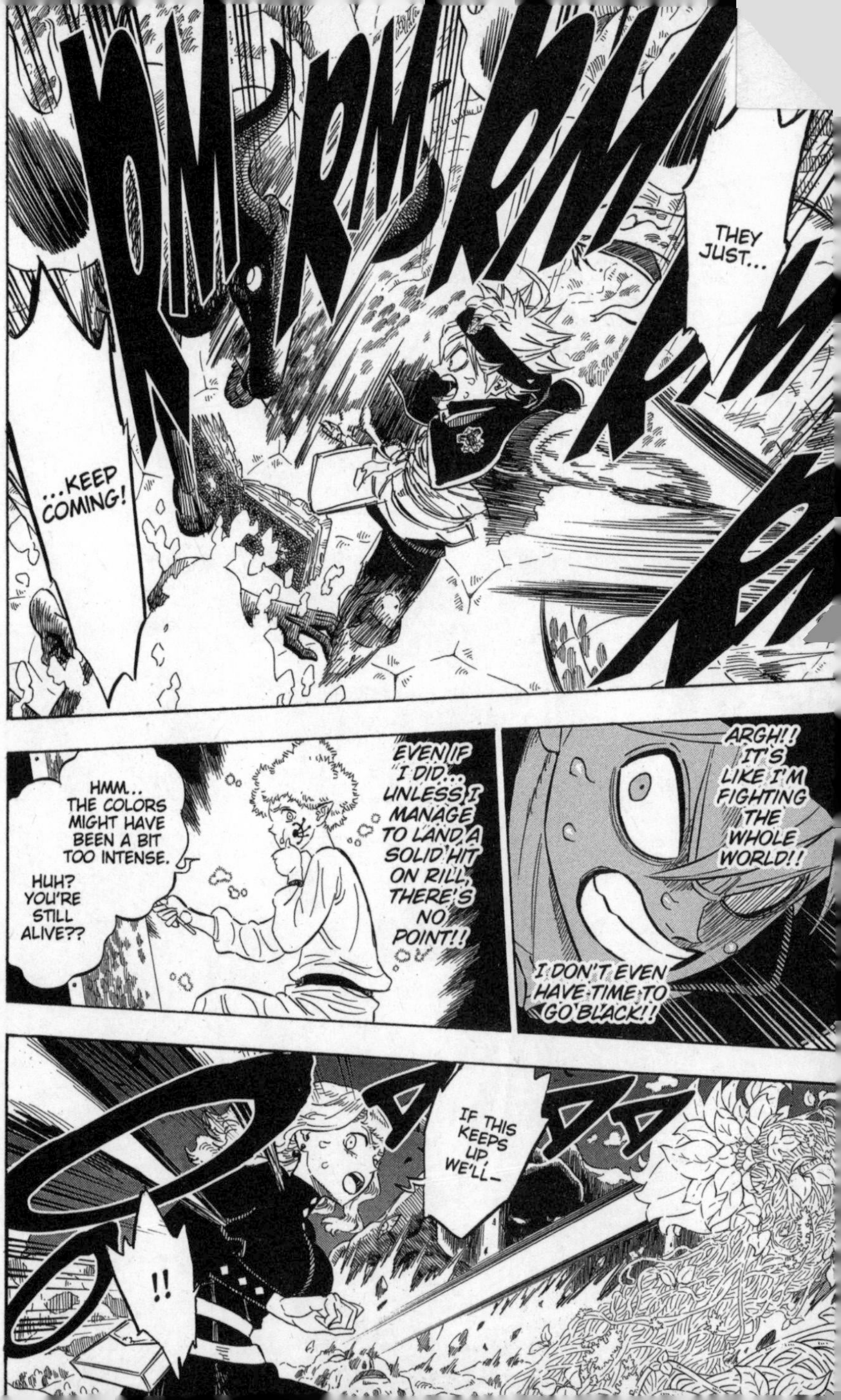
THEY JUST...
...KEEP COMING!
ARGH!! IT'S LIKE I'M FIGHTING THE WHOLE WORLD!!
I DON'T EVEN HAVE TIME TO GO BLACK!!
EVEN IF I DID... UNLESS I MANAGE TO LAND A SOLID HIT ON RILL, THERE'S NO POINT!!
HMM.. THE COLORS MIGHT HAVE BEEN A BIT TOO INTENSE.
HUH? YOU'RE STILL ALIVE??
IF THIS KEEPS UP, WE'LL—
!!

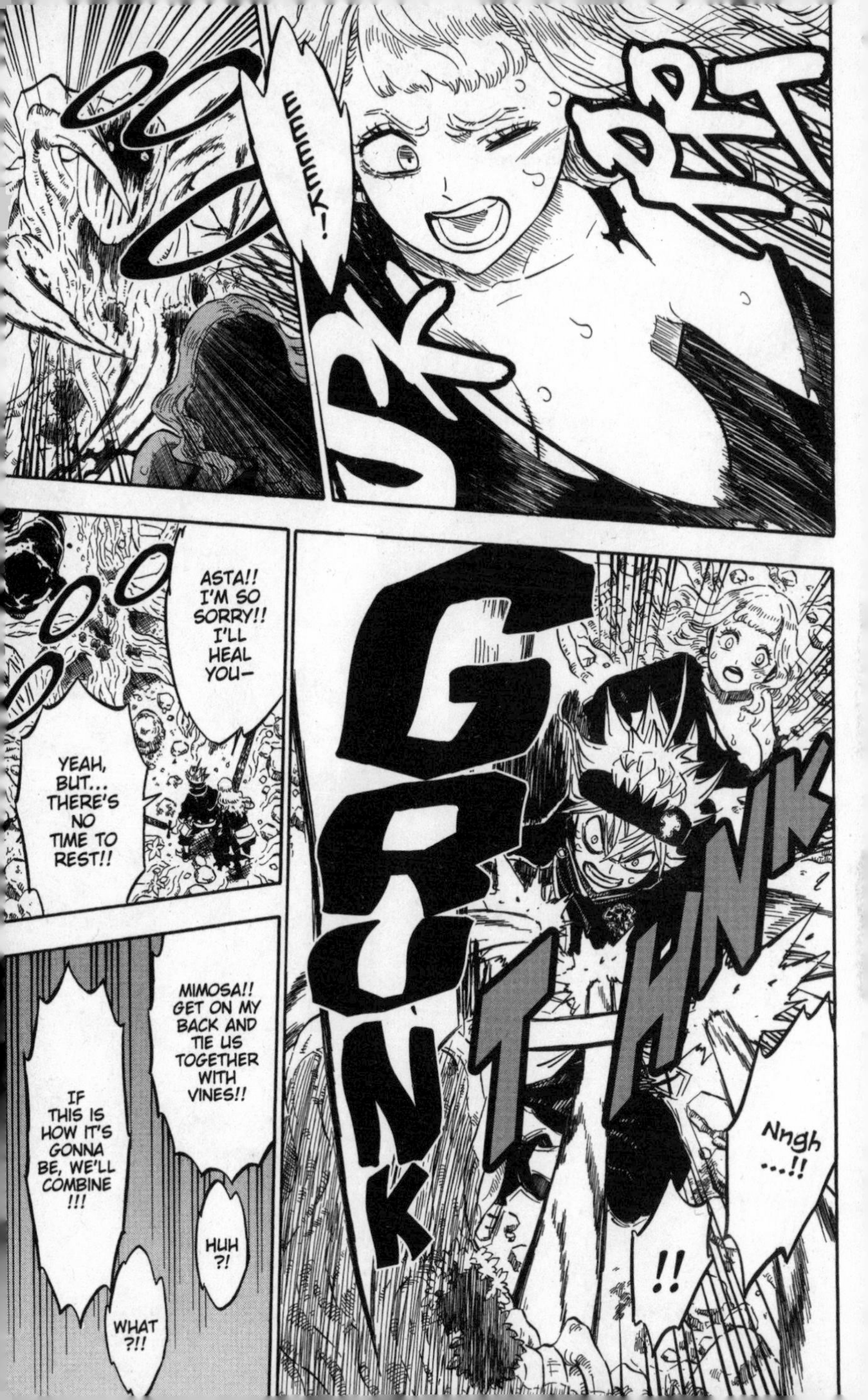
EEEEEK!
THUNK
Nngh ...!!
!!
ASTA!! I'M SO SORRY!! I'LL HEAL YOU—
YEAH, BUT... THERE'S NO TIME TO REST!!
MIMOSA!! GET ON MY BACK AND TIE US TOGETHER WITH VINES!!
IF THIS IS HOW IT'S GONNA BE, WE'LL COMBINE !!!
HUH ?!
WHAT ?!!

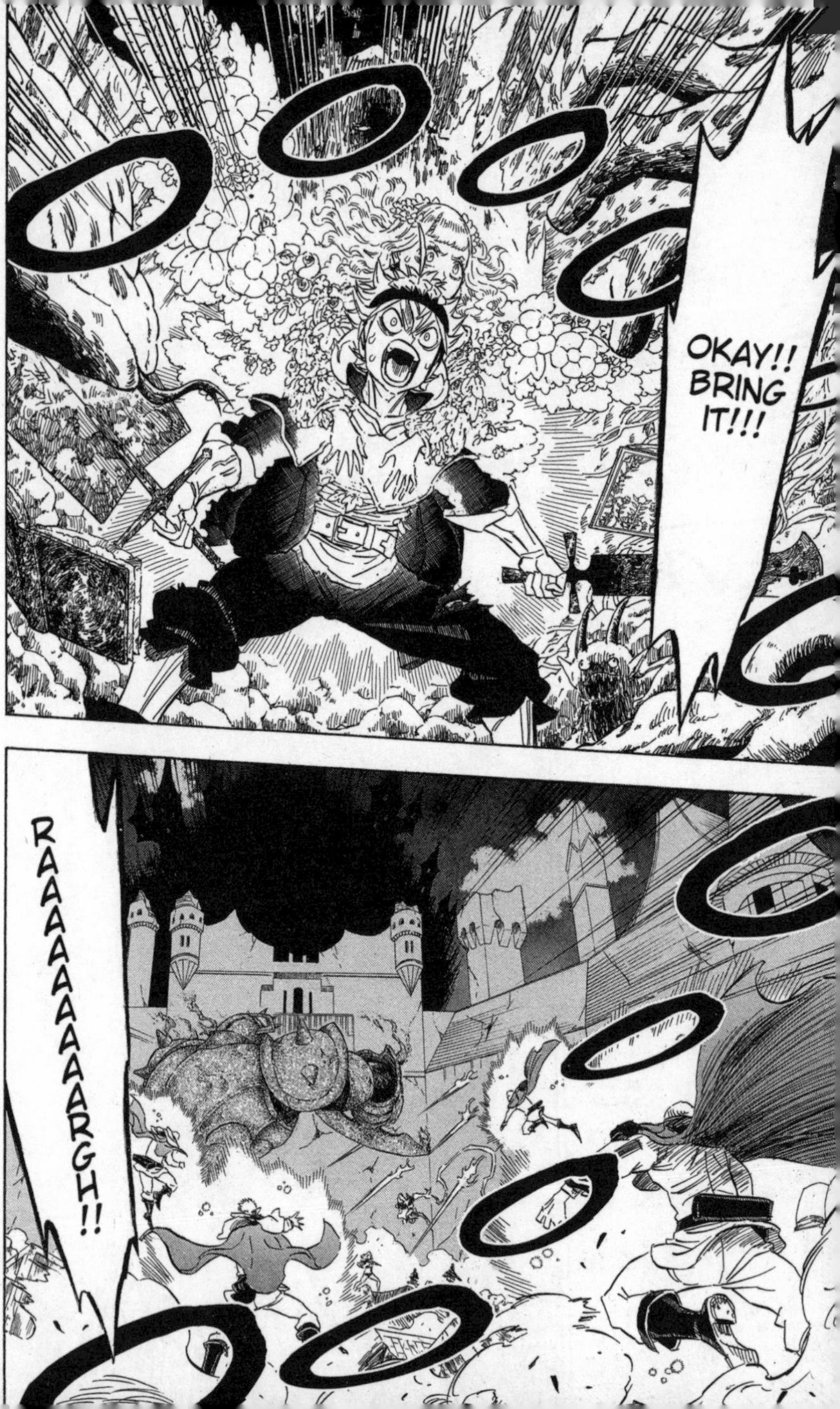
OKAY!! BRING IT!!!
RAAAAAAAAAAARGH!!

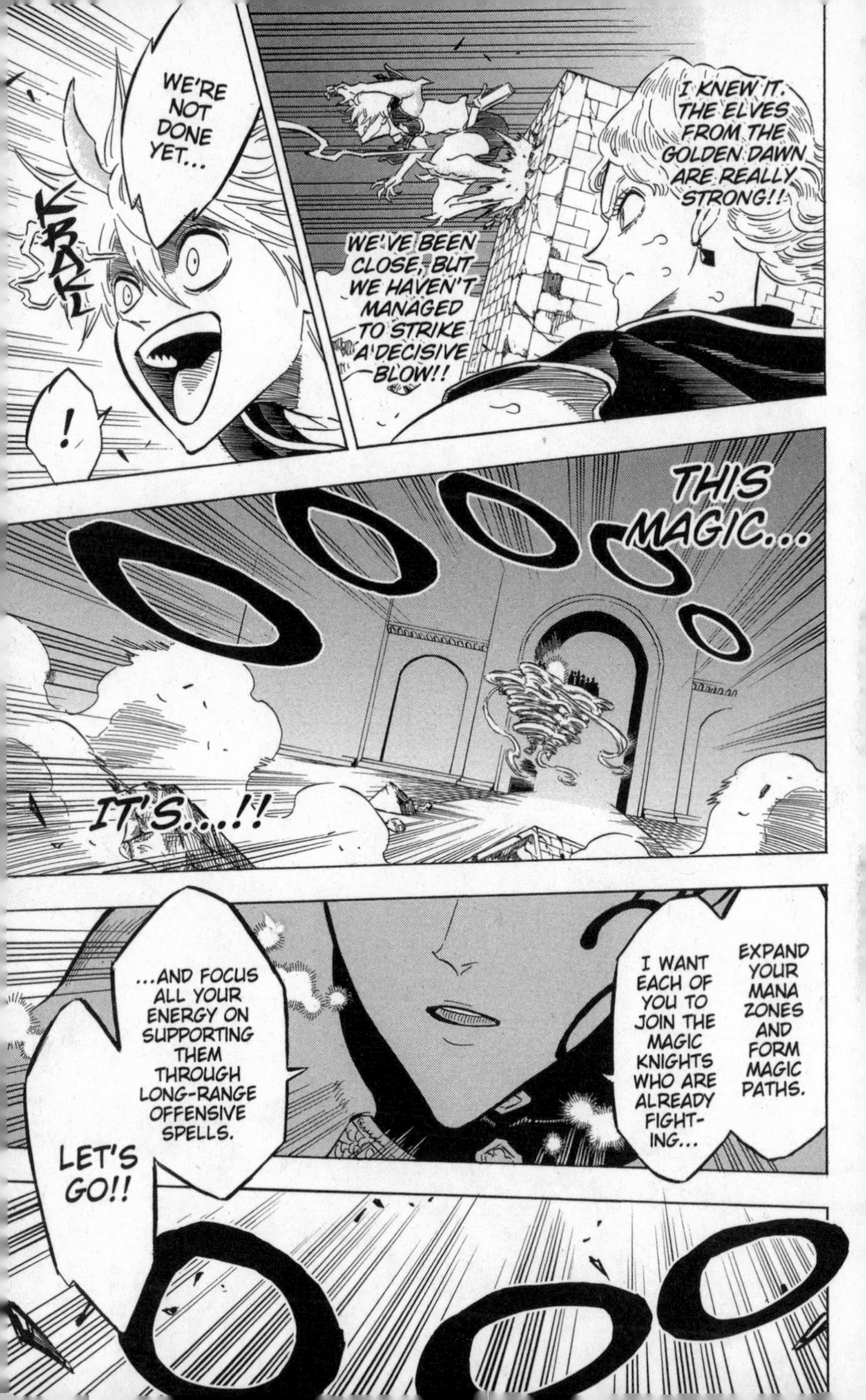
I KNEW IT. THE ELVES FROM THE GOLDEN DAWN ARE REALLY STRONG!!
WE'VE BEEN CLOSE, BUT WE HAVEN'T MANAGED TO STRIKE A DECISIVE BLOW!!
WE'RE NOT DONE YET...
KRAKL
!
THIS MAGIC...
IT'S...!!
EXPAND YOUR MANA ZONES AND FORM MAGIC PATHS.
I WANT EACH OF YOU TO JOIN THE MAGIC KNIGHTS WHO ARE ALREADY FIGHTING...
...AND FOCUS ALL YOUR ENERGY ON SUPPORTING THEM THROUGH LONG-RANGE OFFENSIVE SPELLS.
LET'S GO!!

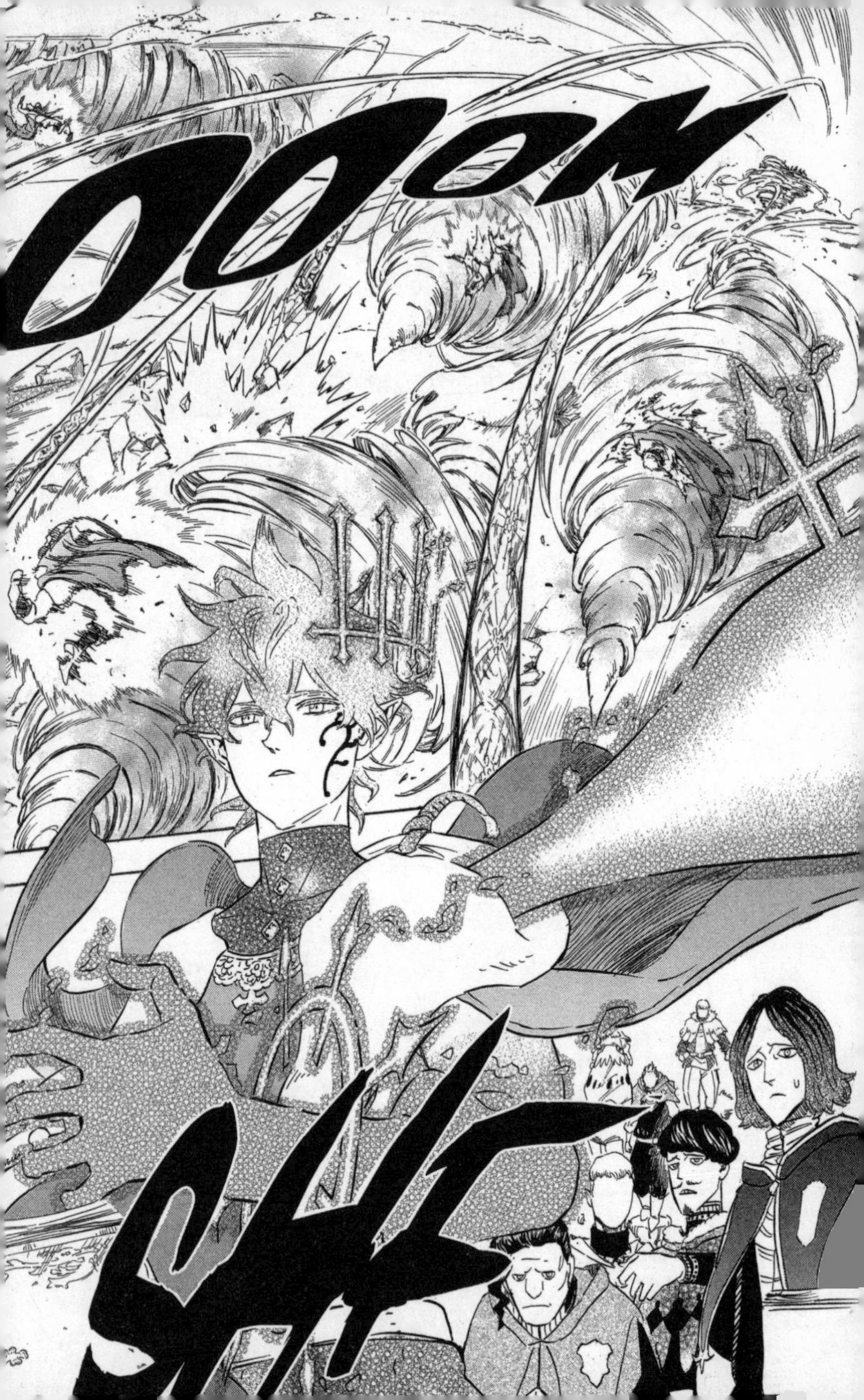

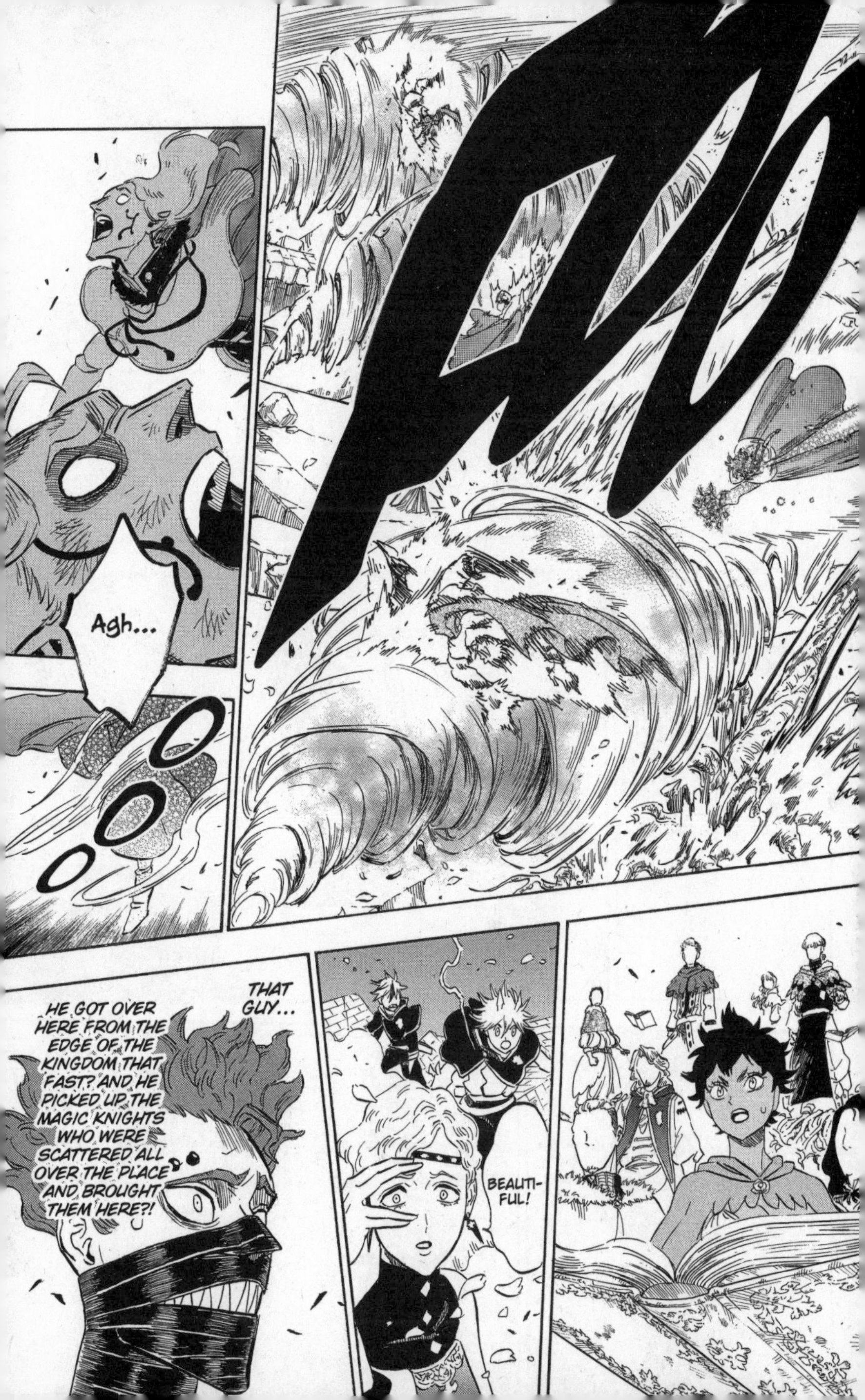
Agh...
BEAUTI-FUL!
THAT GUY...
HE GOT OVER HERE FROM THE EDGE OF THE KINGDOM THAT FAST? AND HE PICKED UP THE MAGIC KNIGHTS WHO WERE SCATTERED ALL OVER THE PLACE AND BROUGHT THEM HERE?!

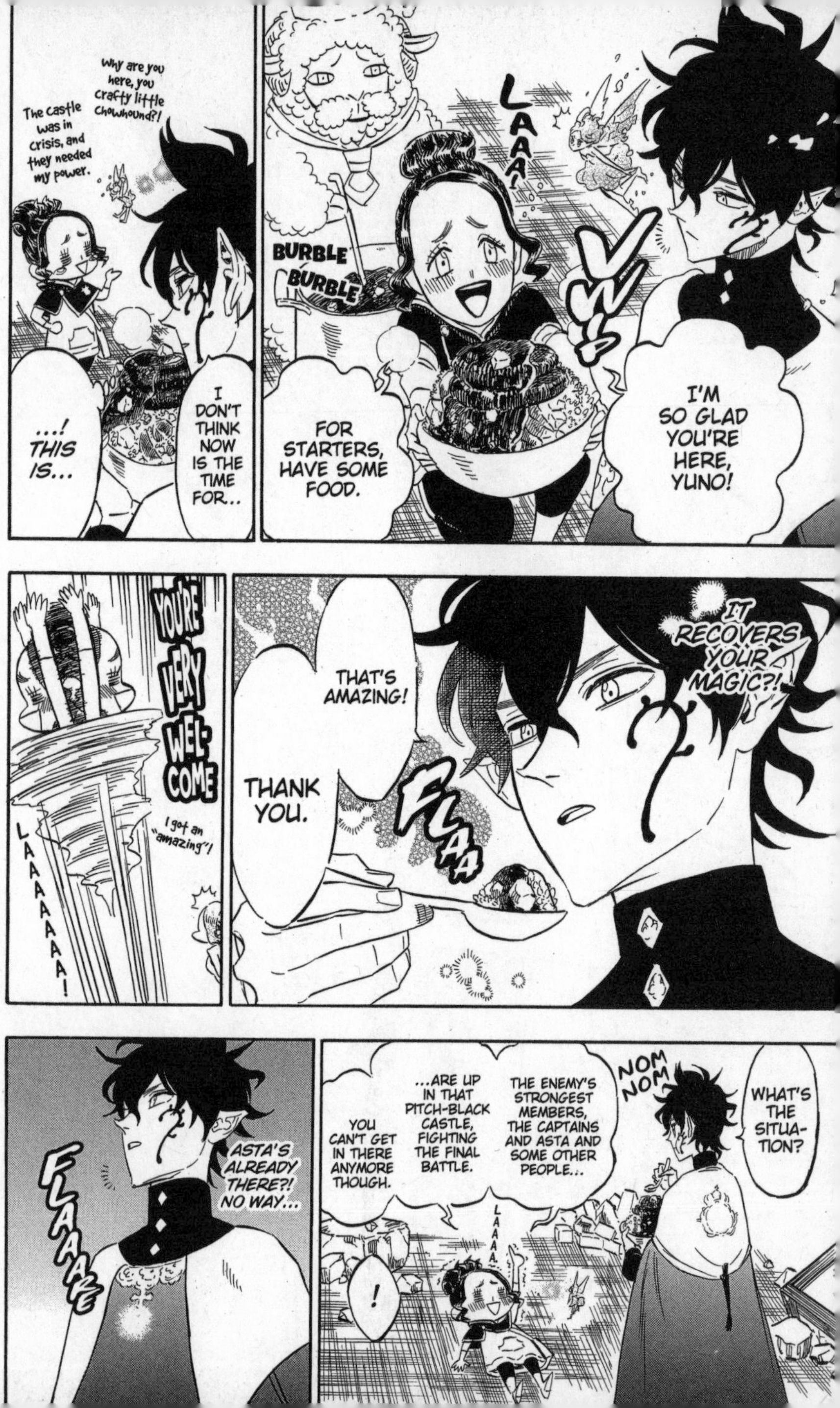
I'M SO GLAD YOU'RE HERE, YUNO!
VWIP
LAAA!
FOR STARTERS, HAVE SOME FOOD.
BURBLE BURBLE
Why are you here, you crafty little chowhound?!
The castle was in crisis, and they needed my power.
I DON'T THINK NOW IS THE TIME FOR...
...! THIS IS...
IT RECOVERS YOUR MAGIC?!
FLAA
THAT'S AMAZING!
THANK YOU.
YOU'RE VERY WEL-COME
I got an "amazing"!
LAAAAAAAA!
WHAT'S THE SITUA-TION?
NOM NOM
THE ENEMY'S STRONGEST MEMBERS, THE CAPTAINS AND ASTA AND SOME OTHER PEOPLE...
...ARE UP IN THAT PITCH-BLACK CASTLE, FIGHTING THE FINAL BATTLE.
YOU CAN'T GET IN THERE ANYMORE THOUGH.
LAAAA...
!
ASTA'S ALREADY THERE?! NO WAY...
FLAAAAA

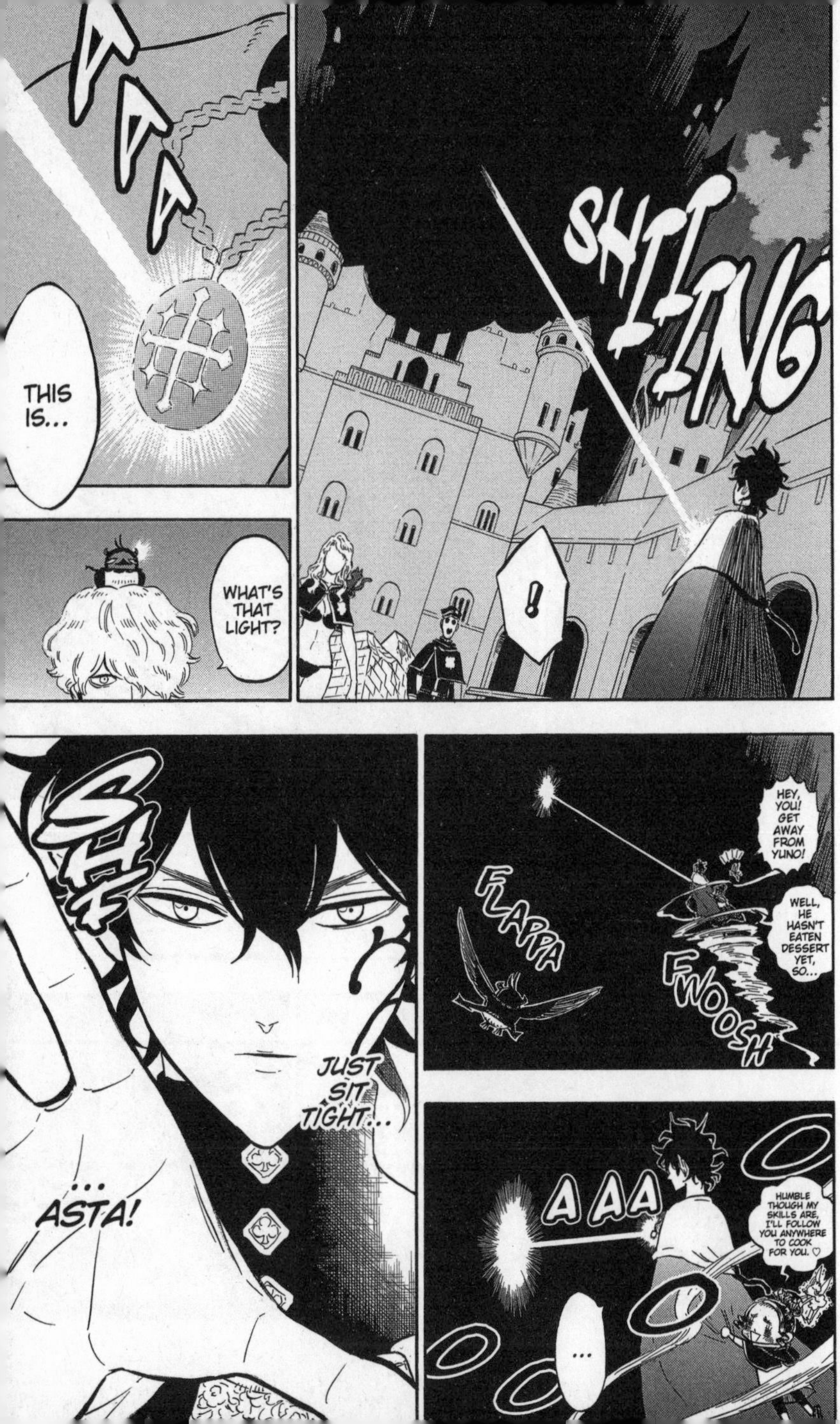
SHIIING
!
AAA
THIS IS...
WHAT'S THAT LIGHT?
HEY, YOU! GET AWAY FROM YUNO!
WELL, HE HASN'T EATEN DESSERT YET, SO...
FLAPPA
FWOOSH
HUMBLE THOUGH MY SKILLS ARE, I'LL FOLLOW YOU ANYWHERE TO COOK FOR YOU. ♡
AAA
...
SHK
JUST SIT TIGHT...
...ASTA!

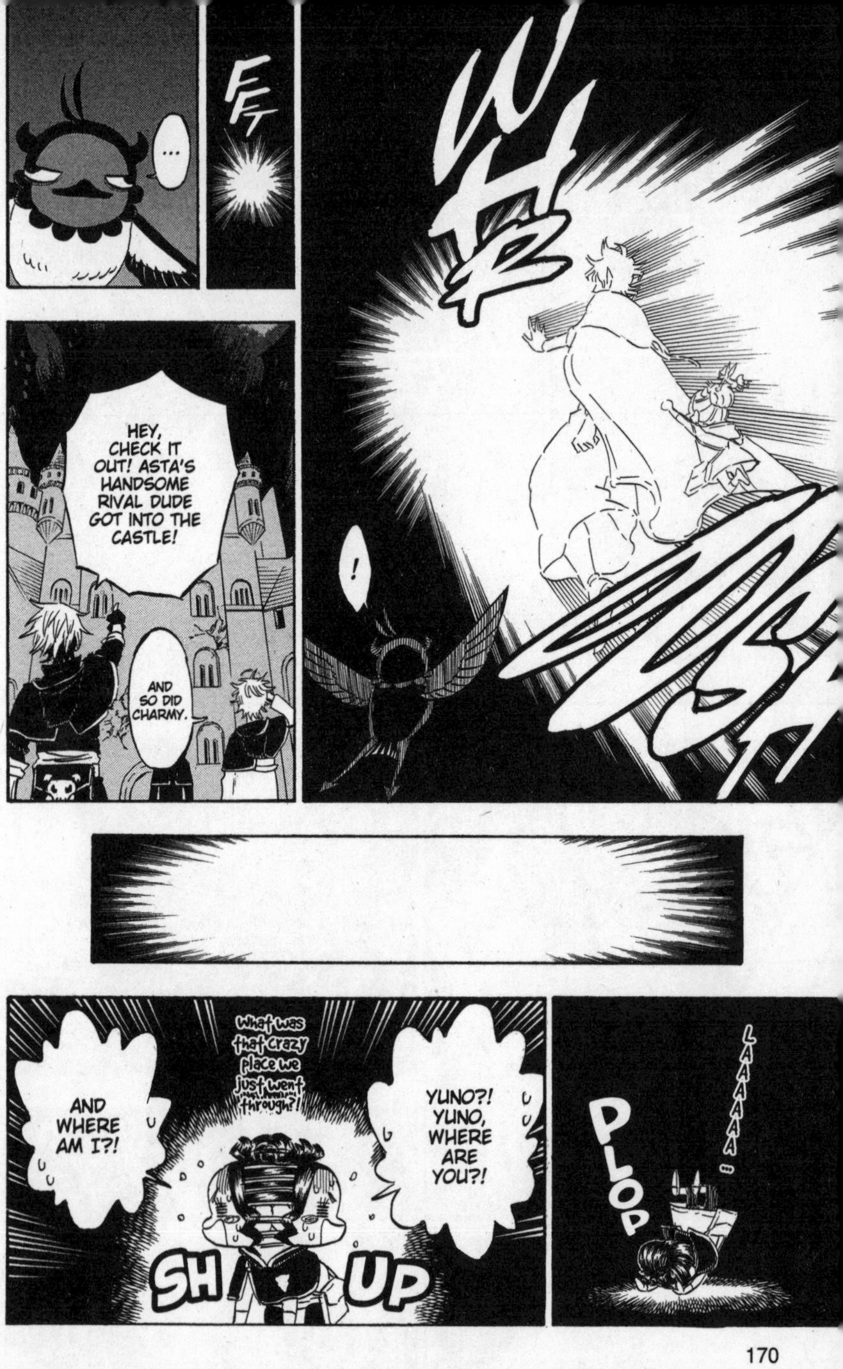
WHOOSH
!
FFT
...
HEY, CHECK IT OUT! ASTA'S HANDSOME RIVAL DUDE GOT INTO THE CASTLE!
AND SO DID CHARMY.
LAAAAAA...
PLOP
YUNO?! YUNO, WHERE ARE YOU?!
What was that crazy place we just went through?!
AND WHERE AM I?!
SHUP

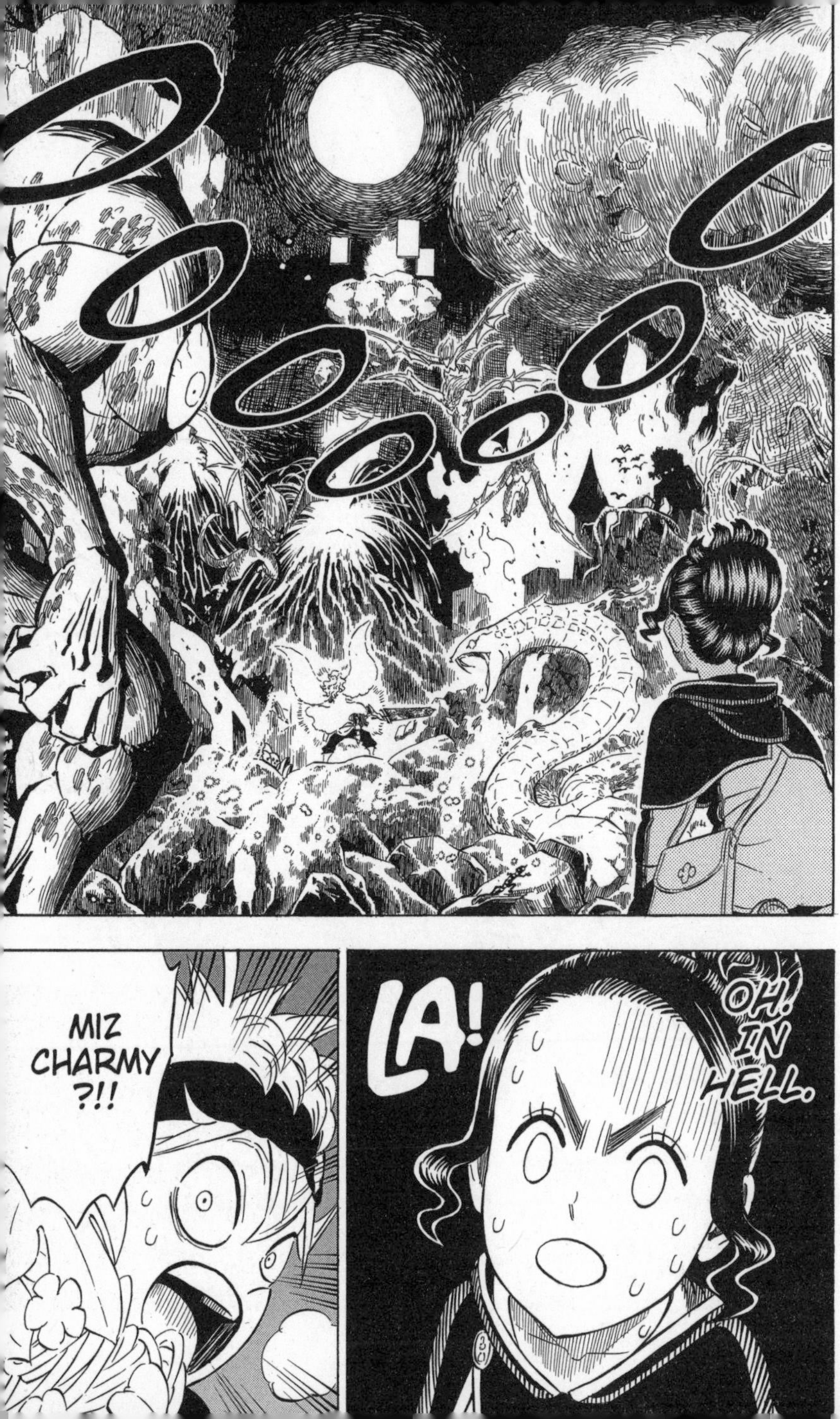
OH. IN HELL.
LA!
MIZ CHARMY ?!!

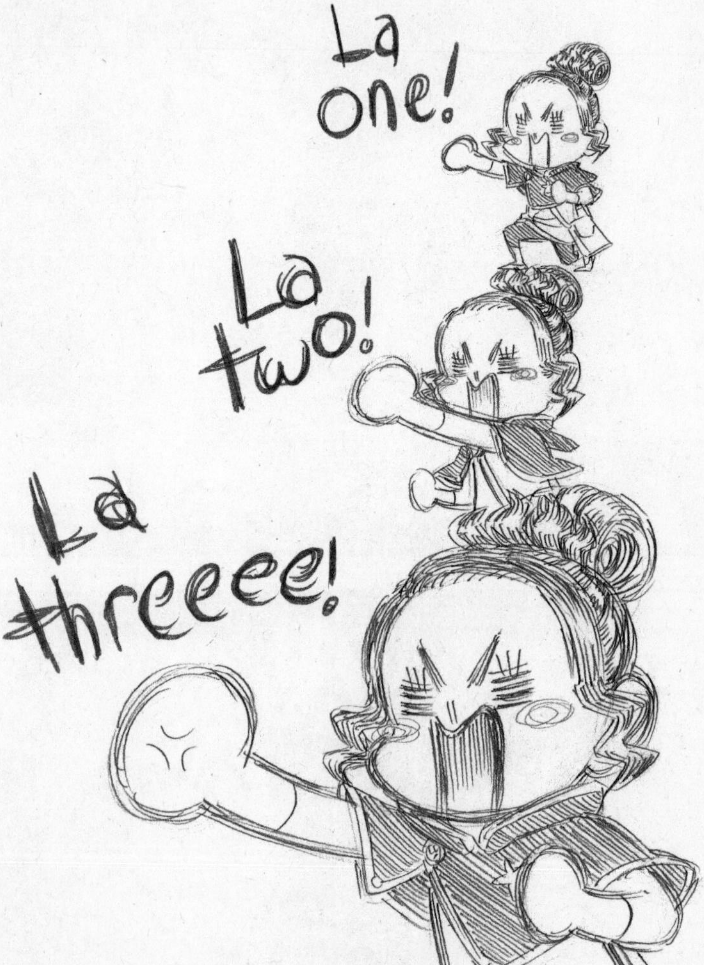
La one!
La two!
La threeee!

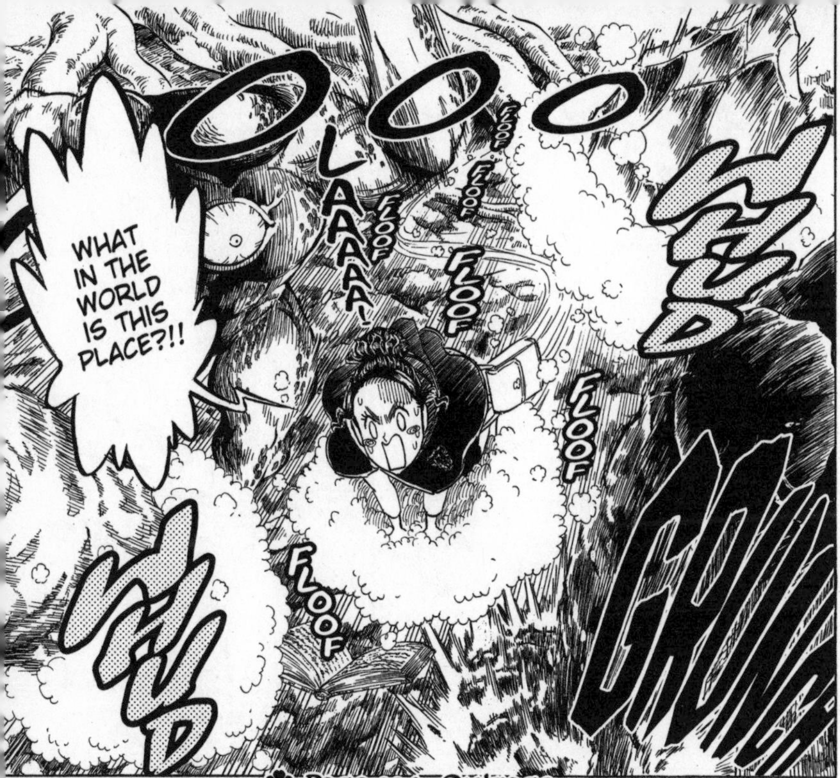
WHUD
FLOOF
FLOOF
FLOOF
FLOOF
LAAAAAA!
WHAT IN THE WORLD IS THIS PLACE?!!
FLOOF
WHUD

Page 194: Outrage

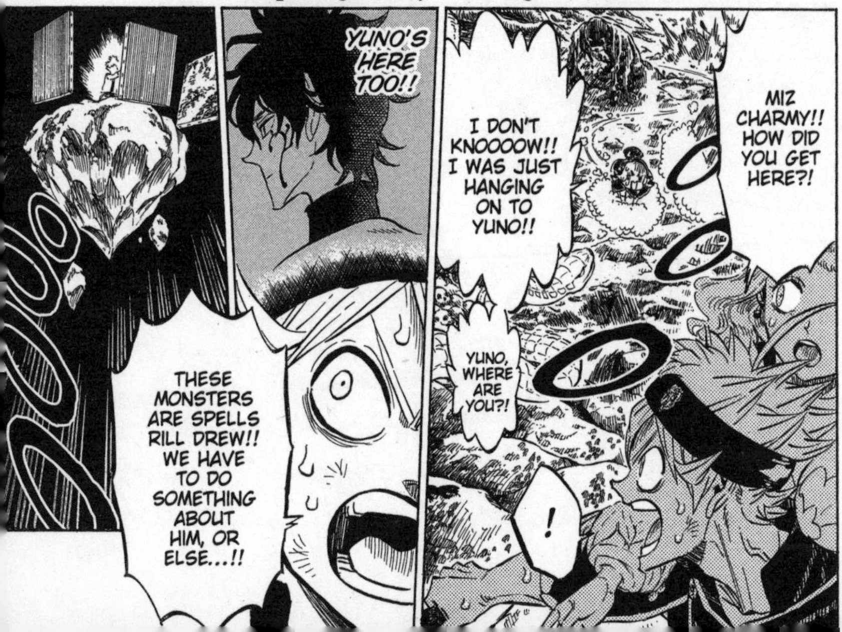
MIZ CHARMY!! HOW DID YOU GET HERE?!
I DON'T KNOOOOW!! I WAS JUST HANGING ON TO YUNO!!
YUNO, WHERE ARE YOU?!
!
YUNO'S HERE TOO!!
THESE MONSTERS ARE SPELLS RILL DREW!! WE HAVE TO DO SOMETHING ABOUT HIM, OR ELSE...!!

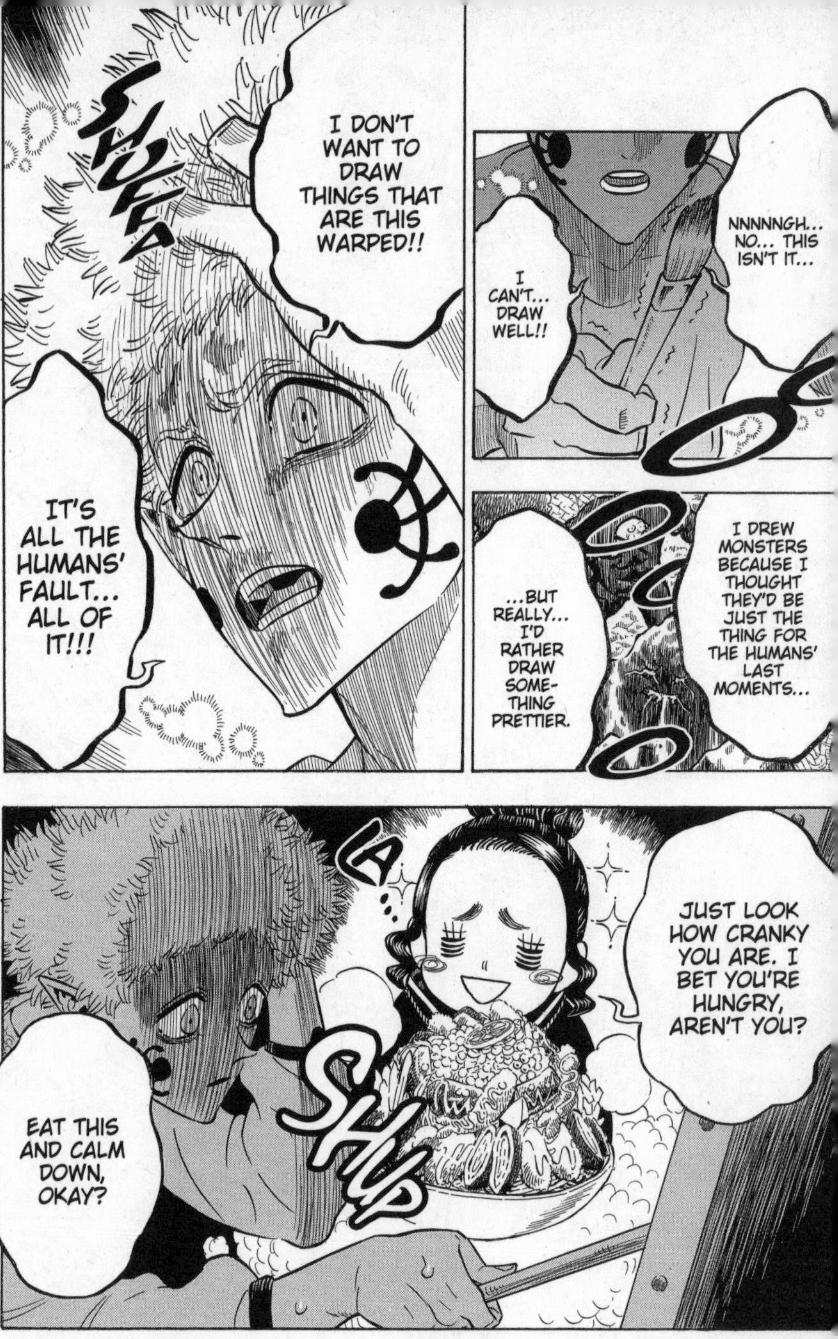
NNNNNGH... NO... THIS ISN'T IT...
I CAN'T... DRAW WELL!!
I DREW MONSTERS BECAUSE I THOUGHT THEY'D BE JUST THE THING FOR THE HUMANS' LAST MOMENTS...
...BUT REALLY... I'D RATHER DRAW SOME-THING PRETTIER.
SHUFFA
I DON'T WANT TO DRAW THINGS THAT ARE THIS WARPED!!
IT'S ALL THE HUMANS' FAULT... ALL OF IT!!!
JUST LOOK HOW CRANKY YOU ARE. I BET YOU'RE HUNGRY, AREN'T YOU?
LA...
SHUP
EAT THIS AND CALM DOWN, OKAY?

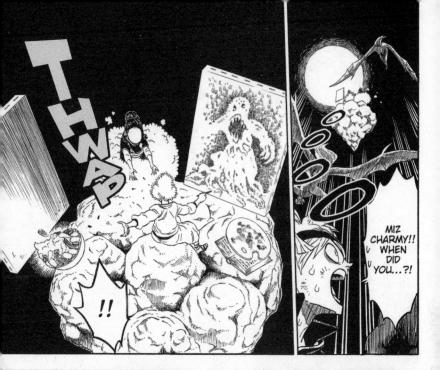

MIZ CHARMY!! WHEN DID YOU...?!

!!

Get away from me, human !!

I'm not eating anything you people made!!

HEY...

Shut up.

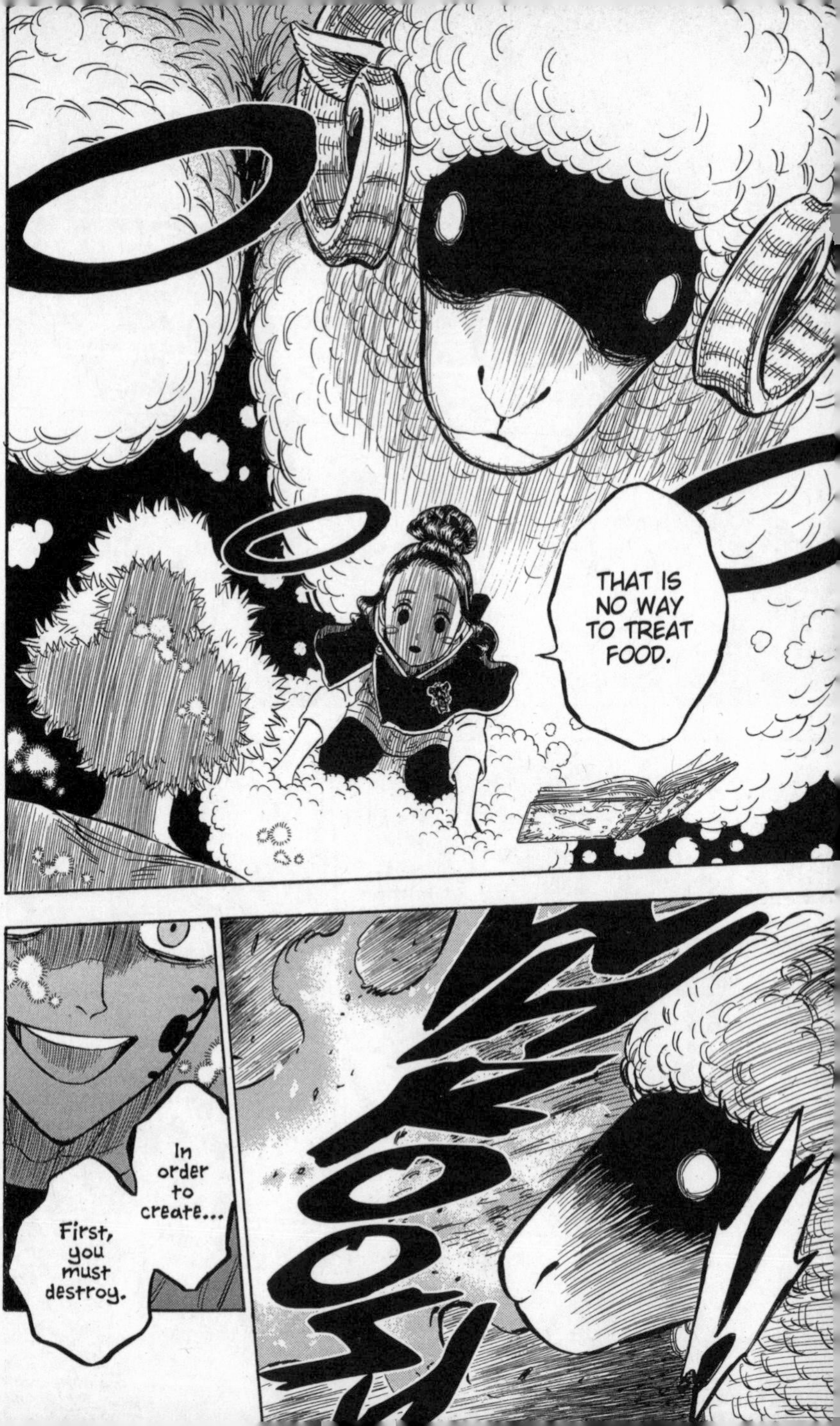
THAT IS NO WAY TO TREAT FOOD.
In order to create...
First, you must destroy.

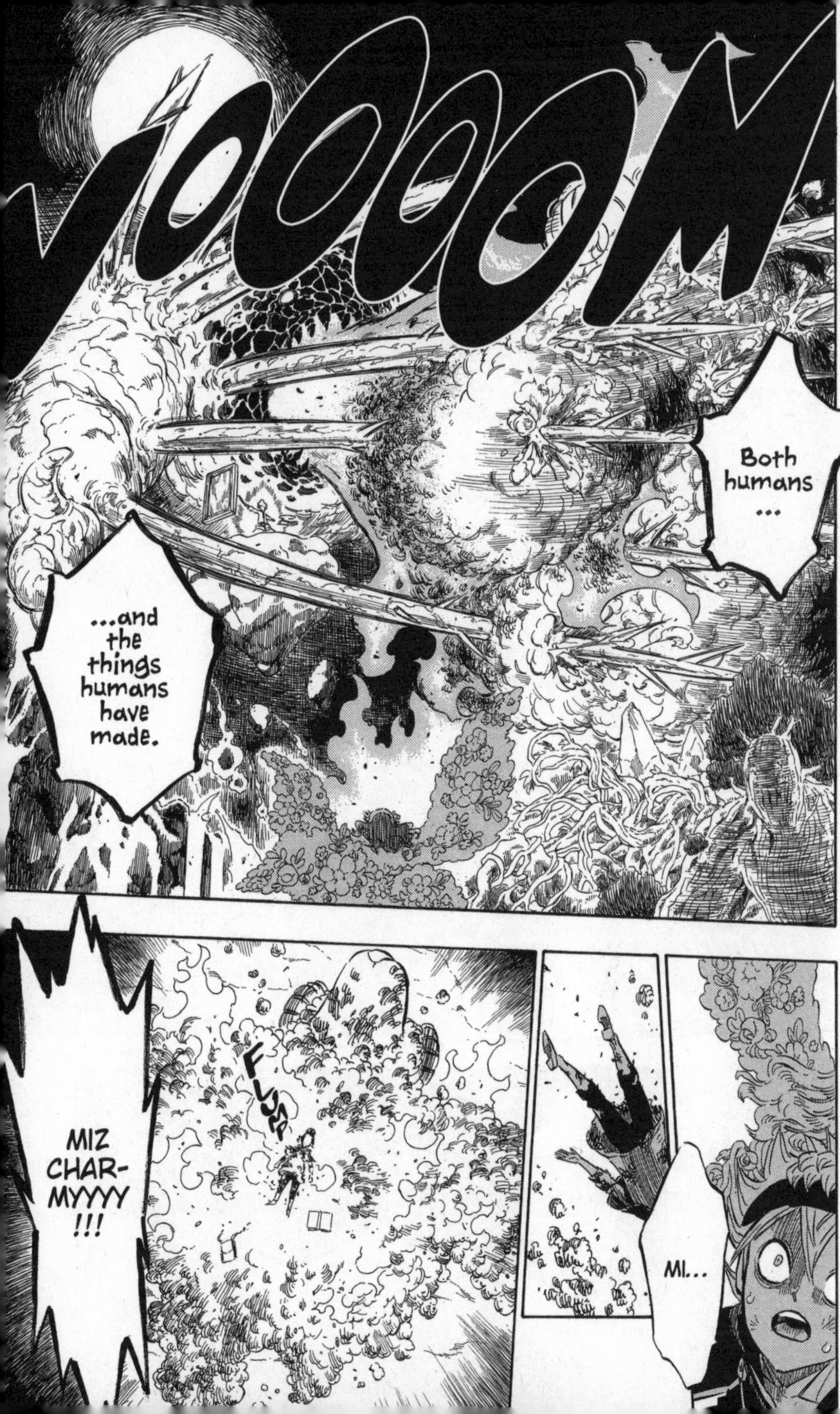
Both humans...
...and the things humans have made.
MI...
MIZ CHAR-MYYYY!!!

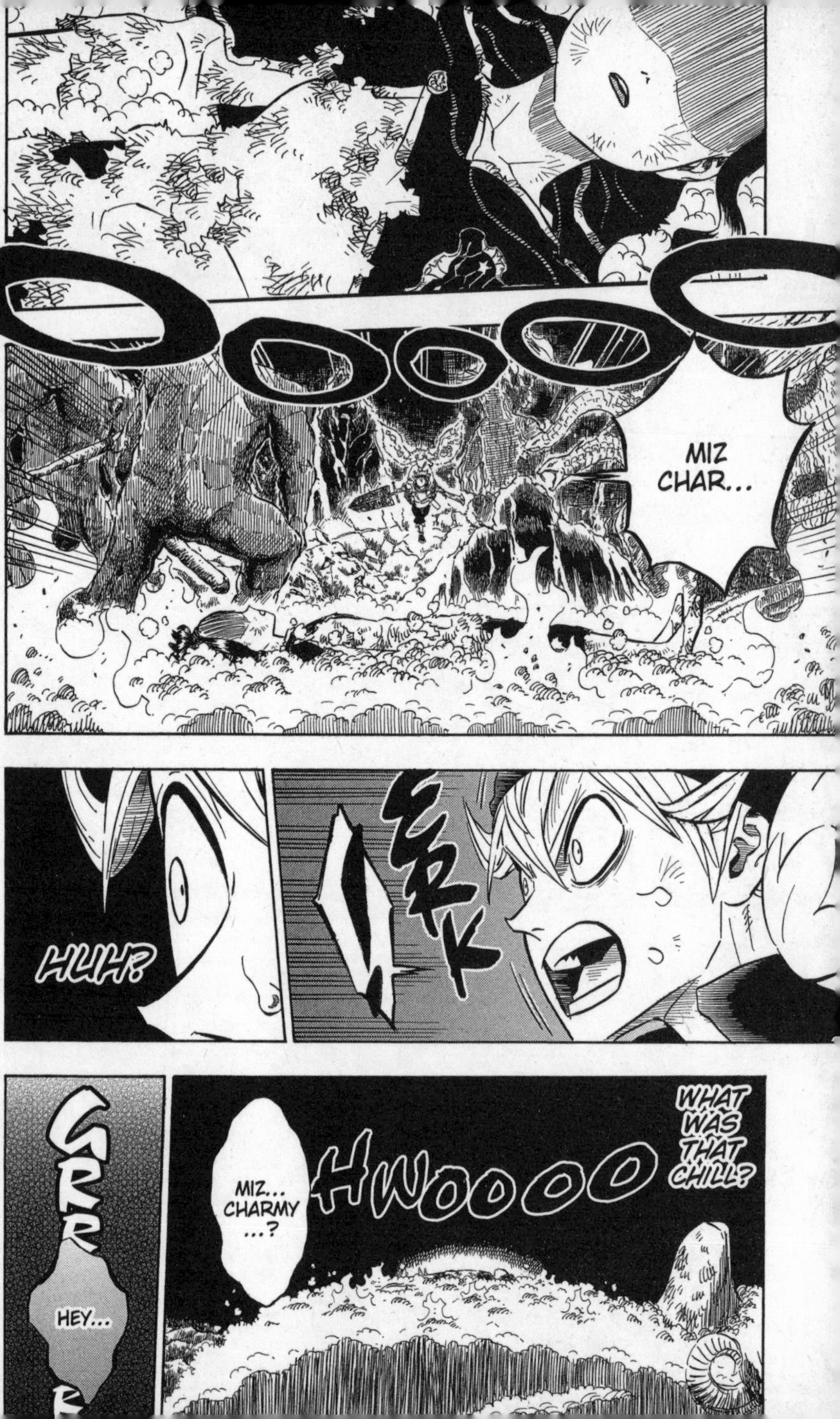
MIZ CHAR...
ERK
HUH?
WHAT WAS THAT CHILL?
HWOOOO
MIZ... CHARMY ...?
GRR
HEY...

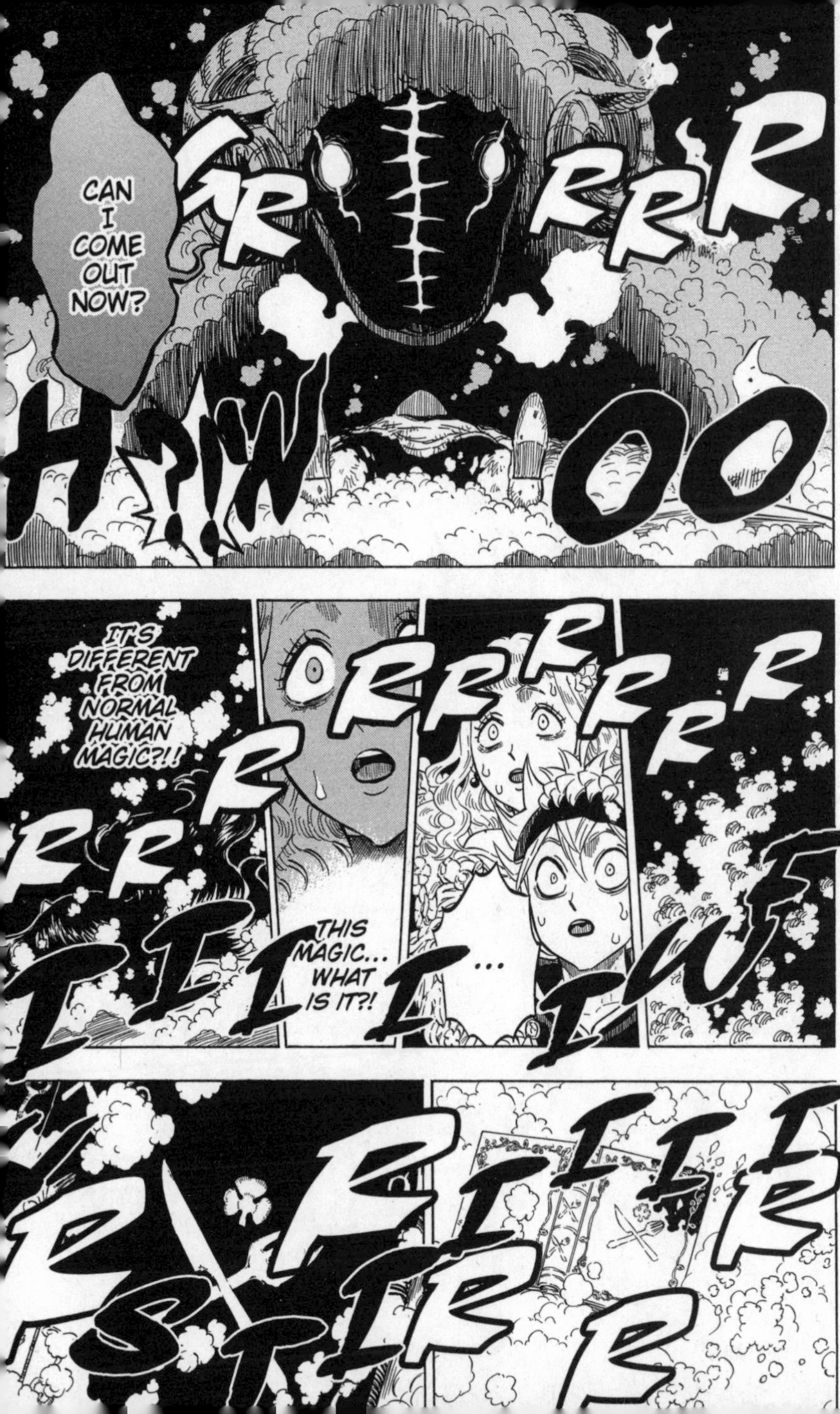
CAN I COME OUT NOW?
!?!
...
THIS MAGIC... WHAT IS IT?!
IT'S DIFFERENT FROM NORMAL HUMAN MAGIC?!!

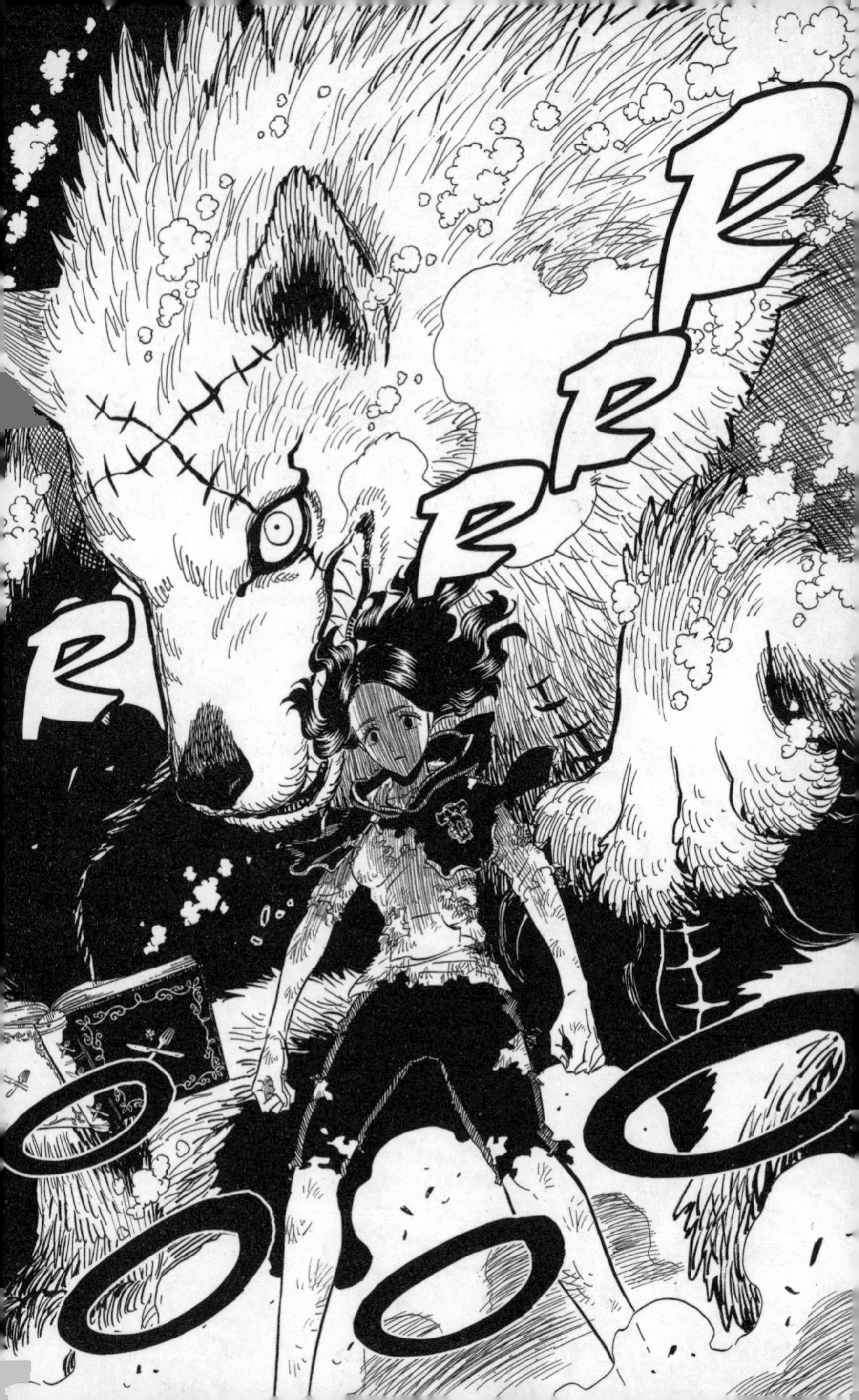
RRRR
OOOO

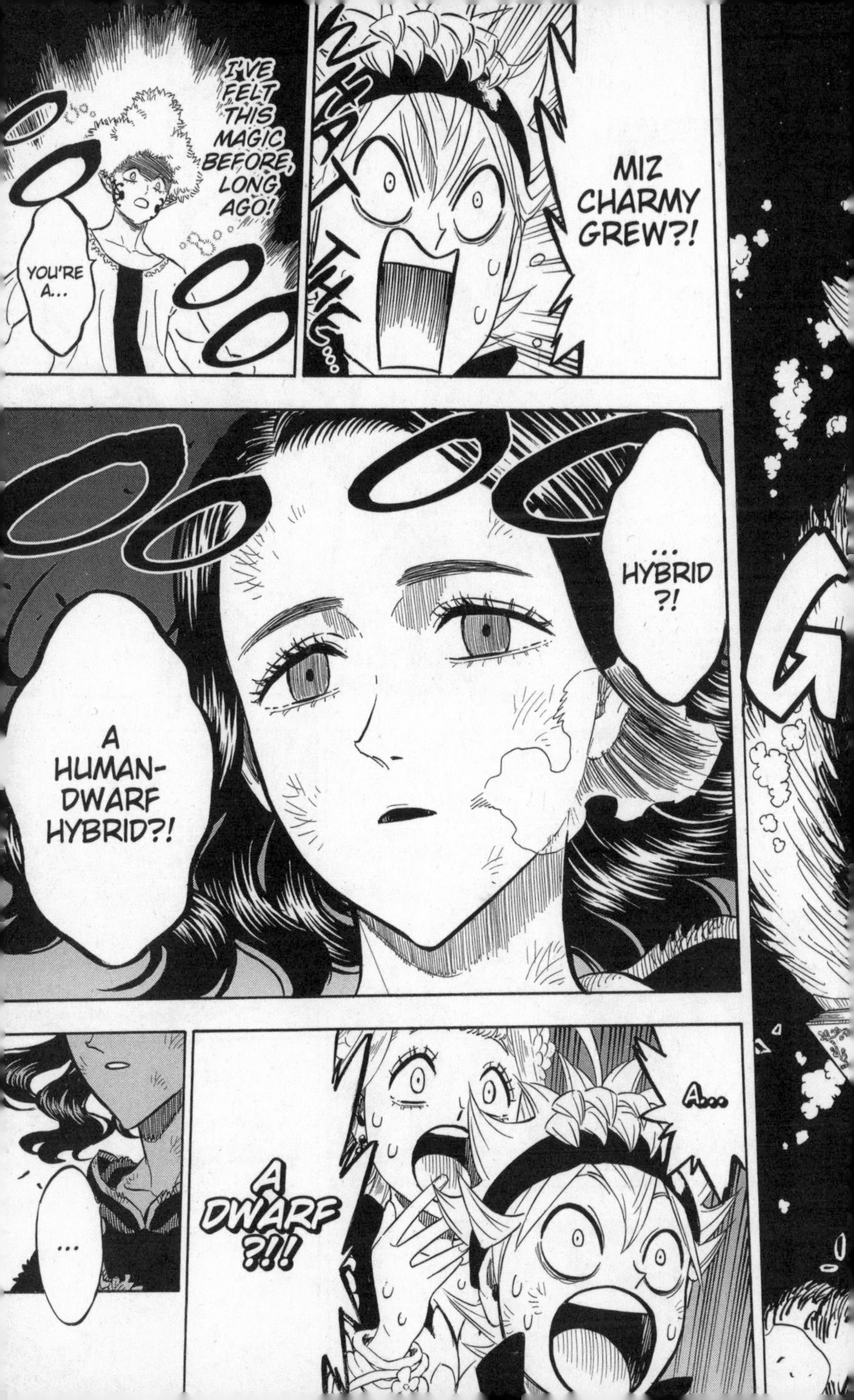
WHAT THE...
MIZ CHARMY GREW?!
I'VE FELT THIS MAGIC BEFORE, LONG AGO!
YOU'RE A...
... HYBRID ?!
A HUMAN-DWARF HYBRID?!
A...
A DWARF ?!!
...

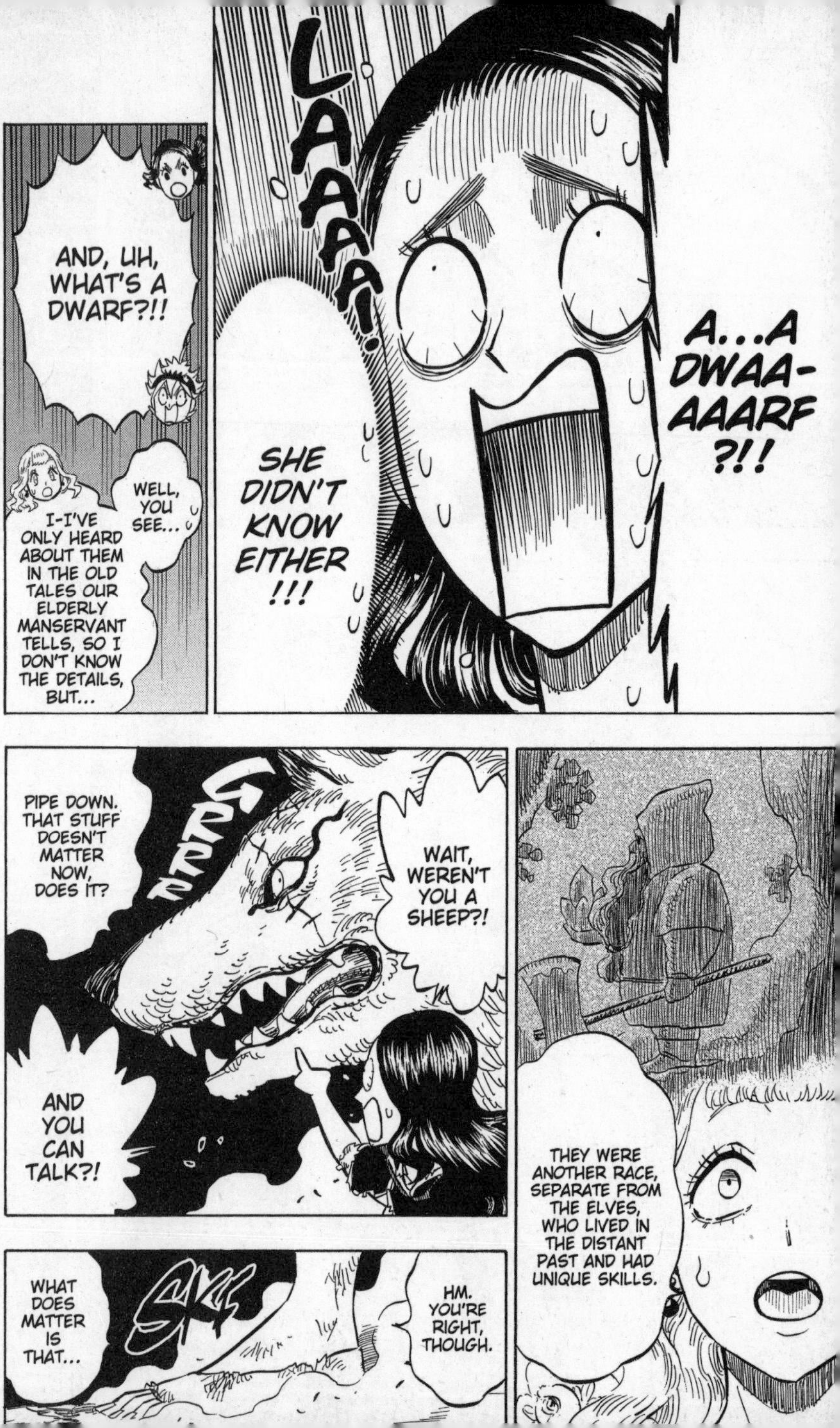
A...A DWAA-AAARF?!!
LAAAA!
SHE DIDN'T KNOW EITHER!!!
AND, UH, WHAT'S A DWARF?!!
WELL, YOU SEE...
I-I'VE ONLY HEARD ABOUT THEM IN THE OLD TALES OUR ELDERLY MANSERVANT TELLS, SO I DON'T KNOW THE DETAILS, BUT...
THEY WERE ANOTHER RACE, SEPARATE FROM THE ELVES, WHO LIVED IN THE DISTANT PAST AND HAD UNIQUE SKILLS.
WAIT, WEREN'T YOU A SHEEP?!
GRRR
PIPE DOWN. THAT STUFF DOESN'T MATTER NOW, DOES IT?
AND YOU CAN TALK?!
HM. YOU'RE RIGHT, THOUGH.
WHAT DOES MATTER IS THAT...

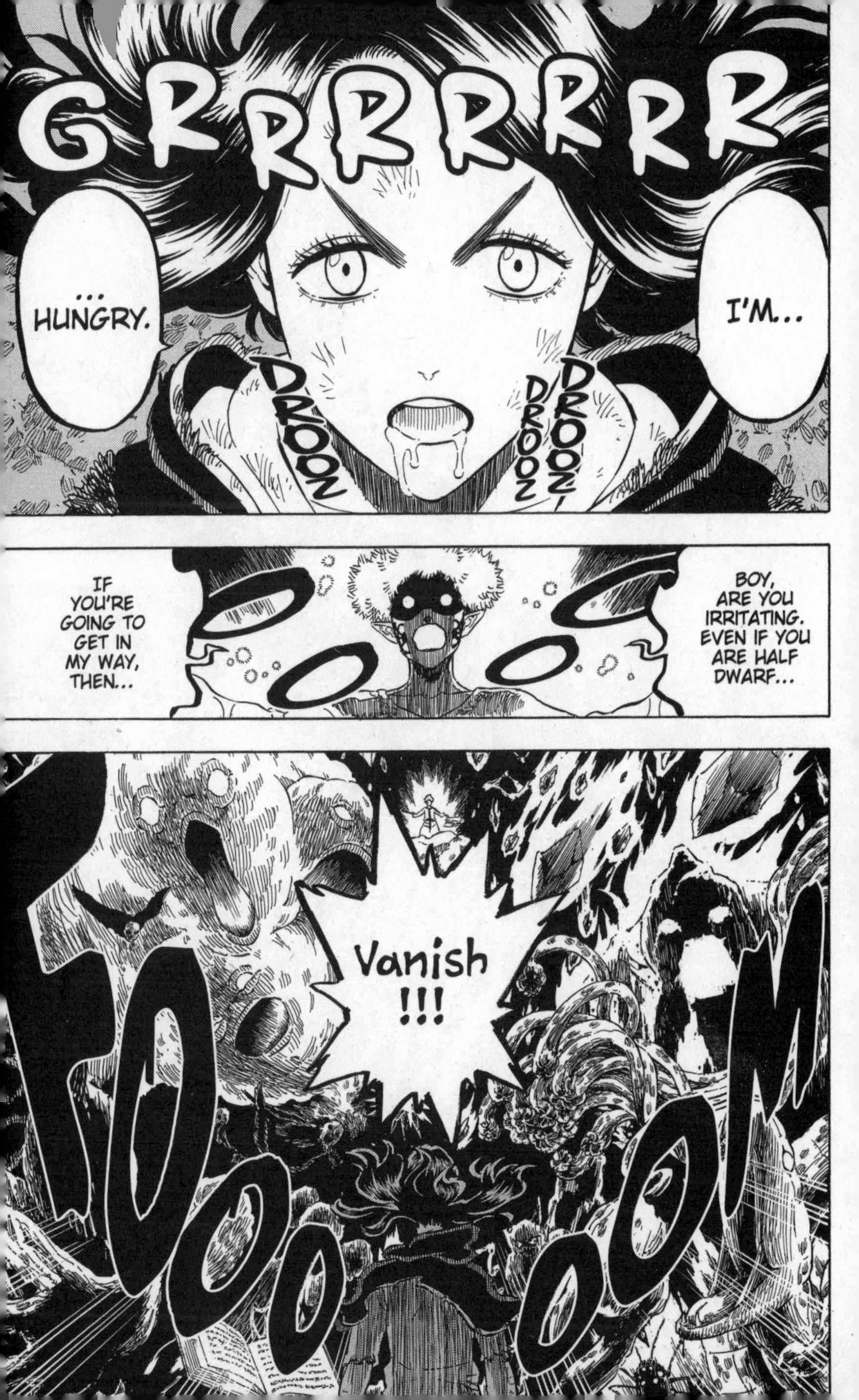
GRRRRRRR
I'M...
...HUNGRY.
DROOOZ
DROOOZ
DROOOZ
BOY, ARE YOU IRRITATING. EVEN IF YOU ARE HALF DWARF...
IF YOU'RE GOING TO GET IN MY WAY, THEN...
Vanish !!!
GOOOOOOOM

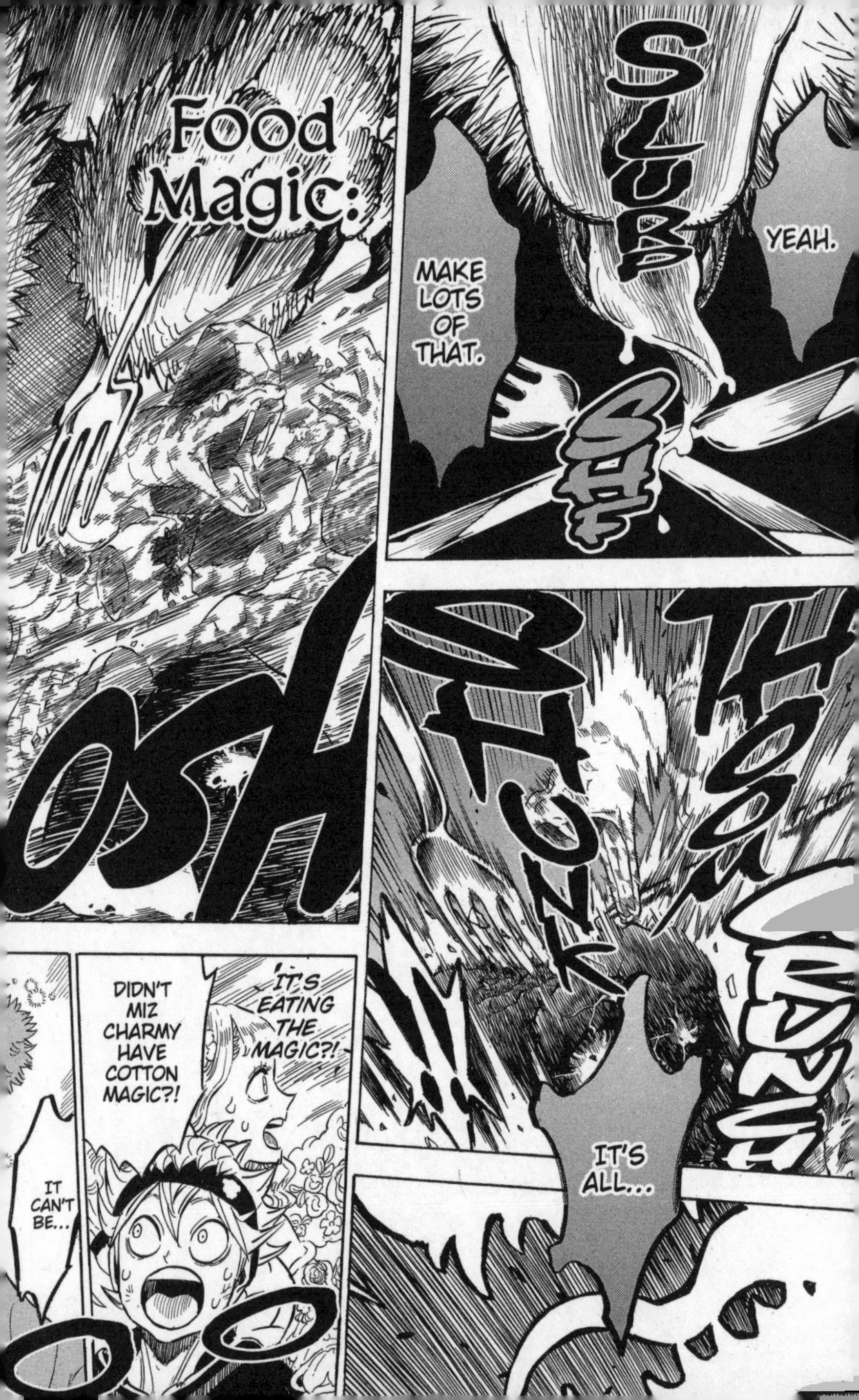
YEAH.
MAKE LOTS OF THAT.
Food Magic:
IT'S ALL...
IT'S EATING THE MAGIC?!
DIDN'T MIZ CHARMY HAVE COTTON MAGIC?!
IT CAN'T BE...

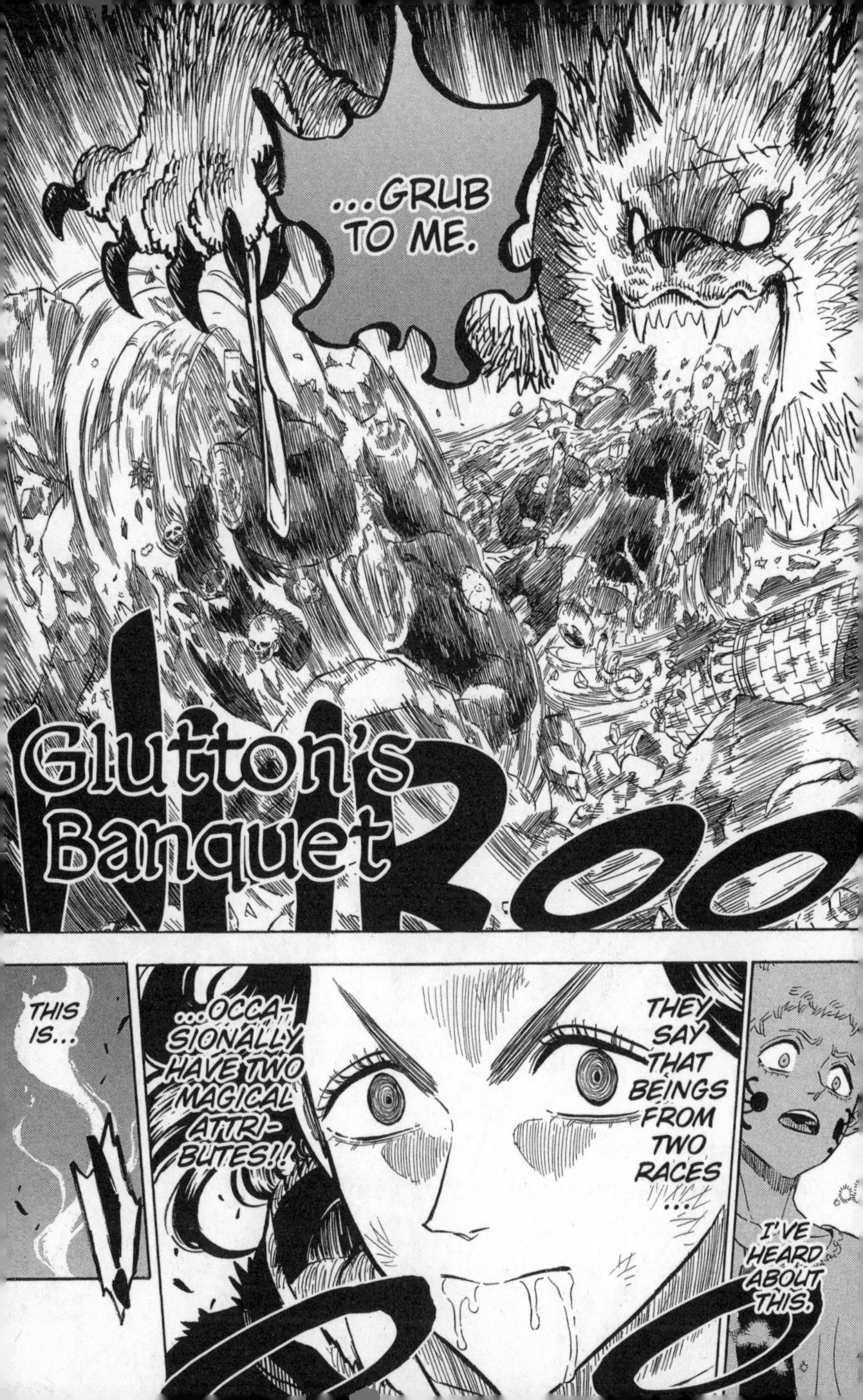
...GRUB TO ME.
Glutton's Banquet
I'VE HEARD ABOUT THIS.
THEY SAY THAT BEINGS FROM TWO RACES...
...OCCASIONALLY HAVE TWO MAGICAL ATTRIBUTES!!
THIS IS...

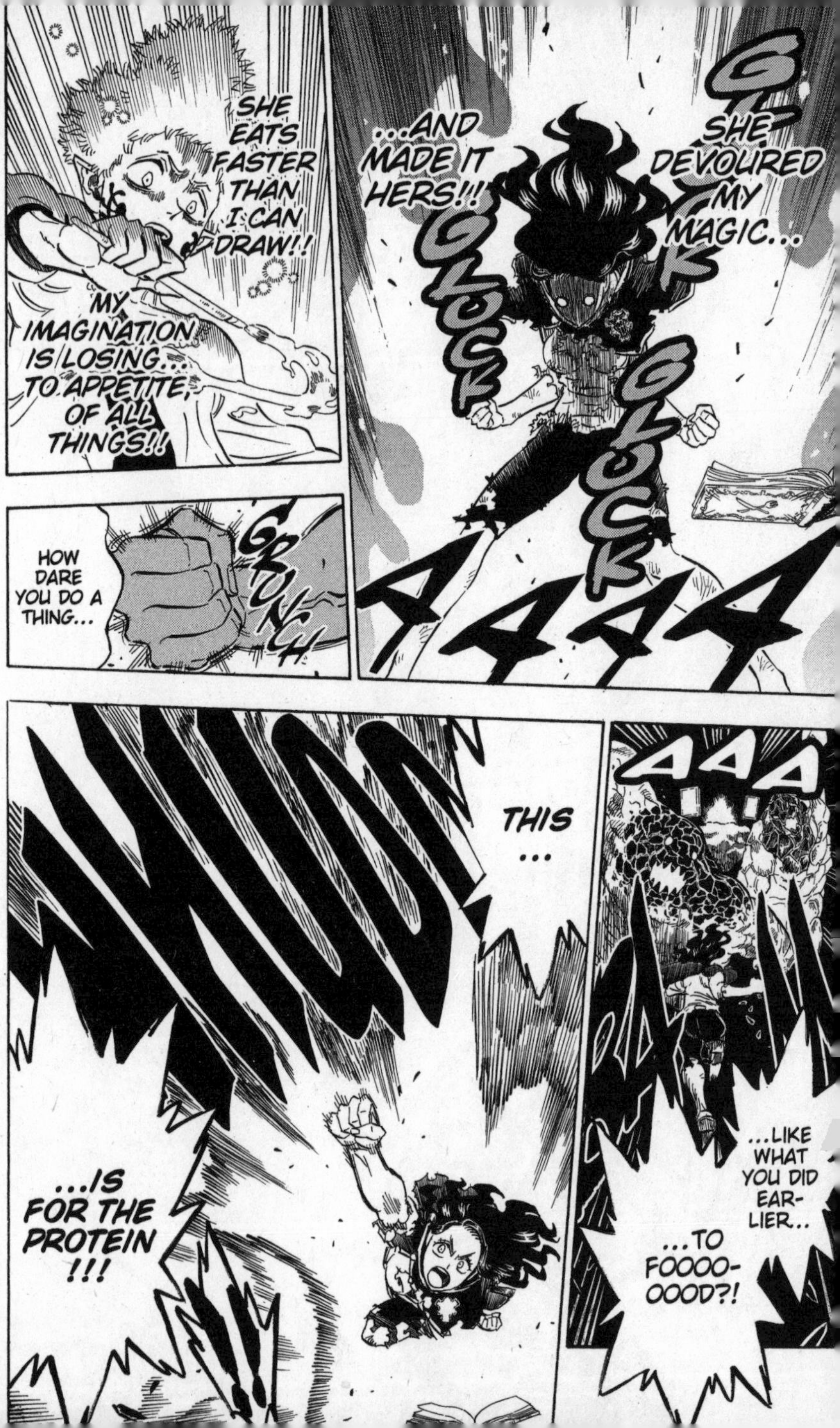
SHE DEVOURED MY MAGIC...
...AND MADE IT HERS!!
GLOCK
GLOCK
AAAA
SHE EATS FASTER THAN I CAN DRAW!!
MY IMAGINATION IS LOSING... TO APPETITE, OF ALL THINGS!!
GRUNCH
HOW DARE YOU DO A THING...
AAA
...LIKE WHAT YOU DID EARLIER...
...TO FOOOOOOOD?!
WHUD
THIS...
...IS FOR THE PROTEIN!!!

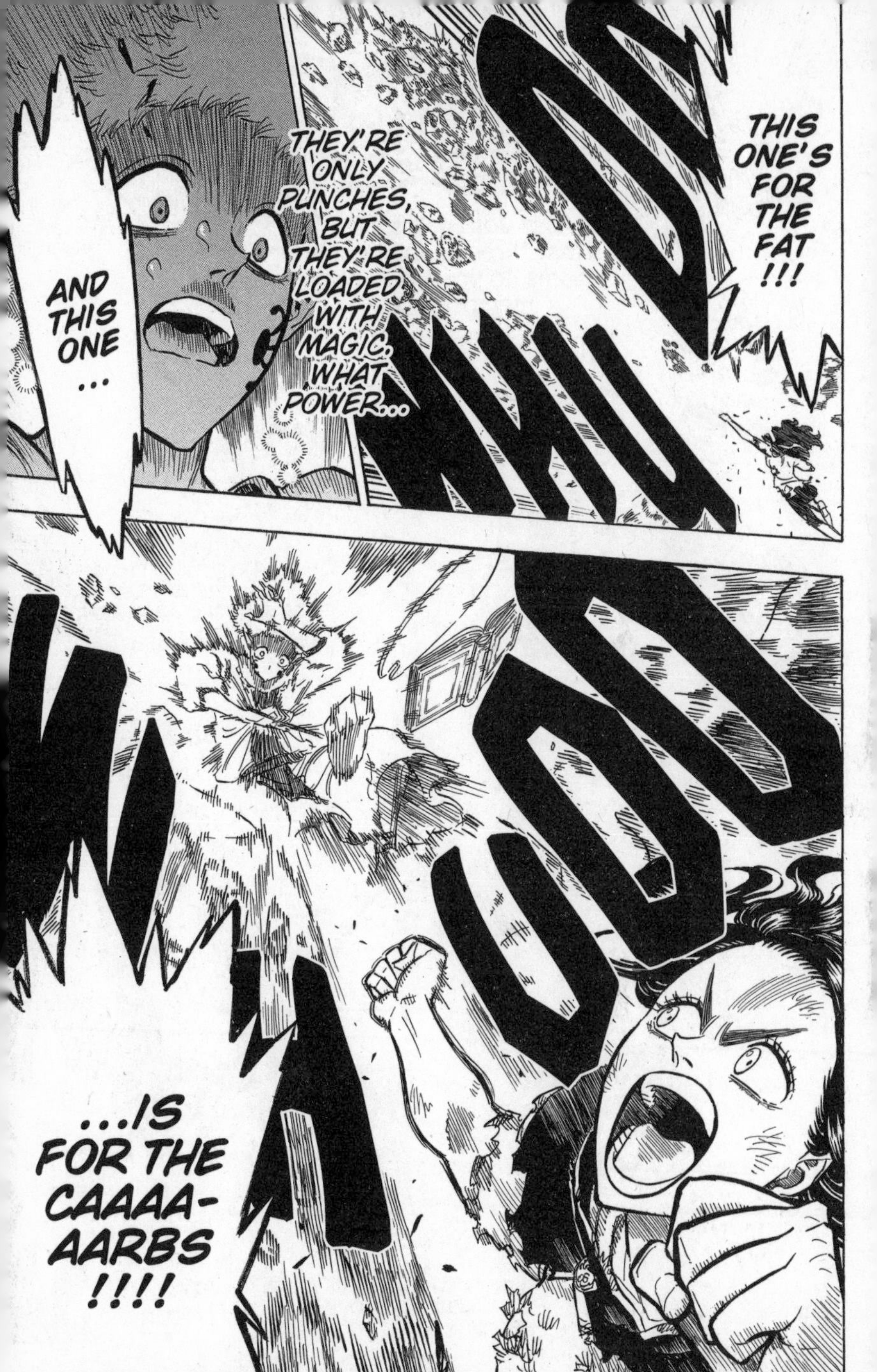
THIS ONE'S FOR THE FAT!!!
THEY'RE ONLY PUNCHES, BUT THEY'RE LOADED WITH MAGIC. WHAT POWER...
AND THIS ONE ...
...IS FOR THE CAAAA-AARBS!!!!

TO BE CONTINUED IN VOLUME 21!

The Blank Page Brigade

This volume's topic:
What three school lunch items do you have fond memories of?

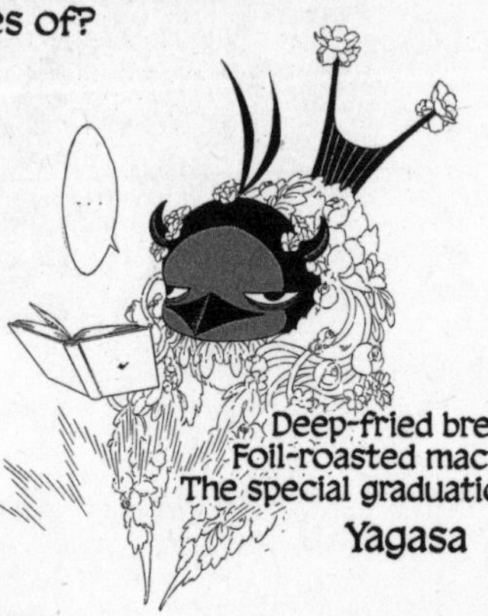
...

Deep-fried bread
Foil-roasted mackerel
The special graduation menu

Yagasa

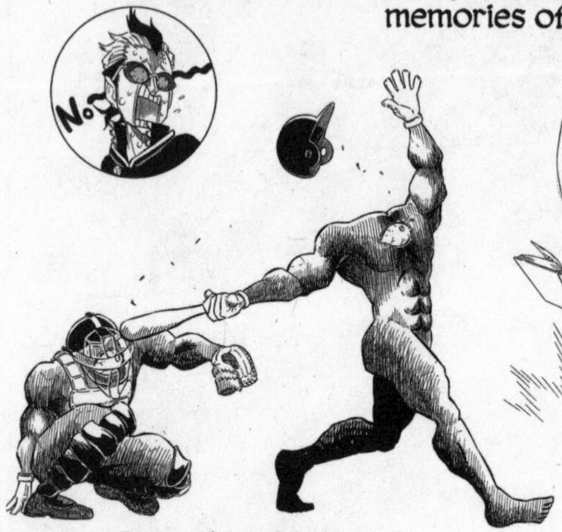
No

Cocoa deep-fried bread
Ginger pork
Chirashi-zushi

Hayato Gotō

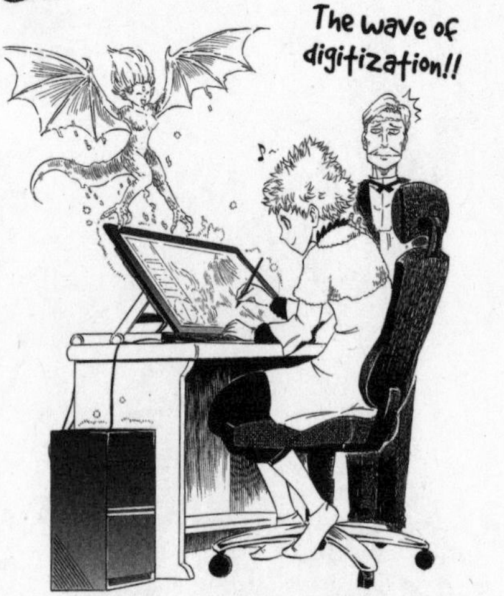
The wave of digitization!!

Deep-fried bread
Frozen tangerines
Soft noodles

Teruaki Mizuno

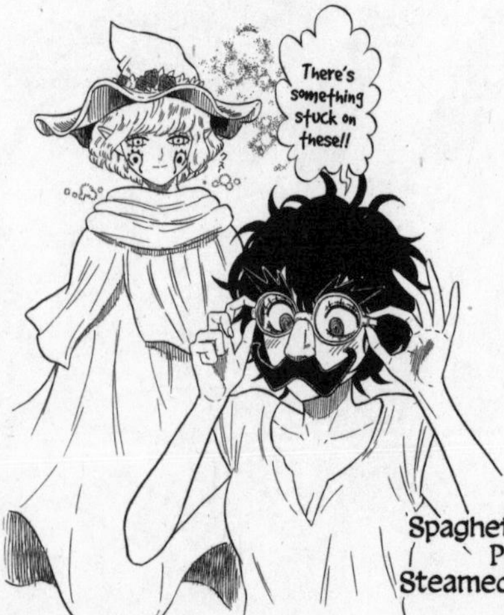
There's something stuck on these!!

Spaghetti with meat sauce
Pumpkin soup
Steamed sweet potato buns

Kazuhiro Wakao

Mackerel stewed in miso
Milk in a bottle
Rolls with toasted soy flour

Masayoshi
Satoshō

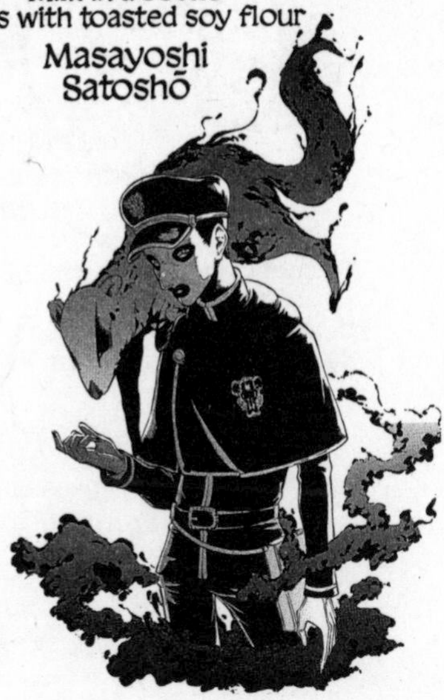

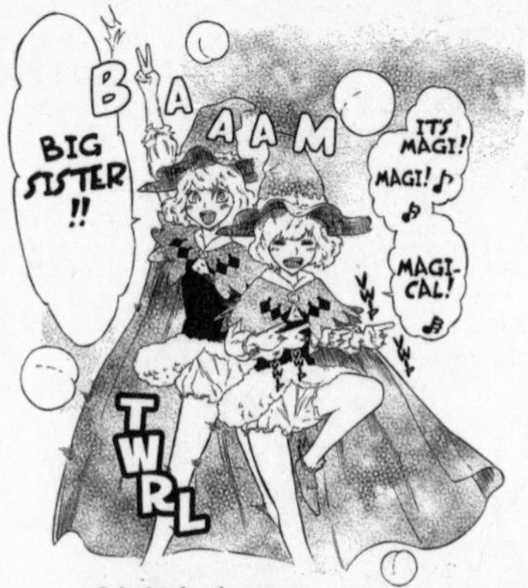
BIG SISTER!!
B A A A M
IT'S MAGI! MAGI! ♪ ♪
MAGICAL! ♪
TWRL

Alphabet soup
Raisin Danish
Haskap jelly

Yōtarō
Hayakawa

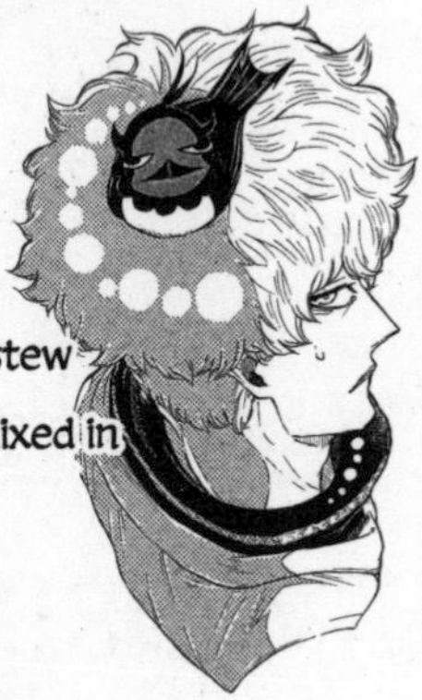

Meat and potato stew
Curry rice
Milk with Milmake mixed in

Sōta
Hishikawa

You'd figure curry, but it's hash
Milk with tops you couldn't open
if your fingernails were short
Fish salad with vinegar and miso

Seiya
Miyamoto

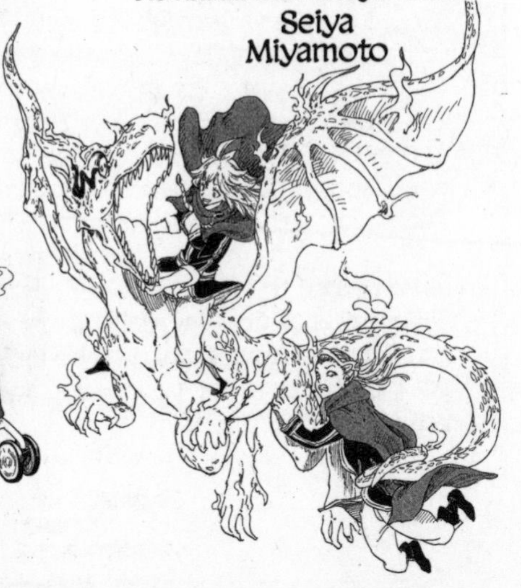

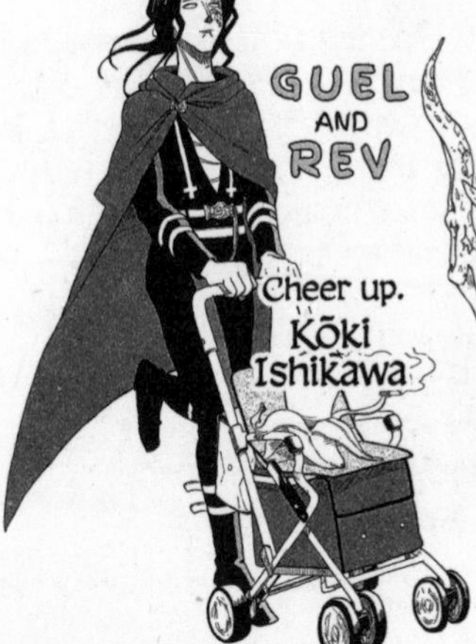
GUEL AND REV
Cheer up.
Kōki
Ishikawa

Common hake with lemon
Deep-fried bread
Dried-up yakisoba

Kōki
Ishikawa

The ultimate "big side dish": beef rice bowl
The ultimate "little side dish": spicy roasted fish
The ultimate bread that totally dries out your mouth: Butter Snacky

Captain Tabata

"Three-color jelly,"
served only during the
Girls' Festival.
Spaghetti with meat sauce
Seasoned fried chicken
©

Rice with wakame
seaweed
Soup with lots of
wheat gluten
Hand-rolled sushi
Comics
Editor
Koshimura

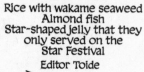

Rice with wakame seaweed
Almond fish
Star-shaped jelly that they
only served on the
Star Festival

Editor Toide

*Incredibly, it turns out that these two are
from the same part of the country.

AFTERWORD

After I finished my pages for 2018, for the first time in two years, I got to participate in the Jump Festa Super Stage! That meant I got to talk up a storm with everybody, and it was a whole lot of fun!! While I was there, I ran a "Learn How to Draw Nero" corner, and all the voice actors drew really good, sharp-looking Neros, so I put them in the book! Thank you very much!!

Right before this volume, Iwai the designer moved to a different project... I'm really sorry for all the trouble I caused you!! Also, thank you so much!! I'll never forget your enthusiasm for your work, and the impressive way you drank!!

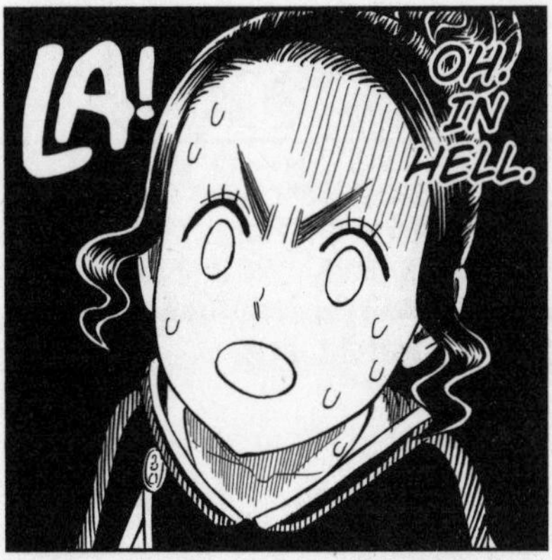
OH! IN HELL.
LA!

Special Bonus Materials

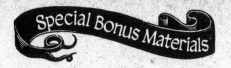

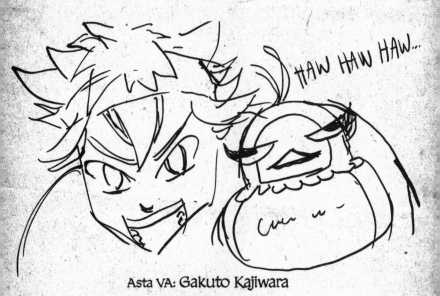

HAW HAW HAW...

Asta VA: Gakuto Kajiwara

At the *Black Clover* Super Stage at Jump Festa 2018, I taught people how to draw Nero! Here, just for you, I'm publishing the versions of Nero the anime's voice actors drew!!! Thank you, voice actors! (Everybody except Kajiwara drew something different, and Konishi actually drew Hanae, but...) You're all fantastic!!!

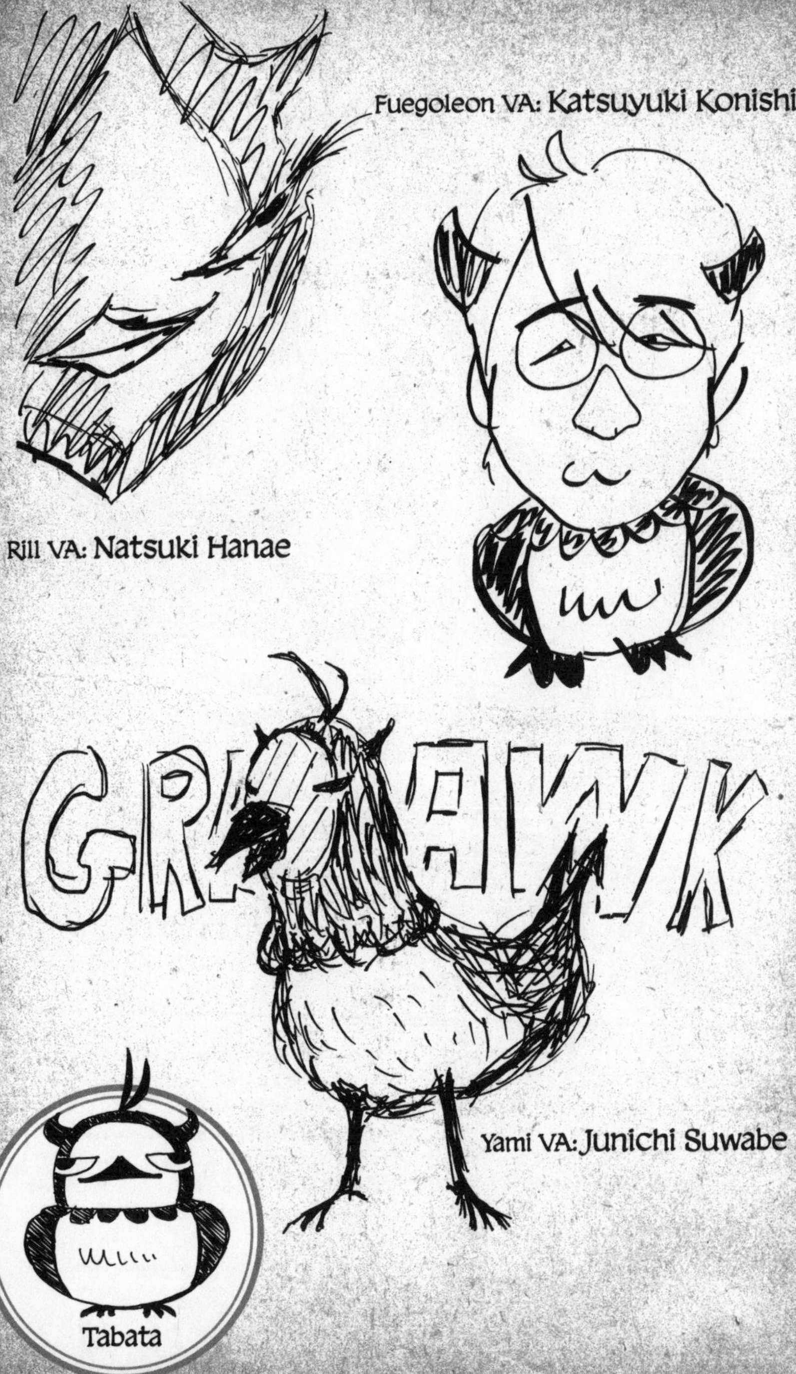

Fuegoleon VA: Katsuyuki Konishi
Rill VA: Natsuki Hanae
GRAWK
Yami VA: Junichi Suwabe
Tabata

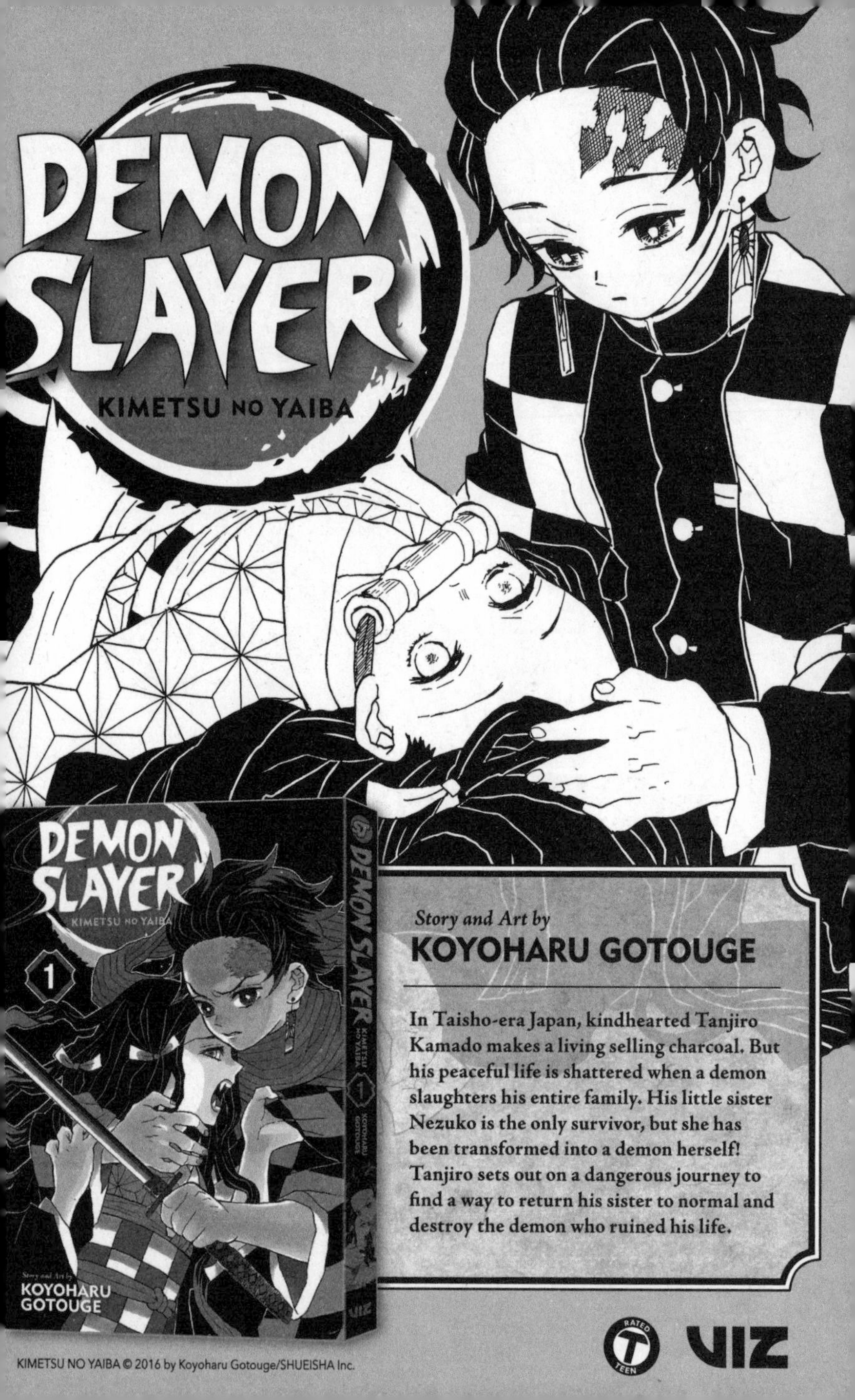
DEMON SLAYER
KIMETSU NO YAIBA
DEMON SLAYER
KIMETSU NO YAIBA
1
Story and Art by
KOYOHARU GOTOUGE
Story and Art by
KOYOHARU GOTOUGE
In Taisho-era Japan, kindhearted Tanjiro Kamado makes a living selling charcoal. But his peaceful life is shattered when a demon slaughters his entire family. His little sister Nezuko is the only survivor, but she has been transformed into a demon herself! Tanjiro sets out on a dangerous journey to find a way to return his sister to normal and destroy the demon who ruined his life.
RATED T TEEN
VIZ
KIMETSU NO YAIBA © 2016 by Koyoharu Gotouge/SHUEISHA Inc.

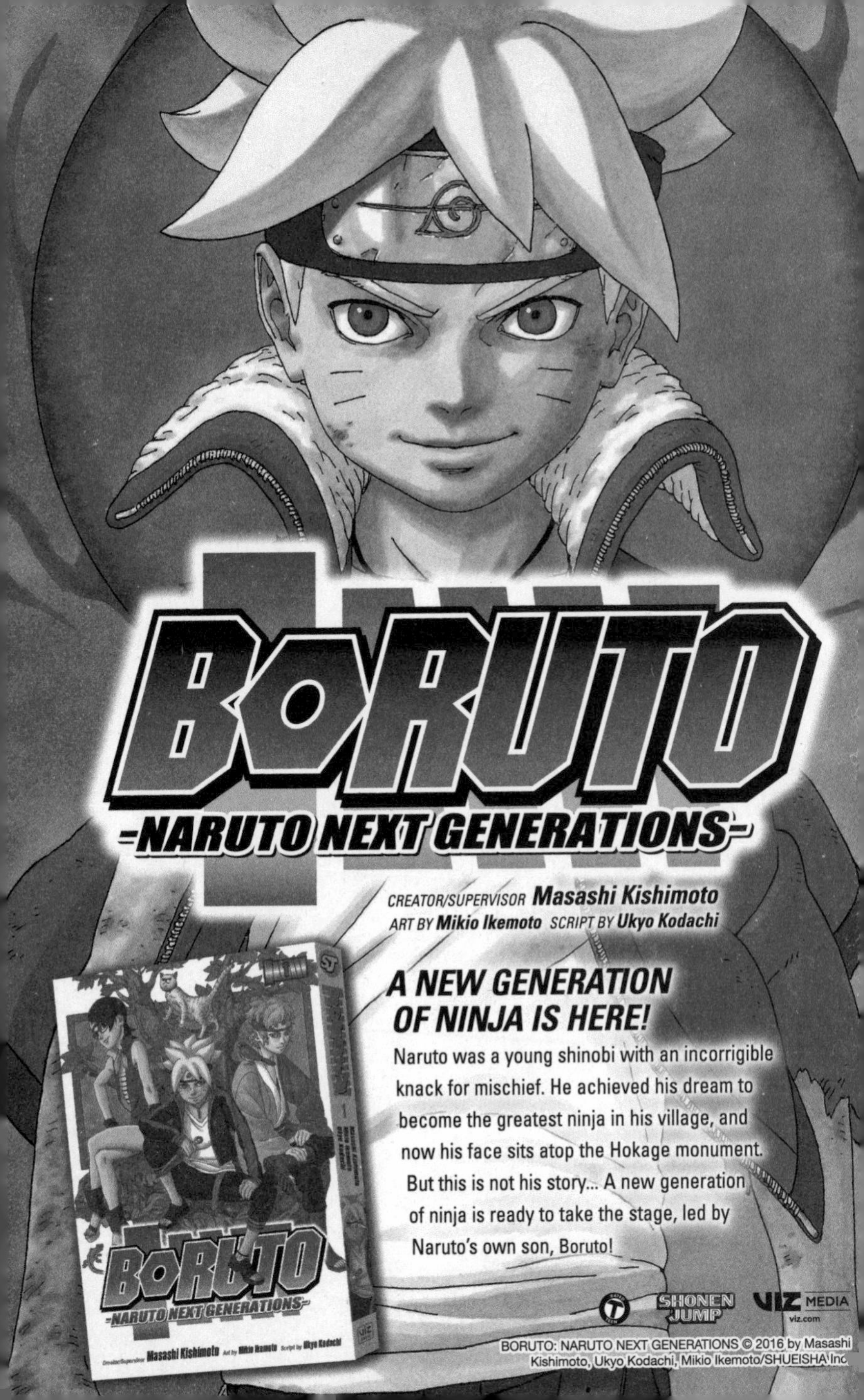
BORUTO
-NARUTO NEXT GENERATIONS-
CREATOR/SUPERVISOR Masashi Kishimoto
ART BY Mikio Ikemoto SCRIPT BY Ukyo Kodachi
A NEW GENERATION OF NINJA IS HERE!
Naruto was a young shinobi with an incorrigible knack for mischief. He achieved his dream to become the greatest ninja in his village, and now his face sits atop the Hokage monument. But this is not his story... A new generation of ninja is ready to take the stage, led by Naruto's own son, Boruto!
SHONEN JUMP
VIZ MEDIA
viz.com
BORUTO: NARUTO NEXT GENERATIONS © 2016 by Masashi Kishimoto, Ukyo Kodachi, Mikio Ikemoto/SHUEISHA Inc.

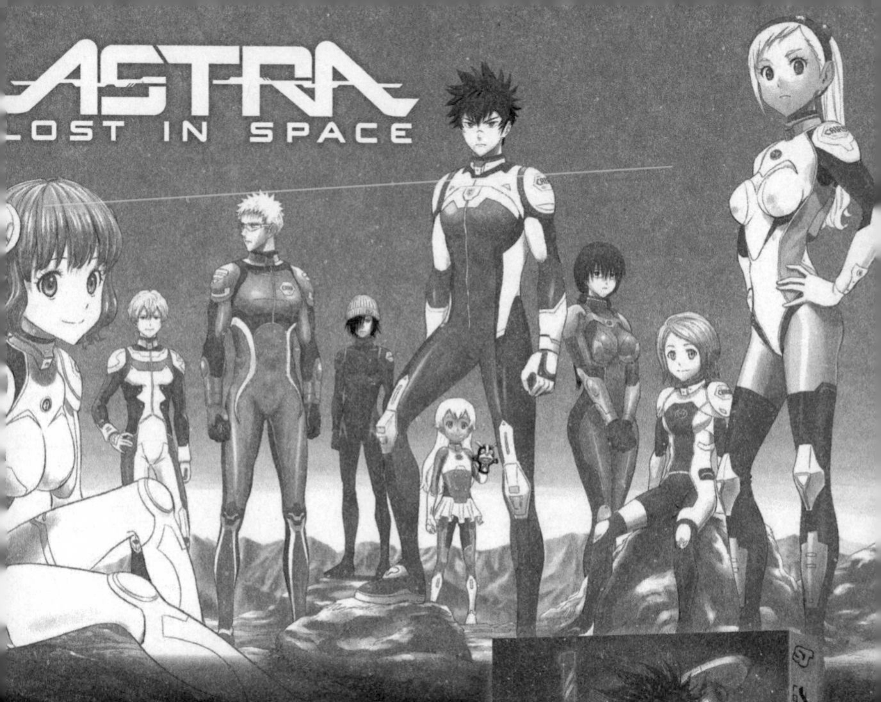
ASTRA
LOST IN SPACE

CAN EIGHT TEENAGERS FIND THEIR WAY HOME FROM 5,000 LIGHT-YEARS AWAY?

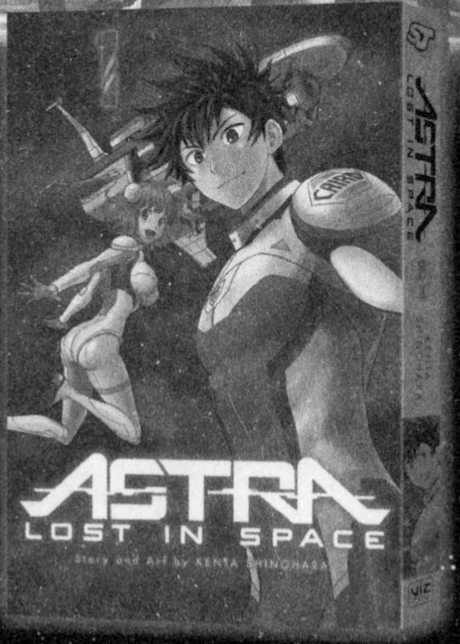
ASTRA
LOST IN SPACE
Story and Art by KENTA SHINOHARA
VIZ

t's the year 2063, and interstellar space travel has ecome the norm. Eight students from Caird High chool and one child set out on a routine planet camp xcursion. While there, the students are mysteriously ransported 5,000 light-years away to the middle of owhere! Will they ever make it back home?!

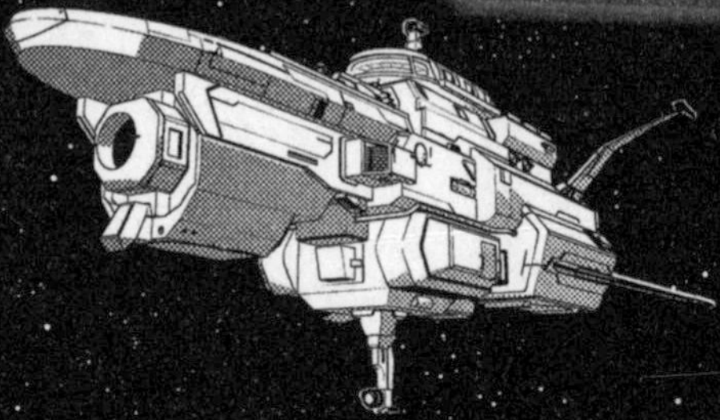

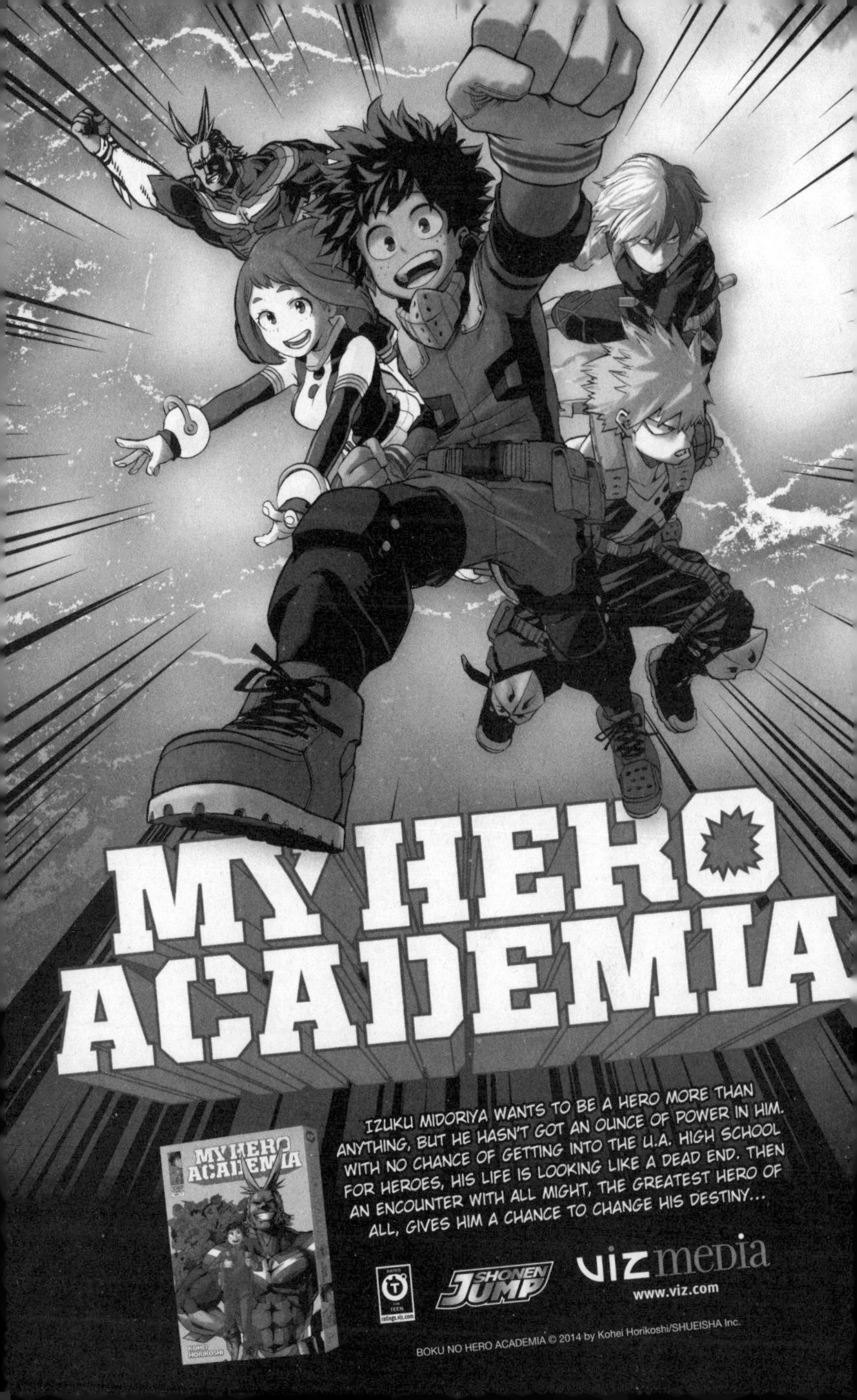
MY HERO ACADEMIA
IZUKU MIDORIYA WANTS TO BE A HERO MORE THAN ANYTHING, BUT HE HASN'T GOT AN OUNCE OF POWER IN HIM. WITH NO CHANCE OF GETTING INTO THE U.A. HIGH SCHOOL FOR HEROES, HIS LIFE IS LOOKING LIKE A DEAD END. THEN AN ENCOUNTER WITH ALL MIGHT, THE GREATEST HERO OF ALL, GIVES HIM A CHANCE TO CHANGE HIS DESTINY...
MY HERO ACADEMIA
KOHEI HORIKOSHI
TEEN
ratings.viz.com
SHONEN JUMP
viz media
www.viz.com
BOKU NO HERO ACADEMIA © 2014 by Kohei Horikoshi/SHUEISHA Inc.

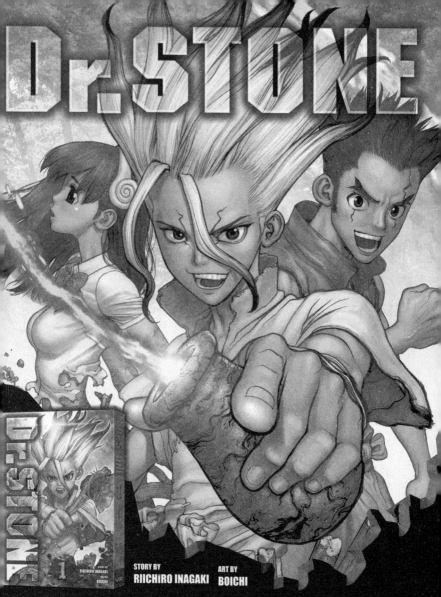

Dr.STONE

STORY BY
RIICHIRO INAGAKI

ART BY
BOICHI

One fateful day, all of humanity turned to stone. Many millennia later, Taiju frees himself from petrification and finds himself surrounded by statues. The situation looks grim—until he runs into his science-loving friend Senku! Together they plan to restart

𝔖top

YOU'RE READING
THE WRONG WAY!

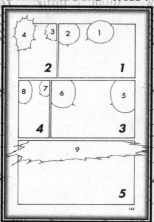

BLACK CLOVER
reads from right to left, starting
in the upper-right corner. Japanese
is read from right to left, meaning
that action, sound effects, and
word-balloon order are completely
reversed from English order.